Discourse Research and Religion

Discourse Research and Religion

Disciplinary Use and Interdisciplinary Dialogues

Edited by
Jay Johnston and Kocku von Stuckrad

DE GRUYTER

ISBN 978-3-11-099145-1
e-ISBN (PDF) 978-3-11-047343-8
e-ISBN (EPUB) 978-3-11-047264-6

Library of Congress Control Number: 2020946760

Bibliographic information published by the Deutsche Nationalbibliothek
The Deutsche Nationalbibliothek lists this publication in the Deutsche Nationalbibliografie;
detailed bibliographic data are available on the Internet at http://dnb.dnb.de.

© 2022 Walter de Gruyter GmbH, Berlin/Boston
This volume is text- and page-identical with the hardback published in 2021.
Cover image: Scott Webb / pexels.com
Typesetting: Integra Software Services Pvt. Ltd.
Printing and binding: CPI books GmbH, Leck

www.degruyter.com

Contents

Jay Johnston and Kocku von Stuckrad
Introduction —— 1

Russell T. McCutcheon
**Discourse Analysis as an Anthropology of the Mundane:
An Interview** —— 7

Reiner Keller
**Entering Discourses: A New Agenda for Qualitative Research and the
Sociology of Knowledge** —— 23

Dominique Maingueneau
Religious Discourse and Its Modules —— 57

Kocku von Stuckrad
Historical Discourse Analysis: The Entanglement of Past and Present —— 77

Frans Wijsen
**Whose Voice Is This? The Multicultural Drama from CDA and DST
Perspectives** —— 89

Anne Koch
**Some Important Conceptual Lines of Discourse Theories in Cultural Studies
of Religion** —— 107

Erin K. Wilson
**The Power Politics of 'Religion': Discursive Analysis of Religion in Political
Science and International Relations** —— 125

Guy Redden
**Religion, Discourse, and the Economy Question: Fraught Issues in Market
Societies** —— 145

Hans G. Kippenberg
**Dynamics of the Human Rights Discourse on Freedom of Religion – Observed
from the Religious Studies Angle** —— 169

Morny Joy
Gender and Its Vicissitudes —— 183

Jay Johnston
'Beyond' Language? Ecology, Ontology, and Aesthetics —— 231

Index of Key Terms —— 243

Index of Places —— 247

Index of People —— 249

Jay Johnston and Kocku von Stuckrad
Introduction

The origins of this volume go back to the year 2015, when De Gruyter invited us to think about a *Handbook* that would cover the field of discourse research and religion in an interdisciplinary way. We were torn between two different responses: On the one hand, producing a handbook for a certain field of research means that enough knowledge, theory, and method has been accumulated to sit down and put it all together in an integrative way. So we were thrilled to have the opportunity of doing exactly this with an established press. But then there was hesitation on our side too: Isn't the genre of a handbook itself something that discourse research should critically address? Handbooks – very much like encyclopedias (Sullivan 1990; von Stuckrad 2005) – are tools (or, as some discourse theorists would say, 'dispositives') that present knowledge in a normative way; they pretend to provide the 'standard' interpretation and view of a certain field, which should be used in classrooms and should be considered state of the art. They tend to come with a closing vocabulary, not an opening one; the very genre pretends to have all the answers, instead of asking questions that may stimulate interesting debates and reflections. How should we position ourselves between these two responses?

When it comes to discourse research and religion, a point can be made for both views. This disciplinary (sub)field has certainly gained increasing attention since Hans G. Kippenberg in 1983 published his programmatic article on "Discursive study of religion: Thoughts on a study of religion that is based neither on a generally valid definition of religion nor on a superiority of science." More than thirty years later, in 2016, Frans Wijsen and Kocku von Stuckrad opened their introduction to a volume on the topic with the statement:

> Discursive approaches to the study of religion have gained momentum in recent years. Closely linked to developments in linguistics, historiography, and sociology, discourse research has slowly but steadily become an accepted way of addressing theoretical and methodological issues in the study of religion. It is time to take stock of the state of the art in the discursive study of religion, to identify its strengths and weaknesses, and to explore new directions for future research – hence this book.[1]

That discourse research has established itself within the academic study of religion can also be seen in the fact that recent handbooks and critical overviews of method and theory in the study of religion include a chapter that engages with discursive approaches (e.g., Hjelm 2011; Neubert 2014; Carrette 2018). What is more, the concept of 'discourse' figures prominently in many academic publications, even though

---

[1] Introduction to Wijsen and von Stuckrad 2016, 1; see also the overview presented in that introduction, which we do not repeat here.

authors often leave it undefined or seem to use it mainly as a way to signal affinity with a certain intellectual milieu. Despite – or perhaps because of? – its popularity, there still is need for clarification about what the study of discourse is and isn't.

This observation brings us to that other impression of the status of discourse research in the study of religion. Engaging with 'religion' as a discourse is sometimes still met with negative, even hostile, responses. The idea that you can study something that people call religion without having a general definition of 'it,' or that you need to include your respective position of power and your perspective in the very analysis of what we 'know' about religion, and how this knowledge materializes in societal arrangements – these, and other, characteristics of a discursive understanding of religion (and the disciplinary system that produces that knowledge) regularly trigger allegations of being vague, relativist, unscientific, or naïve.

Regardless of where scholars position themselves on this spectrum of responses to discourse research, one thing seems to be clear: In a world that is challenged by massive transformations on ecological, social, political, and economic levels, it is difficult to uphold an ideal of independent and objective scholarship (if such an ideal had ever been realistic in the first place). Today, it is impossible to escape the entanglement of academic activity and societal realities. Scholars and their publics (Patton 2019) form a discourse community that in mutual engagement creates orders of knowledge, the implications of which materialize on a planetary scale. We need frameworks of interpretation and tools of analysis that actually capture those entanglements and open them up for reflection and learning. Discourse research is an attempt at providing exactly these frames and tools.

Consequently, this volume is not a handbook. It does not present a codified body of knowledge to readers who simply absorb that knowledge. Rather, the knowledge presented here is in constant flux; while discourse research can provide some structure in which a hermeneutical process can unfold – including themes to be addressed, as well as levels and steps of analysis to be incorporated – the way scholars engage with these structures, formulate their own research questions, and arrive at new vistas and answers that others find useful, too, is a creative process of learning.

The chapters that follow engage both with those overall structures that mark this kind of reasoning as discursive, and with new vistas that creatively build up knowledge in an open societal setting. All of them build bridges to adjacent disciplinary fields that often have more experience with discourse research than the academic study of religion. The entanglement of discourses on religion with discourses on identity, gender, law, history, culture, ecology, politics, and many others has a strong impact on contemporary worlds, as well as on the perception of the past. Over against this strong entanglement of discourses, however, the entanglement of the various disciplines that study those factors still needs to be enhanced. This volume contributes to such an endeavor. Its authors discuss the use of discourse research in various disciplines and gauge the possible application of this knowledge within the academic study of religion.

For a project like this, it makes sense to use a definition of discourse that is open to various applications and disciplinary contexts. A good example of such an understanding of discourse is Franz X. Eder's definition: Discourses are practices "that systematically organize and regulate statements about a certain theme; by doing so, discourses determine the conditions of possibility of what (in a social group at a certain period of time) can be thought and said" (Eder 2006, 13; our translation). Hence, discourse analysis does not only look at the textual and linguistic dimension of a topic but also at the practices that carry or change orders of knowledge. This includes institutions such as governments, courts, scientific associations, religious organizations, the media, as well as universities. These practices determine "the conditions of possibility of what can be thought and said" from identifiable positions of power. That is why discourse research always pays attention not only to an analysis of what is being said or done, but also of who says or does it, and from which position and institutional background this is said or done. It turns out that discourses on 'religion' are an excellent example of such an exercise – there simply is no 'objective' understanding of religion; since antiquity, religion has been a terrain on which perspectives with clear institutional and intellectual interests have been acted out. These power-related discourse strands, entangled and intersected with many other tools and concepts, still regulate and determine orders of knowledge about religion today. As this book makes clear, studying such multi-layered processes through the lenses of discourse research can significantly improve our understanding of the place of religion in global contexts today, as well as the history and genealogy of these contexts. It also demonstrates the importance and usefulness of interdisciplinary collaboration. The study of religion can learn a lot from the experiences of other disciplines; in turn, experts on religion can enhance the understanding of the place of religion in many discursive arrangements.

'Mapping the Volume'

The volume opens with an interview with Russell T. McCutcheon, which reflects on both his own engagement with discourse research, its impact and importance for the development of studies in religion, as well as related critiques and controversy. It is pleasing to be able to present these reflections from such a pivotal and influential scholar on the discourse approach. They are particularly welcome at the outset of the volume, enabling both a conceptual tracing and reflection on the development of the 'discourse' of discourse approaches.

To follow are ten discrete chapters each which engage discourse approaches while also paying particular attention to interdisciplinary engagement: formative or potential. Rainer Keller proposes a sociology of knowledge approach to discourse studies (SKAD), which, he argues, places the "politics of knowledge" center stage.

His chapter articulates not only the relevance of this approach for qualitative research but illustrates applicable devices and provides further reflection on the method being proposed. Closing with a salient reminder of the ubiquitous nature of knowledge–power relations, Keller makes clear the interdisciplinary relevance of his approach.

Established on the disciplinary base of linguistics, Dominique Maingueneau presents an innovative framework for integrating various discourse analysis approaches to the study of religion. This chapter expertly outlines and reflects upon the dominant approaches to religion within the discipline of linguistics and opens out a new subfield of study by devising a holistic, text-orientated approach to religious corpora.

Taking historiography as his remit, Kocku von Stuckrad brings a critical eye to discourse studies in the context of historical analysis. He asks questions regarding its valiancy and potential for illuminating relations of entanglement, material agency, and the spaces of productive slippage between past and present that both render periodization unstable. It is exactly in these interstices, he argues, that discourse analysis has the most to offer historical knowledge production.

Frans Wijsen reflects on the more concrete method of Critical Discourse Analysis (CDA), providing an overview of dominant approaches, and offers an extension of the utility of CDA via consideration of Dialogical Self Theory (Hermans and Hermans-Konopka 2010; Hermans 2018).

Anne Koch investigates the centrality of Foucauldian discourse studies to cultural studies approaches to religion. Acknowledging the slippery nature of both terminology and recognized 'bodies' of disciplinary knowledge, she deftly provides an overview of the cultural study of religion and articulates its critical terms (governance, discipline, etc.), and – via a discussion rich with examples – reflects on the necessarily interdisciplinary engagement that has produced such scholarship. Importantly, her analysis concludes with reflection on the limits and critiques of the examined discursive approaches.

Scrutinizing the recent 'turn' to religion in political science and international relations, Erin Wilson articulates the innovation and the benefits of interdisciplinary engagement between these disciplines and the critical, discursive study of religion. In particular she elucidates the impact of 'relational dialogist' approaches and the relevance of the discursive study of religion for global politics.

Continuing this focus on interdisciplinary engagement, Guy Redden brings a cultural studies approach to understanding the engagement between discourses of religion and those of economics: the "fraught issues of market societies" as his chapter title frames the concern. His analysis is both a call to take the relevance of economics, and in particular marketing, for the discursive study of religion seriously, and a challenge to dominant conceptualizations that view each as being mutually exclusive realms of life experience.

Renowned scholar of discourse approaches in religious studies Hans G. Kippenberg makes a significant contribution to the volume through his analysis of the 'practices' of law and religion as they coalesce via examination of the United Nations legal discourses on religious freedom. Studying the legal framing of religion provides new insights into attempts to regulate the religious field in times when intolerance and violence pervade it. Hence, as Kippenberg elucidates, the freedom of religion requires a discourse on regulations.

Morny Joy furnishes the volume with an insightful and comprehensive account of discourse analysis in gender studies and its particular impact on religious studies scholarship. Combining an innovative heuristic and detailed interdisciplinary knowledge, she clearly articulates the complex interrelations between disciplines enabled by the discourse approach.

The volume concludes with Jay Johnston's necessarily playful exploration of the serious topic of the relevance of discursive approaches beyond the domain of human linguistic forms. She explores the pertinent question if 'beyond' really is the right term to use here, or if language should rather be uncoupled from human spoken and written systems.

References

Carrette, Jeremy. 2018. "Foucault and the Study of Religion." In *Religion – Theory – Critique: Classic and Contemporary Approaches and Methodologies*, edited by Richard King, 487–495. New York: Columbia University Press.

Eder, Franz X. 2006. "Historische Diskurse und ihre Analyse – eine Einleitung." In *Historische Diskursanalysen: Genealogie, Theorien, Anwendungen*, edited by Franz X. Eder, 9–23. Wiesbaden: VS Verlag für Sozialwissenschaft.

Hermans, H. 2018. *Society in the Self: A Theory of Identity in Democracy*. New York: Oxford University Press.

Hermans, H., and A. Hermans-Konopka. 2010. *Dialogical Self Theory: Positioning and Counter-Positioning in a Globalizing Society*. Cambridge: Cambridge University Press.

Hjelm, Titus. 2011. "Discourse Analysis." In *The Routledge Handbook of Research Methods in the Study of Religion*, edited by Michael Stausberg and Steven Engler, 134–150. London and New York: Routledge.

Kippenberg, Hans G. 1983. "Diskursive Religionswissenschaft. Gedanken zu einer Religionswissenschaft, die weder auf einer allgemein gültigen Definition von Religion noch auf einer Überlegenheit von Wissenschaft basiert." In *Neue Ansätze in der Religionswissenschaft*, edited by Burkhard Gladigow and Hans G. Kippenberg, 9–28. Munich: Kösel.

Neubert, Frank. 2014. "Diskursforschung in der Religionswissenschaft." In *Diskursforschung: Ein interdisziplinäres Handbuch*, 2 vols., edited by Johannes Angermuller, Martin Nonhoff, Eva Herschinger, Felicitas Macgilchrist, Martin Reisigl, Juliette Wedl, Daniel Wrana, and Alexander Ziem, vol. 1, 261–275. Bielefeld: Transcript.

Patton, Laurie. 2019. *Who Owns Religion? Scholars and Their Publics in the Late Twentieth Century*. Chicago: University of Chicago Press.

Stuckrad, Kocku von. 2005. "Encyclopedias." In *Encyclopedia of Religion*, edited by Lindsay Jones (ed. in chief), vol. 4, 2782–2785. 2nd ed. Detroit etc.: Thomson Gale.

Stuckrad, Kocku von. 2013. "Discursive Study of Religion: Approaches, Definitions, Implications." *Method and Theory in the Study of Religion* 25: 5–25.

Sullivan, Lawrence E. 1990. "Circumscribing Knowledge: Encyclopedias in Historical Perspective." *Journal of Religion* 70: 315–339.

Wijsen, Frans, and Kocku von Stuckrad (eds.). 2016. *Making Religion: Theory and Practice in the Discursive Study of Religion*. Leiden and Boston: Brill.

Russell T. McCutcheon
Discourse Analysis as an Anthropology of the Mundane: An Interview

1. You have used the term 'discourse' regularly throughout your work. Can you briefly explain what you mean by it and how you apply it in your research?

I recall a lunch at University College, while doing my Ph.D. at the University of Toronto, sometime around 1990 I guess, when my friend Stephen Heathorn (who was then doing his Ph.D. in History and who is now a faculty member at McMaster University in Canada) and I were working through our readings of Michel Foucault, processing it and making sense of it for our own interests and projects, and, as we talked, we stumbled upon 'discursive field' as our preferred term; I can't speak for Stephen but I recall thinking that we'd come up with it on our own. I open with that anecdote just as an example of a time when, at least in the study of religion, this notion of discourse was still pretty new for our field. The works we were reading were 20 or 30 years old by then, sure (though Said's *Orientalism* was just a little over ten years old at that point), but they had not yet been much applied in the study of religion. You have to recall, this was just a couple years after the first edition of Mircea Eliade's multi-volume *Encyclopedia of Religion* came out (in 1987 – I recall well it being new and Neil McMullin's really useful review of it, among others, that appeared soon after), so that model – represented by a focus on hierophanies, the dialectics of the sacred, religion as irreducible, the priority of experience, the camouflaged meaning of symbols, the New Humanism, etc. – still dominated the field. (As it does today, by the way; it's just that some of the terms have changed, with many of us now talking about religion being *embodied* and its meaning *expressed*.) So reading Foucault, among others, was a pretty new experience for many scholars of religion back then (something I started doing in the late 1980s, thanks to the recommendations by McMullin, who became my doctoral advisor) and the challenge was how to transpose those methods to our data, as a way to answer our questions. So by that point I'd read so much of the material, including a bunch of literary critical theory and historiography, that I was losing track of whose ideas were whose, hence me thinking that we'd coined a new term: discursive field.

But that technical term standing out for us during lunch that day (when I recall that we were, quite literally, scribbling notes from our conversation onto napkins), to name a diffuse but interrelated set of items, procedures, assumptions, styles, and institutions – whose iceberg tip could be just a misleadingly simple word – starts to get at the work this term discourse does for me. It's much like the term social formation, which I've also favored in some of my work; as I wrote long ago, it can function as a gerund, moving us from talking about the seemingly settled results of processes to the processes themselves, switching from nouns to verbs, as it were (looking back, it's something my first book's title, *Manufacturing Religion*, aimed to register). For instance, sure, we can use 'society' as a convenient shorthand when we talk to one another, but if we agree on our social theory then, as we talk about society doing this or that to us, we'll both know that we're actually talking about a series of ongoing and thus dynamic practices and actions, as well as sub-groups and sub-sub-groups, etc. – some of those acts seem intentional and some of those sub-groups seem homogenous, but many are not, with some explicitly interrelated but some not so much. The result of which, should we not pay attention to their workings (which we probably won't do, if they are working well!), is the impression of this thing we call the group, society, identity, self, etc.

The task for scholars, though, is to pay attention. (Sometimes to the moments when things break down, as Bruce Lincoln so nicely told us in his book *Authority*, for that's when we might see what's happening a little better.) So I tend to use the technical term discourse, or discursive field, in that fashion, to name an interconnected series of tangible items (e.g., books on a shelf), practices (e.g., someone coming by my office to chat), and institutions (e.g., a degree program's rules, which were not made any one individual, by the way) that, when working in concert, constitute a domain that we can occupy and which can shape how we act and interact. For instance, the above parenthetical list starts to get at that discursive field that we call higher education or academia, in which the display of books arranged on shelves or framed diplomas on walls, not to mention a person behind a desk asking their visitor a series of questions, in the good old Socratic style, are taken to implicitly signify all sorts of things, allowing us to sort ourselves as specific sorts of interrelated subjects, inasmuch as we inhabit that field (or it inhabits us!) along a hierarchy of authority and thus rank. I'm now a professor. You're now a student. So let's get on with this thing that we call school …

What this helps me to do in my work is, to put it simply, historicize that many of us (but not all!) think and act like religion is an easily identified domain of life. Again thinking back to the model that has long reigned in our field, it's easy to find analyses that start talking about some historical item as "that which is believed to be a conduit for the sacred" (as did the credit for a photo used not long ago on the cover of the *Journal of the American Academy of Religion* [86/4, 2018]). I won't go into the problems of this term 'the sacred' (of which there are many – first and foremost is the manner in which people today seem to confuse Durkheim's usage of it, as an adjective, with Eliade's, as a noun …. [a difference nicely identified by Bill Paden long ago]), but here we have a seeming statement of fact which is not just a highly theoretically-informed interpretation but which takes the result of a series of process for granted, as if we can just talk about beliefs instead of discussing the contingent, structured conditions in which one *believes* something or, better yet, with a nod to Slavoj Žižek, comes to believe that they have things called beliefs that cause them to do things. And that's what I mean by historicization – not far off from paying attention to the gerunds, i.e., the settled nouns that might actually be contestable verbs – to try not just to trace the chronological development of something but, rather, to see things, like the so-called beliefs that the photo credit presumes people just to have and then express, as products of prior, sometimes unnoticed, sometimes planned, and sometimes happenstance, processes that can be studied.

2. Related to this, was there already a concept of discursive approaches in the study of religion when you started to get interested in this, or did that develop later?

As suggested above, I'd say no. Although certainly influenced by a number of people publishing in our field, with regard to other aspects of my work, in terms of discourse analysis the influences back then (at least in my case) were generally from outside the field, from literary critical theory, etc. Remember, books now seen as pivotal in this area, let alone critiquing "religion" as a category, were yet to be published (not counting Cantwell Smith's early 1960s theological critique of 'religion'; for instance, Tim Fitzgerald's *The Ideology of Religious Studies* was still several years from publication) and the so-called theory wars in Departments of English, at least here in North America, had taken place only in the decade prior to this, though their reverberations were still being felt, so the effort to rethink claims about such things as literariness, intentions, authors, aesthetic value, and meaning became the – at least I thought at the time – easily transposed models for how to rethink the key disciplinary-organizing concepts of our work, e.g., religiousness, sacredness, experience, faith, etc. (For example, *Critical Terms for Literary Study* was the model for the *Guide to the Study of Religion* that Willi Braun and I co-edited, an idea that we came up with not knowing that Mark Taylor was also using it as a model for his own handbook on the study of religion – making them the first two modern handbooks in this now incredibly crowded genre.) In fact, I don't even think of myself doing discourse analysis since, when I started doing this, there was no such organizing concept in our field, so I saw myself doing what we at Toronto then just called 'method and theory' – admittedly a vague, catch-all category that captured anyone interested more in our tools than in the data that many scholars take for granted (giving some of us no good answer to the still inevitable "so, what religion do you study" question at job interviews). My interest in the fabrication process (i.e., those gerunds I talked about a little earlier) involved the links between words and institutions – an interest surely indebted to Jonathan Z. Smith's work too, I now realize, given that famous line of his from the preface to *Imagining Religion* having come only a few years before. So could we zero in on what was required to even talk or think about, say, 'the primitives' as if it actually named some stable thing in the world, let alone the practical (usually self-beneficial) implications of arranging the world in that fashion (i.e., culturally-evolved and thus civilized people over here and primitives over there)? It's a question that seems to have landed me in a group that developed some years later, and so we arrive at me apparently doing discursive analysis in the study of religion – itself a great example of how discourse on origins are always a project done in hindsight from some invested present moment. I'm happy to be included, of course.

3. What do you think is the main advantage of using discursive approaches in the study of religion? Is it different here than, say, in historiography, the social sciences, or in cultural studies? Can you give examples from your own research?

That long opening answer affords me the opportunity now to keep saying "As I said above ..."; so yes, I think it is different. Working on a genealogy, in Foucault's sense, is not looking to craft a narrative of chronological development from past to present, or simply aiming to demonstrate the social basis of this or that practice. The advantage of making the shift, as I see it, is developing a way to take both agents and structures seriously, as mutually informing, as co-constitutive (or a recursive formation as some might say), neither of which predates the other in some definitive or ontological sense. Although we surely see this tendency in our field, too many in our field strike me as opting for agential studies, focusing on actors, their supposed intentions, their meanings, their supposed experiences, and criticizing anyone who fails to take the so-called devotee 'seriously,' a code word for irreducible, self-evident, etc. To my way of thinking, such a view hampers scholarship, for it's not difficult to examine the prior or wider conditions that helped to make the person *into* a devotee, which means to be seen by either themselves or others *as* a devotee – and all that this entails in their lives and relationships.

The classic, or at least easily digested, example, I think, is what I referenced above: Slavoj Žižek's discussion (drawing on both Louis Althusser and Blaise Pascal) – none of whom I'd place too squarely in the discursive tradition, but bear with me ... – of kneeling in a Roman Catholic mass (he writes briefly about this in the opening to his edited collection, *Mapping Ideology*). The institution (in this case the Roman Catholic Church), which predates the individual, provides the conditions in which one not only is taught to kneel at certain times, but in which one comes to think of oneself *as* a believer when one does it, thereby eventually coming to see the action as an outward expression of some original, inner causation, yet that inner sentiment was surely not there when one first knelt, or the second time, or ..., since one did it by imitating others, or was just told to do it by an authority figure – well-meaning but firm hands pressing down on little shoulders at a key moment in the mass, etc. (Think here of the tremendous apparatus that we've devised to teach children to experience and thereby define themselves *as* French or British or Canadian or Mexican ...) But that institution didn't spring from the ground fully formed; instead, it resulted from prior actors, with various goals in mind, working in concert as well as against each other (as I said earlier, social institutions are complex, multi-layered things, right?), and doing so within a no less complex institution that predated them (after all, none of them invented table manner and mating rituals, let alone English or Spanish ...), and so on and so on ... . But of course this is not determinism for, like the variations of jazz or table manners, once you learn the rules you can tweak the system, change it for those who come after you – all within certain parameters, of course (otherwise you go to jail, all depending which set of rules you're adjusting or subverting).

Now, why I like the e.g. of kneeling during that mass is that, with a little analysis, we not only see what I take to be the constant oscillation between agent and structure but, more importantly, we begin to see that, unless we do this sort of analysis, the taxon 'believer' is doing considerable, philosophically idealist work, conserving and thereby normalizing a specific set of historical, social, etc., conditions that led to it but, importantly, that all could have been different (that little child didn't have to be born into a Roman Catholic world in France, non?). So the taken-for-granted way that scholars in our specific field talk about 'believers,' or the way pollsters try to determine how different beliefs supposedly make you act in different ways (such as how the so-called evangelicals voted in the 2016 US election of Donald Trump – that's recently been a popular one in the US) is the tip of a complex iceberg of interrelated assumptions, artifacts, practices, institutions, ranked social relations, all of which can become apparent if we historicize that person kneeling and our commonsense reading of them as motivated by their faith and so doing it because they say they believe this or that. So it's a great example, I think, to make evident that the thing that we call belief arrives long after the act, long after the institution – making belief an artifact of prior social situations. Or to put it simply for a change: the discourse on belief makes claims about belief and believers possible.

4. Critics of discursive approaches often argue that if you only study "what people think religion is" and not "religion itself/religion proper," you will leave the confines of rigorous scholarship and undermine the very basis the study of religion as a discipline is built upon. How do you respond to that?

Yes, I've heard that before. "Let's just get on with it" is what I'd call this viewpoint. In fact, this morning on Twitter I was told that studying the category religion was "navel-gazing" and that scholars have a political responsibility to challenge and correct the way government agencies use the term today. And sure, sometimes we just get on with studying this or that group's rituals, for instance. But it doesn't take much to realize that without a definition of ritual you can't do much of that work, and that different people have different definitions, since they want to do different things in their work, and that definitions really are just theories in miniature (that is, a Freudian certainly doesn't use a Marxist definition of ritual when doing their work …) and voila, "just getting on with it" turns out to be far more complicated than anyone might have thought at the outset. (Failing to do this sort of examination, by the way, strikes me as an authorizing move to enable scholars just to assert their interests and curiosities along with their common-sense or folk ontologies, as if they were all obvious and thus we all ought to share and promote them. Or, to come at it from another direction, adopt and un-ironically use a previous generation's once self-evident terms and you'll quickly learn that categories involve interests and that interests are historically discrete – they come and go – making the "let's just get on with it" something you'd likely not entertain if you bumped into a colleague who wanted to go to fieldwork to study, let's say, the heathens ...)

So I respond by saying that it strikes me that being a scholar is a specific social role some of us happen to play, along with our many other roles (I'm also a son, for example, and a citizen, and a brother, and a department chair, and a ..., well, you get the picture), and that role of scholar – to tip my hat to Bruce Lincoln's closing section of *Theorizing Myth* – entails, among other things, showing your work (as math teachers once told us when we were learning how to do long division): making your assumptions as evident as you can, which means defining things explicitly, making evident where you got this or that idea (as I've tried to do with the few citations I'm putting into even these answers, by the way, let alone the number of times I'm adding "for me" or "as I see it," thereby trying to make evident that none of this is eternal truth or self-evidently right – instead, it is open to debate and so how shall we discuss it and settle the differences ...? What are the rules of our discourse ...? Peer review is one of them. What are the others ... ?). And so, though it'll surely sound too bold to put it this way, the sort of analysis of the field that I try to model for readers is an invitation to people who strike me as not showing their work to be better scholars.

I recall Robert Orsi's review of my earlier book, *The Discipline of Religion*, in which he made what I took as some pretty strong criticisms of me dehumanizing the people I study by not taking them seriously in their own right, such as describing them as they supposedly understood or described themselves. Well, that claim provided a wonderful opportunity to examine how he goes about *his* work and, wouldn't you know it, I was able to demonstrate (in a 2006 essay in the *Journal of the American Academy of Religion*) that his representations of the people he studies also function at a distance from what they seem to say about themselves (if the people we study are even engaged in self-representation as opposed to just living their life, as most of us do each day of our lives), all of which makes pretty evident that the role of scholarship is to say something new about the world, based on curiosities specific to the scholar and, ideally, shared by enough colleagues to constitute a field or a discipline. For if it is just repetition and paraphrase of what people already think or say about themselves then, as Jonathan Z. Smith said on a number of occasions, it's pretty uninteresting, since the people are already saying or thinking this or that and so who are we to think that they need our help.

5. Also, how do you respond to the somehow related critique that discursive approaches, while they often refuse to provide definitions of 'religion,' apply tacit definitions by describing something as a 'discourse on religion'? It is better, they claim, to make definitions explicit. What is your take on that?

I don't feel a need to define religion if my interest is in studying what other people are doing when they define it and study the it that their definitions makes it possible for them to talk about – that is, when they create a discursive object, religion, as if it was an actual item in the world. There's no tacit definition of religion in such approaches, if you ask me – one can study the discourse on beauty or the discourse on justice without ever needing to implicitly or explicitly take a stand, in one's role as scholar, on what either of these discursive objects actually are or whether talking about such objects is something we *ought* to be doing, if only we could do it in some better fashion.

But that having been said, of course, as I noted above: one must always work to make one's definition explicit (show your work, as I quoted above). Often we assume a shorthand, of course, as I also noted earlier ('society' being one instance of that, an example I picked up from J. Z. Smith's little essay, "The Necessary Lie: Duplicity in the Disciplines" that I'm happy to have been able to include as an Afterword to my own intro book, *Studying Religion*) but the trouble is that many fail to see our terms as convenient shorthands since we often just assume that, to return to another topic that I discussed earlier, our word belief or the word faith necessarily pairs up with actual things in the world that are somehow internal and thus private states or dispositions that are primary and thus causal of actions. Instead, I'd like an explicit definition of those terms, a recognition that they usually function as part of a popular discourse (that, in many moments of our own day-to-day lives, many of us [at least English language users] rely upon, to be sure) that needs to be retooled if it is to be employed by scholars as a cross-culturally useful category. (As I've said in classes before, if you think 'soul' means something eternal in you that goes either to heaven or hell after you die then you'd likely better retool it significantly to make it a more useful analytic term or, perhaps, just drop it entirely from your cross-cultural studies, seeing it as a word that works only at the descriptive level.) But for much of our work we don't do that; instead, we often work with a common-sense vocabulary to which we're already very accustomed, much like how scholars often use this word 'religion.'

In fact, that's one of my criticisms of cognitive science of religion: for all its attempts at technical precision it generally just adopts the common definition of religion and uses it as if it is analytically helpful – after all, we all just seem to know that religion exists, that it is different from non-religious things, and it involves belief in superhuman actors, right? That the term has a limited history, when used in this fashion, and develops from much earlier Latin terms that had nothing necessarily to do with how we use it today, well, even if someone acknowledges that they'll probably turn around in the next sentence and talk about ancient religion or a religious impulse or some such universalized, non-historicized notion that, as I read it, reverts back to the taken-for-granted view of the world they've adopted inasmuch as they're members of certain social groups. But scholarship, being a different discourse from that, has requirements, I'd argue. As I've often remarked, there's a good reason why chemists drink water but study H_2O. Unfortunately, many scholars of religion fail to see themselves moving between discourses and thus roles, both of which have very different conditions and requirements.

6. It seems that today discourse research still stimulates very strong negative reactions within the field of religious studies. What is your experience with that? And why is discourse research so controversial within the discipline?

Whether it's in essays and books or in social media posts, yes indeed: discursive analysis gets critiqued from all sides. It's a form of self-involved, politically irresponsible navel-gazing, as I said I was told today, of all places, on Twitter. I've heard some version of this many times over the years. (I think of the times I was regularly critiqued for my work, as being too alienated from the real stuff of our field, by the same person, who ended up with several C.V. lines criticizing my work, until I told him at a conference that because his work took mine as its data, instead of the real stuff of religion, then he must be more alienated than even me!)

I tend to think it's because the social formations in which we live and by means of which we act ourselves into identities and agencies (some form of a liberal democratic nation state, in many of ours cases) require a certain degree of naïve realism in order just to work – pretty much what I meant above when talking about studying the fabrications, as if they arose of their own volition, as opposed to studying the fabricating processes. Take the common example of money, for instance: in order to just work, making possible our daily exchange systems, we likely can't think too much about what all is going on that allows both of us to think that the papery stuff in our pockets 'has value' or 'represents our labor'; quite a few people in Canada know that a penny, representing 1 cent, costs more to make than it symbolized (back in 2012 it cost 1.6 cents to make one), so they got rid of it in the Fall of 2012, making the 5 cent piece the smallest unit in their currency (though some want to get rid of that too), but that's a pretty abstract thing with which to grapple and it probably gets in the way of just leaving a tip at the cafe.

So I'd suggest that any approach that calls the folk realism of our fabrications into question, any approach that does not succumb to the good Dr. Johnson's famous stone-kicking retort (as an attempt to refute Bishop Berkeley's immaterialism) is (rightly, perhaps) seen as a threat of grave consequence to the conditions that make the group possible. So, whether on the right or the left, all sides rally to expel the unorthodox position, inasmuch as it threatens the playing field on which the left gets to be left and the right gets to be right. So while theologians and humanists are not friendly recipients of this sort of analysis, neither are social or behavioral scientists or those working in the natural sciences.

Now, in citing that "I refute you thus!" episode form the history of philosophy, I don't want to make it seem that I'm an anti-realist, for there's all sorts of ways to practice a discursive approach without maintaining that we're all figments in someone else's imagination and that nothing therefore matters. I recently published a collection of essays with De Gruyter and for one of the chapters I decided to write a new piece that tackled the way people are today using this word 'critical' in our field, such as critical religion or critical realism, for it seems counter-intuitive to many to find someone engaged in a discursive approach also to be a realist – I think of Craig Martin, Merinda Simmons, Vaia Touna, and Leslie Dorrough Smith, for example, as all being people very influenced by discursive/social constructionist approaches yet who, like me, get rather frustrated with what I can only characterize as dismissive responses that accuse them of being an anti-realist. But, again, it seems to me that anything which troubles that seemingly intuitive realism (which, I'd suggest, is not intuitive but acquired over time), the one that we all probably walk around with when navigating daily life – you know, assuming that there's no gap between signifier and signified, that authorial intentions determine meanings, that there's a right and a wrong way to talk about the past, that identity is a uniform internal trait expressed publicly by means of symbolic codes or actions, etc. – calls far too much about day-to-day life into question.

That's why I sometimes think of my work (with a bow to Michel de Certeau's book *Culture in the Plural*) as not just on the politics of classification systems (something greatly influenced by Mary Douglas's work, by the way, such as her early essay collection, *Purity and Danger*) but also as an anthropology of the credible or the mundane: investigating the practical and often overlooked conditions that make the most seemingly uninteresting of things possible and persuasive – things like saying this is religious and that isn't.

7. Many scholars of religion respond to discourse research with skepticism and sometimes even very strong rejection. Why do you think there is this general hostile response?

Well, to build on the above answer, my work proposes that the modern (i.e., post seventeenth-century) category religion – defined as it usually is: as signifying an inner, experiential, and thus private yet universally-shared trait that is only secondarily expressed in public – plays a central role in helping to make possible both the large scale social formations in which many of us today live, which is another way of saying that it plays a central role in helping to define what is generally thought to constitute a truly human being and thus a legitimate member of the group (in our case, we could call that thing a citizen, if adopting a political approach, or a consumer, if adopting an economic approach, etc.). We can see this as soon as we study, say, the history of European colonialism and the great difficulty that early imperialists (those we once called 'explorers') had deciding whether 'the natives' had religion or not and, moreover, were human beings or not.

In the new edition of my intro book I included a number of practical examples where readers could apply what each chapter was about and, as an example of the practical implications of classification I used a quotation from David Chidester's rightly celebrated book *Savage Systems: Colonialism and Comparative Religion in Southern Africa* (1996), concerning the seventeenth- and eighteenth-century Dutch understandings of the Indigenous Hottentots (also known as the Khoikhoi, the preferred term today), specifically whether they had religion or not. Chidester's conclusion? Throughout the period the Dutch concluded that these Others had religion *only when the two groups were not in open conflict* – as they were on a variety of successive occasions. As I concluded there: "Chidester argues that using this term to name certain of Khoikhoi claims and behaviors was one of the tools (or might we just say weapons?) that the Dutch employed to make sense of and thereby manage these others."

Here we have a very nice example, I think, of how handy this term religion is, defined in the usually idealist way – and if we add to this the later development of the liberal nation-state (something on which Naomi Goldenberg has done some interesting work lately), premised on the assumption of maximizing its individual members' happiness, opportunities, etc., then this tool, religion, defined in a particular way, not only can be used to name the irreducible item that made members unique but also used to name those actions that are best left in the private domain, just so that the public realm could get on with running on time (and thereby maximizing just some people's happiness, opportunities, etc.). So we arrive at the modern notion of separating church and state, whether as modeled in the US Constitution or, say, in its own way, in France's notion of *laïcité* – what Goldenberg characterizes as a technique of statecraft.

So what I'm arguing is that religion (again, defined in a certain but also common way) can be understood to play a crucial role in the day-to-day life that so many of us take for granted – whether we think we're religious or not, whether or not we attend a mosque or a synagogue, etc. So what happens when you call that taken-for-grantedness into question by studying the discourse on religion itself, such as when you try to historicize it or develop its genealogy? Or study the wider discursive field of which religious belief, religious experience, religious faith, etc., is a part … ? If my analysis is persuasive then we arrive at a situation where much of that daily life gets called into question, is potentially seen as contingent upon far wider operations that are themselves far from necessary or inevitable. If that's the case – and I know there's a number of ifs up and running here – then a hostile reaction from a variety of sites is pretty predictable. After all, could you imagine suggesting to those Dutch settlers that their continuing efforts to decide whether their southern African neighbors had religion or not was actually a hegemonic management device and thus part of an arsenal being used to conquer them?

8. Major directions within discourse research, particularly Critical Discourse Analysis, see the uncovering and critique of power relations as an important task of their work. Do you agree with that?

I do, but not in the way that some might think.
In other words, the relationship between discourse analysis and Marxist analysis is sometimes evident at this very point and the question is whether the identification of

power relations is the first step to overturning them and putting in place a more just alternative. At this particular moment in history there seems to be a number of scholars of religion who see their role *as* scholars necessarily to involve them in this very sort of overt political action – think back to that tweet that I mentioned earlier, in which it was claimed that work on categories was politically irresponsible. Now, to me, discourse analysis is intimately linked with identifying relationships of authority, since historicizing something makes it profoundly evident that, if something turns out to be contingent then *why* do we so easily see it as necessary? Think back to that penny – if we start with the view that there's no necessary link between its exchange value and its production cost, then we can become curious about why it represents one cent. Why not 10 cents? Or 20? Maybe 50? For the moment that the gap between signifier and signified becomes apparent, one can start to ask why things are the way they are, why aren't they otherwise, and just how otherwise could they be …? And here is where power comes in, I think, for one might now start to see the tremendous effort it takes not simply to keep things on track but on a specific track, so that – to stick with this one example – those pennies continue to be seen *as being worth* one cent – there's an awful lot riding on not questioning that linkage. So discourse analysis, by making what I'll just call contingency apparent, turns our attention to why certain relationships (between symbol and meaning, for example, or item and value) endure and, importantly, what it might take to create new ones.

The Confederate flag's contemporary use and place in the US is another helpful example (have you noticed that none of my examples are religious?), for in this case we have two opposed sides each equally certain about its real meaning, each presuming a necessary link between the flag and 'what it represents' – for one, it's a rich spirit of independence and, for the other, a tragic history of enslavement. Much is at stake in which of these we opt to endorse, of course, but I'd argue that, inasmuch as we are being scholars, our role is not to endorse but, instead, to make the alternatives apparent, to historicize the seeming necessity of the options, and to thereby make clear the interests, choices, and actions – in a word, the human situations – needed for, for example, statues honoring Confederate heroes to remain in place, in cities across the US South, or, as they are now in so many cases, to be toppled from where they once stood. It amounts to not just showing our work but showing the work it takes to make this thing we call society run and, at least in our classes, inviting our students to see how messy it is and then to take that knowledge and go make the world into something.

On this I'm quite close to J. Z. Smith, in fact: I'm not here to make the choices for them but, instead, to try to let them in on the secret that choices are being made, all the time, that there always are alternatives, that things are always at stake, that the world could be rather different – for what I might personally consider good or ill, to be sure – and thereby trying to empower them to step up and make their choices, whether they wish to become a scholar or in whatever other future they try to make for themselves. As I sometimes say in class, it takes tremendous effort to look the same each day – we all know how messy we look when we awake in the morning.

That effort, that exercise of power to create the impression of uniformity, deserves attention if we're wondering why things are the way they are. And that attention likely gives us a clue to how things could change.

So, as I've written over the years, I don't think my role is to critique power relations in the items I study, if by that it means to identify their flaws and then correct them (so, yes, what do we mean by critique or being critical?); instead, discourse analysis helps to make clear the elaborate authorizing systems that it takes to make any apparent link between symbol and meaning seem natural, inevitable, or correct. As a scholar, I think that's my job – again, what I meant earlier by historicization. What I take Roland Barthes to have been up to by trying to find the way we present things to each other as natural.

9. Discursive approaches are usually informed by a constructivist paradigm that has been very prominent in the social sciences since the 1970s. Recently, a strong critique of constructivist approaches has been raised in the fields of cultural studies, ecocriticism, biosemiotics, new materialisms, with repercussions in anthropology, science and technology studies, and archaeology. Do you think we see today a new trend against constructivist approaches? And how should discourse research respond to that criticism?

I don't think it's a new trend, since it's been pretty clear all along that there are those who are not pleased with considering that, as I said above, things could be otherwise – or, let me correct that: they are very pleased that things can be otherwise when it comes to overturning views with which they disagree but that their own associations are contingent and situation-specific as well is not something of interest to them. It's for this reason that I tend to think that discourse analysis will likely always be on the fringe, identifying overlooked gaps between words and things. At least in my experience, this sort of approach does not win you too many friends, for it can identify a certain sloppiness in other scholars' approaches.

I think of a point I once made in a review essay on a recent book by Anne Taves, commenting on a cognitive science experiment cited in our field, in which counter-intuitiveness was being tested, and the stimulus "A sick rock" was presented to test subjects, to see if they caught the fact that it confused domains, inasmuch as inanimate objects cannot get sick. But all one has to do is point out that, for a certain English-speaking generation who might be taking that test, "sick" could be synonymous with good, as in something being cool (not meaning the temperature, of course), hip (a term well divorced from anatomy), wicked (though not at all in the moral sense), or crazy (with no relation to insanity, to be sure). In other words, the test presupposed as normative a certain sort of standard English, which is well enough, but not if the test is trying to discover supposedly universal or genetically inevitable cognitive traits in human beings; for we have not controlled for the fact that language is itself a contingent, social phenomenon but, instead, presented it as meaningfully transparent and unambiguous, which – as the sick rock makes plain – it is not. So, to my way of thinking, the test's design was quite sloppy and, if nothing else, discourse analysis identified this, thereby functioning within a field akin to a quality control department, looking at our peers' work and suggesting that we all could do it better. Though not all who are interested in discourse analysis may be content with this role – and it certainly is not the only one available – it is an important one nonetheless, I think.

10. What do you think is the future for discursive studies in the discipline of religious studies? Given that nature of academic 'fads' and the recent turn to the affective, material and agential, do you consider it likely that discursive approaches will flourish or remain as an accepted – if not overly utilized – part of the discipline's academic 'furniture'?

I'm not sure; if some of my above answers were persuasive – such as the role I proposed for the idealist notion of religion within liberal democracies – then we not only have a way to understand the (re)turn toward the affective, the embodied, and the material but also a way to see the fringe (but, I think, important nonetheless) role that discursive approaches might always play. In our department, at the University of Alabama – one in which we are explicitly experimenting with new ways to organize and practice the field (my preferred term, as you may have noticed, though I'll happily call it a discipline too, but with little emphasis placed on the specificity of that term) – the faculty represents a broad range of critical approaches that we group together as social theory, with discourse analysis certainly being one among them, but inasmuch as we're trying to train our M.A. students in a way that will help make them competitive for doctoral programs at other universities (should that be their aim), it is clear that they need to be conversant with more (traditional) models for the field than just discourse analysis. After all, they're applying to Religion in America programs or Asian Religion specialties or Religion and Culture programs, etc., each run by faculty who hope to recognize their applicants as some version of themselves – not to mention the hiring departments that are several years in the future of a new Ph.D. student, whose members, when making decisions on job applicants, will surely aim to hire someone who can teach the world religion course or the course on myth or the one on science and religion, etc.

Until such a time that the field is reorganized, from top to bottom – and I'm not optimistic that it will be, given my above thoughts on the wider role played by the modern category religion – that world religions model (and what some are now calling religious literacy) will continue to define what many of us do, ensuring that the discursive approach is not in the lead. The dominant model may be tweaked a little in response to our work, such that more things will be admitted into the world religions club (question: should Indigenous religions have a chapter of its own in those books, and what about New Age or maybe even the Nones and spirituality ...?). Also, due to recent critiques of categorization many no longer study, say, Judaism but, rather, they now study Judaisms, but despite such gains, sooner or later, you just know that you'll still find the term 'radical Islam' or 'political Hinduism' making their appearance in their respective fields, signifying the (often unspoken) apolitical, idealist norm against which these variants are being compared and, yes, judged – a judgment scholars regularly make and one which reinforces an orthodox norm or, as my colleague at Alabama, Steven Ramey, phrases it, an accidental favorite.

So my hope is that the discursive approach remains, of course, but given my use of that approach to study the discourse on religion I'm not optimistic for its ability to change the field entirely. That doesn't make me a pessimist, of course, but, instead, I'd say a realist who recognizes that the luxury of occupying a small, creative lacuna where we can do this different sort of work comes at the price of inhabiting the larger structure that makes these very gaps possible.

References

Barthes, Roland. 1972. *Mythologies*. New York: Farrar, Straus and Giroux.
Braun, Willi, and Russell T. McCutcheon (eds.). 2000. *Guide to the Study of Religion*. London: Bloomsbury.
Certeau, Michel de. 1997. *Culture in the Plural*, edited by Luce Girard and translated by Tom Conley. Minneapolis: University of Minnesota Press.
Chidester, David. 1996. *Savage Systems: Colonialism and Comparative Religion in Southern Africa*. Charlottesville: University of Virginia Press.
Douglas, Mary. 1966. *Purity and Danger: An Analysis of Concepts of Pollution and Taboo*. Routlege and Kegan Paul.
Fitzgerald, Timothy. 2000. *The Ideology of Religious Studies*. New York: Oxford University Press.
Goldenberg, Naomi. 2015. "The Category of Religion in the Technology of Governance: An Argument for Understanding Religions as Vestigial States." In *Religion as a Category of Governance and Sovereignty*, edited by Trevor Stack, Naomi Goldenberg, and Timothy Fitzgerald, 280–292. Leiden and Boston: Brill.
Lincoln, Bruce. 1994. *Authority: Construction and Corrosion*. Chicago: The University of Chicago Press.
Lincoln, Bruce. 1999. *Theorizing Myth: Narrative, Ideology, and Scholarship*. Chicago: The University of Chicago Press.
McCutcheon, Russell T. 1997. *Manufacturing Religion: The Discourse on Sui Generis Religion and the Politics of Nostalgia*. New York: Oxford University Press.
McCutcheon, Russell T. 2003. *The Discipline of Religion: Structure, Meaning, Rhetoric*. New York: Routledge.
McCutcheon, Russell T. 2006. "'It's a Lie. There's No Truth in It! It's a Sin!': On the Limits of the Humanistic Study of Religion and the Costs of Saving Others from Themselves." *Journal of the American Academy of Religion* 74: 720–750.
McCutcheon, Russell T. 2010. "Will Your Cognitive Anchor Hold in the Storms of Culture?" *Journal of the American Academy of Religion* 78: 1182–1193.
McLaughlin, Thomas, and Frank Lentricchia (eds.). 1990. *Critical Terms for Literary Study*. Chicago: The University of Chicago Press.
McMullin, Neil. 1989. "*The Encyclopedia of Religion*: A Critique From the Perspective of the History of the Japanese Religious Traditions." *Method & Theory in the Study of Religion* 1: 80–96.

Orsi, Robert A. 2004. "Fair Game," *Bulletin of the Council of Societies for the Study of Religion* 33: 87–89.
Paden, William E. 1991. "Before 'the Sacred' Became Theological: Rereading the Durkheimian Legacy." *Method & Theory in the Study of Religion* 3: 10–23.
Ramey, Steven R. 2015. "Accidental Favorites: The Implicit in the Study of Religion." In *Claiming Identity in the Study of Religion: Social and Rhetorical Techniques Examined*, edited by Monica R. Miller, 223–238. Sheffield: Equinox Publishers.
Said, Edward. 1978. *Orientalism*. New York: Pantheon Books.
Smith, Jonathan Z. 1982. *Imagining Religion: From Babylon to Jonestown*. Chicago: The University of Chicago Press.
Smith, Jonathan Z. 2019. "The Necessary Lie: Duplicity in the Disciplines." In Russell T. McCutcheon, *Studying Religion: An Introduction*, 2nd ed., 124–129. New York: Routledge.
Smith, Wilfred Cantwell. 1963. *The Meaning and End of Religion*. Minneapolis: Fortress Press.
Taves, Ann. 2011. *Religious Experience Reconsidered: A Building-Block Approach to the Study of Religion and Other Special Things*. Princeton: Princeton University Press.
Taylor, Mark C. 1998. *Critical Terms for Religious Studies*. Chicago: The University of Chicago Press.
Žižek, Slavoj (ed.). 1994. *Mapping Ideology*. London: Verso.

Reiner Keller
Entering Discourses: A New Agenda for Qualitative Research and the Sociology of Knowledge

1 Introduction

The following text argues for a new agenda in qualitative research and the sociology of knowledge. Taking up the concept of discourse and embedding it in the social constructivist approach – itself largely anchored in the interpretive paradigm and sociological pragmatism – I present theoretical foundations, methodological implications, and some practical tools for a *sociology of knowledge approach to discourse* (SKAD). This qualitative approach to discourse has been established in German sociology since the late 1990s and has been presented in several books (for example, Keller [2005] 2021; [2003] 2013; for additional recent presentations, see Keller 2011; Keller, Hornidge, and Schünemann 2018). Since then, it has influenced research across the social sciences.[1] This chapter first sets up the arguments for entering discourses from sociology of knowledge perspectives; it then presents theoretical grounds for and methodological reflections on SKAD, discusses some knowledge-orientated tools for doing SKAD research, and concludes with reflections on methods of discourse research.

---

[1] The full argument is presented in Keller (2005) 2021. Studies using the SKAD framework focus on environmental politics (Keller [1998] 2009; Cantoni et al. 2018; Boettcher 2019), the symbolic production of space and cityscapes (Christmann 2004), healthcare policy (Bechmann 2007), the acknowledgement of competency in employment strategies (Truschkat 2008), public discourse on Satanism (Schmied-Knittel 2008), identity-building in left-wing social movements in Germany and Great Britain (Ullrich 2008) and Chinese migrant communities in Romania (Wundrak 2010), criminology (Singelnstein 2009), same-sex marriage TV controversies in the US (Zimmermann 2010), or political sciences' mapping of suicide terrorism (Brunner 2011). For compilations of these different applications of the approach, see Keller and Truschkat 2012; Bosančić and Keller 2016; Keller, Hornidge, and Schünemann 2018.

Updated reprint of Keller, Reiner. 2012. "Entering Discourses: A New Agenda for Qualitative Research and Sociology of Knowledge." *Qualitative Sociology Review* 8, no. 2: 46–75, http://www.qualitativesociologyreview.org/ENG/archive_eng.php. Reprinted with the kind permission of the *Qualitative Sociology Review*.

https://doi.org/10.1515/9783110473438-003

2 Entering Discourses

For some decades now, sociology has broadly acknowledged the ascendancy of knowledge societies. According to Anthony Giddens' diagnosis of reflexive modernity, these kinds of societies are special in the way they rely on expert knowledge (Giddens 1991, 36–44). Such knowledge, gained through organized procedures, shapes every detail of everyday life as well as organizational processes and institutions, from the way we 'do orgasm' to the daily practices of education, sports, food, and drink; to our ways of working and organizing production and consumption; all the way to the higher spheres of political governance at national or global levels of action in a "world risk society" (to borrow Ulrich Beck's phrase; see Beck 1999). As Stuart Hall and his colleagues in the Birmingham School of Cultural Studies argued in the 1990s, we are living in a period of "circuits of culture" – a phrase Hall used to indicate that meaning-making activities and the social construction of realities have become effects of the organized production, representation, marketing, regulation, and adaption of meaning (Hall 1997a). In making this statement, the Birmingham School was heavily influenced by the interpretive tradition in sociology, primarily by symbolic interactionist and Weberian theorizing and research (see, for example, Blumer 1969; Weber [1904] 1949). However, in their insistence on organized or structured means of processing circuits of culture, the Birmingham School referred to rather different theoretical traditions as well, including some of Michel Foucault's concepts:

> [r]ecent commentators have begun to recognize not only the real breaks and paradigm-shifts, but also some of the affinities and continuities, between older and newer traditions of work: for example between Weber's classical interpretive "sociology of meaning" and Foucault's emphasis of the role of the "discursive." (Hall 1997b, 224)

Here it is interesting to see Hall arguing for an integrated perspective on meaning-making, including both Weberian and Foucauldian thinking – bearing in mind that common sociological (and poststructuralist) debates seem to draw a sharp line between these two authors. However, if we look more closely, we can indeed assert that Max Weber's work on *The Protestant Ethic* (Weber [1905] 2002) is no less and no more than an *avant la lettre* discourse study of religious discourse and its power effects in capitalist societies. In making his claim regarding the connection between *The Protestant Ethic and the Spirit of Capitalism*, Weber analyzed several kinds of texts: religious books, advice books, and sermons. It was from such textual data that he developed his ideas on "worldly asceticism" (Weber [1905] 2002, 53–125) and deeply structured ways of living everyday life, whether at home or at work. While Weber insisted on the subject's role in meaning-making, for him this never denoted individual or idiosyncratic activities. *The Protestant Ethic* delivered a deeply social "vocabulary of motives" (to borrow Charles W. Mills' phrase) and an institutionally preconfigured "definition of the situation" (in William I. Thomas' and Dorothy Thomas' sense). Mills (1940) was well aware of this implication of Weber's sociology when he argued, with strong references to Weber and the sociology of knowledge, for a sociological analysis of vocabularies of motives and situated actions. And Thomas and Thomas (1928) – together with George Herbert Mead (1934) and others in the Chicago tradition – were at least familiar with the German context of *verstehen* and meaning(-making), to which Weber was deeply committed.

As far as I know, Weber never used the term discourse, but the Chicago pragmatists did. They argued that social collectivities produced and lived in 'universes of discourse' – systems or horizons of meaning and processes of establishing and transforming such systems. In the 1930s, George Herbert Mead stated: "This universe of discourse is constituted by a group of individuals [. . .] A universe of discourse is simply a system of common or social meanings" (Mead [1934] 1963, 89).

Alfred Schütz, the main proponent of social phenomenology, also referred to this notion – for example in the 1940s, when he considered the conditions of possibility for scientific work:

> [a]ll this, however, does not mean that the decision of the scientist in stating the problem is an arbitrary one or that he has the same "freedom of discretion" in choosing and solving his problems which the phantasying self has in filling out its anticipations. This is by no means the case. Of course, the theoretical thinker may choose at his discretion [a particular scientific field.] But, as soon as he has made up his mind in this respect, the scientist enters a preconstituted world of scientific contemplation handed down to him by the historical tradition of his science. Henceforth, he will participate in a universe of discourse embracing the results obtained by others, methods worked out by others. This theoretical universe of the special science is itself a finite province of meaning, having its peculiar cognitive style with peculiar implications and horizons to be explicated. The regulative principle of constitution of such a province of meaning, called a special branch of science, can be formulated as follows: Any problem emerging within the scientific field has to partake of the universal style of this field and has to be compatible with the preconstituted problems and their solution by either accepting or refuting them. Thus, the latitude for the discretion of the scientist in stating the problem is in fact a very small one. (Schütz 1973, 250)

And a few pages later, he writes: "[t]heorizing [. . .] is, first, possible only within a universe of discourse that is pregiven to the scientist as the outcome of other people's theorizing acts" (Schütz 1973, 256).

While later work in the tradition of Alfred Schütz – as well as of Peter L. Berger and Thomas Luckmann (1966), who built on Schütz's work – only marginally took up this concept (if at all), the symbolic interactionist perspective has indeed informed several research agendas which turned to discourse-related subjects and questions, whether implicitly or explicitly. Without offering an exhaustive list, one could mention Joseph Gusfield's study on the *Culture of Public Problems* (1981), Anselm Strauss' attention to "ongoing negotiated orderings in social worlds/arenas" (1979; 1991; 1993), or broader work on the social construction and careers of social problems. Stephen Hilgartner and Charles L. Bosk have presented certain essential assumptions involved in the latter:

In its most schematic form, our model has six main elements:
1. a dynamic process of competition among the members of a very large 'population' of social problem claims;
2. the institutional arenas that serve as 'environments' where social problems compete for attention and grow;
3. the 'carrying capacities' of these arenas, which limit the number of problems that can gain widespread attention at one time;
4. the 'principles of selection' or institutional, political, and cultural factors that influence the probability of survival of competing problem formulations;
5. patterns of interaction among the different arenas, such as feedback and synergy, through which activities in each arena spread throughout the others; and
6. the networks of operatives who promote and attempt to control particular problems and whose channels of communication crisscross the different arenas. (Hilgartner and Bosk 1988, 56)

In the context of the symbolic interactionists' social movements research in the 1980s and 1990s, such ideas were closely linked to a concept of public discourse, referring to the issue-framing activities of competing collective actors in public struggles for the collectivities' "definition of the situation" (see Gamson 1988). However, despite these efforts and multiple studies, it seems that this interpretive paradigm's analysis of discourses did not succeed in establishing an approach of its own – one that would integrate the different usages and elaborate on the proposed initial frameworks. Nor did cultural studies in the Birmingham tradition succeed in this arena; concrete research in this tradition made use of social semiotics or argued for critical discourse analysis, as established by Norman Fairclough and others (see Hall 1997a; Barker 2000; Barker and Galasinski 2001).

Discourse research in today's social sciences is mostly attributed to the work of the French philosopher Michel Foucault (see Keller 2008; 2018b). Such a diagnosis might be sustained by Norman Denzin's ongoing insistence on the importance of poststructuralist or postmodernist thinking for interpretive sociology (see Denzin 1992). Moreover, Adele Clarke's impressive book on *Situational Analysis* (2005) clearly indicates this influence.[2] In her manifesto for a "grounded theory after the postmodern turn," Clarke convincingly shows how grounded theory's focus on situation and interaction can be inspired and "complexified" not only by Anselm Strauss' social worlds/arenas model, but by introducing discourses as important elements of the situation under analysis. Clarke then refers to Michel Foucault as her major "modest witness" to qualitative sociology's discursive turn. She proposes various tools – such as situational maps, positional maps, and social world/arena maps – to account for the "discursive elements" of situations. *Situational Analysis* was developed at almost

---

2 A revised edition was published in 2018 by Clarke, Friese, and Washburn.

the same time as my plea for an original sociology of knowledge approach to discourse, between 1999 and 2003, which made use of many of the same references in interpretive sociology and discourse research, although Clarke and I were several thousand miles apart and did not know of each other. However, while Clarke zeroes in on the complexity of situations, my own work (Keller [2005] 2020) takes discourse (s) as the central starting and focal point. Therefore, I refer to Clarke's approach as complementary to SKAD.

Having thus far outlined the interpretive paradigm's basic arguments on social actors' meaning-making in universes of discourse, and before diving more deeply into the theoretical foundations and methodology of the sociology of knowledge approach to discourse, let us now turn to discourse and discourse analysis, as these terms are widely used in today's social sciences. No exhaustive account is possible in this case either (see Keller 2013). At present, various notions of discourse are used in the humanities. In Germany, Jürgen Habermas (1985) extensively contributed to the dissemination of the term discourse. But in the Habermasian tradition, discourse is hardly an object of inquiry to be empirically analyzed. Instead, it is regarded as an organized, ordered deliberative process to which a normative ethics of discourse is applied. A case in point concerns conflicts emerging around environmental issues or technological risk, where roundtables are set up to bring together concerned and committed actors in order to discuss what should be done. This usage, which is current today primarily in the political sciences, has created – and continues to create – some confusion in debates on discourse research. The traditional political sciences approach to discourse is mainly concerned with the relationship between arguments (ideas) and interests: in short, discourse matters if the better argument wins over the material interests of (the most) powerful actors. However, this argumentative approach to discourse has (thus far) rarely analyzed the politics of knowledge.[3] More common among sociological perspectives is discourse analysis as a label for the micro-orientated analysis of language in use, which is based either in pragmatic linguistics or – more closely aligned with sociological traditions – in conversation analysis and ethnomethodology. Here the focus is on concrete "text and talk in (inter)action" (to borrow Teun van Dijk's phrase), with more or less attention to either linguistic issues or 'sociological' questions – including, for example, turn-taking in group discussion or the interactional construction of references to larger social or mental entities. Today's linguistics uses concepts of discourse in order to address linguistic questions of language change and usage in larger social contexts (see Frans Wijsen, chapter 6, this volume). Corpus linguistics, for example, has built up enormous corpuses of textual data around selected word items (e.g., related to political issues such as migration or climate change) in order to search for statistical correlations between words.

---

[3] It should be noted that there are approaches to discourse in political science which are closer to interpretive thinking, which space does not allow me to discuss here.

Somewhere between linguistics and social sciences stands *Critical Discourse Analysis* (Norman Fairclough's concept; see, for example, Fairclough 1995), along with the British-Austrian version of this approach, *Wiener Kritische Diskursanalyse* (initiated by Ruth Wodak and others; see, for example, Wodak and Meyer 2015), and its German counterpart, *Kritische Diskursanalyse* (as developed by Siegfried Jäger; see, for example, Jäger 2012). These approaches are all based in linguistics but have slightly different discourse-theoretical elaborations; they direct discourse research mainly toward 'unmasking' the ideological functions of language in use or discovering and 'healing' instances of 'asymmetrically biased communication' and 'disorders of discourse.'[4]

If we consider them more carefully, we can state that none of the approaches to discourse research mentioned thus far is interested in larger societal and historical meaning-making or questions of power/knowledge, which are central to Foucault's arguments on discourse (see below). These approaches cannot (and, to be honest, do not aim to) account for the socio-historical processing of knowledge and symbolic orderings in larger institutional fields and social arenas. It is evident that discourse research anchored in linguistics addresses linguistic questions – and Foucault's main purpose was to pivot discourse away from such issues. The lack of focus on knowledge analysis is also particularly clear in research that employs critical discourse analysis. Instead, such research implies that the researcher identifies and unmasks the illegitimate, ideological, strategic use of language by 'those in power' to 'manipulate the people.' This often results in a 'proof' of the presence of ideological notions and functions in a concrete body of spoken or written language (discourse). There is no room to derive any surprising results or insights from such empirical research, because the discourse theorist always already knows how the ideology in question works. The ethnomethodologically inspired tradition of discourse analysis investigates the situational production of ordered verbal interaction and communication. This is very useful for in-depth analyses of singular discursive events, but it does not (and does not seek to) grasp larger historical processes of knowledge circulation.

As far as I can see, there are two further candidates that could address questions of meaning-making via the concept of discourse. I suggest calling them, for want of a better expression, *discourse theories* – including the work of the philosopher Michel Foucault or the political scientists Ernesto Laclau and Chantal Mouffe. Discourse theories are designed to analyze the social formation of circuits of culture, power/knowledge relationships, or political struggles for hegemony and the articulation of collective identities on more global levels of social orderings. The Laclau and Mouffe tradition combines a rather extensive definition of discourse – the discursive and the social are but one[5] – with a reductionist analysis of the

---

4 For SKAD's engagement with concepts of critique, see Keller 2016a.
5 It seems that what has been called (for a hundred years now) 'symbolic ordering' and 'meaning-making' or 'social signification systems' in sociology is here referred to as 'the discursive.'

'hegemonic functions' of texts and articulations, mainly focused on political identity building around a particular issue. Here, attention is drawn to political claim-making in the name of the 'common good' (Laclau and Mouffe 2001).

The main point I want to make against the Laclau and Mouffe approach to discourse refers back to Foucault's interests in the discursive constitution of knowledge – to which they either do not or cannot draw our attention. So why could and should this part of Foucault's thinking be of interest for interpretive sociology? How did he refer discourse to knowledge and meaning-making? This merits closer examination. As a philosopher turning to empirical and historical studies, Foucault developed his approach to discourse and the complexities of power/knowledge quite apart from sociological positions (which where rather marginal in the French context in the early 1960s). Nevertheless, he invented his own "historical sociology of knowledge" (see Keller 2008; 2018b). While in the German discussion the works of Michel Foucault were long placed in stark contrast to the sociology of knowledge, in the Anglo-American debates, affinities, parallels, and connections were seen early on. This becomes particularly clear in the following quotation, which reflects an early, precise, comprehensive assessment by Philipp Manning:

> Foucault explores the domain of the sociology of knowledge: ideas in their social context and the explanation for their continuity and change, as seen against the changing significance of history, politics, and economics. [. . .] Foucault attempts to construct a history not of ideas, but of events, and these events are critical insofar as they serve to show the disruption of previous modes of discourse. [. . .] He is interested in the ways discourse is represented in documents in his historical guise and how these, in turn, become important or significant, or statements of entire sets of conflicting times, durations and spatial forces. [. . .] The document provides an anchor with which Foucault grounds his work on the classification of the world [. . .]. Language does not guide Foucault to a consideration of the distinctions between the sign and the signifier, or between language as a system of rules and speech as competence or performance. Rather Foucault distinguishes rules and practices [. . .]. The sociology of knowledge in Foucault is represented in the search for the concept that will show how certain practices within a field of regulation or control vary, revealing the effect of power and of invisible forces on the practices. [He] introduces the material and political forces that shape and are sedimented in structures of knowledge.
> (Manning 1982, 65)

In a certain way, Foucault can definitely be understood as a representative of the Durkheimian ([1912] 2008) tradition, which advances a genuine sociology of knowledge analysis of social 'systems of thought.' However, he did so in somewhat abductive ways, which are closer to qualitative research in sociology. By this I mean that he worked 'from the bottom up,' starting with certain methodical devices and sensitizing concepts in order to analyze in detail certain historical (textual) data representing past institutions, practices, actors, and knowledge – what Hubert Dreyfus and Paul Rabinow called an "interpretive analytics" (1982). Foucault's fundamental achievement was first to look at discourses as socio-historically situated 'practices,' manifest as textual data, and not as the development of ideas or lines of argumentation, and second to 'liberate' discourse analysis from linguistic issues.

In so doing, he laid important foundations for a sociological analysis of discourses. When he argued that his main concern was the "analysis of problematisations" (Foucault 1984) – that is, the appearance of central breaking or turning points in the history of social constitutions of subjectivities or particular orders of practice – he came quite close to the interests of the symbolic interactionists.

Although Foucault's work is often presented in a rather monolithic way, I would like to insist on (and point to) his varied uses of the term discourse. In his seminal book for discourse research, *The Archaeology of Knowledge* (1972a), which reflects his own previous studies (especially the *Order of Things*, a historical analysis of the sciences; see Foucault [1966] 1970), Foucault proposes a theoretical framework which takes discourse as its central concept. Discourses are considered as historically situated, real social practices – not *representing* external objects, but *constituting* them. This implies looking at concrete data – oral and written texts, articles, books, discussions, institutions, disciplines – in order to analyze 'from the bottom up' how discourses are structured and how they structure knowledge domains and claims. Foucault speaks of "discursive formations" (1972a, 34–78) – for example, the "formation of concepts" (which concepts are used and how they relate to each other) or the "formation of enunciative modalities" (such as the "places for speakers" and the established criteria – for example, academic careers and titles – by which they are accessed). His notion of the "statement" (Foucault 1972a, 79–117) refers to the typified core elements of discursive events and concrete utterances – that is, what makes them part of a particular discourse and sets up a particular knowledge claim. The analysis of discursive formations leads us, via empirical data, to the rules and regularities which operate – and are operated by socialized actors – in a given or emerging disciplinary field, including rules directing (rather than determining) who is allowed to speak, how a particular discourse is to be performed, and what can be said. This idea can easily be shown in the present text, where I am following social sciences discursive formation, which excludes, for example, gossiping about my adventures yesterday evening or changing the language setting to *der deutschen Sprache*, in which I could also pursue my arguments (if permitted to do so).

In his later works, Foucault never realized the kind of analysis he projected (or stated retrospectively) in *The Archaeology of Knowledge*. Nevertheless, he returned to discourse several times: *L'ordre du discours* (The Order of Discourse), presented as oral communication in 1970 and strangely translated as *The Discourse on Language* (which was included as an appendix in the American translation of *The Archaeology of Knowledge* [1972b, 215–238]), in fact pursues the framework of discourse research by more explicitly introducing ideas of power and the mechanisms of the 'inner structuration' of discourses (such as the 'commentary,' for example, which differentiates between important statements and the rest). Most interesting for interpretive social research, in the context of the Rivière case (see *I, Pierre Rivière* [1973] 1982), Foucault addresses discourses as "battlefields," as power struggles around the legitimate definition of phenomena. This lesser-known work comes very close to symbolic interactionist positions. Here, Foucault and his team are dealing with a case of parricide in early nineteenth-century French Normandy: Pierre Rivière killed his mother, sister, and brother in an act of revenge, in order to recover his father's 'lost honor.' The interesting point is that this person presents an extensive written account of his motivation – and he really wants to be punished. But there are some other accounts, too: the police, the doctors, different psychological schools – they all produce their own, often contradictory versions of 'what the Rivière case is.' This is all highly consequential: Is he responsible for this act? Should Rivière be accused and put to death for murder, or labelled 'insane' and sent to a psychiatric hospital? Thus we can observe a classic struggle for the common, institutionally acceptable definition of the situation and the corresponding actions to be taken.

Foucault's implicit affinities with pragmatist and interpretive sociology are very clear here. Indeed, Richard Rorty (1982, xviii) and Nancy Fraser (1997) asserted Foucault's relation to pragmatist philosophy very early on, referring to pragmatist notions of discourse. "Foucault and Pragmatism" is taken up in detail in a recent special issue of *Foucault Studies* (Koopman 2011), with contributions discussing Foucault and Dewey, among other themes. In symbolic interactionism and interpretive sociology, Lindsay Prior (1989), Brian Castellani (1999), Stevi Jackson and Sue Scott (2007), Adele Clarke (2005), and others have drawn attention to the interest Foucault's work holds for interpretive sociology. We hear echoes of Herbert Blumer's, Anselm Strauss', and many other's writings on symbolic interactionism when Prior states:

> Indeed, for Foucault the familiar objects of the social world (whether they be death, disease, madness, sexuality, sin or even mankind itself) are not "things" set apart from and independent of discourse, but are realized only in and through the discursive elements which surround the objects in question. Things, then, are made visible and palpable through the existence of discursive practices, and so disease or death are not referents about which there are discourses, but objects constructed by discourse. As the discourse changes, so too do the objects of attention. A discourse moreover, is not merely a narrow set of linguistic practices which reports on the world, but is composed of a whole assemblage of activities, events, objects, settings and epistemological precepts. The discourse of pathology, for example, is constructed not merely out of statements about diseases, cells and tissues, but out of the whole network of activities and events in which pathologists become involved, together with the laboratory and other settings within which they work and in which they analyze the objects of their attention. (Prior 1989, 3)

Despite these engagements, discourse research, whether situating itself in 'Foucault's footsteps' or more generally in the tradition of poststructuralism, does not usually refer to pragmatist traditions in sociology, and interpretive sociology and qualitative research have not thus far invested very much effort in elaborating a discourse research agenda of their own. However, as Adele Clarke has convincingly argued, discourses are not contexts of situations, but rather constituting aspects of situations.

Qualitative research has to pay attention to this if it aims to better address the complexities of today's social phenomena.

> Today the qualitative research enterprise is moving beyond field notes and interview transcripts to include discourses of all kinds. We dwell [. . . in] explosions of images, representations, and narrative discourses that constitute cultures of consumption as well as production, of politics writ a million ways, of diverse individual and collective social and cultural identities, including racial, ethnic, gendered, religious, and subcultural identities, of dense histories, of old and new technologies and media from television to the Internet, and so on. Because *we and the people and things we choose to study* are all routinely both producing and awash in seas of discourses, analyzing only individual and collective human actors no longer suffices for many qualitative projects. Increasingly, historical, visual, narrative, and other discourse materials and non-human material cultural objects of all kinds must be included as elements of our research and subjected to analysis because they are increasingly understood/interpreted as both constitutive of and consequential for the phenomena we study.[6]
>
> (Clarke 2005, 145)

The following section presents the sociology of knowledge approach to discourse, which aims to deepen such proposals.

3 The Sociology of Knowledge Approach to Discourse

3.1 General Outline

Once again, it was Stuart Hall (among others) who prominently argued in favor of a knowledge-oriented concept of discourse in the 1990s: "Discourses are ways of referring to or constructing knowledge about a particular topic of practice: a cluster (or *formation*) of ideas, images and practices, which provide ways of talking about, forms of knowledge and conduct associated with, a particular topic, social activity or institutional site in society" (Hall 1997a, 4). The hypothesis I want to pursue here is as follows: Berger and Luckmann's sociology of knowledge provides a theoretical framework which makes it possible to integrate (or elaborate within) a sociology of knowledge approach to discourse.[7] In the 1960s, Peter L. Berger and Thomas Luckmann brought together sociology of knowledge traditions, the interpretive

---

[6] See also Clarke, Friese, and Washburn 2018; Clarke and Keller 2018.

[7] Despite some minor differences, I believe this sociology of knowledge approach goes hand-in-hand with symbolic interactionist thought. The whole argument on SKAD is presented in Keller (2005) 2020; see also Keller 2011; the methods are discussed in Keller (2003) 2013. In addition, see the detailed presentation of SKAD and several case studies in Keller, Hornidge, and Schünemann 2018. For the usage of SKAD in social movement research and comparative cultural studies, see Ulrich and Keller 2014.

paradigm (including symbolic interactionist thinking and social phenomenology), and neighboring fields in their influential book, *The Social Construction of Reality* (1966). In this work, the authors differentiated between society as an objective reality which is sedimented within institutions and stocks of knowledge, on the one hand, and the way in which the acting subjects appropriate this reality in diverse socialization processes, on the other. It should be noted here that the term knowledge refers to all kinds of symbolic orderings and institutionalized symbolic orders (including common-sense knowledge, religion, theory, ideology, scientific knowledge, and so on). Above all, Berger and Luckmann emphasize the role of language and the daily 'conversational machinery' in the construction of a shared social reality. They discuss how knowledge is typified and realized through interactions and socially objectified in differing processes of institutionalization. Knowledge is also reified and becomes the foundation of social worlds differentiated by their symbolic horizons. Next, they talk about the legitimization of these knowledge/institutional complexes, and also about forms or steps of legitimization, which extend from the simple usage of particular vocabularies through theoretical postulates and explicit legitimization theories to elaborate symbolic sub-universes. These legitimizations are supported by various forms of social organization. Together with this analysis regarding the structure of knowledge come questions about the individuals, groups, actors, organizations, practices, artifacts, and institutional structures that fix (or transform) such orders. The historically situated order of knowledge within a society is internalized by the actors via socialization processes and is then reproduced (and occasionally transformed) through the permanent use of language or other systems of signs, as well as through nonverbal practices.

Indeed, Berger and Luckmann integrated a more Durkheimian view of society as institutionalized facticity with a more Weberian interest in social actors' meaning-making activities and Meadian perspectives on socialization processes and (wo)man's use of significant symbols. They temporalized and neutralized the older antagonism between structure and action by replacing it with a more dialectical perspective, arguing for structures (institutions) as the historically situated, emerging (side) effects of social actors' practices, 'doings,' and negotiations, and for social actors' agency and creativity as constituted by a socio-historical *a priori* – that is, existing social contexts, particularly "symbolic universes" (Berger and Luckmann 1966, 110–120) or "sub-universes of reality" and "finite provinces of meaning" (Schütz 1973, 230).

Although Berger and Luckmann highlighted the role of 'theoretical conceptions' (ideas, theories, and others) in social processes, they placed much more emphasis on the fact that their main interest (and therefore also the main interest of the sociology of knowledge inspired by these two authors) was in 'common sense,' since in the end, this seemed to them the most relevant level of social knowledge (1966, 14–15). The Berger and Luckmann legacy in Germany at present uses the label *Hermeneutische Wissenssoziologie* (the hermeneutical sociology of knowledge;

see Hitzler, Reichertz, and Schröer 1999; 2020)[8] to mark the difference between this and other social science approaches to knowledge. Since Schütz's, Berger's, and Luckmann's sociology of knowledge has always paid great attention to the connection between language and knowledge, it has recently been presented by some of its proponents as the "communicative paradigm" in knowledge research (Knoblauch 1995; see also Knoblauch 2020 on the "communicative construction of reality"). In taking up foundational work on social construction, including the tenet that everyday knowledge should be the central point of reference for research, the *Hermeneutische Wissenssoziologie* has unfortunately concentrated primarily on micro-levels of knowledge analysis. It has directed its interests toward ethnographies of the "small lifeworlds of modern man" (to borrow Benita Luckmann's phrase) or laypersons' and professional actors' interpretations of their everyday activities, as well as toward common-sense knowledge and individuals as the knowledge actors of daily life. However, as we have seen with regard to the original argument on institutionalization and legitimization, this is a rather contingent and by no means necessary elaboration on their work.

SKAD, although situated within this paradigm of knowledge research, constitutes both an extension and a correction, elaborating on the 'objective reality' side of Berger's and Luckmann's theory – that is, on the (institutional) processes and structures in social relations of knowledge – and taking the *discursive* construction of highly consequential objective realities into consideration. Nevertheless, as we have seen, Berger and Luckmann's original work offers a rather comprehensive view of society as symbolic order and ordering, including both institutional levels and actors' agency, as well as the interplay between them. Their *insistence* on Mead and Schütz explains the 'priority' these two scholars assume here over Foucault's argument for discourses, which only addresses institutional settings and practices. Foucault's perspective has to be grounded in a general pragmatist theory of the conditions of possibility of the human use of symbols, of the "animal symbolicum" (to borrow Ernst Cassirer's phrase; see Cassirer 1977). Without such an argument, the notion of discourse itself – as used by Foucault in the different ways we have seen – would lose its sense.

I do not have space here to elaborate on the relations between Mead and Schütz; I shall merely note the strong argument presented by Ilja Srubar (1988) regarding the close connection between Schütz and Chicago pragmatist thinking. Following Alfred Schütz, SKAD assumes that meaning is constituted in human consciousness, in the transformation of sensual experience into conceptual experience. The process by which we ascribe meaning to our actions and interactions, social situations, and/or the world is necessarily located in embodied human consciousness. Without a process

---

8 See Hitzler, Reichertz, and Schröer 2020. This approach is indeed very close to symbolic interactionist perspectives (Keller 2012), but it insists on phenomenological foundations (e.g., the work of Alfred Schütz) as well as on strong reflection on the researcher's interpretive activities.

such as the layering or the constitution of meaning, there is no separation between the self and the world, no perception of space, time, the social, and so on. However, this capacity of consciousness is not a genuine, extra-worldly 'production capacity,' as if consciousness creates the existence and the meaning of the world out of nothing in an act of solitary, productive creativity. As social phenomenology and symbolic interactionist thinking have largely shown, consciousnesses do indeed draw on social interpretation schemata in a fundamental typification process in order to instantiate their capacity for orientation. This occurs by means of signs – that is, significant symbols or knowledge schemata, which are taken from the socio-historically generated and established collective stocks of knowledge/universes of discourse, primarily within socialization processes. A particular individual's specific, subjective stocks of knowledge are inconsistent, heterogeneous, complex sedimentations and actualizations of knowledge triggered from the outside, which always exist in a situational, pragmatically motivated relation between focalization and blurry horizons, actualized by 'external' stimulation.

George Herbert Mead and the tradition of symbolic interactionism considered in more depth how individual competence in the use of signs/knowledge or of significant symbols develops within socialization processes. Above all, Mead emphasized the primacy of communication and of the universe(s) of discourse that always historically 'comes before' the individual. The existence of social-symbolic orders – never ultimately achieved, but always being in the 'process of ordering' – and the corresponding communication processes are a necessary prerequisite for the development of individual consciousnesses that are capable of intellectual reflection. Thought is therefore a form of communication turned inward. Research into the social phenomenon of discourses is obsolete without such a theory of sign-processing consciousnesses (which does not mean that everything is already said here).[9] Significant symbols, as well as the 'legitimate ways of using them,' are processed discursively, and the corresponding social rules work as instructions in discursively embedded utterances. Historically, they make up the more or less solidly fixed pre-existing 'supply' to be used by particular individuals and consciousnesses. The language system of meaning is a pre-condition of the inevitable, necessary 'desubjectification' of the individual's interpretive practice – in other words, the historical-social assignation of the possibilities for a 'subjective' orientation of individuals in the life-world. Its usage always presupposes the participating actors' capacity for interpretation. Every long-term use of significant symbols is a social practice regulated by social conventions. These conventions form the basis of discourse practices as a set of more or less powerful, more or less institutionalized instructive rules. They are actualized in practical usage, thus simultaneously reproduced and altered, or transformed, as needed. So individual or collective actors' complex involvement in discourses is socially regulated, but not

---

9 Consider, for example, the (widely forgotten) work of Florian Znaniecki on *Cultural Reality* (1919).

determined. There is therefore, in principal, a certain amount of freedom in interpretation and action in concrete situations, as well as a surplus of forms of communication and models for the attribution of meaning. Societies differ in the available spectrum and in their ways of producing such choices.

Following Foucault, I identify discourses as regulated, structured practices of sign usage in social arenas, which constitute smaller or larger symbolic universes. Discourses are simultaneously both an expression of and a constitutional prerequisite for the (modern) social; they become real through the actions of social actors, supply specific knowledge claims, and contribute to the liquefaction and dissolution of the institutionalized interpretations and apparent unavailabilities. Discourses crystallize and constitute themes in a particular form as social interpretation and action issues. Discursive formations are discourse groupings, which follow the same formation rules. For example, a scientific discourse is manifest in texts, conferences, papers, talks, associations, and so on, which can all be studied as data. Such discourses emerged historically out of actions and interactions committed to 'telling the empirical truth' about phenomena 'in the world,' both in form or formal appearance as well as in content: what could – and should – be said about these phenomena. Once institutionalized and generally legitimated, such discourse pre-structures (as Alfred Schütz indicated in the citation above) what can be said and done in this particular discourse arena. Michel Foucault, in the seminal works I have already mentioned, identified the ways in which dimensions of discourse can be analyzed as emergent discourse formations without recourse to the unmasking of the 'real' or 'covert' reasons and intentions of particular social interest groups or actors. He then proposed corresponding dimensions of analysis of discursive formations which, when combined with historically situated institutionalization processes and the interwoven actions of social actors therein, can benefit interpretive sociology. In discourses, social actors' use of language or symbols constitutes the sociocultural facticity of physical and social realities. The meaning of signs, symbols, images, gestures, actions, or things is more or less fixed in socially, spatially, and temporally or historically situated (and therefore transformable) orders of signs. This meaning is affirmed, conserved, or changed in the concrete usage of these signs. In this respect, every fixed meaning is a snapshot within a social process that is capable of generating an endless variety of possible readings and interpretations. Discourses can be understood as attempts to freeze meanings or, more generally speaking, to freeze more or less broad symbolic orders – that is, to fix them in time, and by so doing, to institutionalize a binding context of meaning, values, and actions/agency within social collectives.

SKAD is concerned with this correlation between sign usage as a social practice and the (re)production/transformation of social orders of knowledge. It is called the sociology of knowledge approach to discourse (analysis) because the perspective on discourses implied in SKAD can be situated in the sociology of knowledge tradition founded by Berger and Luckmann. This is mainly due to SKAD's research focus on knowledge and symbolic orderings, and also because it benefits from its connection to this tradition, which is close to qualitative research. More specifically, this approach proposes a perspective on discourse that bridges the gap between agency and structure-oriented traditions within the sociology of knowledge. Indeed, just as Berger and Luckmann addressed the manifestation of institutions out of processes of institutionalization, we can consider the processing of discourses through society as a dialectical interplay between actors producing statements and the established as well as emerging structurations and socio-historical means they have to draw upon.

SKAD is not a method, but rather a research program embedded in the sociology of knowledge tradition that examines the discursive construction of symbolic orders, which occurs in the form of competing politics of knowledge. Social relationships of knowledge are complex socio-historical constellations of the production, stabilization, structuration, and transformation of knowledge within a variety of social arenas. SKAD examines discourses as performative statement practices and symbolic orderings, which constitute orders of reality and also produce power effects within a conflict-ridden network of social actors, institutional dispositifs, and stocks of knowledge. It emphasizes the fact that discourse is concrete and material; it is not an abstract idea or a free-floating line of arguments. This means that discourse appears as speech, text, discussion, visual image, and use of symbols, which have to be performed by actors following social instructions; therefore, discourses are a real social practice.

SKAD research is concerned with reconstructing the processes which occur in the social construction, objectivization, communication, and legitimization of meaning structures in institutional spheres and issue-specific arenas. It is also concerned with the analysis of the social effects of these processes. This includes various dimensions of reconstruction: sense-making as well as subject formation, ways of acting, institutional/structural contexts, and social consequences; how, for example, they become apparent in the form of a dispositif. The latter refers to a kind of material, practical, and symbolic/immaterial infrastructure designed to solve a problem (for instance, consisting of a law, administrative regulations, staff, or things like cars, computers, and so on – which are all kinds of disposals) or in social actors' adoption or rejection of such dispositifs in their everyday lives. For example, actors might refuse to behave 'in an environmentally-friendly way,' to act as "enterprising selves" (to borrow Nicolas Rose's phrases; see Rose 1992), to become a "flexible man" (to borrow Richard Sennett's phrase; see Sennett 1998), or to identify as 'a true African-American.' This perspective presumes the normality of symbolic battles, contested problematizations, and controversies – of competitive discourses, the manifestations and effects of which can be traced back only in the rarest cases to the dominance and intentions of individual actors (although one should perhaps not dismiss them upfront).

The (more or less institutionalized) speaker positions which are available within discursive battles and their corresponding discourse or issue-specific arenas, as well as the social actors who are involved in these arenas, are not 'masters of the discourse universe,' but are rather (co-)constituted by the existing structuring of discursive orders or formations. Nevertheless, they in no way act as "cultural dopes" (as Harold Garfinkel (1967, 68) put it a long time ago), but rather as lively, interested producers of statements, as articulators with more or less strong potential in terms of resources and creativity. The symbolic orders that are produced and transformed in this process constitute the aggregated effects of their actions; unambiguous, temporary forms of dominance or hegemony are probably rare, but they are nonstandard configurations that should not be excluded from an empirical point of view.

I describe discursive fields as social arenas, constituting themselves around contested issues, controversies, problematizations, and truth claims in which discourses are in reciprocal competition with one another. SKAD's topics of analysis are both *public discourses* and *special discourses* performed in closed arenas for special publics. They are analyzed with regard to their bearer, to their matching or differing formation rules and content positionings, as well as to their effects. In the processing of discourses, specific *discourse coalitions* and statement-bearers can 'win out' over others using a wide range of means. As Thomas Kuhn (1970) long ago demonstrated with regard to scientific revolutions, paradigm shifts do not have to emerge out of arguments; there are many other kinds of reasons. This holds true for discourses, too. However, the discursive formation that occurs as a result of this process cannot be understood as an intended, controlled effect achieved by individual actors. What is at stake in these discourses is the fixing of collective symbolic orders through a more or less accurate repetition and stabilization of the same statements in singular utterances. Argumentative consensus-building processes, as projected in Habermas' normative discourse ethics, in which all participants are equal and the best argument wins, may appear as very particular and rather rare cases of discourse processing. Therefore, SKAD addresses discourses as complexes of power/knowledge which should be the objects not of pre-established normative judgment, but of empirical inquiry and analysis.

SKAD proposes additional terms to use in the analysis of utterances that are assumed to be part of the same discursive formation. The term discourse itself indicates a structuration context, which is the basis for disseminated discursive events. The unity of the structuring context – that is, of the discourse in question – should be considered as a necessary hypothetical construct for sociological observation, an essential research hypothesis. This means that discourses indeed exist as/in performances: if we, the observers, state that there is such a thing as a scientific or religious discourse, or an issue-driven discourse in public or specialized arenas, then we assume that very different usages of signs and things pertain to the same phenomenon – and then we try to give accounts of that phenomenon. Much the same thing occurs in every field of sociology. For example, research on families is rather similar: it presumes that assemblages of individual persons can be regrouped, researched, compared, and analyzed if they are considered 'families' (rather than, for instance, a group of friends or biological organisms).

Just as concrete families are performances of 'doing family,' discursive orders are the results of a continuous communicative production within individual language and action events, which should not be understood as spontaneous or chaotic, but rather as interwoven, structured practices which refer back to one another. A pamphlet, a newspaper article, or a speech in the context of a demonstration, for instance, actualizes an environmental policy discourse in different concrete forms and with different empirical scope. Discourses are subject to the conditions of institutional inertia: individual discursive events never actualize and reproduce a discourse's structure in a completely identical way, but always in a more or less varied form. 'Actualization' can therefore be understood in two ways: as the transfer of discourse-structuring patterns onto a real event, and as the accompanying modification or adaptation to the current conditions of a situational context. Consequential discourse transformations can rarely be related to such an individual event. Rather, they originate in the sum of the variations, in a kind of switch from the quantitative to the qualitative effect. The materiality of discourses (such as discursive or non-discursive practices, 'real' speakers, texts, speeches, discussions, and things) simply means: the way discourses exist in societies.

In producing/articulating interpretations, *social actors* use the rules and resources that are available as discourses in their discursive practice – not as deterministic regulation, but as *instruction* – or they react to them as *addressees*. Only if discourse research accounts for the agency of these actors can we understand how the more or less creative implementation of such practices takes place. SKAD does not hastily mistake the discourse level as a condition of the possibilities or limitations of utterances for the factual interpretations and practices of social actors. Social actors are not merely the empty addressees of knowledge supplies and the value assessments embedded therein, but are also socially configured incarnations of agency – according to the respective socio-historical and situational conditions – who more or less obstinately interpret social knowledge supplies as 'available rules' in their everyday interpretive activities (Hitzler et al. 1999), standing in the crossfire of multiple, heterogeneous, perhaps even contradictory discourses, trying to handle the situations they encounter.

3.2 Subject Positions

In what follows, I will give short illustrations – inspired by my own research on waste issue discourses in Germany and France (Keller [1998] 2009) – of some further SKAD concepts before finally turning to questions of method. Firstly, social actors are related to discourse in two ways: on the one hand, as the holders of a *speaker position* and *statement producers* who speak within a discourse; and on the other hand, as *addressees of the statement*. The sociological vocabulary of institutions, organizations, roles, and strategies of the individual or the collective – but always of social actors – can be used in a corresponding analysis of the structuration of speaker positions within discourses. However, actors generally appear on the discursive level, too: *subject positions/identity offerings* depict the positioning processes and 'patterns of subjectivization' that are generated in discourses and that refer to (fields of) addressees. Imagine for a moment, for example, the multiple evil figures and bad guys/bad citizens in visual and textual green action mobilizations who illustrate 'what not to do' – on billboards, in guidebooks, in children's books, etc. It is not necessary to enter into details of interpretation and meaning-making here. I merely want to point out how a subject position might appear in a given discourse. Here, the bad citizen is the one who pollutes, the wild waste-maker, the one who takes the plane and uses plastics, the 'simple wo/man from the street' littering, thereby destroying nature while others are trying to save and enjoy it. S/He is the one who needs to be 'disciplined,' punished, corrected. But such bad citizens are not alone. They have a strong and powerful counterpart, the eco-citizen who has appeared in public discourses all around the western world since the late 1960s. The good subject of environmental discourse and her or his perfect behavior is likewise addressed in countless advice books, education and teaching programs, etc.

3.3 Practices

The term practice(s) depicts very generally conventionalized action patterns, which are made available in collective stocks of knowledge as a repertoire for action – in other words, a more or less explicitly known, often incorporated recipe or knowledge script about the 'proper' way to act. This knowledge can originate, establish, and develop itself (further) in fields of social practice by experimenting and testing actions in relation to specific issues. SKAD considers several forms of practice: discursive practices are communication patterns that are bound to a discourse context. They are not only interesting for discourse research – such as genre theory and conversation analysis – so far as their formal process structure is concerned, but also equally in considerations of what Foucault called the (socio-historical emergence of) rules of formation, their adoption by social actors, and their function in discourse production. Discursive practices are observable, describable, typical ways of acting out statement production, the implementation of which requires interpretive competence and active shaping on the part of social actors. SKAD differentiates between the latter and model practices generated within discourses – that is, exemplary patterns (or templates) of action which are constituted in discourses, fixed to subject positions, and addressed to a particular discourse's public or to some 'counter-discourse.' To build on the above-mentioned examples of environmental discourse, this includes recommendations for eco-friendly behavior (such as turning the shower off while shampooing one's hair, riding a bike, or preparing slow food). Similarly to the subject positions discussed above, one should not suppose that the model practice will actually be implemented in the way it was imagined in a discourse. Its 'realization' has to be considered in its own right. The idea of 'model practices' can be illustrated by the numerous and locally varying information sheets explaining – often with the help of color schemes and diagrams – how to separate your household waste, which material category has to be put into which container (in order to be transformed from waste to value), how to prepare it, etc. In Germany at least, such diagrams often show us a rather complicated system of waste classification in order to guide our behavior concerning waste separation at home or in the office: there might be the blue bin for paper (which has to be flattened before it is thrown away) – but only for certain kinds of paper (such as newspapers and cartons, but not for tissues, dirty paper, or tampons). There is a yellow bin for all items marked with a green dot (the German recycling label), except paper and glass. There is a green bin for all organic waste (except meat, fish, cheese, and certain other items). There is grey for everything else (such as meat, fish, and condoms). And there might be many more differentiated kinds of waste (glass, bulk garbage, electrical appliances, and special or hazardous waste). What is more, such diagrams provide us with a large number of instructions about how to classify different kinds of waste and they indicate the correct actions that should be performed. Sometimes, a new actor of surveillance, control, and reporting is introduced. This could be a special job position (the waste care taker) or just 'we' towards one another, in the battlefield of environmental governmentality.

3.4 Dispositifs

The social actors who mobilize a discourse and are mobilized by discourse establish a corresponding infrastructure of discourse production and problem solving, which can be identified as a dispositif. Michel Foucault (1980, 194–228) introduced different notions of dispositifs. SKAD takes up the one which is most common in everyday French (and which, in a certain way, can be linked to the English terms 'disposal' or 'device'). Thus dispositif refers to what could be called an infrastructure established by social actors or collectivities in order to resolve a particular situation, with its inherent issues of action. Consider the state's need to obtain some 'money of its own': the combination of financial laws, administrative regulation, tax authorities, tax assessment, and tax investigators, together with texts, objects, actions, and persons, constitute the dispositif in question – an ensemble of heterogeneous elements, drawn together and arranged in order to manage a situation, to respond to a kind of 'urgency' (in Michel Foucault's sense). SKAD distinguishes between *dispositifs of discourse production* and *dispositifs* or infrastructures *that emerge out of a discourse* (or several discourses) in order to deal with the real-world phenomena addressed by the discourse in question. A dispositif is both the *institutional foundation* – the sum total of all the material, practical, personal, cognitive, and normative infrastructures of discourse production – and also the *infrastructures of implementation* that emerge out of discursively configured problematizations of fields of practice.

Consider the issue arena of 'household waste,' recycling, and so on – important issues in public debates and policy decisions in recent decades: with reference to the discourse (re)production level, we should mention the discursive interventions of the various administrators, spokespersons, and press committees, and also the research centers that diffuse and legitimize a specific construction of waste issues through their statements, brochures, and so on. With regard to implementation, one could also include the legal regulation of responsibilities, formalized proceedings, specific objects, technologies, sanctions, courses of study, and personal and other phenomena. For instance, waste separation systems are part of the dispositif and effects of discourses on waste. This includes the corresponding legal regulations, the waste removal company's staff, and also the waste separation and waste cleaning practices to which people submit (or which they refuse). Dispositifs mediate between discourses and fields of practice. SKAD is therefore not simply the textual analysis of signs in use, communication, text, or image research. It is simultaneously case studies, observations, and even dense ethnographic descriptions which consider the links between statements (as situated events), practices, actors, organizational arrangements, and objects as more or less historical and far-reaching socio-spatial processes. From the beginning, SKAD has argued for a focused ethnography of discourses and dispositifs – that is, for particular attention to discourse production and the performative elements and effects of dispositif structures. Such an ethnography is one point of entry in SKAD's reaction to recent debates on new materialisms (see Keller [2005] 2021; see also the special issue of the *Journal for Discourse Research* on "Discourseethnography," ed. by Elliker, Wundrak, and Maeder 2017; on discourse research and new materialisms, see Keller 2017, 2018a, 2019).

Here is another appeal to your imagination, in order to illustrate the concept of dispositive: What do we need to address the 'urgencies' of waste proliferation, scarcity of natural resources, and environmental degradation? We need texts – laws, rules, regulations, numbers and statistics, books, reviews, information sheets, all of which make accessible the collective level of waste production. We need concrete material devices such as garbage cans, garbage trucks, waste disposal sites, incinerators, and recycling plants. We need people for collecting, transporting, and processing material flows and transformations. And we need some kind of (more or less organized) relations between all such elements.

3.5 Symbolic Ordering and Symbolic Orders

Thus far, we have discussed certain core conceptual elements of SKAD. We shall now focus on the 'knowledge side' of discourse – that is, the symbolic ordering proposed and performed in singular discursive events and series of such events. Discourse includes both form and content. Discourse research may concentrate on the socio-historical genealogy, variation, and transformation of such forms, pursuing questions such as: In what way does a speech or a text have to be formally constructed to count as being part of political, religious, or scientific discourse at a given historical moment and in a particular context? Second, at least in sociology, there is an enduring interest in what is being said, by whom, with what effects – that is, in terms of content, actor, and power. We should remember Max Weber and his analysis of *The Protestant Ethic* – a study not about the formal aspects of sermons, prayers, and religious books, but rather about their content – and its effects. Naturally – like all forms – contents, actors, and powers will change over time.

Nevertheless, discourse-oriented research tries to account for the processes by which different, often conflicting ways of symbolic ordering compete – which is what content is all about – and why some of them are more consequential than others. This means, roughly, that there is no longer a need to show that everything is social construction or contingency, but to illuminate, interpret, and thereby understand (or render understandable) how and with what effects such contingency is reduced in social engagements. This holds true for scientific discourses as well as for discourses in the public realm or in special issue arenas. Therefore SKAD does not address singular, isolated, individualized discursive events for their own sake, but always as part of a series of such events. Foucault proposed a very useful idea here, one that is close to qualitative research agendas. In his *The Archaeology of Knowledge*, he asserted that discourse research is about statements, not about singular utterances. This idea of the 'statement' refers to what could be called the typical core element of knowledge configuration processed by a given discourse. To give but one example from interpretive sociology: William Gamson (1988) speaks of "discursive frames" (for example, a certain way of considering nature, be it as a sophisticated "clockwork" or as "our great mother"), argumentative reasoning, and rhetorical framing devices as means to identify and analyze such statements. SKAD proposes a slightly different framework of sensitizing concepts, which are closer to the sociology of knowledge, for analyzing the content of discourses – distinguishing between *interpretive schemes, classifications, phenomenal structures* (*Phänomenstrukturen*), and *narrative structures*. Together, these elements create the *interpretive repertoire* of a discourse.[10] I shall now consider these concepts more closely.

The term interpretive scheme (*Deutungsmuster*), which is close to Gamson's idea of frame but situated in the German traditions of *Deutungsmusteranalyse*, conveys meaning and action-generating schemata, which are combined in and circulated through discourses. Such interpretive schemes can be applied to different

---

[10] The term "interpretive repertoire" was coined by Margaret Wetherell and Jonathan Potter (1988); see Keller (1998) 2009, 36.

kinds of phenomena or events, and indeed, they undergo historical and social transformations. Interpretive schemes are part of society's stocks of knowledge. Discourses differentiate in the ways they combine such schemes in specific interpretive frameworks. They are able to generate new interpretive schemes and different ways of positioning these within a social agenda – which is exactly what characterizes discourses. An example of this is the interpretive scheme of the 'irreducible risk' of complex technologies, which has found its way into social stocks of knowledge over the last few decades, within and because of various environmental discourses (and disasters). This frame can be applied to nuclear power plants (as evidenced by the events in Fukushima/Japan in 2011) as well as to waste disposal infrastructures, nanotechnologies, GMOs, hydraulic fracturing, and many other instantiations. It might be opposed by framing certain events in terms of a 'deficient political system' (as was the case with Chernobyl) or 'singular human error.' In contrast to Gamson and certain social movement research, SKAD argues that such framings are of interest far beyond the singular question of their strategic use, because they always aspire to configure reality. Furthermore, against Gamson's and others' empirical research procedures, I would argue that such interpretive schemes may appear in very different ways, and analytical strategies have to address this: they require careful reconstruction,[11] which cannot be reduced to a quantified 'measurement' of key words or expressions (a strategy adopted by William Gamson and his colleagues in their analysis of media discourses), and which has to expand beyond media platforms in order to reach for complexities in arenas of discourse.

A second element which allows for a content-focused analysis of discourses is the exploration of the *classifications* (and therefore qualifications) of phenomena, which are performed both within discourses and by discourses. Classifications are a more or less elaborate, formalized, institutionally fixed form of social typification. Like every form of symbolizing, sign usage within discourses classifies the world and separates it into particular categories, which create the basis for conceptual experiencing, interpreting, and addressing it. Competition for such classifications occurs, for example, between discourses about how (potential) technological catastrophes should be interpreted, which identity offerings can be considered legitimate, the differences between correct and condemnable behavior, and whether or not perpetrators are certifiably sane (one could consider Foucault's Rivière case here; see Foucault 1982; see also *The Order of Things*). Classifications have specific impacts on action. Although this was shown in the groundbreaking work of Geoffrey S. Bowker and Susan L. Star (2000) in the interpretive paradigm, discourse research thus far has rather seldom addressed the work of classification.

---

[11] Keller and Truschkat (2014) explore sequential analysis as a procedure for analyzing such interpretive schemes. Case studies can be found in Keller, Hornidge, and Schünemann 2018.

Alongside interpretive schemes and classifications, the concept of phenomenal structure (*Phänomenstruktur*), which corresponds in some ways to Karl Mannheim's classical notion of *Aspektstruktur*, offers a complementary third point of access to the levels of content-related structuring of discourse (see Table 1 below). For instance, constructing a theme as a problem on the public agenda requires that the protagonists deal with the issue in several dimensions, referring to argumentative, dramatizing, and evaluative statements; determining the kind of problem or theme of a statement unit; defining characteristics, causal relations (cause-effect), and their links to responsibilities; identifying the human and non-human actors involved; establishing the dimensions of the problem, the values, the moral and aesthetic judgments, the consequences, and the possible courses of action, among other aspects. The phenomena which are constituted by phenomenal structures do not necessarily appear as a 'problem to be solved,' even if they always relate to 'meaning-making' and 'problems of action' in a very general way. The existing state of discourse research provides insight into certain elements of such phenomenal structures, as mentioned above. For example, the subject positions constituted by a discourse can be differentiated in a variety of ways. Discourses carry out social actors' positioning as heroes, rescuers, individuals who act sensibly or responsibly, problematic individuals, villains, and so on. Social actors are not pre-determined or pre-fixed entities with clear interests, strategies, and resources. SKAD discourse research is very much about the discursive processes in which actors emerge, engage themselves or are engaged by others, claim or perform reciprocal positionings, and are involved in discursive structuring in multiple ways. This also includes discourse-generated model practices, which provide templates for how one should act with regard to issues that the discourse has defined. The concept of phenomenal structure takes on these kinds of considerations and links them to the fact that discourses, in the constitution of their referential relation (their 'theme'), designate different elements or dimensions of their topic and link these to a specific form or phenomenal constellation. This does not describe any essential qualities of a discourse topic, but rather describes the corresponding discursive attributions. Both the structural dimensions and the concrete implementation of such a phenomenal structure have to be depicted using empirical data; this constitutes a major difference from the concept of the "conditional matrix," as established by Anselm Strauss and Juliette Corbin (1990) in their grounded theory approach.

One final element that is part of the content-related shaping of discourses should be discussed here. The structuring moments of statements and discourses – through which various interpretation schemes, classifications, and dimensions of the phenomenal structure (such as actors and problem definitions) are placed in relation to one another in a specific way – can be described as narrative structures. Narrative structures are not simply techniques used to assemble linguistic elements, but a *mise en intrigue* ('emplotment,' in the sense Paul Ricœur uses the term), a configurative act, which links disparate signs and statements in the form of

Table 1: Phenomenal Structure: Administrative Discourse on Waste Issues, France, 1995. Source: Keller 2009, 232.

Dimensions	Concrete Implementation
Causation	– Waste as a sanitary issue; discrepancy between the amount produced and disposal or recycling infrastructure – Increased wealth, economic and technical advances, consumption needs of consumers → rise in waste produced – Waste as a problem of deficient waste disposal at landfills – Waste as a problem of a lack of citizen responsibility and discipline – Waste as a problem of national autonomy/foreign trade balance/ usage of raw materials – Waste as a problem of international competitive conditions – → *waste as a 'quasi-natural' by-product of progress and wealth*
Responsibilities	– Politics/government/national administration (must develop and enforce a waste policy framework program in coordination with the economy) – Regional corporations, economy (individual responsibility for the implementation of the political specifications) – Citizens/society (giving up irrational fears and selfish denials; taking on responsibility for waste; accepting technologies)
Need for action/ problem-solving	– Low problem level; technical mastery of the waste issue is possible through recycling and elimination → *nature is governable* – Large-scale technological expansion and optimization of the waste disposal and recycling infrastructure → *interpretive pattern of socio-technical mastery* – Obtaining acceptance of removal infrastructure through the use of communication and participation – Comprehensive mobilization of citizens' responsibility (local authorities, economy, consumers) for the *national interest in resource importation reduction*
Self-positioning of speakers	– Representatives of scientific-technical, economic, and pragmatic reason, or of civil (socio-cultural/socio-technical) progress – Government as the administrator of the collective interest – → *The French state as representing civilization, modernity, and progress in behavior and technology, as incorporating pragmatic reasoning*
Othering	– French civil actors (regional corporations, economy, citizens) show a *lack of consciousness of their responsibility as citizens of France* – Irrationalism and fundamentalism of German waste politics as a disguise for economic protectionism
Thing culture	– Not a topic in the waste discussion; follows seemingly 'sacrosanct' modernization dynamics and market rationalities – Material model of affluence; the state does not control people's desires and needs (with regard to production and consumption)

Table 1 (continued)

Dimensions	Concrete Implementation
Values	– Government secures collective interests (affluence, progress, modernity) – (Actual and moral) cleanliness of public space – Nature as a (scarce national) resource, the usage of which can be optimized – *Society as it is, right here and now*, as a realization of the 'good life'

narratives. They can be considered a basic modality by which humans order their experience of the world (Ricœur 1984, 5). In the seriality of discursive events that constitutes a discourse, the above-mentioned elements of knowledge configuration are tied together in a particular 'narration' and are integrated via a common thread, a storyline. Narrative structures link the various interpretive elements of a discourse into a coherent, portrayable, and communicable form. They provide the plot for the narration, with which the discourse can address an audience in the first place, and with which it can construct its own coherence over the course of time.

It should be noted here that the elements for analyzing the 'knowledge side' of discourse presented thus far can each be used separately or all together in empirical research. They indicate what to look for and how to 'order' the results of analysis. SKAD proposes further kinds of ordering devices, such as maps of engaged actors, maps relating actors and competing discourses, or more general maps that attempt to account for the processing of discourses in the public sphere. Consider the following example in Table 2 (modified version, based on Keller 2009, 287).[12]

4 On Methods

SKAD aims to direct qualitative research's attention in sociology, the sociology of knowledge, and interpretive traditions toward the field of discourses. As Adele Clarke (2005) argued in *Situational Analysis*, discourses are not external to situations, but

---

[12] My work in Keller 2009 uses several tables or 'maps' to account for the discursive arena of waste politics in Germany and France, which cannot be included here. These mappings refer to relations between opposing discourses and economic, political, administrative, and civil society actors/entities and the public sphere, as well as to the arena of actors involved in these processes, according to their 'statement producing activity,' which might be central to or on the margins of a given discursive field. Related to this are Clarke's ideas of 'mapping,' as well as Michel Foucault's, Gilles Deleuze's, and Bruno Latour's arguments on 'cartography' (on Foucault and Deleuze, see Deleuze 1988; on Latour, see Venturini 2010).

Table 2: The Public Discursive Field of Legitimate Statements and Articulators in (West) Germany (Discourse on Waste) in the 1980s—Some Examples. Source: Keller 2009, 287.

Actors	Structurally conservative discourse on garbage: technical-ecological modermization	Culturally critical discourse on garbage: political-ecological restructuring
Politics/Administration (e.g.)	Discourse Coalitions *Federal Government (Ministry Of Economics) *Federal States (Baden-Wuettemberg, North Rhine-Westphalia) *Parties *FDP *CDU/CSU *SPD *local authority	*Federal stage government (Lower Saxony, Hesse) *Parties *SPD *Die Grünen *PDS
Economy/ environmental organizations (e.g.)	*Trade associations (BDI, DIHT, VCI) *individual large companies *Disposal and utilization industry (Initiative Sichere Abfallbehandlung, BDE, DSD) *Labour unions	*Enivronmental organizations (BUND, Greenpeace, Robin Wood, Das bessere Müllkonzept)
Experts(e.g.)	*Experts from public authorites and science *Federal environmental agency *Advisory council on the enivironment	*Expert from public authorities and science *Office for Technology Assessment of the German Federal Parliament *Environmental institutes
Media(e.g.)	*FAZ *Die Welt *Handelsblatt *Rheinischer Merkur *SZ *Wirtschaftswoche	*SZ *Der Spiegel *Der Zeit, DAS *FR *taz *nature, global garbage journal
	Way of profiling	

should be considered internal components of discourses. This means that whenever qualitative sociological research analyzes concrete phenomena and empirical questions, it should address this discursive dimension in order to provide more complex accounts of 'what is going on.' SKAD research even takes discourses under consideration as the 'situation to address.' Strategies of qualitative research are highly interesting here, as discourses are ways of meaning-making which manifest in concrete textual data. If sociology seeks to be an empirical science – that is, a specifically accountable form of reality-related analysis – rather than a writer's novel or journalist's report, then certain claims regarding general disclosure and transparency of the steps one takes in research and interpretation must be maintained. This requires a systematic analytical procedure and applies independently of whether or not subjective or collective stocks of knowledge (or the forms of externalization/articulation which document them or are indicative of them, such as books, speeches, newspaper articles, and films) are being analyzed.

Therefore, like certain other qualitative approaches, SKAD favors sequential analysis of textual data directed toward its own research questions to give an account of discursive claims and statements beyond the single utterance or discursive event: a line-by-line, step-by-step development, debate, and choice of interpretations in order to build up an accountable analysis of frames (*Deutungsmuster*), phenomenal structures, classifications, and storylines. The open coding procedure elaborated in grounded theory is helpful in indicating this procedure, as it demands the careful checking of interpretation and categories against the data at hand. In this sense, SKAD is part of the newer hermeneutical tradition in the sociology of knowledge, which pays attention to the fragile relation between 'questions to' and 'answers given by' empirical data. For example, in my own research on waste issues, a 'risk' frame was elaborated from newspaper data. This interpretive scheme entered German discourses on waste in the early 1980s and appeared in many different ways: as textual utterances, as front-page newspaper illustrations, as scientific analyses of waste incineration. In French discourse on waste, the main organizing frame was the importance of French engineers mastering all kinds of technological procedures, including types of waste disposal.

I speak of interpretive analytics in order to emphasize that discourse research places various types of data and interpretive steps in relation to one another – for example, more traditional sociological strategies for individual case analysis or case studies, combined with detailed close analyses of textual data. I also speak of interpretive analytics because, in contrast to other qualitative approaches in sociology, SKAD is not interested in the 'consistency of meaning' inherent to one particular document of a discourse *per se*, but rather assumes that such data is articulating some (but not all) of the heterogeneous elements of discourse, or that perhaps they appear as the points where several discourses cross (as in many books or newspaper articles). So discourse research has to break up the material surface unity of utterances. The mosaic of the analyzed discourse or discourses develops incrementally out of this process – this is certainly one of SKAD's most important modifications of traditional qualitative approaches in the social sciences, which very often take one interview, for example, as a 'coherent' and 'sufficient' case of its own.

In order to work through complex fields of discursive data, SKAD uses ideas of theoretical sampling and concepts of minimal and maximal contrasting (see Strauss 1987, 22–40; Strauss and Corbin 1998, 201–216). Theoretical sampling means the step-by-step building up of data – by beginning the analysis early, then following the criteria that emerge from the first data to inform further data collection – aiming to explore the whole range of the discourse or the discursive field of interest, the positions taken, and the actors who appear (or, surprisingly, do not appear). Minimal and maximal contrasting is a systematic strategy for crossing the field of inquiry in order to establish the range of important findings and to achieve detailed accounts of particular elements of analysis. To be clear: SKAD, unlike classic grounded theory, does not aim to explore particular 'situations and (inter)actions' along with their basic social processes, but rather explores ongoing discourses in social arenas. In addition to these strategies borrowed from grounded theory, the rich tradition of qualitative data analysis, of case studies and fieldwork methods, as developed in symbolic interactionism and interpretive sociology, can be usefully referred to in order to grasp the materialities and dispositifs of discourse, since social sciences discourse research deals – to a great extent – with current issues. In addition to documents (of all kinds), interview and ethnographic research strategies can therefore be part of empirical SKAD work on discourses. Such interview data and observations are not available for historical discourse analysis (as in Foucault's work). Nevertheless, SKAD can surely be used to analyze historical discourses as well; its heuristic framework allows for a wide range of questions in this field, too. As Kocku von Stuckrad (see chapter 5, this volume) and other work on historical discourse analysis (Eder 2006; Landwehr 2009) show, there is no proper historical approach to discourse – there are simply particular documents and contexts which must be respected, but very different perspectives can also be applied to historical questions.

Like all discourse-focused approaches, SKAD is itself a discourse about discourses, which follows its own discourse production rules, its own means of enabling and disciplining. Statements about individual data – as well as generalizing hypotheses, formulations, and conclusions – must be argued and explained. However, the criteria for the evaluation of evidence and inconsistencies are themselves part of discourses, and in this way, there is no escape from the network of meanings. We cannot ignore the fact that SKAD's reconstructive work is also irreducibly constructive work. The interpretation can be called reconstructive because it refers to data, and its goal is to reveal something about that data's interrelations and peculiarities. In this general sense, all discourse research necessarily proceeds in a reconstructive way. Such analyses also proceed constructively because they generate interpretations, conceptual schemata, and observations out of the data, and in so doing, they generate types of statements that were not – and indeed could not have been – in the actual data as such. Since the process of construction is determined first of all by the relevancies – the questions, analytical concepts, and strategies – of sociological discourse research, these are geared toward giving the 'field's own relevancies' a chance.

I would like to add one final point: When analyzing discourses, competing discursive meaning-making, and the discursive construction of reality, one major interest is in reconstruction – understanding and thereby explaining situated discursive processes and concrete cases (in Max Weber's sense). But we should not forget the more general questions: What are our cases 'cases of'? This is not to forget our interest in power/knowledge, in relations of knowledge/knowing, and in the politics of knowledge/knowing. Thus SKAD research can also be informed by and contribute to core debates and theoretization in every arena where questions of knowledge and power are relevant. This not only concerns sociology, but also the broad field of disciplines and studies where SKAD is used, which now ranges from (to name a few examples) Chinese studies to criminology, education to gender studies, history to Japanese studies, media and communication to political science, postcolonial studies to studies of religion, and beyond.

References

Barker, Chris, and Dariusz Galasinski. 2001. *Cultural Studies and Discourse Analysis: A Dialogue on Language and Identity*. London: Sage.
Barker, Chris. 2000. *Cultural Studies: Theory and Practice*. London: Sage.
Bechmann, Sebastian C. 2007. *Gesundheitssemantiken der Moderne. Eine Diskursanalyse der Debatten über die Reform der Krankenversicherung*. Berlin: Sigma.
Beck, Ulrich. 1999. *World Risk Society*. Cambridge: Polity Press.
Berger, Peter L., and Thomas Luckmann. 1966. *The Social Construction of Reality*. Garden City, NY: Anchor Books.
Blumer, Herbert. 1969. *Symbolic Interactionism: Perspective and Method*. Englewood Cliffs, NJ: Prentice Hall.
Boettcher, Miranda. 2019. "Cracking the Code: How Discursive Structures Shape Climate Engineering Research Governance." *Environmental Politics*. DOI: 10.1080/09644016.2019.1670987.
Bosančić, Saša, and Reiner Keller, eds. 2016. *Perspektiven wissenssoziologischer Diskursforschung*. Wiesbaden: Springer VS.
Bowker, Geoffrey S., and Susan L. Star. 2000. *Sorting Things Out: Classification and Its Consequences*. Cambridge: Cambridge University Press.
Brunner, Claudia. 2011. *Wissensobjekt Selbstmordattentat. Epistemische Gewalt und okzidentalistische Selbstvergewisserung in der Terrorismusforschung*. Wiesbaden: VS-Verlag.
Cassirer, Ernst. (1944) 1977. *An Essay on Man: An Introduction to a Philosophy of Human Culture*. New Haven: Yale University Press.
Castellani, Brian. 1999. "Michel Foucault and Symbolic Interactionism." *Studies in Symbolic Interaction* 22: 247–72.
Christmann, Gabriele B. 2004. *Dresdens Glanz, Stolz der Dresdner. Lokale Kommunikation, Stadtkultur und städtische Identität*. Wiesbaden: VS-Verlag.
Clarke, Adele E., Carrie Friese, and Rachel Washburn, eds. 2018. *Situational Analysis: Grounded Theory After the Interpretive Turn*. 2nd ed. Thousand Oaks, CA: Sage.
Clarke, Adele. 2005. *Situational Analysis: Grounded Theory After the Postmodern Turn*. London: Sage.
Deleuze, Gilles. 1988. *Foucault*. Minneapolis: University of Minnesota Press.
Denzin, Norman. 1992. *Symbolic Interactionism and Cultural Studies: The Politics of Interpretation*. Oxford: Blackwell.
Dreyfus, Hubert L., and Paul Rabinow. 1982. *Michel Foucault: Beyond Structuralism and Hermeneutics*. Chicago: University of Chicago Press.
Durkheim, Émile. (1912) 2008. *The Elementary Forms of Religious Life*. Oxford: Oxford University Press.

Eder, Franz X., ed. 2006. *Historische Diskursanalysen: Genealogie, Theorien, Anwendungen*. Wiesbaden: VS Verlag für Sozialwissenschaft.

Elliker, Florian, Rixta Wundrak, and Christoph Maeder. 2017. "Introduction to the Thematic Issue and Programmatic Thoughts on the Sociology of Knowledge Approach to Discourse Ethnography." *Journal for Discourse Studies* 5, no. 3: 232–48.

Fairclough, Norman. 1995. *Critical Discourse Analysis: The Critical Study of Language*. London: Pearson Education Ltd.

Foucault, Michel, ed. (1973) 1982. *I, Pierre Rivière, having slaughtered my mother, my sister, my brother . . . A Case of Parricide in the 19th century*. Lincoln: University of Nebraska Press.

Foucault, Michel. 1970. *The Order of Things*. New York: Pantheon Books.

Foucault, Michel. 1972a. *The Archeology of Knowledge*. London: Routledge.

Foucault, Michel. 1972b. *The Archeology of Knowledge & The Discourse on Language*. New York: Pantheon Books.

Foucault, Michel. 1980. *Power/Knowledge. Selected Interviews and Other Writings 1972–1977*. Ed. by C. Gordon. New York: Pantheon Books.

Foucault, Michel. 1984. "Polemics, Politics and Problematizations. Interview with Paul Rabinow." In *The Foucault Reader*, ed. by Paul Rabinow, 381–98. New York: Pantheon Books.

Fraser, Nancy. 1997. "Structuralism or Pragmatics? On Discourse Theory and Feminist Politics." In *The Second Wave: A Reader in Feminist Theory*, ed. by Linda Nicholson, 379–394. New York: Routledge.

Gamson, William A. 1988. "The 1987 Distinguished Lecture: A Constructionist Approach to Mass Media and Public Opinion." *Symbolic Interaction* 2: 161–74.

Garfinkel, Harold. 1967. *Studies in Ethnomethodology*. Englewood Cliffs, NJ: Prentice-Hall.

Giddens, Anthony. 1991. *Consequences of Modernity*. Oxford: Blackwell.

Gusfield, Joseph. 1981. *The Culture of Public Problems: Drinking-Driving and the Symbolic Order*. Chicago: University of Chicago Press.

Habermas, Jürgen. 1985. *The Theory of Communicative Action*. 2 vols. Boston: Beacon Press.

Hall, Stuart, ed. 1997a. *Representation: Cultural Representations and Signifying Practices*. London: Sage.

Hall, Stuart. 1997b. "The Centrality of Culture: Notes on the Cultural Revolutions of Our Time." In *Media and Cultural Regulation*, ed. by Kenneth Thompson, 208–38. London: Sage.

Hilgartner, Stephen, and Charles L. Bosk. 1988. "The Rise and Fall of Social Problems: A Public Arena Model." *American Journal of Sociology* 94, no. 1: 53–78.

Hitzler, Ronald, Jo Reichertz, and Norbert Schröer, eds. 1999. *Hermeneutische Wissenssoziologie*. Konstanz: UVK.

Hitzler, Ronald, Jo Reichertz, and Norbert Schröer, eds. 2020. *Kritik der Hermeneutischen Wissenssoziologie*. Weinheim: Beltz/Juventa.

Jackson, Stevi, and Sue Scott. 2007. "Faking Like a Woman? Towards an Interpretive Theorization of Sexual Pleasure." *Body & Society* 13, no. 2: 95–116.

Jäger, Siegfried. 2012. *Kritische Diskursanalyse. Eine Einführung*. 6th rev. ed. Münster: Unrast-Verlag.

Keller, Reiner. 2008. *Michel Foucault*. Konstanz: UVK.

Keller, Reiner. (1998) 2009. *Müll – Die gesellschaftliche Konstruktion des Wertvollen*. 2nd ed. Wiesbaden: VS-Verlag.

Keller, Reiner. 2011. "The Sociology of Knowledge Approach to Discourse (SKAD)." *Human Studies* 34, no. 1: 43–65.

Keller, Reiner. 2012. *Das Interpretative Paradigma*. Wiesbaden: VS-Verlag.

Keller, Reiner. 2013. *Doing Discourse Research: An Introduction for Social Scientists*. London & Thousand Oaks, CA: Sage.

Keller, Reiner. 2016a. "Has Critique Run Out of Steam? On Discourse Research as Critical Inquiry." *Qualitative Inquiry*, July 2016: 1–11.

Keller, Reiner. 2016b. "Die komplexe Diskursivität der Visualisierungen." In *Perspektiven wissenssoziologischer Diskursforschung*, ed. by Saša Bosančić and Reiner Keller, 75–94. Wiesbaden: Springer VS.

Keller, Reiner. 2017. "Neuer Materialismus und Neuer Spiritualismus? Diskursforschung und die Herausforderung der Materialitäten." *Österreichische Zeitschrift für Volkskunde Neue Serie* Band LXXXI, vol. 120, nos. 1 and 2: 5–32.

Keller, Reiner. 2018a. "Der fliegende See. Wissenssoziologie, Diskursforschung und Neuer Materialismus." In *Wissensrelationen: Beiträge und Debatten zum 2. Sektionskongress der Wissenssoziologie*, ed. by Angelika Poferl and Michaela Pfadenhauer, 94–107. Weinheim: Beltz/Juventa.

Keller, Reiner. 2018b. "Michel Foucault: Discourse, Power/Knowledge and the Modern Subject." In *The Routledge Handbook of Language and Politics*, ed. by Ruth Wodak and Bernhard Forchtner, 67–81. London & New York: Routledge.

Keller, Reiner. 2019. "New Materialism? A View from Sociology of Knowledge." In *Discussing New Materialism: Methodological Implications for the Study of Materialities*, ed. by Ulrike T. Kissmann and Joost van Loon, 151–72. Wiesbaden: Springer VS.

Keller, Reiner. (2005) 2021. *The Sociology of Knowledge Approach to Discourse: Outline of a Research Program*. New York: Springer.

Keller, Reiner, and Adele E. Clarke. 2018. "Situating SKAD in Interpretive Inquiry." In *The Sociology of Knowledge Approach to Discourse: Investigating the Politics of Knowledge and Meaning-Making*, ed. by Reiner Keller, Anna-Katharina Hornidge, and Wolf Schünemann, 48–72. London: Routledge.

Keller, Reiner, and Inga Truschkat, eds. 2012. *Methodologie und Praxis der Wissenssoziologischen Diskursanalyse*. Wiesbaden: VS-Verlag.

Keller, Reiner, and Inga Truschkat. 2014. "Angelus Novus: Über alte und neue Wirklichkeiten der deutschen Universitäten. Sequenzanalyse und Deutungsmusterrekonstruktion in der Wissenssoziologischen Diskursanalyse." In *Diskursforschung. Ein interdisziplinäres Handbuch. Vol. 2.*, ed. by Johannes Angermuller, Martin Nonhoff, Eva Herschinger, Felicitas Macgilchrist, Martin Reisigl, Juliette Wedl, Daniel Wrana, and Alexander Ziem, 294–328. Bielefeld: transcript.

Keller, Reiner, Anna-Katharina Hornidge, and Wolf Schünemann, eds. 2018. *The Sociology of Knowledge Approach to Discourse: Investigating the Politics of Knowledge and Meaning-Making*. London: Routledge.

Knoblauch, Hubert. 1995. *Kommunikationskultur: Die kommunikative Konstruktion kultureller Kontexte*. Berlin: Aldine De Gruyter.

Knoblauch, Hubert. 2020. The Communicative Construction of Reality. London: Routledge.

Koopman, Colin, ed. 2011. "Foucault and Pragmatism." Special issue, *Foucault Studies* 11.

Kuhn, Thomas. 1970. *The Structure of Scientific Revolutions*. 2nd enl. ed. Chicago: University of Chicago Press.

Laclau, Ernesto, and Chantal Mouffe. 2001. *Hegemony and Socialist Strategy: Towards a Radical Democratic Politics*. London: Verso.

Landwehr, Achim. 2009. *Historische Diskursanalyse*. 2nd ed. Frankfurt am Main: Campus.

Manning, Philipp K. 1982. "Structuralism and the Sociology of Knowledge." *Knowledge: Creation, Diffusion, Utilization* 4, no. 1: 51–72.

Mead, George H. (1934) 1963. *Mind, Self and Society*. Chicago: University of Chicago Press.

Mills, Charles W. 1940. "Situated Actions and Vocabularies of Motive." *American Sociological Review* 5, no. 6: 904–913.

Prior, Lindsay. 1989. *The Social Organization of Death: Medical Discourses and Social Practices in Belfast*. London: Macmillan Press.
Ricœur, Paul. 1984. *Time and Narrative, Vol. 1*. Chicago: University of Chicago Press.
Roberto Cantoni, Matthias S. Klaes, Simone I. Lackerbauer, Claudia Foltyn, and Reiner Keller. 2018. "Shale Tales: Politics of Knowledge and Promises in Europe's Shale Gas Discourses." *The Extractive Industries and Society* 5, no. 4: 535–46, https://doi.org/10.1016/j.exis2018.09.004.
Rorty, Richard. 1982. *Consequences of Pragmatism*. Minneapolis: University of Minnesota Press.
Rose, Nicolas. 1992. "Governing the Enterprising Self." In *The Values of the Enterprise Culture: The Moral Debate*, ed. by Paul Heelas and Paul Morris, 141–64. London: Routledge.
Schmied-Knittel, Ina. 2008. *Satanismus und ritueller Missbrauch. Eine wissenssoziologische Diskursanalyse*. Würzburg: Ergon.
Schütz, Alfred. 1973. "On Multiple Realities." In *Alfred Schütz Collected Papers I: The Problem of Social Reality*, ed. by Maurice Natanson, 207–59. Den Haag: Nijhoff.
Sennett, Richard. 1998. *The Corrosion of Character: The Personal Consequences Of Work In the New Capitalism*. New York: Norton.
Singelnstein, Tobias. 2009. *Diskurs und Kriminalität*. Berlin: Duncker & Humblot.
Srubar, Ilja. 1988. *Kosmion. Die Genese der pragmatischen Lebensweltheorie von Alfred Schütz und ihr anthropologischer Hintergrund*. Frankfurt am Main: Suhrkamp.
Strauss, Anselm L. 1979. *Negotiations: Varieties, Contexts, Processes and Social Order*. San Francisco: Jossey-Bass.
Strauss, Anselm L. 1987. *Qualitative Analysis for Social Scientists*. Cambridge: Cambridge University Press.
Strauss, Anselm L. 1991. *Creating Sociological Awareness: Collective Images and Symbolic Representation*. New Brunswick, NJ: Transaction Publications.
Strauss, Anselm L. 1993. *Continual Permutations of Action*. New York: Aldine De Gruyter.
Strauss, Anselm L., and Juliette Corbin. 1990. *The Basics of Qualitative Analysis: Grounded Theory Procedures and Techniques*. Newbury Park, CA: Sage.
Strauss, Anselm L., and Juliette Corbin. 1998. *Basics of Qualitative Research*. London: Sage.
Thomas, William I., and Dorothy S. Thomas. 1928. *The Child in America*. New York: A. A. Knopf.
Truschkat, Inga. 2008. *Kompetenzdiskurs und Bewerbungsgespräche. Eine Dispositivanalyse (neuer) Rationalitäten sozialer Differenzierung*. Wiesbaden: VS-Verlag.
Ullrich, Peter. 2008. *Die Linke, Israel und Palästina. Nahostdiskurse in Großbritannien und Deutschland*. Berlin: Dietz.
Ulrich, Peter, and Reiner Keller. 2014. "Comparing Discourse Between Cultures: A Discursive Approach to Movement Knowledge." In *Conceptualizing Culture in Social Movement Research*, ed. by Britta Baumgarten, Priska Daphi, and Peter Ulrich, 113–39. Hampshire: Palgrave.
Venturini, Tommaso. 2010. "Diving in Magma: How to Explore Controversies with Actor-Network Theory." *Public Understanding of Science* 19, no. 3: 258–73.
Weber, Max. (1904) 1949. *On the Methodology of the Social Sciences*. Illinois: The Free Press of Glencoe.
Weber, Max. (1905) 2002. *The Protestant Ethic and the Spirit of Capitalism*. New York: Penguin Books.
Wetherell, Margaret, and Jonathan Potter. 1988. "Discourse Analysis and the Identification of Interpretive Repertoires." In *Analysing Everyday Explanation: A Casebook of Methods*, ed. by Charles Antaki, 168–83. Newbury Park, CA: Sage.
Wodak, Ruth, and Michael Meyer. 2015. *Methods of Critical Discourse Studies*. London: Sage.

Wundrak, Rixta. 2010. *Die chinesische Community in Bukarest. Eine rekonstruktive diskursanalytische Fallstudie über Immigration und Transnationalismus*. Wiesbaden: VS-Verlag.

Zimmermann, Christine. 2010. *Familie als Konfliktfeld im amerikanischen Kulturkampf. Eine Diskursanalyse*. Wiesbaden: VS-Verlag.

Znaniecki, Florian. 1919. *Cultural Reality*. Chicago: University of Chicago Press.

Dominique Maingueneau
Religious Discourse and Its Modules

When they study utterances that are considered 'religious,' linguists follow a variety of paths. Some claim to study 'religious language' the same way they would study 'legal' or 'medical language' – from a sociolinguistic (Ferguson 1973, 1982) viewpoint, or as a 'register,' a 'style,' a specialized use of language that links text function and the use of specific linguistic forms (Crystal 1964; Crystal and Davy 1969; Banks 2008; Adam 2009; Ruetten 2011). The interaction between religious practices and language throughout history is also a prominent research theme (Mühleisen 2007; Kohnen 2010). Other linguists, undoubtedly the most numerous, use linguistic concepts and methods to help interpret texts, or edit manuscripts from a philological perspective.[1]

As for discourse analysts, they claim to study religion *as discourse*. Unlike many researchers in religious studies who use 'religious discourse' in a superficial manner,[2] they consider 'discourse' as a key concept.[3] In fact, according to their interpretation of the term, they tend to follow one of two main routes. According to the first one, drawing upon Foucault's line of thought, they see discourse as "the totality of thought-systems that interact with societal systems in manifold ways" (von Stuckrad 2010, 158).[4] According to the second one, they practice "'textually oriented discourse analysis'[5] against (although drawing in some aspects from) Michel Foucault's more abstract and broadly historical approach" (Hjelm 2011, 134).

In this chapter, I shall not try to define religion (in any case, as a discourse analyst, I very much doubt that this is possible), nor will I present a painstaking study of texts. I will simply emphasize some basic characteristics of 'religious discourse'

---

1 I do not have space here to mention the multitude of articles that deal with these topics; readers can find an extensive list (about 300 references, but only up to 2013) on the website http://www.discourses.org/resources/bibliographies/. Regarding religious studies and discourse analysis, see in particular the two different points of view illustrated in Kocku von Stuckrad's (2003, 2011) and Titus Hjelm's (2011) work.
2 "Despite much talk of 'discourse', few scholars of religions have used the methodological tools of discourse analysis" (Stausberg and Engler 2011, 13). For example, in the philosopher M. Scott's book *Religious Language* (2013), the section bearing the title "Religious Discourse" does not deal with texts, but only with "the use of religious sentences," "the information that a sentence is used to communicate" (2013, 153). On the website http://www.discourses.org/resources/bibliographies/, many of the books and articles that are supposed to belong to the field of discourse studies do not, in fact, fall within this domain.
3 Here we make a distinction between text and discourse. This is not always the case. R. B. Terry's book *A Discourse Analysis of First Corinthians*, for example, is a study that falls within the domain of text linguistics: "discourse analysis is roughly equivalent to text analysis or textlinguistics" (1995, 3).
4 See also von Stuckrad 2003, 2011.
5 Helm borrows this expression from N. Fairclough.

in a narrow sense of the term – that is, as a regime organized around sacred texts and associated with a field (Bourdieu 1971). Although anthropologists can consider one or another practice in any kind of society 'religious,' the very possibility of delimiting 'religious discourse' as a specific, recognized area of discourse production implies particular socio-historical conditions. If we adopt this narrow sense, then the rites and beliefs of Amazonian tribes or ancient Greek society, for example, would not constitute 'religious discourse.' Of course, I am not claiming that one cannot find in ancient Greek religion or Amazonian tribes rites, beliefs, or rules (among other aspects) that anthropologists may consider 'religious'; I am not even claiming that one may not consider them as pertaining to 'religious discourse.' By using the term 'religious discourse' here, I give 'discourse' a more restricted meaning than it has in Foucault's line of thought; according to my use of the term, it refers to a network of genres within a specified area of society. The boundaries of this network are constantly negotiated by the actors, who at the same time oppose various positions in their own field and distinguish it from others (such as the political or the philosophical). From a historical viewpoint, such a configuration is possible only when religious practice is structured around sacred texts.

By focusing on 'religious discourse' in this way, my purpose is not to present new data or new interpretations, but to integrate well-known elements into a general frame, with the aim of contributing to linking a holistic perspective and a 'textually oriented' analysis, "to transcend the division between work inspired by social theory which tends not to analyze texts, and work which focuses upon the language of texts but tends not to engage with social theoretical issues" (Fairclough 2003, 3). I will proceed in two stages. First, I will consider religious discourse as an element of a broader category, that of 'self-constituting discourses'; second, I will describe it as the interaction of three components. This way of analyzing religious discourse differs from the standard practice of most discourse analysts who study genres (Groeger 2010; Kohnen 2010, 2012; Maingueneau 2009), which by their very nature are deeply anchored in socio-historical contexts. I think both approaches are necessary and complementary.

1 The Paradox of the French Situation

Frans Wijsen (2013, 1) rightly states that "whereas discourse analysis has become a well-respected method in a variety of disciplines, it is rarely used in religious studies in a systematic and methodical way." But one may be surprised to find that this is also the case in French discourse analysis,[6] which, given its theoretical background, ought to favor research on this subject.

---

[6] Here I make a distinction between 'French discourse analysis' and 'discourse analysis in France,' which is highly diversified.

Although we cannot speak of a "French school,"[7] in much of the research currently done within the frame of 'French' discourse analysis, there is nevertheless a family likeness based on some specific *tendencies*:
1. The style of research is non-empiricist: 'facts' or 'data' are not considered as given, but as the product of the researcher's construction. The emphasis is placed on the conceptual coherence of the investigation.
2. There is an interest in 'constrained' corpora – whether oral or written – which are bound to *institutional* frames and often associated with the *memory* of other texts. As a consequence, political debates on TV or in parliament are much more likely to be studied than everyday speech. From this viewpoint, French-speaking discourse analysis differs greatly from North American trends, as it does not focus on conversation and does not draw on micro-sociological theories.
3. Researchers are supposed to take linguistic forms (morphology, syntax, and enunciation phenomena) into account, and not merely focus on their social function. Language is not considered a passive tool to aid in the achievement of social or psychological purposes; it has its own rules and its own history.
4. Interdiscourse has primacy; the identity of a discourse is seen as a constant process of determining its borders. Discourse is always crisscrossed by manifold forms of other discourses, be they virtual or real. From this viewpoint, meaning is not a mere projection of communicative intention, but a move within a radically conflicted space. Reflection on interdiscourse relates to the question of 'dialogism' and 'polyphony,' as developed by Mikhail Bakhtin.
5. There is a close relationship with the question of subjectivity *in* language. This preoccupation is closely connected to "enunciative pragmatics" (Angermuller, Maingueneau, and Wodak 2014), mainly inspired by the French linguist Émile Benveniste (1966). As a result of the essential reflexivity of language, enunciation is the reference point of an utterance, which bears many of its traces: person, time, place, determination, modality. The 'speaker' and the 'enunciator' are not considered synonymous. The speaker is the individual, regarded as someone who belongs to the world outside of language, whereas the enunciator appropriates language and sets it in motion during the process of enunciation. Since enunciators exist only through enunciation, many enunciators are not speakers (Ducrot 1984); for example, the enunciator of proverbs is 'popular wisdom' or 'common sense,' not a flesh-and-blood being.

Within such a landscape, one would assume that the analysis of religious discourse was bound to develop in France. Of course, as in many other countries, researchers in sociology or anthropology have made extensive use of notions from linguistics to

---

[7] In particular, we cannot ignore the considerable differences between its two main founding authors, M. Pêcheux (1969) and M. Foucault (1969).

study religious phenomena, but most of them do not claim to practice discourse analysis.[8]

The paucity of research in discourse analysis on religion can be explained by the history of the field and the cultural context. When discourse analysis appeared in the 1960s, it marked its difference from traditional practices of text commentary by studying corpora that had been ignored prior to that point, such as conversations, TV programs, advertisements, and newspapers. As for the specialists who studied 'great texts' or 'works,' they were reluctant to adopt these new approaches, which they considered reductionist. This situation was aggravated by the fact that in France, discourse analysis has been perceived as a left-wing approach. For a long time, the political left has been associated with the rejection of religion, together with the principle of secularism (*laïcité*). Indeed, most French discourse analysts have perceived religion as an ideology, in the Marxist sense of the term (Althusser 1972; Pêcheux 1975),[9] and are not familiar with religious culture. Most of the time, when they happen to study religious texts, they do so not in order to understand the function of religious discourse, but because religion impacts political or social problems.[10]

Independently of the French situation, the reluctance of many discourse analysts to study religious corpora may also be epistemologically motivated. Discourse analysts prefer to study texts from the arenas of media, politics, education, law, or health because with such corpora, it is much easier to fulfill the basic requirement of discourse analysis: linking linguistic and social phenomena. They seem to believe that this is less the case with religious texts, especially when such texts deal with theological matters. In this respect, it is significant that my research on religious controversies of the seventeenth century (Maingueneau 1983, 1984) did not receive attention because it improved the understanding of religion, but because it proposed a semantic model of polemics. The priority most discourse analysts accord to micro-sociological approaches and to oral interaction also plays a part. If one considers oral interaction to be the core of discourse activity, then one is

---

[8] Concerning the role of language in sociological and anthropological approaches to religion, see Obadia 2009.

[9] There was not the same reluctance in French semiotics (see, for example, A.-J. Greimas), which was very influential until the 1980s. Unlike discourse analysis, semiotics claimed to study *texts*, not social practices; despite its structuralist assumptions, this approach was more easily compatible with traditional commentary practices. 1971 saw the publication of a special issue of *Langages*, the most prestigious French journal of linguistics, edited by C. Chabrol and L. Marin, on the study of the Bible: "Sémiotique narrative : récits bibliques." This was followed by other publications (Marin 1972; Marin and Chabrol 1972; Groupe d'Entrevernes 1977; Almeida 1978). 1975 saw the founding of the journal *Sémiotique et Bible*, edited by L. Panier. Since the 1980s, semiotics has lost much of its influence, and the linguists interested in religious studies have increasingly used tools from enunciative pragmatics (see, for example, Rabatel 2007a, 2007b, 2015).

[10] This is particularly clear in the bibliography published on www.discourses.org (see fn. 1).

induced to push religious discourse to the fringes because of its strongly scriptural dimension and its special relationship with memory.

The marginalization of religious discourse in discourse analysis can be observed in two prominent journals of the field: *Discourse & Society* and *Discourse Studies*. In the former, among the 200 articles published between 2010 and 2015, not one deals with religious topics. In the latter, over the same six years (36 issues), only one article addresses religion: "Call and Response: An Anatomy of Religious Practice" (Loeb 2014). This study "details the interactional practices of 'call and response' using conversation analysis to analyze video data gathered from Bible study meetings" (Loeb 2014, 514) in a Catholic community made up of African Americans and Latinos. Significantly, the author studies these oral interactions with the toolkit typically used for ordinary conversation. This kind of research is undoubtedly necessary, but religious discourse analysis cannot focus on conversational practices alone.

2 Religious Discourse as a Self-Constituting Discourse

To broaden our perspective, instead of focusing on those aspects of religious discourse that can be studied with the help of certain concepts and methods used to study conversation or media, I think a reflection in terms of "self-constituting discourses" (Maingueneau 1999) can be fruitful.

2.1 Ultimate Discourses

Integrating religious discourse into this wider category – alongside aesthetic, philosophical, or scientific discourses, for example – means that many of the features of religious discourse are not specific to it. To clarify the notion of 'self-constituting discourses,' one can start with a commonplace observation. Philosophers or scientists are not supposed to appeal to the authority of journalists when they address philosophy or science; but when a debate is organized in the mass media about important issues, particularly ethical issues, journalists may request intervention on the part of priests, scientists, philosophers, or writers, among others. These people are perceived as authorities because they are the spokespersons of 'ultimate' discourses: discourses upon which others are based, and which have a particular relationship with the foundations of society. Self-constituting discourses, by their very nature, claim to be above any other type of discourse. As discourses bordering on unspeakable meanings, they must negotiate the paradoxes such a status implies. To found other discourses without being founded by them, they must set themselves up as intimately bound up with a legitimizing transcendent Source and show that they are in accordance with it, owing to the operations by which they structure their texts and legitimate the ways in which they emerge and develop. Discourse analysts can study the textual operations by which they manage such a self-foundation: only a discourse that constitutes itself can found others.

In the expression 'self-constituting discourses,' the word 'constituting' connects two dimensions: 1) constituting as the act of establishing something legally, of giving legal form to some entity: self-constituting discourses emerge by instituting themselves as legitimated to say what they and the way they say it; and 2) constituting as forming a whole, an organization: self-constituting discourses are sets of texts whose structure must be legitimized by discourse itself.

Self-constituting discourses produce texts dedicated to embodying norms, to guaranteeing certain community behaviors, and to drawing the boundaries of good and evil, falsehood and truth, among other things. They take charge of what could be called the *archeion* of discursive production in a given society. In my view, this Greek word has an interesting polysemy: derived from *arché* ('source,' 'principle,' 'order,' 'power'), the *archeion* is both the center in which authority sits – a group of magistrates – and also refers to public archives (*archivum* comes from *archeion*). So this notion tightly binds *founding* in and by discourse to the determination of a *place* for legitimate speakers and addressees as well as the management of *memory*.

In modern societies, as in classical Greece, *various* self-constituting discourses exist at the same time, thus competing with each other. The common-sense belief is that each self-constituting discourse is autonomous and has contingent relations with other discourses. In reality, their relation to other discourses is part of their core identity: they must manage their impossible coexistence, and the way in which they manage this *is* their very identity. For a few centuries in Europe, philosophical discourse claimed to be prevalent: it attributed to itself the privilege of assigning boundaries to all other discourses. Theological discourse did this in a previous era, as did scientific discourse in a later period.

2.2 The Three Dimensions of Self-Constituting Discourses

Self-constituting discourses can be viewed as three-dimensional: they are at the same time an *apparatus*, a *field*, and an *archive*. But each self-constituting discourse combines these three elements in a specific way.

The first element is an *apparatus* by which individuals can be instituted as legitimate speech producers or addressees, and in which a network of discourse activities is stabilized. In the case of religious discourse, these activities can be private or collective (such as rites) and imply various places (such as holy mountains, monasteries, or temples) as well as categories of participants (in particular, a structured clergy).

The second element is a *discursive field* (Maingueneau 1984[11]) in which various *positions* compete, and in which frames are continually discussed. The content of this notion of 'position' (for example, a doctrine, a school, or a party) is very poor; it only implies that no position can occupy the whole space within a given self-constituting discourse, and that the identity of each position emerges and is maintained through this interaction, often in conflict with the others. In order to understand the 'contents' of texts, we must refer to the place that their producers attempt to hold in the field at a given moment.

The third element is an *archive*. Self-constituting discourses imply a memory by which they are dominated, but which they also constantly rework. This is especially true with regard to religious discourse, which draws on founding texts and commentaries. The link between the discursive field and the archive is essential: each position implies taking an original route through the archive; by claiming filiation and by excluding others, religious speakers can validate their own enunciation and show what they consider to be the legitimate way of being a legitimate member of the community.

However, we must be careful when we use notions such as 'field,' 'apparatus,' and 'position.' Self-constituting discourses, by their very nature, are basically *paratopic* (Maingueneau 2004a, 70–117) – that is, they are part of society without fully belonging to it. Paratopy is a never-ending negotiation between locality and un-locality. Without locality, there are no institutions to legitimate discourse, but without un-locality, there is no privileged relationship with a transcendent reality. Paratopy also characterizes those great personalities (such as Jesus, Rousseau, Van Gogh . . . XX) who elaborate their doctrine or their works through the very impossibility of their occupying a well-established position in society.

2.3 Position and Discourse Community

When we study texts falling within the frame of self-constituting discourses, we are addressing highly structured discourses that speak of notions such as humankind and society, rationality and beauty, good and evil – notions with a large scope or *global* aims. But these discourses are produced *locally*, by a few people who belong to a small sector of society. A position in a field is not only a more or less systematic set of ideas; it also implies a certain way of life for these groups of people, for *discourse communities* (Maingueneau 1987, 37–51) structured by the texts they produce and put into circulation, which are both the product of discourse communities and the condition of their existence. Inventing a new way to relate to members of the community and producing new discourses are two dimensions of the same phenomenon. The ways in

---

11 This notion of a 'discursive field' draws on Bourdieu's theory of fields (Bourdieu 1971, 1992).

which people do science, practice philosophy or religion, or lead an artistic life are inseparable from the ways in which they produce discourse (De Certeau 1975; Debray 1983, 1991; Maingueneau 1984). But this principle must be diversified according to the type of discourse considered: communities that belong to a scientific field behave differently than communities that belong to a theological field. Moreover, sub-fields must be distinguished: theology does not imply the same type of community as piety.

2.4 Hierarchies

A self-constituting discourse is not a genre; it forms a network of genres, which are distributed over a scale. More precisely, two complementary hierarchies must be distinguished. The first sets 'archetexts' in opposition to 'ordinary texts'; the second opposes 'top' to 'secondary' genres.

Archetexts are singular texts reputed to have a privileged relation with the 'archeion' – for instance, Plato's *Dialogues* or Descartes's *Meditations* in philosophical discourse, Homer's *Odyssey* in literature, or the gospel in Christianity. But the notion of an archetext varies according to each self-constituting discourse. In literature, archetexts are 'chefs-d'oeuvre'; in scientific discourses, archetexts exemplify the norms of scientific activity at a given moment in time; whereas in religious discourse, archetexts are the eternal source of truth. Two kinds of archetexts can be distinguished: those that are acknowledged as such by everyone, and those that are acknowledged only by some members of a given discursive field. In fact, this distinction is not clearcut. From the viewpoint of Muslims, the Bible is an indirect archetext in that it prefigures the Qur'an. For philosophers, Hume's, Kant's, or Husserl's greatest works are archetexts, but not all philosophical positions attribute the same value to each. The definition of archetexts is indeed controversial: each position has its own archetexts, its proper textual pantheon, and establishes its own identity by modifying the prevailing hierarchies. Hierarchies of archetexts can be guaranteed by institutions: literature handbooks oppose 'great' writers to *menores*, while the Catholic Church has drawn up a sophisticated hierarchy of textual authorities.

Although it seems contrary to common sense, the archetexts – which are destined to be commented upon – and their commentaries presuppose each other. Archetexts are accorded a pragmatic status that turns them into texts that are worthy of interpretation but that exceed the abilities of their interpreters. If the interpreters fail to understand them, it is the interpreters – not the texts – who are deficient. This failure is the consequence of their "hyperprotected" pragmatic status (Pratt 1977). The more interpretations a text gives rise to, the more enigmatic it appears.

The second hierarchy sets *top* and *secondary genres* in opposition. This distinction grounds the necessity of popularization in particular: on the one hand, there are texts that are not supposed to be dominated by any other text; on the other hand, one finds genres that clarify, simplify, or diffuse established doctrines. The top genres of theology or basic science, for instance, are disseminated through secondary genres, such as sermons in churches or TV programs about diseases, diets, or beauty. Between these boundaries (of top genres and mass TV programs), we can recognize various intermediate levels, such as academic handbooks, Bible meetings, biographies of great writers,. Our analysis of self-constituting discourses cannot solely focus on archetexts and texts that belong to top genres: self-constituting discourses are basically heterogeneous. They are made up of the interactions between these elements in a network of genres.

3 The Modules of Religious Discourse

Unlike ordinary devotees, most experts – in order to play their role as experts – need to postulate that their religion forms (or can form) a coherent whole. In reality, religious discourse is not a whole organized around a center, as it claims to be. It is more realistic to see it as a constant negotiation between three relatively independent discourse modules: a *thesaurus* (TH) of founding texts, a *regulation* module (RM), and an *indexical* module (IM). Hence, religious discourse proves an unstable system, punctuated by crises of varying intensity.

In order to connect these modules, I had originally thought of using the notion of the *dispositif*, drawing in a personal way on one of Foucault's concepts, which is widely used in the social sciences and philosophy. Foucault characterizes the *dispositif* in the following terms:

> a thoroughly heterogeneous ensemble consisting of discourses, institutions, architectural forms, regulatory decisions, laws, administrative measures, scientific statements, philosophical, moral and philanthropic propositions – in short, the said as much as the unsaid. Such are the elements of the *dispositif*. The *dispositif*[12] itself is the system of relations that can be established between these elements.   (Foucault 1980, 194)

This definition is rather open-ended, but in my view, it has two main drawbacks when we use it to analyze religious discourse: 1) it integrates elements that pertain to various levels of society, and 2) although these elements are heterogeneous, they implicitly converge into a consistent whole, according to a structural conception of discourse. I prefer an approach based on modularity. By this I mean a 'weak' modularity, since the modules I am dealing with are not closed domains.

---

[12] In the English translation, *dispositif* is translated as "apparatus," which is unsatisfactory. I prefer to use the French word.

3.1 Thesaurus, Regulation, and Indexical Modules

A thesaurus (TH) is a set of oral or written archetexts: what has been *said* by the highest authorities. These can be based on a revelation (as in Christianity or Islam) or an illumination (as in Buddhism), but as a rule they mix didactic and hagiographical elements. They are not considered as belonging to a genre, but rather as founding events preserved in collective memory, singular traces of a transcendent 'speech', the meaning of which cannot be exhausted by any interpretation. As a rule, TH is written in an ancient, foreign language (in Christianity, Hebrew and Greek) or in an ancient, prestigious variety of a vernacular language (such as biblical Hebrew for Judaism, classical Arabic for Islam, or Sanskrit for Hinduism). Even the contemporary translations of the Bible that claim to be 'modern' preserve some lexical, syntactic, and pragmatic archaisms.

The regulation module (RM) structures believers' lives. It brings together two sub-modules: the *ritual* and the *prescriptive*. The ritual sub-module includes collective rites, but also the utterances of everyday life (such as prayers and spells). These signifiers are supposed to preserve the religion's identity. Their stability is enhanced and embodied by the use of liturgical language, which is not used for ordinary transactions (such as Slavonic in the Eastern Orthodox Church, Pali in Theravada Buddhism, or Aramaic in the Chaldean Church). In the case of Sanskrit, to ensure that rites remain effective, the priestly caste constantly strives to preserve the original signifiers, which must not be corrupted by everyday language in any way.

Those who participate in a religious service or say a prayer are supposed to be inhabited by a "hyperenunciator" (Maingueneau 2004b) – the spirit of the community, which is activated by the enunciation process. Rituals imply repetition on two complementary levels: the utterances are 1) destined to be reiterated indefinitely and 2) structured by the repetition of signifiers (see, for example, litanies; Rabatel 2015). Reciting the same texts shapes the community, whose members repeat these repetitive texts together.

However, the ritual sub-module takes many forms, according to the circumstances and the type of religion. Whereas Brahmanism precisely fixed the way in which ritual utterances must be enunciated in minute detail, and whereas the Catholic Church – until the Second Vatican Council – tried to maintain tight control over its rites, in American evangelical Protestantism, each church can establish its own rites, within certain limits.

The prescriptive sub-module defines what one must do and not do if one is to be a legitimate member of the community. As a rule, these prescriptions are concentrated into short texts that can be easily memorized: for example, the Ten Commandments, or the Five Pillars of Islam. But these are a small part of the whole set of implicit or explicit prescriptions that a believer must submit to in his or her everyday life. Part of these prescriptions concerns the ritual component (such as which prayers one must say under certain circumstances, or when one must go to the place of worship.

According to the social context and the time period, the tension between these prescriptions and the norms which prevail in society more broadly varies widely. In traditional rural societies, the tension can be weak, but in other contexts, it can be very strong: the Protestant Amish or the Jewish Haredim are good examples of a strong divergence between enforced religious prescriptions and the norms of the society that surrounds the community.

In principle, the regulation module (RM) is, in one way or another, anchored in the thesaurus (TH). In reality, it is the product of a negotiation between anthropological and historical constraints on the one hand and doctrinal constraints on the other, which are themselves shaped by the relations between the positions in the field. In Christianity, for example, the cult of the saints or the Virgin have a problematic relationship with TH; this is one of the key differences between Catholicism and Protestantism, the latter of which holds that the Bible is a higher source of authority than Church tradition. Even when TH seems to give clear instructions about rites, there are always differences between what is said in TH and actual practice in a particular place and at a particular time. But most of the time, the divergence between TH and actual practice does not yield critical conflicts: rites or prescriptions that are no longer widely accepted are not explicitly rejected, but rather progressively marginalized or forgotten.

The function of the *indexical* module (IM) is to make TH or RM relevant in a particular context. The difference between IM, on the one hand, and TH or RM, on the other hand, manifests itself through language: as a rule, IM uses vernacular, living languages. By drawing on the authority of a very limited stock of utterances produced under particular circumstances, a religion must respond to the demands for sense made by people who constantly find themselves in new situations and different historical environments.

The way in which 'indexicalization' is managed depends on the specific constraints of the genre and the doctrinal positioning. IM covers a wide range of genres: from the most hermetic genres of theology to those that involve ordinary believers – such as, in the Christian tradition, religious classes, papal encyclicals, parish bulletins, websites, sermons, and 'Bible meetings.' These genres and the ways in which they are practiced are socio-historical realities and are at one with the doctrine: not all religious faiths tolerate events like Bible meetings, where laypeople discuss the meanings of sacred texts, or where "religious doctrine is made relevant in the interpretation of personal experience" (Loeb 2014, 514). Inferences and categorization play a key role in this kind of session. Consider, for example, Seventh-day Adventist collective Bible readings:

> The participants use words and expressions that recontextualize the Bible story, connect it to categories that are relevant in the world of the participants. Understanding the categorizations is, however, dependent on the skill of inferring. The inferential order of the Bible study relies on cultural resources. The participants must, for example, see themselves as potential believers and as potentially engaged in teamwork. Understanding the recontextualizations is

> dependent on the same resources as producing them. It is important to note, however, that the skill involved is a practical one. There is no need for the participants to draw on any fixed body of cultural knowledge. Rather, they need a skill to make contextual inferences. The contextuality of their work becomes even more evident when the categorizations are explored in their sequential context. (Lehtinen 2009, 22)

Furthermore, IM concerns more than just the people who must give meaning to their lives and make decisions; it also focuses on the institutions, which must constantly legitimate their own organization and their activities. This is especially important at critical moments, when people challenge the legitimacy of certain practices or organizations and may enter into open conflict with orthodoxy.

The most obvious difference between RM and IM is that believers who share the same elements of RM need not ascribe the same meaning to them. This divergence becomes visible when there is a conflict. I will give an example: In the seventeenth century, there was a controversy between the Humanists and the Jansenists about the French translation of the Latin hymn to the Virgin "Ave maris stella," which was part of the Catholic liturgy. Their respective translations in the missals showed that they interpreted the Latin words according to their own doctrines, as we can see by comparing the first stanza.[13]

(1) Original Text	(2) Jansenist Translation	(3) Humanist Translation
Ave maris stella Dei mater alma Atque semper virgo Felix coeli porta	Eclaire, Astre divin, les noirs flots de ce monde Mère du Dieu des Dieux, Toujours Vierge, mais Vierge heureusement féconde, Claire porte des cieux.[14]	Bel Astre Intendant de la mer Dont les regards peuvent calmer L'orgueil des vents les plus farouches Mère de Dieu, porte du ciel.[15]

In (2), the author divides the universe into two worlds (the "black" world of sin, and the "bright" world of God), which are connected by the light of divine grace. In (3), the world is a cosmos where the Virgin, associated with the rhythms of the sea, is a mediator between the human being and God.

If we take into account Thomas Kohnen's distinction between "first-order," "second-order," and "third-order" spheres in religious discourse, then TH and the

---

13 For a detailed analysis, see Maingueneau 1989.
14 Louis-Isaac Le Maistre de Sacy, *L'Office de l'Eglise et de la Vierge en latin et en français avec les hymnes traduites en vers* (Paris: Veuve Jean Camusat & Pierre Le Petit, 1650), 114. Translation: "Light up, divine aster, the black waves of this world / Mother of the God of Gods / Always virgin, but fortunately fruitful virgin / Clear door of the heavens."
15 Jean Adam, *Heures catholiques en latin et en français* (Paris: G. Meturas, 1651), 544. Translation: "Beautiful star intendant of the sea / whose eyes can appease the fiercest winds / Mother of God, door of the Heaven /Virgin before and after your childbirth."

prescriptive component of RM belong to the first-order sphere ("texts that are issued by a superior, binding body or authority and are directed at all the members of the discourse community"); IM mainly pertains to the third-order sphere ("texts with which members of a discourse community, who do not form a superior body or institution, communicate with each other"); and a large part of the ritual component falls within the second-order sphere ("the members of a discourse community address a superior authority or institution").

3.2 The Relationship Between the Modules

IM must satisfy believers' demands while also preserving a link with TH and ensuring the evolution of RM. This is possible because the faithful mostly perceive TH and RM as relatively stable: TH is supposed to remain unchanged, and RM seems to last hundreds of years. Indeed, for laypeople who are immersed in the present, the relation between TH, RM, and IM is experienced as unidirectional: TH directly guarantees the legitimacy of RM, and any legitimate member of the clergy is supposed to proclaim 'the' meaning of TH, which is supposed to have remained unchanged since the origin, in its signifier as well as its signified. In fact, however, both aspects are subject to historical evolution.

In principle, any fragment of TH is sacred. But at a given moment in time, members ot the community ascribe different value to each its utterances. Each position in the field gives priority to some texts or excerpts, to the detriment of others. This is prompted by the fact that TH is constituted by texts from different genres or different periods; their compatibility is problematic. Since the IM experts who produce doctrines must define a coherent position by delimiting a specific space in the field, they have to value some excerpts over others and present this selection as the correct interpretation of TH. As a rule, over a given period, a hegemonic interpretation casts a large part of TH to the fringes, where it is ignored or interpreted in a different way. In the Catholic tradition, for example, the Song of Songs was widely quoted and commented upon in the first half of the seventeenth century, but it was marginalized in the second half of the century, when a strong mistrust of mysticism developed.

For institutional reasons, sometimes texts produced in IM are integrated into TH. Paul's epistles, for example, which clearly belong to IM, were added to the New Testament very early on, together with the Gospels. Likewise, but to a lesser degree, the 'great church fathers' (Augustine, Gregory the Great, Ambrose, and Jerome) were a superior source of authority. For centuries, Saint Augustine's thought on the subject of grace has defined orthodoxy. In this respect, one could also mention the example of rabbinic literature: the Torah denotes both the Pentateuch and the Oral Torah, which consists of commentaries transmitted from generation to generation. Likewise in Islam, the Sunna is made up of two components: the Qur'an and the collection of hadiths which preserve the words and deeds of the Prophet. But a hierarchy has been established: first, between the Qur'an, which is believed to have been directly revealed by God, and the hadiths; and second, among the hadiths themselves, as some are considered authentic while others are not. In reality, this boundary cannot be clear-cut: it depends on which criteria are considered relevant, and this opens up space for conflict. Religious institutions can decide to exclude certain texts from TH (for example, the 'apocryphal' gospels in the first centuries of Christianity). They can also grant them less authority (for example, the Torah includes only five books).

The key role of IM is especially apparent when believers perceive a change in RM the stability of which gives them the feeling that their religion has remained the same over time. They associate the stability of these signifiers with the very identity of the community. They are particularly sensitive to the modification of rituals and prescriptions. Replacing liturgical RM language with another language can trigger sharp controversy, as can the simple act of modifying a translation – for example in 1966, when the Catholic Church imposed a new 'ecumenical' translation of the "Our Father" prayer in French, in which God was called 'tu' instead of 'vous.'

As for the experts, they can employ sophisticated resources to show that, despite appearances, deep transformations of RM actually preserve their religion's identity. The Second Vatican Council was presented by those sympathetic to it as a 'prophetic act' which, rather than innovating, brought the Church back to its foundation:

> The Second Vatican Council is a prophetic event. [. . .] An extraordinary event in purest fidelity to the Good News announced by Jesus Christ, an extraordinary event in that it shows an institution given over – at least for a while – to the powers of prophets, an institution that accepts the consideration of its own reform and exposes itself to the risks of being called into question [. . .] This self-destruction is not a destruction, the refusal of its heritage, a break in continuity, but a moment of reflexivity, of dismantling, a moment of crisis,. (Nault 2011, 461)

4 Community and Embodiment

4.1 The Three Communities

The modules we have sketched thus far are not sufficient to characterize religious discourse. It also implies a community whose members share a cultural background, constituted of heterogeneous elements (such as beliefs, memories, and narratives). This community takes three complementary forms: *transcendent*, *instituted*, and *global*.

The transcendent community is not limited to a specific context; it integrates the living and the dead, the present and the absent. Over time, it must always be the same community. Instituted communities are the multiple groups of people who participate in the same discourse activity: a religious service, a predication, or a prayer. They are legitimized by the transcendent community, which envelops them. When the faithful sing or pray together, the 'I' of each participant also implies all of those who, addressing the same divinity, have said, are saying, will say, or might say the same words in the same situation. Even in solitary practices (such as meditating on a sacred text or praying), the transcendent community gives meaning to the activity.

At a higher level, instituted communities are incorporated into the global community of all believers at a given moment, independently of any particular discourse activity. The global community is structured by the distinction between clerics and non-clerics. The status of the clerics is ambiguous: they are both mediators of the divinity and members of the community. As a result, they are expected to legitimate themselves by behaving in an exemplary manner. Depending on the situation and the moment, they can use discourses to distance themselves from the other members, taking on the point of view of the divinity, or to present themselves as an ordinary community member.

4.2 Embodiment

This leads us to the polysemy of 'body,' which can refer to both the anatomical body of a person and a mystical body, the whole community. The members of the community are supposed to maintain the same disciplined body, especially the same speaking body. Here we can refer to notions like "habitus" or "hexis" (Bourdieu 1972, 1980) in sociology, or "discursive ethos" (Maingueneau 1999, 2014; Amossy 2010) in discourse analysis. Speaking with a certain ethos enhances one's belonging to the community, and one validates the doctrine through one's utterances. In the case of self-constituting discourses, speaking with the right ethos is not a rhetorical strategy: it means being consistent with the world as the divinity intends it to be. In other words, conflicts between doctrines are inseparable from conflicts between discursive ethos. In France in the seventeenth century, the controversy between Christian Humanism and Jansenism was also the opposition between two ethos. For the Humanists, speaking in a 'sweet'[16] way meant conforming to the rules of God's cosmos. This doctrine, which refused rigorous piety and particularly Calvinist discipline, was in a sense embodied in the Humanist ethos. At the beginning of the most famous book representing this trend, *Introduction à la vie dévote* (Introduction to Devout Life) by François de Sales (1609), the author stages a representation of the body of good piety, which is opposed to that of bad piety. According to the medical categorization of the time, the latter is represented by the stereotype of a melancholic character, as opposed to the sanguine temperament of the enunciator: "The people, dear Philothée, defame as much as possible holy piety, depicting devout persons with an unpleasant, sad,

---

16 In French: 'doux.'

and peevish face, and proclaiming that piety causes melancholic and insufferable humors."[17] This 'anti-ethos' indirectly legitimates the enunciator as a good Christian: the person who is speaking so softly and in such a friendly manner is the very person who does not have a "peevish face" or "insufferable humors."

The embodiment of religious convictions is not simply a matter of speech. It also implies a way of dressing and moving one's body that must be in line with the required ethos. This aspect is particularly important for the laity. Catholics were particularly moved when the Second Vatican Council decided to change the way priests and nuns were dressed: many people thought that abandoning the cassock would damage their status. The same thing happened with religious services: the introduction of songs with guitar accompaniment implied a different embodiment of religion. So, depending on the social context, religion can, to a large extent, manage the surveillance mechanisms – both external and internalized – that Foucault described.

However, the problem of ethos cannot be reduced to doctrinal aspects. We must also take into account the specific constraints of the genres, especially those of RM. The nature of a prayer, a song, or a litany implies a specific ethos, which is largely independent of the various doctrines. Moreover, the laity do not have to satisfy the same requirements as clerics do: clerics must embody the doctrine, whereas very few believers adopt a religious ethos. They behave mainly according to the norms of the social groups they belong to (such as family, social class, gender, or profession).

5 Conclusion

I have stressed that religious discourse, in the narrow sense I ascribe to the term, is both stable and unstable. We can explain this with reference to its modularity. The modules are relatively autonomous and subject to a specific history, but at any moment in time, they must interact in order to appear compatible. Discourse practice is constantly engaged in both repeating and forgetting, in preserving signifiers and inventing new meanings and new speech frames, implying new forms of subjectivity and new audiences.

Discourse analysis cannot replace philosophy, sociology, psychology, or anthropology in proposing a theory of religion. But it can contribute to changing the way religion is studied. Its purpose is to overcome the traditional relationship between

---

[17] François de Sales, *Oeuvres* (Paris: Gallimard, 1969), 34. Original text: "Le monde, ma chère Philothée, diffame tant qu'il peut la sainte dévotion, dépeignant les personnes dévotes avec un visage fâcheux, triste et chagrin, et publiant que la dévotion donne des humeurs mélancoliques et insupportables."

'linguistics' and 'religious text' or 'religious language,' in which linguistics is merely an auxiliary discipline that offers help in interpreting texts or analyzing a language register. But most discourse analysts are still reluctant to study religious corpora. When they do, they tend to select those aspects of religious discourse that resemble the data they are familiar with – especially oral interaction and sermons. I think religious discourse must be considered in the full diversity of its practices as well as its components. Undoubtedly, the integration of religious data will have an impact on the theoretical background and methods of discourse analysis, but we cannot simply expand the standard toolkit to encompass corpora that have previously been marginalized. New concepts must be used. Nevertheless, opening up this new field of research is in line with what ought to be its aim: considering the interactions of all manifestations of discourse in society in their full diversity.

References

Adam, Martin. 2009. *Functional Macrofield Perspective: A Religious Discourse Analysis Based on FSP*. Brno: Masarykova univerzita.
Althusser, Louis. 1972. "Ideology and Ideological State Apparatuses." In *Lenin and Philosophy and other Essays*. New York: Monthly Review Press, 121–176.
Almeida, Yvan. 1978. *L'Opérativité sémantique des récits-paraboles. Sémiotique narrative et textuelle. Herméneutique du discours religieux*. Louvain-Paris: Peeters-Cerf.
Amossy, Ruth. 2010. *La présentation de soi. Ethos et identité verbale*. Paris: PUF.
Angermuller, Johannes, Dominique Maingueneau, and Ruth Wodak, eds. 2014. *The Discourse Studies Reader: Main Currents in Theory and Analysis*. Amsterdam/Philadelphia: John Benjamins.
Banks, David, ed. 2008. *La langue, la linguistique et le texte religieux*. Paris: L'Harmattan.
Benveniste, Emile. 1966. *Problèmes de linguistique générale*. Paris: Gallimard.
Bourdieu, Pierre. 1971. "Une interprétation de la théorie de la religion selon Max Weber." *Archives européennes de sociologie* XII, no. 1: 3–21.
Bourdieu. Pierre. 1972. *Esquisse d'une théorie de la pratique*. Genève: Droz.
Bourdieu. Pierre. 1980. *Le Sens pratique*. Paris: Minuit.
Bourdieu, Pierre. *Les règles de l'art. Genèse et structure du champ littéraire*. Paris: Seuil, 1992.
Crystal, David. 1964. "A Liturgical Language in a Linguistic Perspective." *New Blackfriars* 46, no. 534: 148–56.
Crystal, David, and Derek Davy. 1969. *Investigating English Style*. London: Longman.
Debray, Régis. 1983. *Critique de la raison politique*. Paris: Gallimard.
De Certeau, Michel. 1975. *L'Écriture de l'histoire*. Paris: Gallimard.
Ducrot, Oswald. 1984. *Le Dire et le dit*. Paris: Minuit.
Fairclough, Norman. 2003. *Analysing Discourse: Textual Analysis for Social Research*. London/ New York: Routledge.
Ferguson, Charles A. 1973. "Some Forms of Religious Discourse." *International Yearbook for the Sociology of Religion* 8: 224–35.
Ferguson, Charles A. 1982. "Religious Factors in Language Spread." In *Language Spread: Studies in Diffusion and Social Change*, ed. by Robert L. Cooper, 95–106. Bloomington: Indiana University Press.

Foucault, Michel. 1969. *L'Archéologie du savoir*. Paris: Gallimard.
Foucault, Michel. 1980. "The Confession of the Flesh." In *Power/Knowledge Selected Interviews and Other Writings, 1972–1977*, ed. by Colin Gordon, 194–228. New York: Pantheon Books.
Groeger, Dorothee. 2010. *The Pamphlet as a Form of Publication: A Corpus-based Study of Early Modern Religious Pamphlets*. Aachen: Shaker.
Groupe d'Entrevernes.1977. *Signes et paraboles, Sémiotique et texte évangélique*. Paris: Seuil.
Hjelm, Titus. 2011. "Discourse Analysis." In *The Routledge Handbook of Research Methods in the Study of Religion*, ed. by Michael Stausberg and Steven Engler, 134–50. London: Routledge.
Kohnen, Thomas. 2010. "Religious Discourse." In *Historical Pragmatics*, ed. by Andreas H. Jucker and Irma Taavitsainen, 523–47. Berlin: De Gruyter Mouton.
Kohnen, Thomas. 2012. "A Toolkit for Constructing Corpus Networks." In *Developing Corpus Methodology for Historical Pragmatics*, ed. by Carla Suhr and Irma Taavitsainen. Helsinki: VARIENG e-Series, http://www.helsinki.fi/varieng/series/volumes/11/kohnen/.
Lehtinen, Esa. 2009. "Sequential and Inferential Order in Religious Action: A Conversation Analytic Perspective." *Langage et société* 130: 15–36.
Loeb, Laura. 2014. "Call and Response: An Anatomy of Religious Practice." *Discourse Studies* 16, no. 4: 514–33.
Maingueneau, Dominique. 1983. *Sémantique de la polémique*. Lausanne: l'Age d'Homme.
Maingueneau, Dominique. 1984. *Genèses du discours*. Liège: Mardaga.
Maingueneau, Dominique. 1987. *Nouvelles tendances en analyse du discours*. Paris: Hachette.
Maingueneau, Dominique. 1989. "Un conflitto di traduzioni: l'*Ave maris stella* tra umanesimo devoto e giansenismo." In *Lingua, tradizione, rivelazione: le chiese e la communicazione sociale*, ed. by Lia Formigari and Donatella di Cesare, 161–75. Casale Monferrato: Marietti.
Maingueneau, Dominique. 1999. "Analysing Self-Constituting Discourses." *Discourse Studies* 1, no. 2: 175–200.
Maingueneau, Dominique. 2004a. *Le Discours littéraire. Paratopie et scène d'énonciation*. Paris: Armand Colin.
Maingueneau, Dominique. 2004b."Hyperénonciateur et 'particitation'." *Langages* 156: 111–27.
Maingueneau, Dominique. 2009. "Le sermon: contraintes génériques et positionnement." *Langage et Société* 130: 37–60.
Maingueneau, Dominique. 2014. "Retour critique sur l'éthos." *Langage et Société* 149: 31–48.
Marin, Louis. 1972. *Sémiotique de la Passion, topiques et figures*. Paris: Desclée de Brouwer-Aubier-Montaigne.
Marin, Louis, and Claude Chabrol. 1972. *Le Récit évangélique*. Paris: Aubier-Montaigne.
Mühleisen, Susanne. 2007. "Language and Religion." In *Handbook of Language and Communication: Diversity and Change*, ed. by Marlis Hellinger and Anne Pauwels, 459–91. Berlin: De Gruyter.
Nault, François. 2011. "Un concile prophétique au temps des sorciers." *Laval théologique et philosophique* 67, no. 3: 461–75.
Obadia, Lionel. 2009. "Discours et religion : approche synoptique en sociologie et anthropologie." *Langage et société* 130: 83–101.
Panier, Louis. 1984. *Récits et commentaires de la tentation de Jésus. Approche sémiotique*. Paris: Le Cerf.
Pêcheux, Michel. 1969. *Analyse automatique du discours*. Paris: Dunod.
Pêcheux, Michel. 1975. *Les vérités de La Palice. Linguistique, sémantique, philosophie*. Paris: Maspero.
Pratt, Mary Louise. 1977. *Toward a Speech Act Theory of Literary Discourse*. Bloomington: Indiana University Press.

Rabatel, Alain. 2007a. "L'alternance des *tu* et des *vous* dans *Le Deutéronome*: deux points de vue sur le rapport des fils d'Israël à l'Alliance." *Études théologiques et religieuses* 82, no. 4: 567–93.
Rabatel, Alain. 2007b. "Répétitions et reformulations dans *L'Exode*: coénonciation entre Dieu, ses représentants et le narrateur." In *Usages et analyses de la reformulation*, ed. by Mohamed Kara, 75–96. Metz: Université de Metz.
Rabatel, Alain. 2015. "Des répétitions dans le discours religieux: l'exemple des litanies." *Le Discours et la Langue* 7, no. 2: 23–38.
Ruetten, Tanja. 2011. *How to Do Things with Texts: Patterns of Instruction in Religious Discourse 1350–1700*. Frankfurt: Peter Lang.
Scott, Michael. 2013. *Religious Language*. London/New York: Palgrave Macmillan.
Stausberg, Michael, and Steven Engler. 2011. "Research Methods in the Study of Religion\s." In *The Routledge Handbook of Research Methods in the Study of Religion*, ed. by Michael Stausberg and Steven Engler, 3–20. London: Routledge.
Stuckrad, Kocku von. 2003. "Discursive Study of Religion: From States of the Mind to Communicative Action." *Method & Theory in the Study of Religion* 15, no. 3: 255–71.
Stuckrad, Kocku von. 2010. "Reflections on the Limits of Reflection: An Invitation to the Discursive Study of Religion." *Method & Theory in the Study of Religion* 22, nos. 2–3:156–69.
Terry, Ralph Bruce. 1995. *A Discourse Analysis of First Corinthians*. The Summer Institute of Linguistics and The University of Texas at Arlington Publications in Linguistics.
Wijsen, Frans. 2013. "Discourse Analysis in Religious Studies." *Religion* 43, no. 1: 1–3.

Kocku von Stuckrad
Historical Discourse Analysis: The Entanglement of Past and Present

1 History: Forgetting, Selecting, Presenting

Most of history is forgetting. In fact, as Paul Ricoeur reminds us: "There is forgetting wherever there had been a trace. [. . .] Forgetting is the emblem of the vulnerability of the historical condition taken as a whole" (Ricoeur 2006, 284). One reason why human individuals and cultures forget is the sheer fact that there is too much to remember, and that we have learned to perceive pragmatically and selectively. Our brains are geared to delete and destroy information; otherwise we would be lost in an avalanche of data that needs to be processed. Likewise, the lives of humans and non-humans produce a huge amount of traces that subsequent generations may or may not find, read, and engage with. Most of those traces go unnoticed. When later generations notice certain traces, their status changes from traces to sources. They become data, carriers of meaning for people who look back at the past. Most often, people read these sources as meaningful indicators of a coherent line of events that ultimately lead to their own present time. Thus history provides meaning for the present.

Historiography – literally the writing down of history – is a process of selection and prioritization of data that is subsequently written into a meaningful plot. As we know from feminist and other narrative critique, what constitutes a meaningful plot is also socio-culturally created. Historians tell their stories to their contemporaries, not to the people of the past. That is why Hayden White famously compared writing academic histories to writing fiction. The 'emplotment' of history is a creative process, and the tools of classical rhetoric apply to historiography as well, if the authors want to convince their audiences. For White, this historical work is

> a verbal structure in the form of a narrative prose discourse. Histories (and philosophies of history as well) combine a certain amount of "data," theoretical concepts for "explaining" these data, and a narrative structure for their presentation as an icon of sets of events presumed to have occurred in times past. In addition, I maintain, they contain a deep structural content which is generally poetic, and specifically linguistic, in nature, and which serves as the precritically accepted paradigm of what a distinctively "historical" explanation should be. This paradigm functions as the "metahistorical" element in all historical works that are more comprehensive in scope than the monograph or archival report. (White 1973, ix)

Based on this insight, we can deduce that much of what historians write is inspired by questions anchored in their own times. History is a tool to provide answers to present-day questions, rather than a field of information studied solely for its own sake.

Let us consider an example that illustrates this mechanism. All readers of this chapter will be familiar with Sir Isaac Newton (1642–1727), who, as Wikipedia tells us, "is widely recognised as one of the most influential scientists of all time and a key figure in the scientific revolution" (Wikipedia 2018). His major work, the *Philosophiae Naturalis Principia Mathematica* (1687), is considered a cornerstone of modern 'science,' even though its title and content address the mathematical principles of natural philosophy rather than science. What is more, the term "scientific revolution" was introduced many years later and was popularized by Alexandre Koyré only in the twentieth century (see Hall 1987). "Although many seventeenth-century practitioners expressed their intention of bringing about radical intellectual change," Steven Shapin reminds us, "the people who are said to have made the revolution used no such term to refer to what they were doing" (Shapin 1996, 2). Shapin maintains that "[h]istorians have in recent years become dissatisfied with the traditional manner of treating ideas as if they floated freely in conceptual space" (ibid., 4), and he suggests looking at historians' own social and cultural backgrounds to identify the origins of historical theories and narratives.

This also explains the remarkable amount of Isaac Newton's work that has been forgotten. While his 'scientific' work is venerated in museums and libraries, a large part of his writings, consisting of theological and alchemical publications, has been regarded for centuries as unimportant and not representative of Newton's work. An indication of this neglect of scholarly attention is the fact that Sotheby's auctioned some of Newton's unpublished works in 1936, on behalf of Gerard Wallop, 9th Earl of Portsmouth, who had inherited them from Newton's great-niece. At the beginning of the twenty-first century, we see a shift in public and scholarly interest that goes along with a re-evaluation of the history of 'science,' the 'Enlightenment,' and 'modernity,' as well as this history's relevance for the constitution of contemporary culture. The resulting interest in the 'alchemical' Newton,[1] of course, does not mean that we have now come to know the whole truth about this complex figure, but it does mean that we are adding a dimension to the picture, highlighting a feature that is meaningful for understanding our own place in the larger scheme of things and events.

What, then, are the parameters and mechanisms that determine which traces are forgotten and which traces are turned into sources? Historians have discussed this question for a long time and developed theories that are relevant for other disciplines as well. An important contribution to this methodological discussion comes from Reinhart Koselleck, who introduced the distinction between the "space of experience" (*Erfahrungsraum*) and the "horizon of expectation" (*Erwartungshorizont*).

---

[1] See, for instance, "The Chymistry of Isaac Newton" project, run at Indiana University by William R. Newman and colleagues; http://webapp1.dlib.indiana.edu/newton/ (accessed 14 April 2020).

Experience and expectation, because they interweave past and future, are two appropriate categories for thematizing historical time. These categories are suited to finding historical time in the area of empirical research as well, because – enriched in content – they provide the concrete units of action in the execution of social and political movements.²

Historiography distills historical meaning from the tensions between past, present, and future. Historical meaning is always ascribed and generated, a process of meaning-making that German historians refer to as *historische Sinnbildung*. Jörn Rüsen, for instance, distinguishes three elements that together constitute historical meaning: the levels of content, of formal construction, and of function. With regard to contents, historiography has to make sure that the (re)presented past has real empirical grounding – that is, the recipients must recognize the narrated story as factitious. The formal element simply calls for the logical plausibility of the story – for instance, in the temporal relations of its details. Finally, the functional level points to the high significance of the story for contemporary discourse, because the practical application of the presented past is always an inherent part of the narration. In Rüsen's words:

> Hence historical meaning [*Sinn*] is divided into the three components of the empirical, of interpretation, and of orientation. All three refer to the past in a communicated temporal distance to the present. [. . .] "Meaning" [appears] as an adequate term for the coherence that is crucial in this relationship [between past and present]. Meaning is the integration of all three components. They have to refer to one another, converge in one another, and enhance one another. [. . .] The integration is practically realized and applied in narrative operations. Meaning in narrative is the red thread the story follows: it is generated by the respective cultural pattern of interpretation. (Rüsen 1997, 36; my translation)

Rüsen's approach is an example of the possibility of arriving at a theory of history that does not hide its constructive elements and nonetheless is able to correlate the facts of the past with their (re)presentation in the present under the broad conceptual umbrella of history. History, in this perspective, is an analytical term that does not explain anything in itself. It is located on a different level of argument. It is a metaterm necessary for interpretation at the interface of past and present. It should not be mixed up with the "facts" themselves – which would lead to essentialism – but rather should be regarded as a reminder that there are facts "out there," facts which influence our positions or even determine our concepts, even though our representations of history are not a mirror of these actual facts.

Applying "history" in such a way throws some interesting light on a notorious discussion within the academic study of religion. It has become a scholarly trend to quote Jonathan Z. Smith's dictum that *"there is no data for religion*. Religion is solely the creation of the scholar's study" (Smith 1982, xi; italics original). However,

---

2 Koselleck 1995, 353 (my translation). On Koselleck, Paul Ricoeur, and Hayden White see Kippenberg 2002, 187–195. Compare also Ricoeur's response to Koselleck in Ricoeur 2006, 296–305.

most scholars of religion do not seem to read the first part of the italicized sentence, which says that "there is a staggering amount of data, of phenomena, of human experiences and expressions that might be characterized in one culture or another, by one criterion or another, as religious." This fuller picture renders a much more nuanced impression of what Smith is actually arguing. It can be linked to my distinction between 'traces' and 'sources,' which sees history as a set of events that happen, and that we subsequently interpret with our historical imaginations. Our interpretations, contingent and relative as they are, therefore respond to reality. They live up to Sam D. Gill's claim that "writings of the academic study of religion must also be demonstrably grounded in the reality of the subject. Without this grounding, what we do is finally not academic at all" (Gill 2000, 460).

The discussion of constructivism and materialism is a major debate in the humanities today, and I will return to this after addressing the discursive framing of historiography. Much of this has to do with notions of truth and (representations of) reality, a topic about which philosophers also have a lot to say. If we consider Richard Rorty's post-analytical pragmatism, for instance, we see parallel developments in historiography, the sociology of science, philosophy, and cultural studies. Against the realist position, Rorty suggests that we should leave behind our attempt to find an *objectivity* that would mirror the reality of the world. Rather, what we should strive for is establishing *solidarity* among peer-groups. It is not the truth of our models that is at stake, but their power of conviction.

> For the pragmatist [. . .], "knowledge" is, like "truth," simply a compliment paid to the beliefs which we think so well justified that, for the moment, further justification is not needed. An inquiry into the nature of knowledge can, on his [sic!] view, only be a sociohistorical account of how various people have tried to reach agreement on what to believe. (Rorty 1989, 7)

Even our understanding of "objectivity" as a method entirely independent of the observer can be historicized. In their superb study of objectivity, Lorraine Daston and Peter Galison emphasize that this understanding

> first emerged in the mid-nineteenth century and in a matter of decades became established not only as a scientific norm but also as a set of practices [. . .]. However dominant objectivity may have become in the sciences since *circa* 1860, it never had, and still does not have, the epistemological field to itself. Before objectivity, there was truth-to-nature; after the advent of objectivity came trained judgment. (Daston and Galison 2007, 28–29)

For quite some time, discourse research has been engaging with the mechanisms of "how various people have tried to reach agreement on what to believe," as well as the question of the extent to which these mechanisms are based on reality. I will discuss this with reference to the discursive understanding of history.

2 Historical Discourse Analysis

Discourse research has a lot to offer when it comes to understanding the past.[3] Sometimes, however, the use of discourse theory in historical analysis is much more limited. This is the case if scholars stick to the linguistic dimension of their research, like the approach Laurel J. Brinton advocates when he says that it "is the study of discourse forms, functions, or structures – that is, whatever is encompassed by discourse analysis [. . .] – in earlier periods of a language. The attention of the discourse analyst is focused on historical stages of a language, yet the emphasis remains on discourse structure. This approach may be termed *historical discourse analysis* proper" (Brinton 2001, 139; italics original). More relevant for our discussion here are approaches that apply methods of discourse analysis to historical phenomena and investigate how meaning and knowledge are produced in clearly defined historical settings; the only difference would be that our sources are less varied (and mostly limited to textual, visual, and archaeological data) than the sources in an analysis of contemporary discourses. It should be noted, however, that we always require a communicative situation, because otherwise there cannot be any discourse (Landwehr 2009, 128). Examples of such an application are Yoosun Park's analysis of the construction of the 'refugee' in US social work from 1900–1957 (Park 2008) and Jessie Sun's study of 'mindfulness' movements (Sun 2014).

To access the full potential of historical discourse analysis, however, we will have to cut deeper. This is where Michel Foucault comes into play. Throughout his work, Foucault the historian was interested in the genealogy and 'archaeology' of discursive structures, which naturally implies a historical dimension in his analysis of discourse (see Bieder 1998; Bublitz 1999). But Foucault was skeptical of our ability to render a true and neutral image of the past, which created a conflict with historians who argued for a realist approach to historical representation. Only a few historians have seriously explored the implications of discourse research. Even today, "sources are still read as 'documents' of a past reality – perhaps they are read better, more diligently and critically, but nevertheless as a medium with sufficient transparency" (Sarasin 2003, 32; my translation). Most historians would deny that historical meaning is discursively generated, rather than neutrally reconstructed from the facts in a hermeneutical process of understanding. But this is exactly what Foucault wanted to show in his critical reflection on our presupposition that historical truth is accessible in our accounts of it. Since Foucault, "discourse analysis can be understood as the attempt to scrutinize the formal conditions that steer the production of meaning" (Sarasin 2003, 33). Sarasin explains:

> The thing that is meant, the referent, *as a referent* of a certain linguistic sign, is not prior to language; rather, it is the system of signs that ultimately creates it as social reality from the

---
3 For my understanding of discourse, see Keller 2011 and von Stuckrad 2015.

> "chaotic variety" [*chaotische Mannigfaltigkeit*] (Kant) of all possible things in the world: "It is the world of words that generates the world of things" [Jacques Lacan]. Something else is fundamental for discourse analysis: This is not about the abstruse question whether there is more than texts; it is about how the non-linguistic things gain their meaning. No discourse, no grid of classification, however familiar it may appear, has ever been derived "from the things themselves"; it is the other way round, and discourse and classification generate the order of things. [. . .] Even though practices, gestures, and objects are themselves no longer constituted in language, they are relevant in the social world only because meaning has been discursively attributed to them.
>
> (Sarasin 2003, 35–36; my translation)

We will see below that some scholars today would argue, against Lacan and Sarasin, that the world of things generates the world of words – a materialist argument to which discourse theory has to respond. But this does not contradict Foucault's claim that we can understand the workings of discursive structures only if we know their genealogy and formation. Achim Landwehr goes so far as to say that "discourses have no other 'basis' than their own history" (Landwehr 2009, 97; my translation). What is more, only through comparison – in a diachronic or synchronic perspective – we can see the historicity and even singularity of discourses (see also Scott 2007, 8). No discourse emerges 'naturally.' Historical and comparative analysis of how social communicational structures attribute meaning to the world and organize explicit and implicit knowledge is the basis of any analysis of discourse. This is also the approach that many historians who are open to discourse theory share today. See, for example, the broad and yet workable definition Franz X. Eder gives in his volume on historical discourse analyses:

> In this volume, discourses are defined as practices that systematically organize and regulate statements on a certain topic, thereby also determining the conditions of what (in a social group at a certain time) can be thought and said. Which of the three relevant levels – textual, discursive, and social practices – historical discourse research focuses on and how they are related to one another depends on the respective research questions and theoretical positions. In any case, (historical) discourse analysis is by no means a specific method; rather, it is a research program or research perspective: Doing discourse analysis today means applying quite different methods and procedures, all of them scientifically elaborated and explicit.
>
> (Eder 2006, 13; my translation)

Even in the context of the social-scientific study of culture, historical discourse analysis adds a reflection on its own research agenda and politics. Put differently, "historical discourse analysis is a research approach suited to contextualiz[ing] its own research stories and practices" (Jóhannesson 2010, 252). Jóhannesson continues:

> I must acknowledge my resistance against seeing my ways of working as "a method"; I see my research, most of the time, as what can be called a Foucauldian-feminist quest to identify contradictions in the discourses surrounding us, hopefully to be able to exploit these contradictions to interrupt current discourse. This means that I wish to focus more on why research is conducted and under which circumstances, rather than on its methods. Thus, what sparked

the researcher's interest becomes an important part of the story, but what happened to the
research findings is also important and will become part of the story. (Ibid.)

If indeed, following Foucault, we regard discourses as practices that (co-)create the realities they describe, it is important to include the researcher's cultural location in the research itself. In this way, "discourse analysis (also) produces discourses on discourses" (Landwehr 2009, 98), which is not to be regarded as a disadvantage, but as the researcher's acknowledgment of being involved in what I have called the "double-bind of discourse research" (see von Stuckrad 2015, 435).

3 The Materiality of the Past and the Limits of Construction

Including the researcher's contemporary context in our analysis of how historical knowledge is produced, legitimized, sanctioned, and stabilized is a major advantage of discursive approaches. It also means that the analytical focus is on the way knowledge is constructed in social communication. While constructionist approaches in the humanities and the social sciences were very influential in the second half of the twentieth century – mostly thanks to scholars persuaded by the work of Peter L. Berger, Thomas Luckmann, and Alfred Schütz (see Berger and Luckmann 1966; Schütz and Luckmann 1979–1984) – the last ten years have seen a strong critique of constructionism, particularly in its radical forms. New attributions of materialist thinking, along with object-oriented ontologies and theories in philosophy and cultural studies, have challenged what is described as an anthropocentric bias in constructionist arguments. In the introduction to their volume *New Materialisms*, Diana Coole and Samantha Frost point out that

> materialism's demise since the 1970s has been an effect of the dominance of analytical and normative political theory on the one hand and of radical constructivism on the other. These respective Anglophone and continental approaches have both been associated with a cultural turn that privileges language, discourse, culture, and values. While this turn has encouraged a de facto neglect of more obviously material phenomena and processes, it has also problematized any straightforward overture toward matter or material experience as naively representational or naturalistic. (Coole and Frost 2010, 3)

This critique is directed particularly against anthropocentric normativities and radical constructionism (see also Jay Johnston's critical reflections in this volume). But there are many versions of constructionism that try to find a balance between construction and reality. Coole and Frost acknowledge this when they note that it "is entirely possible [. . .] to accept social constructionist arguments while also insisting that the material realm is irreducible to culture or discourse and that cultural artifacts are not arbitrary vis-à-vis nature" (ibid., 27). The question, then, is *how much* constructionism do we need, and how can we include the reality of the world in our hermeneutical equations?

One way out of this predicament is to make clear – as in fact many discourse theorists would emphasize – that discursive approaches do not neglect the reality of the world; it is only that they are more interested in the 'discursivization' of those realities and their transformation into human knowledge. But for them, the world *an sich* will never be accessible to us without the filtering processes of discursivization. From this perspective, knowledge is always precarious and dependent on dynamics of power and perception that humans can only partly control or even understand. The more-than-human world is part of this dynamic and can influence the discursivization of things and events. This leads to the question of whether the more-than-human world – which includes nonhuman animals and objects that humans often deem inanimate – can be part of a discourse, or even get actively involved in a discourse community.

To address this issue, it is helpful to take into account recent discussions about agency, relationality, and object-oriented ontologies. For questions of historical research, the archaeologist Ian Hodder's theory of entanglement is particularly interesting. "The term 'entanglement,'" Hodder explains, "joins the many others that try to bridge the divide between materialism and social construction" (Hodder 2012, 95). Objects and things in history have a natural life that influences what we can know about them; "in many ways things make us. There is an objectness, a stand-in-the-wayness to things that resists, that forms, that entraps and entangles" (ibid., 13). And with reference to Alfred Gell and Bruno Latour, Hodder argues that "[t]hings do have a primary agency, not because they have intentionality but because they are vibrant and have lives and interactions of their own. As they grow, transform or fall apart they have a direct impact on human lives. This is not a secondary agency delegated to things by humans" (ibid., 68). In Hodder's argument, agency emerges from the encounter with humans: "The dependencies are not inherent in the things themselves but in the interactions between humans and things" (ibid., 18).

Similar to entanglement studies, the study of relationality looks at the dynamic interactions of various communication partners, including nonhuman animals and things. The agency of things also emerges from their relations with one another and with human beings (Ingman et al. 2016 weighs this concept in detail). In his most recent work, Bruno Latour introduced the concept of the "metamorphic zone," which refers to the messy area of agency and encounter between humans and the more-than-human world. Building on this, he argues:

> It is the material world that we have rendered mute in order to avoid answering the questions "Who or what is speaking? Who or what is acting?" It is in order to understand this strange situation that I must introduce, in addition to the one of transactions that I have called metamorphic, an entirely different operation through which, *in language and by means of language*, some characters are deprived of any form of agency. This operation is going to *deanimate*

some of the actors and give the impression that there is a gulf between inanimate material actors and human subjects endowed with soul – or at least with consciousness.

(Latour 2017, 67; italics original)

This operation ultimately brings Latour to the concept of 'Gaia,' which he takes from James Lovelock. Gaia refers to the 'world' as a messy and vibrant area of exchange, not a 'system' (as many of Lovelock's interpreters mistakenly assume). Instead,

> I should like to insist on two particularly surprising characteristics of Gaia: first, that it is composed of agents that are neither *deanimated* nor *overanimated*; then, contrary to what Lovelock's detractors claim, that it is made up of agents that are not *prematurely unified* in a single acting totality. Gaia, the outlaw, is the anti-system. (Ibid., 87; italics original)

There is a close relationship between this thinking and the innovative work of Donna J. Haraway. What Latour calls the metamorphic zones of Gaia, Haraway conceptualizes as a zone of entanglement, "worlding," and "co-becoming" among various species and critters. "It is no longer news that corporations, farms, clinics, labs, homes, sciences, technologies, and multispecies lives are entangled in multiscalar, multitemporal, multimaterial worlding; but the details matter. The details link actual beings to actual response-abilities" (Haraway 2016, loc. 2393–2395). Such an understanding of the close encounters and entanglements of acting co-companions naturally leads to the idea of a discourse community consisting of humans, other critters, and things. What I translate into discursive language, Haraway describes in her own way:

> What scientists actually do in the field affects the ways "animals see their scientists seeing them" and therefore how the animals respond. In a strong sense, observers and birds rendered each other capable in ways not written into preexisting scripts, but invented or provoked, more than simply shown, in practical research. Birds and scientists were in dynamic, moving relations of attunement. The behavior of birds and their observers were made, but not made up.

(Haraway 2016, loc. 2624–2627)

Both Latour and Haraway find an excellent way to acknowledge the factuality of the world – as "worlding" and "becoming with," as a zone that is neither deanimated nor overanimated – and at the same time retain the element of construction that is necessary to understand the production of knowledge. They both resist the temptation to set human activities apart from the activities of others or "the world" – a separation that renders most traditional arguments in philosophy, anthropology, and historiography problematic in their anthropocentrism. In contrast to those approaches, Haraway explains: "I am not a posthumanist; I am who I become with companion species, who and which make a mess out of categories in the making of kin and kind. Queer messmates in mortal play, indeed" (Haraway 2008, 19).

Where does all this leave us regarding discourse research? Paraphrasing Haraway's apt formulation, we can say that our historical arguments are made, but not made up. The discursivization of things that happen into events that become elements of historical orders of knowledge – the transformation of traces into sources into narratives – discloses certain mechanisms that discourse research investigates. Human communication is crucial to these mechanisms, but the mechanisms also include the active involvement of the more-than-human world. Historical discourse analysis therefore acknowledges two seemingly paradoxical dependencies: First, it accepts the fragility of historical knowledge, in which the past is a moving target in constant flux. Understanding the past depends on the present as much as on the past; the past – or rather the past *as past*, as explicit part of historical emplotment – is co-created by the present. Second, it recognizes the agency of the more-than-human world, including the power of things that/who have lives and multiple entanglements with the human world. If we frame it as I have done here, historical discourse analysis offers a bridge between constructionism and materialism; it provides a theoretical and methodological tool that acknowledges the contingency of human knowledge without giving up the differentiation between fact and fiction.

References

Berger, Peter L., and Thomas Luckmann. 1966. *The Social Construction of Reality*. Garden City: Doubleday.

Bieder, Ulrich. 1998. *Die Unerbittlichkeit der Historizität: Foucault als Historiker*. Cologne, Weimar, and Vienna: Böhlau.

Brinton, Laurel J. 2001. "Historical Discourse Analysis." In *The Handbook of Discourse Analysis*, ed. by Deborah Schiffrin, Deborah Tannen, and Heidi E. Hamilton, 138–160. Malden and Oxford: Blackwell.

Bublitz, Hannelore. 1999. *Foucaults Archäologie des kulturellen Unbewußten: Zum Wissensarchiv und Wissensbegehren moderner Gesellschaften*. Frankfurt am Main and New York: Campus.

Coole, Diana, and Samantha Frost, eds. 2010. *New Materialisms: Ontology, Agency, and Politics*. Durham and London: Duke University Press.

Daston, Lorraine, and Peter Galison. 2007. *Objectivity*. New York: Zone Books.

Eder, Franz X. 2006. "Historische Diskurse und ihre Analyse – eine Einleitung." In *Historische Diskursanalysen: Genealogie, Theorien, Anwendungen*, ed. by Franz X. Eder, 9–23. Wiesbaden: VS Verlag für Sozialwissenschaft.

Gill, Sam D. 2000. "Play." In *Guide to the Study of Religion*, ed. by Willie Braun and Russell T. McCutcheon, 451–462. London and New York: Cassell.

Hall, A. Rupert. 1987. "Alexandre Koyré and the Scientific Revolution." *History and Technology* 4: 485–495.

Haraway, Donna J. 2008. *When Species Meet*. Minneapolis: University of Minnesota Press.

Haraway, Donna J. 2016. *Staying with the Trouble: Making Kin in the Chthulucene*. Durham and London: Duke University Press. Locations quoted from the Kindle edition.

Hodder, Ian. 2012. *Entangled: An Archaeology of the Relationships between Humans and Things*. Hoboken: Wiley-Blackwell.

Ingman, Peik, Måns Broo, Tuija Hovi, and Terhi Utriainen, eds. 2016. *The Relational Dynamics of Enchantment and Sacralization*. Sheffield: Equinox.

Jóhannesson, Ingólfur Ásgeir. 2010. "The Politics of Historical Discourse Analysis: A Qualitative Research Method?" *Discourse: Studies in the Cultural Politics of Education* 31: 251–264.

Keller, Reiner. 2011. "The Sociology of Knowledge Approach to Discourse (SKAD)." *Human Studies* 34: 43–65.

Kippenberg, Hans G. 2001. "Religious History, Displaced by Modernity." *Numen* 47: 221–243.

Kippenberg, Hans G. 2002. *Discovering Religious History in the Modern Age*. Princeton and Oxford: Princeton University Press.

Koselleck, Reinhart. 1995. *Vergangene Zukunft: Zur Semantik historischer Zeiten*. 3rd ed. Frankfurt am Main: Suhrkamp. English as *Futures Past: On the Semantics of Historical Time*. New York: Columbia University Press 2004.

Landwehr, Achim. 2009. *Historische Diskursanalyse*. 2nd ed. Frankfurt am Main: Campus.

Latour, Bruno. 2017. *Facing Gaia: Eight Lectures on the New Climatic Regime*. Translated by Catherine Porter. Cambridge, UK, and Malden: Polity Press.

Park, Yoosun. 2008. "Making Refugees: A Historical Discourse Analysis of the Construction of the 'Refugee' in US Social Work, 1900–1957." *The British Journal of Social Work* 38: 771–787.

Reisigl, Martin, and Ruth Wodak. 2010. "The Discourse-Historical Approach." In *Methods of Critical Discourse Analysis*, ed. by Ruth Wodak and Michael Meyer, 2nd ed., 87–121. London: Sage.

Ricoeur, Paul. 2006. *Memory, History, Forgetting*. Translated by Kathleen Blamey and David Pellauer. Chicago: University of Chicago Press.

Rorty, Richard. 1989. *Contingency, Irony, and Solidarity*. Cambridge: Cambridge University Press.

Rüsen, Jörn. 1997. "Was heißt: Sinn der Geschichte? (Mit einem Ausblick auf Vernunft und Widersinn)." In *Historische Sinnbildung: Problemstellungen, Zeitkonzepte, Wahrnehmungshorizonte, Darstellungsstrategien*, ed. by Klaus E. Müller and Jörn Rüsen, 17–47. Reinbek: Rowohlt.

Sarasin, Philipp. 2003. *Geschichtswissenschaft und Diskursanalyse*. Frankfurt am Main: Suhrkamp.

Schütz, Alfred, and Thomas Luckmann. 1979–1984. *Strukturen der Lebenswelt*. 2 vols. Frankfurt am Main: Suhrkamp.

Scott, Joan W. 2007. *Politics of the Veil*. Princeton and Oxford: Princeton University Press.

Shapin, Steven. 1996. *The Scientific Revolution*. Chicago and London: The University of Chicago Press.

Smith, Jonathan Z. 1982. *Imagining Religion: From Babylon to Jonestown*. Chicago: University of Chicago Press.

Stuckrad, Kocku von. 2014. *The Scientification of Religion: An Historical Study of Discursive Change, 1800–2000*. Berlin and Boston: De Gruyter.

Stuckrad, Kocku von. 2015. "Discourse." In *Vocabulary for the Study of Religion* (3 vols.), ed. by Robert A. Segal and Kocku von Stuckrad, vol. 1, 429–438. Leiden and Boston: Brill.

Stuckrad, Kocku von, and Frans Wijsen, eds. 2015. *Making Religion: Theory and Practice in the Discursive Study of Religion*. Leiden and Boston: Brill.

Sun, Jessie. 2014. "Mindfulness in Context: A Historical Discourse Analysis." *Contemporary Buddhism* 15: 394–415.

White, Hayden. 1973. *Metahistory: The Historical Imagination in Nineteenth-Century Europe*. Baltimore and London: The Johns Hopkins University Press.

Wikipedia. 2018. "Isaac Newton." https://en.wikipedia.org/wiki/Isaac_Newton (accessed on 9 January 2018).

Frans Wijsen
Whose Voice Is This? The Multicultural Drama from CDA and DST Perspectives

The word 'discourse' seems to have become a fad in academia. More than twenty journals have the word 'discourse' in their titles, and various book series as well. Numerous authors use the word 'discourse' in various ways, often without clarifying what exactly they mean. More or less the same applies to the label 'discourse analysis.' 'Critical discourse analysis' (CDA) is a distinct approach within the broader field of discourse studies that emerged in the early 1990s in the work of scholars such as Teun van Dijk, Ruth Wodak, Norman Fairclough, Theo van Leeuwen, and Gunther Kress. Initially known as critical linguistics, it has become widespread in the social sciences and the humanities (Wodak 2001, 4–9).

CDA takes its main inspiration from Michel Foucault. But within the field of critical discourse analysis, there is a difference between authors who strictly follow Foucault and authors who elaborate on his work, stating that Foucault is too abstract and too deterministic (Fairclough 1992, 56–57). There are authors who are strictly text oriented, authors who focus on cognition and classification, and authors who are interested in the social conditions and social effects of social classifications (Wetherell 2001; Breeze 2011).

In this chapter, I explore the use and usefulness of the three-dimensional model of CDA, as developed by Norman Fairclough (1992, 2001, 2003). I am not the first or the only one to do so. Other scholars who have done so include Jørgensen and Phillips (2002, 60–95), Lock (2004), and Hjelm (2014). Heather (2000), Moberg (2016), and myself (Wijsen 2010), among others, have used this approach in the academic study of religion.

I started using CDA in 2007, in a research project on religious discourse, social cohesion, and conflict, studying the "clash of civilizations" rhetoric in three countries. I was able to employ three junior researchers who successfully completed their doctoral studies using critical discourse analysis. We focused on culturally salient keywords to understand the discursive nature of societal changes in Tanzania (Wijsen and Ndaluka 2012), Indonesia (Wijsen and Cholil 2014), and the Netherlands (Wijsen and Vos 2015).

My contribution to the three-dimensional model involves linking CDA to 'dialogical self theory' (DST), as developed by Hubert Hermans (Hermans and Hermans-Konopka 2010; Hermans 2018). Just as with CDA, DST has been applied in a huge variety of disciplines (Hermans and Gieser 2012; Hermans and Hermans-Konopka 2010, 19–20), particularly also in the field I am interested in: the study of multiple identities or multiple loyalties (König 2012; Buitelaar 2013a, 2013b; Zock 2010, 2013; Buitelaar and Zock 2013; Stock 2014).

Both approaches are rooted in social constructivism (Hjelm 2014) and share concepts such as 'self' (the *I*, identity), 'position' (the self as embodied, bound by space and time), 'voice' (the self as narrative), 'polyphony' (the multiplicity of voices in which *I* constitutes itself), and 'dialogue' (the *I* that constitutes itself in relations). But to the best of my knowledge, they have not yet been linked.

In general, Fairclough (1992, 22–25) is critical of socio-psychological approaches. Such approaches take into account the inconsistency of the self or the multiplicity of *I*-positions, but they neglect the social orientation of the self and demonstrate an individualistic bias. In this chapter, I elaborate on a later version of DST that is capable of bringing DST and CDA together. My hypothesis is that linking CDA and DST is relevant particularly when scholars of religion are dealing with multiple identities or multiple loyalties. Both approaches deal with "different selves" (Fairclough 1992, 25; Fairclough 200, 181) or the "multivoicednes" of the self (Hermans and Hermans-Konopka 2010, 3; Hermans 2018, 3) and link (individual) micro- and (societal) macro-level analyses, mediated by (institutional) meso-level analysis.

My aim is to explore the strengths and weaknesses of both approaches, particularly when it comes to understanding identification and integration in multicultural societies. In the Netherlands, the tension between the identification and the integration of immigrants has been problematized as the "multicultural drama": the idea that a strong national, ethnic, or religious identification on the part of immigrants promotes their segregation and hinders their integration into modern Dutch society (Scheffer 2010, 55–61). This is what we dealt with in the third project mentioned above, analyzing the discursive nature of the "multicultural drama" (Wijsen and Vos, 2014, 2015; Wijsen 2016). In this chapter, I will limit myself to the Dutch case study.

In what follows, I first explain the conceptual frameworks of both CDA and DST. Next I outline the three stages of CDA (analysis of text, intertextuality, and context), identify the conceptual equivalents in DST, and test the usefulness of combining the two for the study of immigrant identification and integration, using a sample from my fieldwork on the multicultural drama rhetoric in the Netherlands. I close with a conclusion and discussion.

1 Fairclough's Critical Discourse Analysis

Having a background in empirical and practical religious studies, I became interested in Fairclough's approach for two reasons. First, his approach is suitable for social-scientific research (Fairclough 1992, 62; Fairclough 2003). Second, it focuses on hegemonic practices and provides tools for innovation to those who may be marginalized by such practices (Fairclough 1992, 9). His approach is most influential in studies that are interested in emancipation.

Fairclough (1992, 99) presents a "three-dimensional framework for discourse analysis" and uses "a variety of theoretical perspectives and methods." I will elaborate on this below, in sections 1.1–1.5. According to Fairclough (1992, 56), discourse has three levels (namely, the interpersonal, the institutional, and the societal level) and three functions (namely, "subject positions," "social relations," and "systems of knowledge and belief"). Moreover, in his view, discourse analysis is based on three assumptions and three traditions, and it has three stages.

Throughout the book, Fairclough gives parent–child relations, teacher–pupil relations, and doctor–patient relations as examples. From Foucault, Fairclough (1992, 3) takes medical practice as an example of how discourses structure areas of knowledge. From Jürgen Habermas, Fairclough (1992, 6) takes the idea of the colonization of the "life world" by economic and political systems.

1.1 Discourse Has Three Levels

According to Fairclough (1992, 56) discourse operates at "three levels." First, there is the "situational" (or "interpersonal") level. Second, there is the "institutional" level ("norms and conventions"). Third, there is the "societal level" ("social structures").

For example, family interactions exist as an interpersonal relationship between parents and children (situational level). But the positions of 'father,' 'mother,' and 'child' go beyond the individuals and are based on conventions, which are more or less shared and formalized (the institutional level) – for example, in family law (Fairclough 1992, 65). Moreover, these positions and conventions are embedded in wider processes such as democratization, by which family relationships – in democratic societies – have become more egalitarian (the societal level).

Classroom communication is first and foremost a communication between the lecturer and the students (the interpersonal level). But their communication is related to and influenced by faculty and university regulations, such as education and examination regulations (the institutional level), and also by processes of "technologization" and "marketization" (Fairclough 1992, 194) in education (the societal level).

1.2 Discourse Has Three Functions

According to Fairclough (1992, 8, 10, 64), discourse has three functions or aspects of constitutive effects: namely, subject positions or social identities ("selves"), social relations ("structures of dialogue"), and social cognitions – that is, shared knowledge or systems of ideas and beliefs ("mental maps"). The ideational function of a text is the way in which the text signifies the world. This ideational function can become ideological (see section 5.1).

For example, classroom communication positions the participants as lecturer and students. There are various modes of being for both lecturers and students. But so long as their relation is defined as classroom communication, they cannot change their positions. Their positions and relations may change if they meet outside of class – for example, at a soccer match or a prayer service.

Moreover, each participant has a "mental map" (Fairclough 1992, 82–83) of what a good lecturer is, or how a good student should behave. These ideas may change in harmony with the definition of what type of class they are in, and this influences their relations. At a lecture, students expect the lecturer to speak, and the lecturer expects them to listen and make notes. In a seminar, the lecturer expects the students to speak, and the students expect the lecturer to listen to them. These expectations are based on the conventions associated with different "types" (lecture, seminar) of classroom communication "genres" (Fairclough 1992, 125–126).

1.3 Discourse Analysis Begins with Three Assumptions

According to Fairclough, discourse analysis begins with three assumptions (Fairclough 1992, 71–72). The first is that discourse is a practice – that is, a real instance of people ("actors") doing, saying, or writing things. In Fairclough's view, practice is lacking in Foucault's analysis (Fairclough 1992, 57, 63); this is what I referred to above: it is too abstract. Discourse 'does' things, just as other practices do; this means that discourse has effects. Discourse not only reflects, but also constitutes entities and relations. What sets discourse apart from other practices is its linguistic form.

The second assumption is that constitutive effects, or the relation between language use and social reality, are mediated through discursive practices – that is, the production, distribution, and consumption of text (Fairclough 1992, 71, 76; Fairclough 2003, 30–31). The third assumption is that the relation between language use and social reality is dialectic. That is to say, language use influences social reality, and the other way around. In Fairclough's view, Foucault's analyses are too deterministic (Fairclough 1992, 60).

According to Fairclough (1992, 72, 80), the central concern of critical discourse analysis is to trace explanatory connections between the way texts are put together (linguistic practice) and the social structures and struggles in which they are embedded (social practice), as well as the ways in which these connections are mediated through processes of production, distribution, and consumption (discursive practice).

1.4 Discourse Analysis Draws on Three Traditions

Discourse analysis draws on three traditions (Fairclough 1992, 72, 85): namely, linguistic analysis of texts, macro-sociological analysis of social practice in relation to social structure (context), and micro-sociological analysis of interactions based on the interpretative tradition. For the linguistic analysis, Fairclough depends on Halliday's systemic grammar and John Austin's speech-act theory. With regard to micro-sociology, he draws on Harold Garfinkel and Ervin Goffman's ethno-methodology and conversation analysis. When it comes to macro-sociology, he draws on critical theory scholars such as Jürgen Habermas, Anthony Giddens, and Pierre Bourdieu.

Fairclough (1992, 72–73) accepts the interpretative claim that analysts must understand participants' perspectives. But participants' perspectives shape and are shaped by social structures. They are heterogeneous and contradictory, and they are contested in struggles which are at least partly discursive in nature. Based on Bourdieu's notion of text production, distribution, and consumption (Fairclough 1992, 67), Fairclough (1992, 226) tries to combine and bridge the humanities and the social sciences.

1.5 Discourse Analysis Has Three Dimensions

Discourse analysis has three dimensions or stages (Fairclough 1992, 56, 73, 198–199, 231). The first stage is "description" – that is, the analysis of the formal features of a text. The second stage is "interpretation" – that is, the analysis of the production, distribution, and consumption of a text. The third stage is "explanation" – that is, the analysis of the social conditions and social effects of a text. Alternatively, these stages are called the analysis of "text," the analysis of "discursive practice" or "interaction," and the analysis of "social practice" or "context" (Fairclough 2001, 21; Fairclough 2003, 21–22).

In a nutshell, this is the three-dimensional concept of discourse. According to Fairclough (1992, 73, 169, 231), overlaps are unavoidable. The analyst performs an in-depth investigation of a limited number of discourse samples and looks at them at different levels and from various perspectives at several stages, which are not exclusive, but complementary.

Critical discourse analysts are aware that they are not above the social practice they analyze; they are part of it. They are conscious of the nature of the social practice of analysis itself (Fairclough 1992, 199). They try to "validate" the analysis (Fairclough 1992, 238) by conducting "dialogical research" and "co-research" (Fairclough 1992, 227–228), collaborating with the people they study and with other researchers, and by exploring the "meta-discourse" – analyzing their own text as if it were another's (Fairclough 1992, 122; Fairclough 2003, 14–15).

2 Hermans' Dialogical Self Theory

In the three studies I mentioned in the introduction to this chapter, we noted that interviewees made various statements that seemed incompatible to us. For example, one Muslim positioned himself as "orthodox," but also as "open-minded" toward believers of other faiths. Another Muslim defined himself as both a Muslim and a believer in indigenous Javanese religion. Fairclough (1992, 24–25) is aware of the issue of 'inconsistency,' but he tends to explain the multiplicity of voices as external. To better understand the internal dialogue within the self, we explored another theory: the dialogical self theory (Wijsen and Cholil 2014, 46; Wijsen and Vos 2015, 55).

2.1 Theoretical Starting Points

This theory combines the concepts of 'self' and 'dialogue' drawn from two sources: American pragmatism and Russian dialogism (Hermans and Hermans-Konopka 2010, 1; Hermans 2018, 9). First, there is William James' notion of the extended self. James goes beyond Descartes' separation of self and body, distinguishing between 'I' and 'me' (Hermans and Gieser 2012, 3–6). 'I' is the self as knower or subject; 'me' is the self as known or object. The self as known is composed of all that the person can call their own: my body, my clothes, my house, my wife, my husband, my children – that is, people and things in the environment belong to my self to the extent that they are felt to be mine (Hermans 2018, 17, 77–79; Hermans and Hermans-Konopka 2010, 137–139).

Second, there is Mikhail Bakhtin's notion of the polyphonic novel. Analyzing Dostoevsky's publications, Bakhtin argued that there is not one author at work in these publications – namely, Dostoevsky himself – but rather a multiplicity of authors, who are represented by the characters. In Bakhtin's view, all utterances are multi-voiced and dialogical. They are multi-voiced because in the act of speaking, there are at least two voices: the voice of the speaker and the voice of the person or group that is represented. And they are dialogical in the sense that in the act of speaking, the speaker can talk to a visible party, with an invisible party as the object of speech (Hermans 2018, 78, 310–312; Hermans and Hermans-Konopka 2010, 35–36; Hermans and Gieser 2012, 67).

2.2 Concepts

DST's conceptual framework (Hermans and Hermans-Konopka 2010, 1–20) has some similarities with CDA. First, there is the "self." The self is part of society; it does not exist separately from society. The self can be conceived of as a dynamic multiplicity of *I*-positions. It is a "mini-society" or a "society of mind." Second, there is "position." The *I* is embodied and bound to particular positions in time and space. The embodied *I* is able to move from one position to another, in accordance with changes in situation and over time. Third, there is "voice." Positions can be voiced or performed linguistically. These voices behave like characters interacting in a story or a movie. Each of them has a story to tell about their own experiences, from their own perspective. Fourth, there is "polyphony." The *I* fluctuates between different and even opposing positions, and these positions are involved in relationships of dominance and power. When the self functions as a multiplicity of unrelated *I*-positions, a confusing cacophony of voices emerges.

Central to this theory is the notion of "dialogue." The polyphonic self is dialogical in that internal dialogues within the self as well as external dialogues with actual others are both necessary in order to achieve a cross-fertilization between the mini-society of the self and the macro-society at large. In this sense, there is a link with Michel Foucault's theory on the relationship between knowledge and power, in which external dialogues are internally reproduced, and vice versa (Hermans and Hermans-Konopka 2010, 92).

2.3 Assumptions

DST first assumes that the self can be conceived of as a (mini) society of mind or a multiplicity of embodied *I*-positions among which a dialogical relationship exists. *I*-positions can be internal (e.g., "*I* as dreamer") or external (e.g., "the voice of my mother") as parts of the extended self (Hermans 2018, 53, 65). Internal *I*-positions can be personal ("*I* as a Muslim") or collective ("we as Muslims"). In multicultural societies, dialogical relationships are required not only between individuals, but also within one and the same individual (Hermans and Hermans-Konopka 2010, 1).

DST's second assumption is that the *I* is capable of shifting from one position to another in accordance with different, even contradictory situations. *I*-positions do not act in isolation. Like individuals and groups in democratic societies, *I*-positions can make compromises and form coalitions (Hermans 2018, 67). If various voices within the self are in harmony with each other, then the self is polyphonic. If the voices conflict and contradict each other without agreement or compromise, then there is cacophony.

Having outlined the conceptual framework of both theories, in the three sections that follow, I first explain the technical framework of CDA; second, I do the same for DST; and third, I combine the two to analyze samples taken from my case study on the identification and integration of immigrants in the Netherlands, conducted between 2012 and 2016. I follow CDA's three-dimensional model of analysis (Fairclough 1992, 73; Fairclough 2001, 21). This comes close to the three-step analytical model of multivoicedness developed from a DST perspective (Aveling, Gillespie, and Cornish 2015; Bourke, de Abreu, and Rathbone 2018). It is only DST's third step that is clearly different from the third dimension of CDA. From the above-mentioned case study, I have selected a corpus of 21 interviews with Indonesian Muslims, which were deposited in the Netherlands' Data Archiving and Networked Services (DANS), and I focus on samples in which the dilemma between identification and integration is at stake.

3 Analyzing 'Text'

In this section, I deal with the first stage of CDA: the description or analysis of the formal features of text and talk. This stage is the implementation of the first assumption mentioned above. Discourse is a form of practice in which people act upon the world and upon each other; it 'does' things. The only difference between this practice (discourse) and other practices is its linguistic form (Fairclough 1992, 57, 63). From a DST perspective, this stage entails identifying *I*-labels or *I*-statements.

3.1 Wording, Over-wording, and Re-wording

In his work, Fairclough pays the most attention to aspects related to vocabulary (Fairclough 1992, 76–77). "It is sometimes useful for analytic purposes to focus upon a single word," he says (Fairclough 1992, 185), or upon "alternative wordings and their political and ideological significance" (Fairclough 1992, 77). This is accomplished via comparison (Fairclough 1992, 193).

The political and ideological function of discourse returns in the third stage of the analysis. According to Fairclough, words are never neutral; they serve political and ideological agendas. For example, in Dutch, it makes a difference whether speakers refer to "newcomers" (immigrants) as *buitenlanders* (foreigners) or *medelanders* (compatriots). It also makes a difference whether newcomers refer to themselves as "Moroccan Dutch" or as "Dutch of Moroccan descent."

In the social sciences, there is a long tradition of focusing on culturally salient 'keywords' (Fairclough 1992, 185–194). The meaning of words – or the wording of meaning – is not individual, but rather social; words are not neutral, but are politically or ideologically invested. For example, the word 'enterprise' is related to the neoliberal agenda.

Hegemonic practice tends to present the dominant wording as the only one. But there is always a multiplicity of ways to word something, and there are also always alternative wordings. For example, it makes a difference whether one describes immigration as an influx or a flood, as opposed to a quest for a better life.

It is useful to compare the wordings in particular contexts in terms of relative density – that is, in terms of the number of different wordings, many of which are almost synonymous (similarities): for example, mastery, skill, competence, and expertise.

This is over-wording. Over-wording demonstrates an intense preoccupation that points to the peculiarities of the group that uses these words – an example of this is technical language in education.

In addition to over-wording, re-wording is the practice of generating new words which are set up as alternatives to – and (usually) in opposition to – the existing words (contrasts). Examples include the use of inclusive language in contrast to sexist – e.g., chairperson instead of chairman – or the way some people in the Netherlands prefer to speak of *prachtwijken* (neighborhoods one can be proud of) or *krachtwijken* (powerful neighborhoods) rather than *probleemwijken* (problematic neighborhoods) as a critique of the multicultural drama rhetoric.

3.2 Personal Position Repertoire

At the descriptive level, the main analytical tool in DST is the personal position repertoire (Hermans 2018, 283–284). The analyst looks at clauses in which the speaker positions or identifies him- or herself as *I* – for example, "*I* am a Muslim," or "*I* am a Dutch person of Moroccan descent." An *I*-position is a position in which one puts oneself toward other positions, either internally within the self (e.g., "I as a rational scientist"; "I as an intuitive dancer") or externally with regard to the positions of other people in the world (e.g., "the voice of my dominant mother"; "the hands of my empathic father").

Referring to Bakhtin, Hermans and Hermans-Konopka (2010, 131) hold that "other beings exist within selves: through the language and tools that we use." According to them, positions can be voiced. However, the concept of 'position' is more fundamental than the concept of 'voice.' The concept of voice as the instrument of speech is intrinsically connected to the use of language and signs, but people already occupy a position even before they learn to speak (Hermans and Hermans-Konopka 2010, 226–228).

3.3 Islam Is Just the Perfect Belief

Despite different priorities, both CDA and DST use Bakhtin's notion of voice and multivoicedness. In my study of the identification and integration of Indonesian Muslims in the Netherlands, some interviewees said that Indonesian Muslims are "more open" and "more flexible" than "other Muslims" who are "more strict": "More than Moroccans and Turks, we easily adjust to modern life in the Netherlands." Other interviewees said that they do not like it when people say that Indonesian Muslims are better integrated than Muslims from Turkey or Morocco because the Islam practiced by Indonesians is "more modern" than that of other Muslims. As one of them said, "Islam is just the perfect belief; what is it that could change? I mean, when you say [that you make Islam] modern, you imply that [Islam] has [been] changed to make it up-to-date."

Young Indonesian Muslims tend to label themselves as "more Muslim" on the one hand, and yet "more Dutch" on the other. According to them, this makes it easier to integrate. Being both "more Muslim" and "more Dutch" is not perceived as a contradiction or an inconsistency. In DST terms, "perfect Muslim" and "modern Dutch" are different *I*-positions or internal voices. They do not think in terms of either–or, but of both–and.

These youngsters identify their interpretation of Islam as purer – that is to say, free of cultural ballast. A second-generation Indonesian Muslim said that he has a stronger bond with other people who are also Muslim because "one understands the other more easily." Referring to his Moroccan girlfriend, he said, "She is really a person who is very non-traditional Islamic, but very much focused on what Islam is, and not on what belongs to a certain country or culture. She is very anti-Moroccan Islam, because there is so much tradition to it." In this case, "non-traditional" Islamic is not used in the same way as "modern" Islamic. The re-wording apparent in the use of the terms "tradition," "non-traditional Islamic," and "much tradition," as well as equating the phrases "non-traditional Islam" and "anti-Moroccan," shows that "tradition" does not refer to belief (Islam), but to culture (Morocco).

This interviewee used the word 'traditional' in a way that runs counter to the way Dutch people and scholars of integration discourses use the word 'traditional.' In the interviewee's usage, "non-traditional" Islam does not mean "modern" Islam, but rather "orthodox" Islam or "perfect" Islam – an Islam that is free of customs and cultural traditions. The analysis thus far depicts a struggle over the meanings of words, or the wording of meanings; it also shows that speakers 'do' something with words.

4 Analyzing 'Intertextuality'

In this section, I address the second stage of CDA: the analysis of discourse as discursive practice. This is the implementation of the second assumption mentioned above. The relation between language and reality is mediated through discursive practice – that is, the production, distribution, and consumption of text. From a DST perspective, this stage entails identifying the voices of 'inner Others.'

4.1 Intertextuality

According to CDA, when people produce (communicate) and consume (interpret) text, they draw on other texts (Fairclough 1992, 82, 83) which are stored in their long-term memory (Fairclough 2001, 8–9). These resources are cognitive in the sense that they are in people's heads, and they are social in the sense that they have social conditions and social effects (Fairclough 2001, 20). These social conditions and effects are what we focus on in the third stage of CDA.

In this second stage, Fairclough (2003, 42; 1992, 102) explicitly draws upon Bakhtin's dialogical theory. Texts are inevitable and unavoidably dialogical in the sense that "any utterance is a link in a very complexly organized chain of utterances" with which it "enters into one kind of relation or another."

There are different forms of intertextuality (Fairclough 1992, 118). Manifest intertextuality is at stake when a text explicitly draws upon other texts. Indirect intertextuality happens when texts are drawn upon in a tacit way. Intertextuality also has horizontal and vertical dimensions. The horizontal dimension implies that the texts drawn upon are contemporary; the vertical dimension implies that they are historical (Fairclough 1992, 101–103).

4.2 Polyphony

According to DST, a dialogical relationship exists not only between individuals, be they past or present, but also within the self of one and the same individual (Hermans and Hermans-Konopka 2010, 1). *I*-positions can be external or internal, and internal *I*-positions can be personal or collective. DST assumes that the polyphonic self is dialogical in the sense that both internal dialogues within the self and external dialogues with actual others are necessary to achieve a cross-fertilization between the mini-society of the self and the macro-society at large.

4.3 A *Burka* Is Really Something Afghan

Both CDA and DST acknowledge "different selves" (Fairclough 1992, 25) or the "multivoicednes" of the self (Hermans and Hermans-Konopka 2010, 3; Hermans 2018, 373). From a CDA perspective, the basic analytic question at this stage is: "Whose voice is this?" (Fairclough 1992, 105)? Or alternatively, whose voice is reproduced, contested, or transformed?

Most of the interviewees referred to the negative image of Islam in the mass media and political discourses, or the presumed incompatibility of Islam and modernity. Nevertheless, they "keep calm," and they "don't express themselves in the media." They said that the (supposed) incompatibility of Islam and modernity does not apply to them because they are "already adjusted" to modern society, they "are different" (as compared to Moroccans or Turks), and they "do not react emotionally" (as Moroccans and Turks do). Thus, in identifying and positioning themselves, they constantly refer to how they are positioned in the mass media and the political discourse, distancing themselves from other Muslims (Moroccans and Turks).

The interviewee who said that "Islam is just the perfect belief" criticized Muslims who separate faith from daily life in their efforts to adjust to modern society. He spoke about them as "part-time Muslims" or "spare-time Muslims" and called them "Muslims in name only." In doing so, he implicitly drew on an Indonesian distinction between *santri* and *abangan*, or those who are serious about their belief (literally 'learned') and those who are not.

The Indonesian Muslim who spoke about his Moroccan girlfriend being "anti-traditional" implicitly drew upon a colonial distinction between *agama* (religion) and *adat* (culture, tradition). In colonial discourse, the word *adat* was used for customs that were considered incompatible with Christian civilization. He and his Moroccan girlfriend refer to a *burka* as a metaphor: "A *burka* is really something Afghan [culture], and anyway has nothing to do with Islam [religion]. As Muslims we are obliged to smile and greet each other in a friendly way, and you cannot see this [smile] when you wear such a thing on your face." Moreover, in saying "Islam is just the perfect belief," the interviewee was referring to a distinction between Islam and Muslims. Islam is pure and cannot fail, but Muslims can fail.

In talking about integration and adjusting to the Dutch situation, Indonesian Muslims explicitly refer to the multicultural situation at home and the Indonesian state philosophy of unity in diversity. As one of them said, "we are already multicultural," and "we are used to adjusting to others."

5 Analyzing 'Context'

In this section, I address the third stage of CDA: the analysis of discourse as social practice, or the social conditions and social effects of texts. This is the implementation of the third assumption mentioned above: discourse 'does' things; it has effects. This third stage of CDA differs from the third stage of DST. Whereas the third stage of DST focuses on interactions between the voices within the self (Bourke et al. 2018, 6), the third stage of CDA focuses on interactions between "text" and "context" (Fairclough 2001, 21–22).

5.1 Reproduction, Contestation, or Transformation

As mentioned above, Fairclough (1992, 64, 238) distinguishes three functions or aspects of the constructive effects of discourse. These are "social identity" or "subject positions," "social relationships," and "systems of knowledge and belief." These aspects are reproduced, contested, or transformed in discourse (Fairclough 1992, 10).

One major concern in Fairclough's book is the constitution of the subject through texts (Fairclough 1992, 105, 168). This is one of the "major insights" that

Fairclough (1992, 55) takes from Foucault. According to Fairclough, subjects are not pre-existent, but are constituted through texts. Furthermore, he expands this insight to all social realities, including institutions and even societies (Fairclough 1992, 133).

Discourses are ideological "in so far as they incorporate significations which contribute to sustaining or restructuring power relations," says Fairclough (1992, 91). In harmony with Antonio Gramsci, he argues that hegemony means "constructing alliances, and integrating rather than dominating subordinate classes" (Fairclough 1992, 92, 58). This is what the "dialectic view" (Fairclough 1992, 93) is all about.

The ideologies embedded in discursive practices are most effective when they become naturalized and achieve the status of "common sense" (Fairclough 1992, 67, 87) or taken-for- granted truth. For example, in a neoliberal era, unemployment is presented as a natural disaster or simply as fate, rather than as a consequence of human decisions. Additionally, manager–secretary or teacher–pupil interactions are ideologically informed by democracy (Fairclough 1992, 89–90, 201–207). Nevertheless, this property of ideologies should not be overstated, as ideologies – and the relations of domination expressed in them – are also contested, redefined, and reshaped. Discursive practices are also ideological struggles in which power relations are transformed (Fairclough 1992, 87–88).

Once again, this demonstrates the dialectical nature of the relation between discourse and reality. According to Fairclough (1992, 91), subjects shape and are shaped by ideology. This is why Fairclough (1992, 60) criticizes Foucault's resistance to the idea of discourse analysis as a form of ideology critique. In Fairclough's view, Foucault is relativistic, in the sense that truth is relative to particular discursive formations. This is why he prefers Gramsci's notion of hegemony (as described above in this section) over Foucault's notion of power (Fairclough 1992, 58).

In conclusion, Fairclough (1992, 223) distinguishes three models of discursive practice: the unilinear, the hegemonic, and the mosaic model. The unilinear model is characterized by ongoing colonization, the hegemonic model by struggle, and the mosaic model by fragmentation. Developing a hegemonic model of discursive practice was one of Fairclough's major objectives in his book *Discourse and Social Change* (1992, 224).

5.2 The Democratic Self in a Democratic Society

According to DST, "a democratic organisation of the self adds value to both the self and society in their interconnectedness" (Hermans 2018, 4). The metaphor of "democracy" is illuminating. Just as people negotiate and compromise with their opponents in democratic societies, there is also room within the democratic self for a dialogue with opposing internal *I*-positions. In the democratic self, different *I*-

positions enrich each other without letting any one position overrule the others (Hermans 2018, 6–7).

Just as in democratic societies, some positions within the self place themselves over against other positions (anti-positions). Other positions promote the coordination of various positions within the self (promoter positions). Sometimes positions are exaggerated to such a degree that the balance of the self is lost (over-positioning). In other cases, certain positions enable a helicopter view of other positions and the relationships between them (meta-positions).

5.3 I Always See Myself as a World Citizen

Both CDA and DST speak of 'positions' – 'subject positions' (in CDA) or '*I*-positions' (in DST) – as effects of positioning and being positioned (Hermans 2018, 47). In my study of the identification and integration of Indonesian Muslims in the Netherlands, all the interviewees positioned themselves (their individual *I*-position) and their group (their collective *I*-position) as being "more open-minded" than Moroccans and Turks. Whereas some of them said that they "adjusted" to modern society by separating faith from daily life (e.g., by not wearing a headscarf), most said that there is no need to separate faith and daily life, because Islam is completely compatible with modern life.

Moreover, integration into modern Dutch society does not require less Islam, but rather more Islam – pure Islam. The interviewee who said that "Islam is just the perfect belief" also said, "I always see myself as a world citizen." In answer to the question of what he says when people ask him whether he is Indonesian, Dutch, or Muslim, another interviewee responded: "I think I would say Muslim, because being a Muslim is not bound to a specific country. Yes, being Muslim is most important for me. It gives me a platform to be a world citizen." These responses suggest that the discourse about the incompatibility of religion and modernity is a typical Dutch, parochial, narrow-minded discourse.

My analysis shows that young Indonesian Muslims in the Netherlands do not want to be either Dutch or Indonesian, but rather global or world citizens. For them, "perfect" or "non-traditional" Islam is an Islam that is not bound by local traditions. Islam as a universal religion provides a platform for its adherents to be "citizens of the world." In DST terms, Islam is a "promoter position" – a position that directs other positions in the position repertoire (Hermans 2018, 65–71). Or, in CDA terms, it is an "ethos" that controls the construction of a particular version of the self from among all possible versions of the self (Fairclough 1992, 166–167).

6 Conclusion and Discussion

This chapter aimed to test the hypothesis that linking CDA and DST is relevant for scholars of religion who deal with multiple identities or multiple loyalties in multicultural societies. Both Hermans (b. 1937) and Fairclough (b. 1941) made their breakthrough in the 1990s and provide 'bridging theories' with a link to Bakhtin. Fairclough bridges language studies and critical theory; Hermans bridges pragmatism and dialogism. Both CDA and DST make use of linguistic data (text and talk) and deal with multiple identities in terms of "different selves" (Fairclough 1992, 25; 2003, 181) or "polyphonic selves" (Hermans and Hermans-Konopka 2010; Hermans 2018).

Both approaches turned to globalization relatively late. Whereas Hermans was primarily focused on personality, Fairclough was focused on nationality. For both scholars, the implications of globalization or internationalization came later. Fairclough (2001, 203–218) added a chapter on globalization to the second edition of his *Language and Power* (first published in 1989). Hermans added this dimension to the book he coauthored with Hermans-Konopka in 2010.

Both scholars make use of 'self,' 'voice,' and 'dialogue' as key concepts. But there are also notable differences between the two approaches. Whereas voice can be defined as a "language performance," it is theorized in two different ways: as an "individual accomplishment" and as a "social/cultural construction" (Sperling 2011, 71). While Hermans mainly represents the former position, Fairclough primarily represents the latter.

Both CDA and DST conceptualize the relationship between personality and social identity (Fairclough 2003, 160, 182). CDA emphasizes social identity, or the society within the self; DST emphasizes personality, or the self in society. In principle, both CDA and DST agree that neither of these approaches excludes the other.

In comparison to Hermans, Fairclough is less concerned with the dialogue among different positions within the self (Hermans and Hermans-Konopka 2010, 1). As an example of "different selves," he gives "various Mr. Blairs" (Fairclough 2003, 181–183). He sees Mr. Blair's personality as a "mix of identities," but he does not conceptualize the dialogue between "various Mr. Blairs" (Fairclough 2003, 182–183). DST succeeds better than CDA in explaining that the "others" are not "strangers," but are already part of "me," and that a dialogue between various "others" within the self is a condition for dialogue with "others" in society (Hermans 2018, 4, 139). This is one of DST's strong points – one that can enrich CDA studies on identification and integration in multicultural and democratic societies.

Both CDA and DST conceptualize the relationship between wording (voice) and positioning. Hermans (2018, 53) emphasizes the positioning of the self. For him, society is a metaphor for understanding how the self functions (Hermans 2018, 65). Combining linguistics with critical theory, Fairclough emphasizes the fact that the self is positioned in discourse. Whereas in Hermans' theory, positioning comes prior to voice (Hermans and Hermans-Konopka 2010, 226–228) and the self is conceptualized "on a deeper prelinguistic level" (Hermans 2018, 51), Fairclough (1992, 137) focuses on "the construction of 'the self' in discourse." For him, discourse is constitutive of the self (Fairclough 1992, 3, 39, 55, 105, 168). He (Fairclough 1992, 133) takes the position that "intertextuality, and constantly changing intertextual relations in discourse, are central to an understanding of processes of subject constitution. This is so on a biographical time-scale, during the life of an individual, and for the constitution and reconstitution of social groups and communities."

In analyzing my interviews, it becomes clear that the shift from "integration retaining identity" to "assimilation" in the multicultural drama discourse is constitutive for how Indonesian Muslims construct their "selves" in the Netherlands. On a more fundamental level, there is quite some evidence for the theory that the language people are taught to speak from their childhood onward structures the way they think and act. Therefore, scholars who study multiple identities or multiple loyalties from a DST perspective (König 2012; Buitelaar 2013a, 2013b; Zock 2010, 2013; Buitelaar and Zock 2013; Stock 2014) could benefit from CDAAs focus on text analysis (Fairclough 1992, 2), moving from storytelling or narrative analysis to discursive analysis.

References

Aveling, E., L. Gillespie, and A. Cornish. 2015. "A Qualitative Method for Analysing Multivoicedness." *Qualitative Research* 15, no. 6: 670–687.

Bourke, K., G. de Abreu, and C. Rathbone. 2018. "'I'm Just Who I Am': Self-continuity and the Dialogical Self in a Study of Migrants." *Journal of Constructivist Psychology*: 1–18.

Breeze, R. 2011. "Critical Discourse Analysis and Its Critics." *Pragmatics* 21, no. 4: 493–525.

Buitelaar, M. 2013a. "Constructing a Muslim Self in a Post-migration Context: Continuity and Discontinuity with Parental Voices." In *Religious Voices in Self-Narratives: Making Sense of Life in Times of Transition*, ed. by M. Buitelaar and H. Zock, 241–274. Berlin/Boston: De Gruyter.

Buitelaar, M. 2013b. "Dialogical Constructions of a Muslim Self through Life Story Telling." In *Religious Stories We Live By: Narrative Approaches in Theology and Religious Studies*, ed. by R. Ganzevoort, M. de Haardt, and M. Scherer-Rath, 43–55. Leiden: Brill.

Buitelaar, M., and H. Zock. 2013. "Introduction: Religious Voices in Self-Narratives." In *Religious Voices in Self-Narratives: Making Sense of Life in Times of Transition*, ed. by M. Buitelaar and H. Zock, 1–7. Berlin/Boston: De Gruyter.

Fairclough, N. 1992. *Discourse and Social Change*. Cambridge: Polity Press.

Fairclough, N. 2001. *Language and Power*. London/New York: Longman.

Fairclough, N. 2003. *Analysing Discourse: Textual Analysis for Social Research*. London/New York: Routledge.

Glaser, B., and A. Strauss. 1967. *The Discovery of Grounded Theory*. Chicago: Aldine & Atherton.

Heather, N. 2000. *Religious Language and Critical Discourse Analysis*. Oxford/Bern/Berlin: Peter Lang.

Hermans, H. 2018. *Society in the Self: A Theory of Identity in Democracy*. New York: Oxford University Press.
Hermans, H., and A. Hermans-Konopka. 2010. *Dialogical Self Theory: Positioning and Counter-Positioning in a Globalizing Society*. Cambridge: Cambridge University Press.
Hermans, H., and Th. Gieser. 2012. "Introductory Chapter: History, Main Tenets and Core Concepts of Dialogical Self Theory." In *Handbook of Dialogical Self Theory*, ed. by H. Hermans and Th. Gieser, 1–22. Cambridge: Cambridge University Press.
Hjelm, T. 2014. *Social Constructionisms: Approaches to the Study of the Human World*. Basingstoke/New York: Palgrave Macmillan.
Jørgensen, M., and L. Phillips. 2002. *Discourse Analysis as Theory and Method*. London: Sage.
König, J. 2012. *Moving Experience: Complexities of Acculturation*. Amsterdam: VU Boekhandel/Uitgeverij.
Lock, T. 2004. *Critical Discourse Analysis*. London/New York: Continuum.
Moberg, M. 2016. "Exploring the Spread of Marketization Discourse in the Nordic Folk Church Context." In *Making Religion: Theory and Practice in the Discursive Study of Religion*, ed. by F. Wijsen and K. von Stuckrad, 239–259. Leiden/Boston: Brill.
Scheffer, P. 2010. *The Open Society: A Story of Avoidance, Conflict and Accommodation*. PhD diss., University of Tilburg.
Sperling, M., D. Appleman, K. Gilyard, and S. Freedman. 2011. "Voices in the Context of Literacy Studies." *Reading Research Quarterly* 46, no. 1: 70–84.
Stock, F. 2014. *Speaking of Home: Home and Identity in the Multivoiced Narratives of Descendants of Moroccan and Turkish Migrants in the Netherlands*. PhD diss., University of Groningen.
Wetherell, M. 2001. "Debates in Discourse Research." In *Discourse Theory and Practice*, ed. by M. Wetherell, S. Taylor, and S. Yates, 380–399. London/Thousand Oaks/New Dehli: Sage.
Wijsen, F. 2007. *Seeds of Conflict in a Haven of Peace: From Religious Studies to Interreligious Studies in Africa*. Amsterdam/New York: Rodopi.
Wijsen, F. 2010. "Discourse Analysis in Religious Studies: The Case of Interreligious Worship in Friesland." *Anthropos. International Review of Anthropology and Linguistics* 105, no. 2: 539–553.
Wijsen, F. 2016. "Indonesian Muslim or World Citizen? Religious Identity in the Dutch Integration Discourse." In *Making Religion: Theory and Practice in the Discursive Study of Religion*, ed. by F. Wijsen and K. von Stuckrad, 225–238. Leiden/Boston: Brill.
Wijsen, F., and T. Ndaluka. 2012. "'Ujamaa Is Still Alive': A Sign of Hope for Africa?" In *Africa Is Not Destined to Die: Signs of Hope and Renewal. The Fifth International Conference on Africa*, ed. by A. Bwangatto, 240–253. Nairobi: Paulines Publications.
Wijsen, F., and S. Cholil. 2014. "'I Come from a Pancasila Family': Muslims and Christians in Indonesia." In *Muslim Christian Relations Observed: Comparative Studies from Indonesia and The Netherlands*, ed. by V. Küster and R. Setio, 29–46. Leipzig: Evangelische Verlagsanstalt.
Wijsen, F., and J. Vos. 2014. "'This is how we are at home': Indonesian Muslims in The Hague." In *Muslim Christian Relations Observed: Comparative Studies from Indonesia and The Netherlands*, edited by V. Küster and R. Setio, 15–18. Leipzig: Evangelische Verlagsanstalt.
Wijsen, F., and J. Vos. 2015. "'Rice and Rice with Sambal': Indonesians and Moluccans in the Netherlands." In *Religion, Migration and Conflict*, ed. by C. Sterkens and P. Vermeer, 53–71. Zürich: LIT Verlag.

Wodak, R. 2001. "What CDA Is About – A Summary of Its History, Important Concepts and Its Development." In *Methods of Critical Discourse Analysis*, ed. by R. Wodak and M. Meyer, 1–13. London: Sage.

Zock, H. 2010. "Voicing the Self in Postsecular Society: A Psychological Perspective on Meaning-making and Collective Identities." In *Exploring the Postsecular: The Religious, the Political and the Urban*, ed. by A. Molendijk, J. Beaumont, and C. Jedan, 131–44. Leiden/Boston: Brill.

Zock, H. 2013. "Religious Voices in the Dialogical Self: Towards a Conceptual-Analytical Framework on the Basis of Hubert Hermans's Dialogical Self Theory." In *Religious Voices in Self-Narratives: Making Sense of Life in Times of Transition*, ed. by M. Buitelaar and H. Zock, 11–35. Berlin/Boston: De Gruyter.

Anne Koch
Some Important Conceptual Lines of Discourse Theories in Cultural Studies of Religion

As cultural studies, discourse analysis, and religious studies are all highly ambiguous terms, used to denote vast fields, I will start by briefly sketching them in the restricted and contingent sense in which they are used here, before proceeding to discuss the potential of particular facets of discourse theory and methodology for cultural studies.

The term 'discourse' is very often used to denote an object of research (see Keller, this volume), but without explaining how their use of the term discourse relates to a particular understanding of discourse theory. One understanding of discourse theory is that it is a perspective and a bundle of very divergent methods. Introductions to discourse analysis regularly distinguish between descriptive and critical discourse analysis (Fairclough 2010, 167) and sometimes come to the irenic conclusion that all discourse analysis is political insofar as language itself is always deeply political (see, for example, Gee 2014, 9). Descriptive discourse analysis can be narrowly restricted to linguistic aspects, with attention to such things as speech and intonation, or it can be applied more broadly, in the pragmatics of language-in-use or even in action theory. Here, following the tradition of Michel Foucault, discourse is understood as a construct consisting of utterances and practices which are institutionally established to different degrees (Foucault 1972). Thinking the Foucauldian perspective in cultural studies means turning all phenomena into practices and investigating these practices with specific questions in mind. This goes beyond approaches that focus solely on the analysis of conversations and speech acts – even if one understands language as a tool or an action, in the intentional-conventionalist sense proposed by John L. Austin (locutionary, illocutionary, and perlocutionary acts), John Searle, and others – since such approaches fail to address culture in all of its complexity, as permanent institutional structures exerting power that becomes relevant for knowledge production. Language-in-use approaches only seldom expand their scope to include the epistemological framework, the episteme, in which what is thinkable, imaginable, and sayable in a particular historical period is embedded (see, for example, Keller's long citation of A. Schütz on the "pre-constituted world of scientific contemplation," and Johnston, this volume).

Religion, as the generally presumed object of the study of religion, requires a second preliminary remark. In the academic and theoretical self-understanding of religious studies today, religion is often regarded as a discourse, or as being 'discursively constituted.' This implies that a particular interpretation of discourse theory has entered into the constitution of religion as an object. Kocku von Stuckrad expresses this idea when he proposes a "discursive study of religion." He indicates the difference between the term "religion" (in lowercase) and the "discourse on religion" by using capital letters ("RELIGION") for the latter, thus indicating the "societal organization of knowledge about religion" (2014, 14). Discourse theory allows us to treat the subject of our investigation and the model we employ equally, historicizing the latter as well. Both are discourses. This makes plain the universalism of this approach, which is comparable to transcendental philosophy, but in this case is applied to empirical culture/s rather than abstract concepts. It is this understanding of discourse analysis, as a discursive practice which itself adds meaning to certain discourse, that von Stuckrad calls its "double-bind" (2013). Through this double-bind, a third order of signification of scientific reflection is added to first-order object or emic discourses and second-order discourses on religion, be it a theological reflexivity or the ways in which other societal subsystems reflect on this field.

A sign that discourse analysis or theory would become central to the study of religion can be seen in the linguistic turn after World War II, which ended the essentialist and phenomenological direction of the discipline. Jonathan Z. Smith, as one exponent of this turn, is mainly interested in discursive norm-building through categorization (what he calls "taxonomies"; see Smith 1996); another is Hans G. Kippenberg, who takes Austin's speech act theory as a point of departure (1983). The sociology of new religious movements was a forerunner in analyzing religion in terms of discourse to better understand why beliefs are so divergent within one and the same culture (Hjelm 2016, 20; Barker 2006).

Cultural studies and the cultural turn are particularly important to today's discourse debates, as this conglomerate of academic disciplines and this perspective reconstruct 'culture' as an all-encompassing web of shared knowledge, contingent habits, and effects, which is thus predestined for studies of the all-embracing concept of discourse. Discourse theory can also profit from certain offshoots in cultural studies: the cultural sciences (*Kulturwissenschaft*) around 1900, the much more influential British Birmingham School from the 1950s onward, and a second wave of cultural sciences and respective debates around the crisis of representation with the 'cultural turn' in the 1970s. Today, with 'cultural studies' in the titles of book series and the names of academic departments, these traditions have mostly been merged to form a few eclectic conceptual mixtures. More conservative – and primarily continental – approaches include metaphorology, the genealogical formation of concepts, cultural history, *école des annales*, history of mentalities, image studies (*Bildwissenschaft*), social structure and semantics, cultures of memory, and many more. Key issues include anthropological debates and postcolonial studies, with their critique of Western modernity and its prioritizing of specific forms of knowledge. Each of these shifts, attentions to, and obsessions with the historicity of language patterns, topics, and the interrelation of social structures with visual as well as semantic forms constitutes an important strand in today's thick cord of discourse theories. Part of the praxeological turn in cultural studies and the analysis of knowledge–power (*savoir–pouvoir*) are linked to the ideology critique characteristic of Birmingham cultural studies, with its Marxist legacy and engagement with race and class – a heritage that some scholars want to carry over into critical discourse analysis, and which comes to a head in laying bare hegemony and ideology (with regard to religious studies, see Hjelm 2016, 21; on linguistics, see Fairclough 2010 and Jäger/Maier 2009; on postcolonial studies, see Laclau/Mouffe 1985; on the sociology of knowledge, see Rainer Keller's work). In the cultural studies approach to religion as a discourse, the theoretical strands outlined above are found in attempts at analyzing conversations, textual content, dispositifs, anthropology, and the sociology of knowledge.

In this chapter, I discuss the reception of these various theoretical strands in religious studies in the light of selected concepts that take their systematics from Foucault's discourse theory. I focus on basic theoretical considerations rather than on the details of individual positions and the differentiation of methods. Space does not permit me to give a complete history of the reception of discursive approaches, or even merely of the most common elements taken from discourse theories in the study of religion.

1 Problem Configuration, Solutions, and Unintended Effects

An extremely interesting insight for the cultural study of religion, taken from Foucault's *Archaeology of Knowledge*, is the concept of problem configuration, as this concept can uncover patterns within the religion discourse when applied to it. Problem configurations emerge on the macro level of interaction in institutional fields and serve as heuristics for underlying challenges to action within historical constellations. Problem configurations prompt reactions – attempts to address a newly perceived reality. This exciting new angle allows us to acknowledge the generic category of religion itself in European discourse as a reaction to such a problem configuration.

What initial situation makes the introduction of the 'religion' category a meaningful practice? History of religion has been kept apart from political theory, as well as from economics. In separating these societal domains, beginning in early modern times, a generic religion was created in the interests of an autonomous state. In Timothy Fitzgerald's words, "the construction of modern discourses on generic religion has been made possible and conceivable by the parallel construction of a number of overlapping discourses on nonreligious/secular science, politics, the nation-state, economics, law, and education" (2007, 7). Fitzgerald contends that, to this day, a specific discourse of religion and of religious studies are to blame for a one-sided and inappropriate line of thinking, which he outlines as discourses on barbarity and civility (2007). Religion "is a modern invention which authorizes and naturalizes a form of Euro-American secular rationality" (Fitzgerald 2007, 6). He argues in favor of embedding the religious studies narrative in the academic discipline of religious studies (and its concept of religion) into a history of early modernity in Europe. Similarly, Kocku von Stuckrad paints a picture of intensified debates in the late nineteenth century on the question of where to draw the lines between religion/science/pseudo-science, a process he calls the "scientification of religion," and one which often descended into polemics against magic, astrology, alchemy, and other areas, at the same time incorporating some of these elements into the newly plausible sciences (von Stuckrad 2014).

Catherine Bell does something very similar to critical discourse analysis, without citing Foucault or introducing a qualified notion of discourse, and may therefore represent work in the study of religion that goes in the same direction as discourse analysis without entering the specific field of discourse debates. As the title of her article indicates, she reveals "Paradigms Behind (and Before) the Modern Concept of Religion," defining a paradigm as a "'knot' operative in our discourses" and "a basic tool for advancing knowledge as a social enterprise" (2006, 28). She also uses the metaphor of archaeological strata of paradigms (ibid.). Thus she acknowledges the force of ideas and models, and sees them as social action. In contrast to Fitzgerald, she accepts the possibility that the process of the reification of religion and religious identities in religious cultures was not "necessarily a logical or internally directed one" (ibid.). In her own work, she uncovers the misleading ideas of smaller models, such as the "uniqueness of ritual action, the cosmological medium of the text, our cultural beliefs about beliefs" (2006, 29), the latter including belief in religion's intrinsic goodness and noblesse. Concerning the level of reflexivity in contemporary theory of religion, she delivers a damning indictment, saying that many variants of the following paradigms are very much alive: Christianity as a prototype, the world religions model, religion as opposed to rationality, the cultural necessity of religion (to which, for instance, the cognitive and evolutionary study of religion are prone), and religion as a Western construct. The latter is of utmost interest to us here, as it seems to explain what discourse theory on religion is all about: deconstructing religion as a Western construct. What is wrong with this? The consequences of postmodernism are ambivalent. On the one hand, Bell criticizes the simplistic relativist assumptions behind this idea, while on the other hand, she argues that it helps to apply the cultural lens that shapes our view of other religions self-reflexively to our own scholarly understanding of the religion category: in both cases, Christianity is the prototype, together with the other paradigms. Moreover, the culturalizing of religion is a strategy intended to keep its continuity under the conceptual roof of culture.

Postcolonial and critical feminist work (such as on the category of gender, on which see Joy, this volume) was very important in helping to explore more of religion's premises. As a descendent of constructivism, discourse theory has deontologizing effects (see Johnston, this volume): cultural and economic orders are only the most salient plausibility structures, and the 'place' of religion is produced in a poststructuralist web of differential signification. Nevertheless, the radical conceptual and historical deconstruction of religion in Jonathan Z. Smith's famous claim that religion "is theirs [the scholars' of religion] to define" (1998, 281) does not render redundant studies of the efficacy and institution-building force of the category of religion in history up to the present. But it does decisively introduce the above-mentioned third-order level of reflexivity.

Scholars can approach contemporary discourses on religion with this requirement for third-order reflexivity. An analysis can come up with distinctions between argumentations, different interests, and different social groups promoting a goal – sometimes with compatible frames of reference, and sometimes not. The recent 'god is back' discourse may serve as an example. Titus Hjelm, for example, critically investigates the secularization theory and distinguishes five relevant discourses: the desecularization debate; talk of deprivatization and post-secularity; the effects of "welfare utopianism" on public religion; a discourse in which religion is seen as a social problem or as an expedient; and finally the mediatization or publicization of religion (2014). For our purposes, it is interesting to see how he evaluates and relates these discourses: he analyzes each of them on its own and then distinguishes between public discursive utterances and the social effects that that are made intelligible in terms of membership numbers; dispositions; correlations between religious belonging and income, nationality, or profession; structural change, such as in new or altered institutions; and, together with this, new procedures for allocating power or resources. In a particular sense, these discourses constitute several meaningful layers above and independent from structural continuity or change. These may involve hectic, short-term evaporations of utterances within social groups that do not receive institutional back-up, a shared interpretation of 'the situation,' or respective elites and their ideas and means of enforcing change, among other things.

This is a recurrent pattern in both the critical and the affirmative use of a variant of discourse analysis: introducing a temporary and a relevant-real distinction. Discursive practices – even when they are loud, frequent, and performed – need not be reflected in institutional structures and social positions (see Keller, this volume, on the dispositive; see also Adele Clarke's focus on "situation" in 2009). Perhaps this distinction is not so much about an ontology of concepts as it is about a detailed, compartmentalized research practice that examines a multiplicity of discourses at a given moment of cultural negotiation, when the outcome or tendency of formative power is not yet decided and not yet materialized in structures.

2 Recurrent Discourse Figurations in the History of Religion from a European Perspective

Generally speaking, discourse theory is a perspective from which to study the structure of categorical orders and the particular ways in which knowledge is organized, legitimized, and used at a specific moment in history, and also as a pattern across history. This is often done with a critical impetus with respect to ideology, society, and culture. In historical terms, therefore, discourse theory has found space and confirmation in the period of postcolonialism. But this is not its only use; within the framework of European thought, discourse theory has also proved to be effective and successful in deconstructing the presumptions of Christianity as a prototype of religion (Bell 2006), alongside further presumptions about Christianity and modernity.

These two areas of application in religion theory and modernity theory are interdependent in many ways. With respect to Christianity, interconfessional disputes between Catholic and Protestant denominations, as fundamental bifurcations in the discourse within the history of religion in Europe, also became significant in defining the Other during the period of colonial expansion. The example of the discourse on 'fetishes' shows how African religious practices are interpreted as conforming to Catholic practices, which Protestants perceive as a characteristic form of material culture. In the same way, a salvific Christian position is attributed to Jews and to Native Americans in the colonization of North America. In this sense, discursive patterns are tools with which to discover the world. Moreover, they are constitutive of worlds in the sense of social constructivism and the new institutional theory. Studies of colonial discourses have revealed quite a bit about European categorizations and axiomatic worldviews, and have made discourse history the most important tool – in the sense of historicizing one's own worldview – linked to a critique of the exercise of power in this colonial worldview.

The cultural study of religion, which will be addressed below, has resulted in countless blended discourses on religion and culture, such as the 'origin of religion in Africa' discourse (Atwood 2015), or alternatively the 'Arian origin' of religion; the 'world religions' discourse, useful for maintaining universalism in times of pluralism (Masuzawa 2005; Bell 2006); the *sui generis* concept of religion (McCutcheon 1997); the 'secularization' discourse; the idea of the 'return of religion'; 'good/bad religion' and 'high/primitive religion' discourses; and many more. Some of the favorite recurrent discourse 'figurations,' 'constellations,' 'knots,' or 'strands' with regard to religion in the context of European history of religion are: pastoral power, with its confessionalism (Protestant or Catholic bias or polemics; see for instance Smith 1998, 180–81); the *longue durée* of the binary cipher of Orientalism–Occidentalism, from the fifth century BCE, with Herodotus and Alexander the Great, up to Edward Said's examination of the political discourse on Islam in 'Western' media (Baker, Gabrielatos, and McEnery 2013); and Samuel Huntington's "clash of civilizations" theory. Further vistas of Central European patterns of discourse on religion include dark/light dualism (Huffer 2012, 21), the female savage/rational male, left-handedness/right-handedness (Knott 2005), insider/outsider perspectives, and reading/deciphering the book of nature.

In such contexts, discourse figuration is used to denote heterogeneous theoretical elements of more limited scope, such as textual pattern (metaphorical lines of right-/left-handedness, for example), or of wider impact, often using the term dispositif. Dispositif has become a significant category and research strand in sociologically oriented discourse analysis. The term refers to socio-material infrastructure, distributive networks for the circulation of knowledge, and recurrent, formalized, or everyday means of knowledge production. A dispositif – like the gender dispositif or the world religion dispositif – is effective on the meso-level of institutions and conventions, and it determines shared structures that are not reducible to the intentions of individual actors. Dispositifs are domain-specific, and each competes and interferes with many others. They therefore also yield unintended (side-)effects in terms of social impact. Dispositifs are interpretive categories which gather and bundle empirical data.

3 *Savoir–Pouvoir*: Knowledge–Power

The previous section deals with the postcolonial critique of the sovereignty of definitional power over central categories and orders of knowledge, and of taking advantage of the mighty machinery of science, media, and technology to circulate specific knowledge to remote localities. This brings another essential element of discourse theory into play: power. For Foucault, categorizations of knowledge are so closely linked to power structures, which go far beyond political organization and permeate the actions and the worldviews behind every action, that he speaks of power–knowledge (Foucault 1977). Discourse theory is not merely an analytical tool for historians and scholars in the field of cultural studies, but has also affected many of the cultural power positions which have been subjected to such a critical examination. In particular, long-established Christian organizations have been robbed of some of their emically ascribed features, such as ethical purity, universalism, justice, and the idea that human nature is innately religious. Russell T. McCutcheon thoroughly examines the US-American discourse on religion and meticulously lays bare the power interests and primarily political agendas of diverse voices in this orchestra (1997). He reveals a hidden agenda predominantly based on Christian interests, in which religion is passed off as morally pure, free of politically compromising practices or corruption, and critically untouchable.

The field of religious studies has also been severely affected by the distinction between or confusion of 'insider/religious' and 'outsider/academic' perspectives. 'Zen studies,' for example, flourished in the US as a reaction to the countercultural attraction to East Asian religious traditions and psychotechniques. In the 1990s, Bernard Faure critically examined this new discourse and revealed its South-East Asian romanticism. He explained common practices as a popularized and in many ways locally adapted form. Post-2000 'modern yoga studies' underwent a similar development, from Eliade's universalist résumé to today's multi-sited ethnographies (Strauss 2002) and reconstructions of multiple influences in a cross-cultural field of modern postural yoga invention (Singleton 2013).

4 Discipline and Regulation

In addition to power, another concept from the Foucauldian tradition has also been consistently important in cultural and religious studies: discipline and disciplining. The exertion of power has often been considered from the point of view of disciplining bodies. Body politics are a common research topic for Foucauldian adepts. Talal Asad's studies are a good example of this. Early on, he interpreted a religious system (Islam) as a discourse, in the sense that the heterogeneous traditions of Islam could be understood as a community of people who referred to the Qur'an as a "certificate of origin" (Asad 1986b; see also the concept of "self-constituting discourses" in Maingueneau's chapter in this volume). Asad also applied another important Foucauldian theorem to religion: *genealogical work*. In *Discipline and Reasons of Power in Christianity and Islam* (1993), and in several essays on attitudes to the body in the medieval Latin Christian church, he compared the Benedictine and Cistercian orders (for instance, with respect to practices related to food, sexuality, and penance; Asad 1983, 1986a).

For Asad, the advantage of a genealogical approach is that it can uncover unconscious "formations" rather than merely expressly symbolical and cultural interpretations or "representations" of the body (1997, 43), thus taking advantage of Foucault's concept of "discursive formations." Religious subjects are regulated and disciplined via their (material or fleshly) bodies. These medieval subjects submitted themselves to a strict code of bodily discipline that ruled their everyday lives. The scope of subjective experience and the modes of regulation are clearly connected to forms of governance. The medieval monastic world – with all of its internal differences between (male and female) monastic orders, which Asad points out – is clearly distinct from the early modern world, in which subjects submit themselves to a new political order ruled by a secular sovereign. In this latter form of governance, individual experiences occupy a much bigger reflective space than tradition, and these experiences gain significance as a result of their difference and variation.

In place of techniques for disciplining the self, it is disciplined more and more by normalizing practices that occur in modern times. Whereas disciplining is based on more or less clear-cut rules and regimes, the procedures and dynamics of normalizing occur within a range; they are informal and situated. Their regime is specialized and adapted to a much wider scope of free action in individualized modernity. The agency of these two types of change therefore differs, even if they occur simultaneously in different social milieus and spheres. In current debates, it remains an open question how far the contemporary regime is still normalizing and how far it constitutes a regime of control and radical data transparency, or whatever one may see as essential trends in the neoliberal cultural ideology of consumerism, in which entrepreneurial selves and 'prosumers' essentially co-align (*pro*duce) their con*sump*tion of products by providing their data in various ways in exchange for certain perceived benefits, such as the free use of communication services, spending time giving feedback to providers to improve their products, and accommodating smartphones to their needs.

5 Governance

> This immediately entails a choice of method that one day I will finally try to come back to at greater length, but I would like to point out straightaway that choosing to talk about or to start out from governmental practice is obviously and explicitly a way of not taking as primary, original and given object, notions such as the sovereign, sovereignty, the people subjects, the state, and civil society, that is to say all those universals employed by sociological analysis, historical analysis and political philosophy in order to account for real governmental practice.
> (Foucault 2008, 2)

This citation mirrors the central concern of Foucault's main argumentative thrust, which is still pivotal for many practitioners of discourse analysis: knowledge and truth are the outcome of social production, of historical contingency as opposed to universal principles – a crucial point being how they are regulated and the scholar's duty to reveal this. The citation also points to a weakness: the lack of an elaborated method, a gap that many sociologists and linguists have tried to fill.

In the field of religion, governance has received increasing attention (Martikainen 2013, 129–34). In recent work, it is mainly conceptually linked to regimes of truth-telling, territory, and neoliberalism. Neoliberalism is an important field, defined as "practices" in Foucault's late work on governmentality and biopolitics (Foucault 2008), the latter replacing earlier dichotomies between liberation and repression in his studies on sexuality, referring instead to gradational biopower. Very recently, closer scrutiny of neoliberal governance has gained ground in the cultural study of religion (see, for example, Martikainen and Gauthier 2013). Tuomas Martikainen develops a systematic approach to the "multilevel and pluricentric network governance of religion" (2013, 129) in order to grasp the many ways of regulating religion besides the church-state model. Religion and immigration is a related field (see, for example, Bradamat and Koenig 2009).

A very illuminating example of a discursive approach to religion in this regard is Breda Gray's Foucault-inspired article on neoliberal governmentality, with a case study of refugee work undertaken by churches and religious organizations in Ireland (2013). Competition between religious and secular organizations, with the state as a stakeholder advertising the projects, leads to a specific institutionalization within the field of refugee work. The pastoral power of care is combined with the rationale of technological and calculative governance, such as efficiency, targets, benchmarking, performance indicators, and an audit culture. Traditionally the pastor is held up as an example and is distinguished by their knowledge of the biographies of those entrusted to their care. Pastoral power is a relationship of obedience. The subordination of those entrusted to this care is realized through confession and the examination of consciences, and at the same time has the merit of individualizing the cared-for person. Within the process of secularization, this pastoral care is widened to social governance, notably through social work and psychological professions. Once a church makes bids for projects in refugee or other social work, it has to adapt to neoliberal, administrative discourse formation, which involves serious changes to the church's former procedural rationality, its human capital portfolio, and its control mechanisms, among other aspects. Therefore, the intermingling of religious organizations in the highly professionalized and socially differentiated subsystems of societies will have a lasting and unforeseeable effect on particular religious dispositifs.

The governance discourse is regularly accompanied by the question of the possibility of resistance. Is practicing yoga or mindfulness an escape from neoliberal governance, or does it stabilize the workforce for further exploitation? Foucault insistently pushed this question in the context of his extensive work on the history of sexuality. When are gender regimes a space for free expression – if indeed this can be seen as freedom, with all the problematics of prescribed confessionalism – and when are they spaces of domination? When do religious regimes enter alliances with psychiatric power or other discourses and the regimes these exert through institutionalized practices? Saba Mahmood's adaptation of Foucault's proof of resistance in discourse points to the agency of Muslim women in Cairo, which disrupts the pattern of female subordination to patriarchy with 'Western' feminist images of freedom (2005).

6 What Room Is There for Subjectivity in the Discourse?

Foucault's conception of the subject is a topic that should not be neglected, and it has been controversial from very early on in the reception of his ideas. A few remarks on the possible importance of the subject in the structure that largely constitutes discourse are therefore called for. What importance do individuals, the 'individual,' late modern subject actors, the self – or however human beings are conceived – have in discourse theory?

Whereas earlier theory-building addressed the cognitive knowing subject, this subject is now embedded or even dissolved in a map of social interactions. Such interaction may now even include animals, non-human beings, material things, or a material vitality. In the above-mentioned work on governance, the subject's self-regulation appears as agency. In recent decades, this regime has been variously characterized as optimizing, privatizing, publicizing, or individualizing. Foucault transposes the individual subject to the more general, historical form of subjectivity. Religion is a well-established political technology used to regulate subjects by inaugurating a form of subjectivity. One of these forms or regimes of subjectivities is truth-telling. Foucault contends that epistemic games of truth-telling enable the renunciation of truth, as in votes or exclamations of feeling and felt bodily experiences.

In the same way, Asad investigates how asceticism uses pain to find out how far the body depends on sensory perceptions. The body is not an obstacle on the way to truth, but rather the arena within which the truth can be brought to light (Asad 1983, 311). From medieval physical torture to the pressure put on penitents with the intention of causing mental pain that will lead to the confession of sins, a bodily sensation (pain) is linked to the revelation of truth (Asad 1983, 321). The habitus of confession "has become an attitude that can have – let's say – simple psychological functions such as an improved knowing of oneself, a better composure of oneself, realizing one's genuine inclinations, the option of leading one's own life" (Foucault 1977, translation mine). To describe this life of one's own and this idealization of authenticity, a history of the contemporary self seems set to become a new discipline, recording practices of subjectification and self-relationships. In this vein, "self-care" and "technologies of the self" are concepts of utmost importance (Foucault 1988).

From the 1960s onward, there is a lacuna with respect to a history not only of the self, but of self-governance (Eitler and Elberfeld 2015). A rising number of therapeutic cultures, which ascribe to subjects a need for therapy, constitute an environment in which the discourse of "vulnerable" or even "traumatized" subjects (Argenti-Pillen 2000) suits the neoliberal industry of supplying support for the vulnerable (for example, migrants; see Gray 2013, 71), whether in the form of anti-trauma therapy (for instance, the new trends in yoga therapy propagated by Price et al. 2017) or mindfulness as a modernist offshoot of Buddhism (Samuel 2014). Discourse theory explains how dispositions work in subjects and what role religions play in connecting affective and ethical dispositions to the more stable formation of a particular historical subjectivity alongside others (on piety, for example, see Mahmood 2005; on the ethics of soundscapes, see Hirschkind 2009).

Altered personal relationships – in families or partnerships – are but one trigger in the discursive changes and interrelated formation of new spiritualities and religious practices; further factors include economization, new forms of networked communication due to globalized digitalization, and transcultural discourses on sustainability and spiritual practice (Strauss and Mandelbaum 2013) that shift and swirl existing discourses, as well as creating new ones.

7 Questions, Limits, and Critiques of Discourse Theory

What are the limits of discourse analysis? Does this approach have a specific operative range within which it is useful, and beyond which it is limited or even unsuitable? Controversies have regularly raged over topics such as the scope of action Foucault's interpretation of culture leaves to agents, the question of non-human agency, the supposed negligence of non-discursive practices, the implosion of 'religion' as a specific category (among others), and claims that discourse analysis is inappropriate for material culture and the body.

Like system theory, discourse theory implies that autonomous subjects are entangled in a structure. Semantic propositions do not equal utterances, but account for a figuration that shapes agents and has influenced their world even before they act upon it. A discourse is more than language as a tool to extrapolate the world. In this sense, subjects are created, maintained, and subordinated to a structure: the discursive web. At the same time, subjects are of the utmost importance in discourse theory. A 'subjectivity formation' conceptualizes the historical conditions of ways of life as well as formative and often oppressive forces and renders them describable on a meso-level. 'Subjectivity' denotes a very important theoretical issue; it is not simply an intentional agent or institution, but indicates the scope of action, options, and feelings – in short, the possible being – of subgroups of people at a given time.

In this regard, discourse theory is very close to what is known in Pierre Bourdieu's structural sociology as field theory, in which critical discourse analysis is a permanent battle over enforcement and hegemony, and it is superior to system theory, where no equivalent conceptual level of subjectivity can be found. The intentionality of actors is limited to the micro-level: the further one moves away from this level, and the more institutionalized the interaction, the more unintended effects take over and develop certain dynamics of the anonymized exertion of power.

The recent debate on the categorization of New Age spirituality serves to provide some insights into how the limits and strengths of discourse theory are currently being discussed. Paul Heelas, for example, opposes Foucauldian interpretations of New Age spiritualties by rooting them in this-worldly "life" (2008). Not very convincingly, he opposes "lived life" to the distanced analytical view. Others examine the transfer of so-called 'psy' discourses into the domain of self-help, therapy, and personal growth, suggesting that these technologies of the self are the product of a form of neoliberal governmentality that reduces personal agency and forecloses political critique and social change. But how can we decide whether spiritual practices are disciplinary techniques that simply reproduce dominant (neoliberal) subject positions, or whether they open up a libertine space? And is liberalism the way to escape regulation? One under-theorized concept is that of a normative bias in some strands of critical discourse analysis, which argues that hegemony is always problematic and constitutes an unjust (unequal) exertion of power (but see Reiner Keller's remarks above, this volume). Very strong hegemonic relations indicate that ex-colonial actors do not have complete and equal freedom to act, and that self-images are interdependent in both Occidentalism and Orientalism. A post-colonial 'bad conscience' may contribute to excessive attempts to justify equality. Social science research is clear on this point; Eileen Barker, for example, points out that there is no way to decide whether frequent sexual intercourse or celibacy is better, or which religious organization "oversteps the boundaries of permissible behaviour" (2006, 391).

A recurring criticism of discourse analysis is that it is logocentric and is not able to take in the embodied quality of agents, since they are rooted in an artificial material world that affects them through affordances, among other things. With a view to the work of Asad and others, the contrary seems to be true: body disciplining and bodies in their materiality have in fact entered the arena of research. At the same time, cognitive and evolutionary approaches were not as common as they are today. Thus this criticism of discourse theory neglects the timeframe. Indeed, linguistic pragmatics was insufficient to give full meaning to practice in discourse theory, whereas ritual theories explicitly link discourse with materiality (Ioannides 2016) and pay attention to body movement, emplacement, and aesthetic delight in practices of text recitation (see the work of one of Asad's pupils in Hirschkind 2009).

Donovan O. Schaefer hints at another important topic, which discourse theory often overlooks: affects. Schaefer still observes a neglect of affect theory, which is why his book on religious affects is "about the ways that intellectual and political circuits are informed by relationships between bodies that are invisible to discursive analytics" (Schaefer 2016, 10). A question that arises from the same background – namely, the evolutionary theory of religion – asks whether animals have discourses, since some primatologists (such as Jane Goodall) argue that they have spirituality, for which Goodall finds proof in a group of primates' spontaneous dance in front of a waterfall. Schaefer gives no reason why a waterfall dance performed by chimpanzees should be religious, rather than an expression of aesthetic taste or a theatrical performance – but the latter would be difficult if not impossible to prove, given that chimpanzees do not found theatre companies, which brings us to the cultural practice argument. Art, like religion, is a discursive conglomerate and not merely a 'massing of affects,' as in Schaefer's work. As primate research has progressed, supposed indicators of human uniqueness – such as cognition, language, tool use, and sociality – have faded away, one after another. Nevertheless, the ascription of religion is not on the same logical level. One would have to presuppose the category of religion, as it is not inevitable to believe that the exceptional *experience of* – or even better, *behavior toward* – a waterfall is a *sui generis* emotion (but a reaction to its rarity, the loud noise, damp air, bright light, fast movement, reflections, etc.).

Religion certainly did not fall out of the blue. There has to be some sort of transition, so we might be forced to indicate some pre-forms of religion – which might be less complex – but even then, it would be necessary to combine contingent forms of living if RELIGION is to be understood as a cultural rather than a genetic phenomenon. A cultural point of view would understand religion as a cultural phenomenon of a higher order, requiring institutions, social ranks, interpretations, misunderstandings, and the wish to regulate others as well as the way the world is represented. The difference between this and any naturalistic, pre-constructivist (or "essentialist"; see McCutcheon 1997), evolutionary discourse is salient here.

The question of how non-discursive practices (such as habits and conventions) constitute the hidden underside of discourses is a question that has been discussed for some time, and it has gained new actuality in recent studies of the aesthetics of religion (Grieser and Johnston 2017; Koch and Wilkens 2019). A crucial developmental step in cultural studies is taking place in embodied cognition. Perhaps recent voices speaking about how to deal with material religion and culture, the body and the senses, images, brains, and media will have a huge impact in pushing discourse theory a step closer to aesthetics.

8 Conclusion

This chapter reviews a small extract of work demonstrating the high, not yet fully exploited potential of Foucauldian discourse research in cultural studies of religion, along the lines of historical configurations of problems and their solutions, as well as their unintended effects; discourse formations; power–knowledge; discipline and regulation; governance; and subjectivity. The special perspective which discourse theory brings to cultural studies is praxeological, genealogical, and juxtaposes differentiated societal domains. Discourse theory has developed in a highly multidimensional manner and is especially successful in creating an entire zoo of conceptual items, such as genres, style, and dispositif. Methodologies for collecting research data can entail focus group discussions (Ndaluka 2012) and expert interviews as well as other sources, such as media articles, religious writings and preaching, and different types of social events, practices, and structures (Fairclough 2010, 164). Thus it is easy to get lost in nomenclature.

It becomes apparent that the history of ideas and the history of concepts have to take a step back from their role as unifying narratives in the light of discourse analysis, paying postcolonial attention to discontinuity, rupture, and new elements brought together from subcurrents of known categorizations (Foucault 1972, 4–6). From the point of view of discourse theory, religious practices interact and overlap with sometimes surprising societal subfields, social movements, and new technologies at any time in history – this is not only typical of (post-)modernity. One considerable impact of discursive approaches is that they lead the cultural study of religion away from a fixed category of religion, away from the history of ideas, and away from a tendency to unify grand narratives, big social theories, and 'great-man' historical reconstructions.

References

Argenti-Pillen, Alexandra. 2000. "The Discourse on Trauma in Non-Western Cultural Contexts: Contributions of an Ethnographic Method." In *International Handbook to Human Response to Trauma*, ed. by Arieh Shalev, Rachel Yehuda, and Alexander MacFarlane, 87–101. New York: Springer US.
Asad, Talal. 1983. "Notes on Body Pain and Truth in Medieval Christian Ritual." *Economy and Society* 12: 287–327.
Asad, Talal. 1986a. "On Ritual and Discipline in Medieval Christian Monasticism." *Economy and Society* 16: 159–203.
Asad, Talal. 1986b. *The Idea of an Anthropology of Islam*. Washington: John Hopkins University Press.
Asad, Talal. 1993. *Genealogies of Religion: Discipline and Reasons of Power in Christianity and Islam*. Baltimore: Johns Hopkins University Press.
Asad, Talal. 1997. "Remarks on the Anthropology of the Body." In *Religion and the Body*, ed. by Sarah Coakley, 42–52. Cambridge: Cambridge University Press.
Atwood, David. 2015. "The Discourse on Primal Religion: Disentangling Regimes of Truth." *Method and Theory in the Study of Religion* 28: 445–464.
Baker, Paul, Costas Gabrielatos, and Tony McEnery. 2013. *Discourse Analysis and Media Attitudes: The Representation of Islam in the British Press*. Cambridge: Cambridge University Press.
Barker, Eileen. 2006. "What Should We Do About the Cults? Policies, Information and the Perspective of INFORM." In *The New Religious Question: State Regulation or State Interference?*, ed. by Pauline Coté and Jeremy Gunn, 371–94. Frankfurt: Peter Lang.
Bell, Catherine. 2006. "Paradigms Behind (and Before) the Modern Concept of Religion." *History and Theory* 45: 27–46.
Bradamat, Paul, and Matthias Koenig. 2009. *International Migration and the Governance of Religion*. Montreal: McGill-Queen's University Press.
Clarke, Adele E. 2009. "From Grounded Theory to Situational Analysis. What's New? Why? How?" In *Developing Grounded Theory: The Second Generation*, ed. by Janice M. Morse, 194–233. Walnut Creek/CA: Left Coast Press.

Eitler, Pascal, and Jens Elberfeld. 2015. "Von der Gesellschaftsgeschichte zur Zeitgeschichte des Selbst – und zurück." In *Zeitgeschichte des Selbst. Therapeutisieung. Politisierung. Emotionalisierung*, ed. by Pascal Eitler and Jens Elberfeld, 7–30. Bielefeld: Transcript.

Fairclough, Norman. 2010. "A Dialectical Relational Approach to Critical Discourse Analysis in Social Research." In *Methods of Critical Discourse Analysis*, ed. by Ruth Wodak and Michael Meyer, 162–171. London: SAGE.

Fitzgerald, Timothy. 2007. *Discourses on Barbarity and Civility*. New York: Oxford University Press.

Foucault, Michel. 1972 [1969]. *Archaeology of Knowledge and The Discourse on Language*. Trans. A. M. Sheridan Smith. New York: Pantheon.

Foucault, Michel. 1977. "Pouvoir et savoir" ("Kenryoku to chi," interview with S. Hasumi, recorded in Paris, 13 October 1977). *Dits et Ecrits* 3, no. 26: 240–56.

Foucault, Michel. 1988. "Technologies of the Self." In *Technologies of the Self: A Seminar with Michel Foucault*, ed. by Martin H. Luther, Huck Gutman, and Patrick H. Hutton, 16–49 ("Les techniques de soi." *Dits et Ecrits* 4, text no. 363). London: Tavistock.

Foucault, Michel. 2008. *The Birth of Biopolitics: Lectures at the College de France, 1978–1979*. London and New York: Palgrave Macmillan.

Gee, James Paul. 2014. *An Introduction to Discourse Analysis: Theory and Method*. New York: Routledge.

Gray, Breda. 2013. "Catholic church civil society activism and the neoliberal governmental project of migrant integration in Ireland." In *Religion in the Neoliberal Age. Political Economy and Modes of Governance* (Religion and Society Series, Series Editors: Linda Woodhead and Rebecca Catto) ed. by Tuomas Martikainen, and Francois Gauthier, 69–90. Farnham: Ashgate.

Grieser, Alexandra K., and Jay Johnston, eds. 2017. *Aesthetics of Religion: A Connective Concept*. Berlin and Boston: De Gruyter.

Hirschkind, Charles. 2009. *The Ethical Soundscape: Cassette Sermons and Islamic Counterpublics*. New York City: Columbia University Press.

Hjelm, Titus. 2011. "Discourse Analysis." In *The Routledge Handbook of Research Methods in the Study of Religion*, ed. by Michael Stausberg, 134–150. London: Routledge.

Hjelm, Titus. 2014. "Understanding the New Visibility of Religion. Religion as Problem and Utility." *Journal of Religion in Europe* 7: 203–222.

Hjelm, Titus. 2016. "Theory and Method in Critical Discursive Study of Religion." In *Making Religion: Theory and Practice in the Discursive Study of Religion*, ed. by Frans Wijsen and Kocku von Stuckrad, 15–34. Leiden and Boston: Brill.

Huffer, Lynne. 2012. "Foucault and Sedgwick: The Repressive Hypothesis Revisited." *Foucault Studies* 14: 20–40.

Ioannides, George. 2016. "The Matter of Meaning and the Meaning of Matter: Explorations for the Material and Discursive Study of Religion." In *Making Religion: Theory and Practice in the Discursive Study of Religion*, ed. by Frans Wijsen and Kocku von Stuckrad, 51–73. Leiden and Boston: Brill.

Jäger, Siegfried, and Florentine Maier. 2009. "Theoretical and Methodological Aspects of Foucauldian Critical Discourse Analysis and Dispositive Analysis." In *Methods of Critical Discourse Analysis*, second Edition, ed. by Ruth Wodak and Michael Meyer, 34–61. London: Sage.

Keller, Reiner. 2013. *Doing Discourse Research*. London: Sage.

Kippenberg, Hans G. 1983. "Diskursive Religionswissenschaft. Gedanken zu einer Religionswissenschaft, die weder auf einer allgemein gültigen Definition von Religion noch auf einer Überlegenheit von Wissenschaft basiert." In *Neue Ansätze in der Religionswissenschaft*, ed. by Burkhard Gladigow and Hans G. Kippenberg, 9–28. Munich: Koesel.

Knott, Kim. 2005. *The Location of Religion: A Spatial Analysis*. London: Equinox.

Koch, Anne, and Katharina Wilkens, eds. 2019. *The Bloomsbury Handbook of Cognitive and Cultural Aesthetics of Religion (HCCAR)*. London: Bloomsbury.

Laclau, Ernesto, and Chantal Mouffe. 1985. Hegemony and Socialist Strategy: Towards a Radical Democratic Politics. Translated by Winston Moore and Paul Cammack. London: Verso.

Martikainen, Tuomas. 2013. "Multilevel and Pluricentric Network Governance of Religion." In *Religion in the Neoliberal Age: Political Economy and Modes of Governance*, ed. by Tuomas Martikainen and Francois Gauthier, 129–142. AHRC/ESRC Religion and Society Series. Farnham: Ashgate.

Martikainen, Tuomas, and Francois Gauthier. 2013. *Religion in the Neoliberal Age: Political Economy and Modes of Governance*. AHRC/ESRC Religion and Society Series. Farnham: Ashgate.

Masuzawa, Tomoko. 2005. *The Invention of World Religions: Or, How European Universalism was Preserved in the Language of Pluralism*. Chicago: University of Chicago Press.

McCutcheon, Russell. 1997. *Manufacturing Religion: The Discourse on Sui Generis Religion and the Politics of Nostalgia*. Oxford: Oxford University Press.

Mahmood, Saba. 2005. *Politics of Piety: The Islamic Revival and the Feminist Subject*. Princeton: Princeton University Press.

Ndaluka, Thomas Joseph. 2012. *Religious Discourse, Social Cohesion and Conflict*. Münster: LIT.

Price, Maggi, Joseph Spianazzola, Regina Musicao, Jennifer Turner, Michael Suvak, David Emmerson, and Bessel van der Kolk. 2017. "Effectiveness of an Extended Yoga Treatment for Women with Chronic Posttraumatic Stress Disorder." *Journal of Alternative and Complementary Medicine* 10, no. 10: 1–9.

Reckwitz, Andreas. 2012. "Affective Spaces: A Praxeological Outlook." *Rethinking History: The Journal of Theory and Practice* 16: 241–258.

Said, Edward. 1997. *Covering Islam: How the Media and the Experts Determine How We See the Rest of the World*. New York: Vintage Books.

Samuel, Geoffrey. 2014. "The Contemporary Mindfulness Movement and the Question of Nonself." *Transcultural Psychiatry*, published online 5 December 2014. DOI: 10.1177/1363461514562061.

Schaefer, Donovan O. 2015. *Religious Affects: Animality, Evolution, and Power*. Durham: Duke University Press.

Singleton, Mark. 2013. "Transnational Exchange and the Genesis of Modern Postural Yoga." In *Yoga Traveling: Bodily Practice in Transcultural Perspective*, ed. by Beatrix Hauser, 37–56. Heidelberg: Springer.

Smith, Jonathan Z. 1996. "A Matter of Class: Taxonomies of Religion." *Harvard Theological Revue* 89, no. 4: 387–403.

Smith, Jonathan Z. 1998. "Religion, Religions, Religious." In *Critical Terms for Religious Studies*, ed. by Mark Taylor, 269–284. Chicago: University of Chicago Press.

Strauss, Sarah. 2002. "'Adapt, Adjust, Accommodate': The Production of Yoga in a Transnational World." *History and Anthropology* 13, no. 3: 231–251.

Strauss, Sarah, and Laura Mandelbaum. 2013. "Consuming Yoga, Conserving the Environment: Transcultural Discourses on Sustainable Living." In *Yoga Traveling: Bodily Practice in Transcultural Perspective*, ed. by Beatrix Hauser, 175–200. Heidelberg: Springer.

Stuckrad, Kocku von. 2014. *The Scientification of Religion: An Historical Study of Discursive Change, 1800–2000*. Berlin and Boston: De Gruyter.

Sutcliffe, Steven J., and Ingvild S. Gilhus. 2013. "Introduction: 'All Mixed Up.' Thinking About Religion in Relation to New Age Spiritualities." In *New Age Spirituality: Rethinking Religion*, ed. by Steven J. Sutcliffe and Ingvild S. Gilhus, 1–16. Durham: Acumen.

Wijsen, Frans, and Kocku von Stuckrad, eds. 2016. *Making Religion: Theory and Practice in the Discursive Study of Religion*. Leiden and Boston: Brill.

Erin K. Wilson
The Power Politics of 'Religion': Discursive Analysis of Religion in Political Science and International Relations

That political science and International Relations (IR) have 'found religion' has become a common trope in recent times. After years of neglect, scholars have, so the story goes, '(re)discovered' religion and its significance in contemporary global politics. This continued relevance of religion flies in the face of predictions of secularization theory, which had significant influence on the field and led to the long neglect of religion as a factor of importance in understanding global political dynamics. The initial (and still largely predominant) interest in religion in political science and IR was as something that could be clearly labeled and identified, measured and analyzed, despite there being no agreed definition of what exactly religion is. The majority of mainstream approaches to religion within political science and IR utilize a 'you know it when you see it' kind of approach to the study of religion.

More recently, however, a growing collective of scholars working at the intersection of religious studies and political science and IR have introduced more critical approaches. To study religion critically in political science and IR is to contest the very idea of 'religion' as some *thing*, an specific object, space, structure that can be clearly identified, and its associated assumptions, along with its binary opposite, 'the secular' (Wilson 2012, 10). Rather than exploring what 'religion' does in IR, critical approaches to the study of religion instead examine what 'religion' is in IR, who gets to define what 'religion' is, how they define it, why they define it as they do, and what the consequences are in real world law and politics of defining it in one way and not another. Religion is understood as an unstable "practice, discursive formation and analytical category" (Agensky 2017, 2), rather than a fixed unchanging entity. As such, discursive analysis is a central component of critical approaches to religion within political science and IR.

This chapter outlines key features of the discursive approach to the study of religion within political science and IR. It begins with a brief overview of the history of the study of religion within the field, noting the almost ideological sway that secularization theory held (and in many cases continues to hold). Political science and IR are concerned with the study of power in domestic and international politics. According to secularization theory, the social and political power of religion was/is in continual and inexorable decline, making it a largely irrelevant topic for scholars of politics and IR. That influence began to be challenged in the post September 11 2001 environment, when scholars of IR realized that they had failed to predict both the end of the Cold War and September 11 and that perhaps religion was not as irrelevant to understanding global events as had previously been thought.

A key innovation in this respect was the engagement with discourse analysis that had taken place in the field since the 1980s and in the 2000s was utilized in the study of religion in political science and IR. The chapter provides a general overview of these developments, before turning specifically to the question of the discursive analysis of religion. The chapter outlines the 'relational dialogist' discursive analysis approach, which draws on the work of Julia Kristeva and Raia Prokhovnik to unpack and take account of oft-neglected dimensions of 'religion' as a discursive phenomenon. Throughout this discussion, I provide relevant examples from the United States of America (USA), which is arguably the most well-known case in which these factors come into play and thus requires the least introduction and background. The chapter concludes by reviewing the ways in which the discursive study of religion in political science and IR contributes to our understanding of power relationships in contemporary global politics.

1 The Study of Religion in Political Science and IR: A Marginal Endeavor

Up until the 1990s, if religion were mentioned at all in IR scholarship, it was usually as an anomaly or as a dangerous, irrational and dogmatic influence on the political sphere.[1] For the most part, however, religion is hardly mentioned at all prior to the end of the Cold War. While there are a number of reasons for this neglect, the prevalence of secularization theory within the social sciences is one of the main contributing factors. With its overarching view that religion would continue to be less significant in public life, secularization theory contributed to the marginalization of the study of religion in Euro-American dominated political science and IR.

Several events contributed to a revision of this approach, however. The increased significance of religious actors in domestic political life, particularly in the USA, contributed to an increased interest in the role of religion in political science. Within IR, the Iranian revolution in the late 1970s caught many analysts unawares. The significant role of religious actors in the civil society movements that contributed to the fall of communism in Eastern Europe and ultimately the end of the Cold War was a further signal that perhaps IR scholars were missing something by not taking religion into account in their analysis. The failure of IR scholars to foresee the possibility of an event such as the terrorist attacks of September 11 2001, however, was the key event that opened up the field to greater interest in analyzing religion (Philpott 2002).

---

[1] See, for example, Carr 1946, Morgenthau and Thompson 1985 and Waltz 1959.

Much of this renewed interest in religion was, however, uncritical. It took religion as something that could be clearly labeled, identified, measured, and analyzed, separated from other socio-political and economic factors. The primary goal of these 'face value' approaches was to understand under what conditions religion contributed to violence, discrimination and conflict and under what conditions religion contributed to building peaceful and inclusive societies. Elizabeth Shakman Hurd has termed this "the two faces of faith approach" (Hurd 2015, 22), or more simply "good" religion vs. "bad" religion. According to this narrative, rather than religion disappearing, it has become increasingly more prominent, both as a source of peace and tolerance and as a source of violence and terrorism. The issue now is to facilitate contributions from religion that support peace, human rights, development, gender equality, and so on, while minimizing those aspects of religion that contribute to violence, intolerance, and chaos. One of the earliest examples of this narrative within IR is R. Scott Appleby's *The Ambivalence of the Sacred*, in which he argues that religion can be both a source for violence and conflict, as well as a source for peace and conflict transformation and it is difficult to determine how, why and under what circumstances religion will contribute to either conflict or peace (Appleby 2000, 5). This narrative has emerged with even more force in politics and public life in the context of the perceived rise of religiously inspired terrorism (Mamdani 2004, 11).

While the increased attention to religion as an issue of significance in contemporary IR brings much-needed analysis to a long neglected area, the new mainstream approach of good religion and bad religion continues to uphold the key assumptions of secularism and secularization theory (Hurd 2015, chapter 2). This means that while there is more attention being given to religion as a phenomenon in global politics, analyses are still limited by the same assumptions about what 'religion' is – and, indeed, what 'secularism' is – that contributed to the neglect of religion in the first instance. The identification and critique of these assumptions concerning religion and secularism is one of the most groundbreaking contributions to come from critical perspectives on religion in political science and IR. It is here that the discursive study of religion has been most significant.

2 Discursive Analysis and the Power Politics of Religion in Political Science and IR

Language is one of the key sites through which to analyze the place of religion in politics, in particular religion's relationship with power. Some of the ways in which religion influences politics are embedded within the values, identities, and worldviews that are assumed to be natural or normal within specific contexts. These embedded influences from religion have become inextricably entwined with elements that have, until recently, predominantly been considered 'secular' by social scientists and IR theorists.

Discourse analysis has enabled scholars of religion, political science, and IR to draw out and unravel these seemingly tangled, deeply embedded cultural assumptions and explore their impact on constructions of identity, dominant worldviews, and, in turn, decision-making processes and outcomes. This discursive analysis thus allows scholars to acknowledge subtle, implicit ways that ideas about 'religion' permeate worldviews through which identities are constructed and enacted as part of policy practice. Language is a potent site for the construction of national and civilizational identity and the development, justification, and implementation of policy, as well as being a primary way through which ideas about religion influence politics.

Within IR, discourse analysis has gained salience in the post-Cold War era as a part of the general broadening of theoretical approaches. Critical and reflectivist scholars utilizing discourse analysis challenged traditional IR approaches that focused on identifying external 'natural' causes for state action. Instead, reflectivist scholars were concerned with modes of interpretation and representation and the consequences of choosing one mode of interpretation and representation over others (Milliken 1999, 225–226; Campbell 1998, 7–8). Discourse analysis in IR focuses on the manifestations of particular ideologies and how these ideologies impact the perceptions and actions of actors in world politics.

Milliken argues that three key assumptions underpin the work of discourse analysts in political science and IR (Milliken 1999, 229). Firstly, discourse analysts hold that discourses are "structure[s] of signification which construct social realities" (ibid.). Discourses are viewed as different series of words, actions and/or symbols, or, as Weldes and Saco suggest, "linguistic and non-linguistic practices" that constitute a particular way of articulating a specific interpretation and/or representation of phenomena (Weldes and Saco 1996, 374). As Milliken points out, such an understanding of discourse reflects a largely constructivist view of how meaning is generated (1999, 229).

Second, Milliken highlights that discourses not only provide the means for interpreting and understanding the world, but also produce ways of being in and responding to the world (ibid.). Milliken refers to this as "discourse productivity." Discourses emphasize certain interpretations of identity and action while excluding other possible ways of being in and responding to the world (ibid.). Following on from Milliken's statement, it is also possible to argue that, as well as producing some means of interpreting the world and closing off other interpretations, discourse serves to reproduce "collectively held subconscious ideas" concerning what constitutes "normal and natural reality" (Galtung 1996, 211). The use of discourse analysis highlights the role of ideas about 'religion' in opening up some ways of being in and responding to the rest of the world whilst closing off others in domestic and foreign policy contexts.

The third commitment of discourse analysts develops out of the second. Discourses are not static but require constant work to be maintained and to uphold the hegemonic practices and status quo that discourses engender. Milliken refers to this as "the play of practice" (Milliken 1999, 230). Discourse analysts identify how hegemonic discourses attempt to "fix" meaning and silence alternative discourses (ibid.). Discursive analysis of religion within political science and IR is thus interested in the ways in which narratives, images and ideas drawn from religious traditions and/or ideas about 'religion' in general or specific 'religions' in particular (usually Christianity and Islam) play in efforts to maintain one interpretation of events and exclude or silence other interpretations in order to open up and justify one set of policy options over others.

The foundational work of David Campbell, Diana Saco and Jutta Weldes, and Michael Barnett reflect these theoretical commitments of discourse analysts. Discourses manufacture ways of responding to the world and attempt to maintain or 'fix' particular meanings and interpretations while subordinating alternatives. Campbell notes that discourse works in conjunction with state actions to reproduce and reinforce traditional representations of state identity (Campbell 1998, 69). The practice of foreign policy, Campbell posits, is an exercise in nation building and national identity construction, but, further, it is an exercise in who is included and excluded from the nation (ibid.). Religious narratives and ideas about 'religion' play a critical role in such discursive constructions.

National discourses aim to privilege one 'official' representation of the nation-state's identity that encompasses its values, purpose and goals, all the while excluding other possible interpretations or representations. Consequently, viewing a state in a particular way becomes 'natural,' while competing representations of state identity are viewed as unnatural, unpatriotic, 'un-American,' for example. Through producing and privileging one identity over others, a particular set of policy options are made available while others are closed off. By privileging one conception of a state's identity over another, particular avenues of state action are opened up, and these choices are made to appear 'logical' and 'rational,' 'natural' and 'common sense' within the privileged identity discourse. Other policy options are excluded, made to seem 'illogical,' 'irrational,' or 'impossible.'

Jutta Weldes and Diana Saco note, in their discussion of the nexus of identity and action in relation to the USA and Cuba, that through particular discursive formations, the USA was able to justify a continued state of hostility towards Cuba into the post-Cold War period. This hostility persisted despite the fact that, in realist power politics terms, Cuba did not pose a significant threat to US power and interests (Weldes and Saco 1996, 374). This is a significant insight, since it points us to the importance of the power politics of language and identity within political science and IR. Power politics is not only about material reality, but about the ways in which that reality is discursively represented and interpreted.

Michael Barnett's study of Israel and the Oslo Peace Accords also demonstrates how discourse works to produce one mode of identity and action over another (Barnett 1999). The case Barnett examines is particularly important, however, because Yitzhak Rabin sought to depart substantially from traditional representations of Israeli identity. Consequently, the discourse utilized was central to Rabin's success in gaining support for a different set of policy options and actions.

Barnett's study emphasizes frames and narratives as important components of the construction of identity and state action. These frames and narratives are social and cultural resources that policy makers and speechwriters can rely on to give added meaning and context to the linguistic and rhetorical devices they utilize in speeches and policy pronouncements. These devices are used in the construction of national identity and then further used to articulate specific avenues of state action consistent with the purpose, goals, and values contained within the construction of national identity. Discourse analysis identifies "representational practices" that serve the purpose of opening up some policy options and closing down others (Shapiro 1989, 72). These representational practices "have an ideological depth to the extent that they engage a stock of signs with which people make their everyday lives intelligible" (ibid., 73).

In other words, the representational practices utilized by policy makers and speechwriters deliberately draw on discourses commonly used within the culture and population of the nation that are representative of the way in which the nation, its identity, purposes, and goals are thought about or, alternatively, are representative of the ideology of the nation. These discourses are ways of thinking about politics and the nation, so deeply embedded within society that they have become subconsciously held and understood belief systems across the majority of members of that nation, constituting a kind of tacit or implicit knowledge (Foucault 1996, 13). Policy makers and speechwriters use these discourses to invoke specific meanings and ideas without explicitly stating them.

A further insight to be gained from discourse analysis is the importance of the relationship between identity, power and state action. Discourse analysis emphasizes the construction of power through language and the reproduction of power in action. For scholars employing discourse analysis, primarily those from constructivist, feminist, critical theory and postmodern perspectives, power is not simply the product of material resources, as the more traditional theoretical approaches within IR, particularly realism, would suggest (Snyder 1999, 1). Power is constructed in multiple ways and operates at multiple levels. Language is a crucial part in that process. Weldes and Saco (1996, 371) argue that one form of power revolves around the ability to define or be defined, that is, to define one's own identity or be defined by another.

This ability to define oneself is related to what Janice Bially Mattern refers to as "the power politics of identity" (2001, 351). Through utilizing discourse analysis, Mattern suggests that power politics is not restricted to physical force but also occurs through "representational force," a function of discourse. In contrast to the realist power politics of physical force, Mattern describes this practice as a power politics of identity, occurring through discourse (ibid.). In important ways, these insights from Mattern and Weldes and Saco suggest a significant link between power, identity, and state action. Further, Strenski (2010) has argued that power, as well as being a crucial component of politics, is also inextricably tied to religion. Thus, discursive analysis of religion is a crucial tool for political science and IR scholars interested in exploring the implicit connections amongst identity, state action, power and religion.

3 Religion and Discourse Analysis

Images, ideas, and narratives connected with 'religion' and various 'religious' traditions provide unique linguistic and discursive tools through which this relationship between power, identity, and state action is activated. The distinctive characteristics often associated with religion – its relationship with the transcendent, its narrative dimensions, institutional and communal authority – imbue religion with different forms of power that can be effectively utilized in discourse to make certain modes of identity and action possible over others. 'Religion' can endow the state (and also the individual) with an identity that is closely connected to the supernatural or the deity of a dominant religious tradition (in the case of the USA, for example, the God/gods of Judaism and/or Christianity).[2] This identity can carry with it notions of being chosen, exceptional, and special, possessing a unique calling or mission in the world, which in turn provides a source of legitimacy and justification for the state. Whilst this is a trope commonly associated with the USA (see, for example, Cherry 1971) it is also one that emerges in constructions of national identity in other contexts (Smith 2000). In turn, this sense of 'chosen-ness' can be used to justify a myriad of actions. 'Religion' consequently can be used to exercise power over those outside the state, subordinating them to the state through the use of discursive elements that demonize or satanize the "other" (Juergensmeyer 2000, 176). Examples of this type of discourse have been abundant in the context of recent debates about migration, where the words 'refugee,' 'migrant,' 'criminal,' 'terrorist,' and 'Muslim' have become inextricably entangled with one another in Euro-American contexts (Wilson and Mavelli 2016, 2). While the state and individuals within the state carry the status of being chosen and possessing a special calling or mission, by implication other states and individuals outside the state do not.

---

[2] It is important to bear in mind the complex, at times antagonistic, at times supportive relationship between particularly Protestant Christianity and Judaism in the USA throughout its history.

4 A Relational Dialogist Approach to the Discursive Study of Religion

There are multiple methods and approaches for engaging in the discursive study of religion within political sciences and IR.[3] In this section, I outline one such approach, the relational dialogist approach, which draws on the work of Raia Prokhovnik and Julia Kristeva. It builds on previous analysis of the ways in which political scientists and IR scholars have understood 'religion,' through a series of binary oppositions. These binary oppositions are: institutional/ideational, individual/communal, and irrational/rational. Dualistic approaches prevalent within political science and IR have predominantly emphasized only one half of each dichotomy, leading to a limited understanding of religion as institutional, individual, and irrational. A relational dialogist understanding of religion considers all six elements equally, as well as adapting and expanding how some of the elements are conceptualized.

Kristeva's engagement with Mikhail Bakhtin's notion of dialogism provides the starting point for this particular discursive approach. Dialogism highlights the ongoing interaction of ideas, emphasizing fluidity and change, rather than rigidity (Kristeva 1986, 39–40). In Kristeva's analysis, dialogism is both "subjectivity and communication." The text is telling a story, describing a series of events, but also communicating with texts and events that have come before and will come after. Kristeva refers to this as intertextuality (39). The aim of dialogism, she argues, is not to arrive at a finite point of understanding and definition, but to strive "toward harmony, all the while implying an idea of rupture (of opposition and analogy) as a modality of transformation" (58). This approach recognizes that ideas are constantly developing and changing. Changes occur through interactions with other ideas within and across texts and historical events. There will be moments of agreement and 'harmony' about what ideas mean and what their implications are for analysis and for broader society. Yet dialogism highlights that such moments are not conclusive. There is always the possibility of shifts and changes in ideas and how they interact, how texts communicate with each other and with broader society.

Dialogism suggests that religion understood as institutional, individual, irrational, and irrelevant to politics and IR is not a fixed permanent definition, but one that will shift through interactions with other ideas. Thus, dialogism refracts established

---

[3] These include, but are not limited to, the so-called 'traditional method,' which focuses on how the language and actions of states are co-constitutive of what we refer to as 'International Relations'; the contextualized approach, which considers these macro-level interactions alongside 'micro contexts and daily practices' that contribute to discursive identity construction, and poststructuralist approaches that not only reconceptualize who is being studied but also how 'discourse' and 'identity' should even be understood within the critical study of discourse in IR. See Godinho 2016–2017, 5.

understandings of religion and politics. Dialogism represents a condition of constant rupture, with few moments of agreement or fixity. This situation is, however, somewhat debilitating. Prokhovnik's model of relational thinking provides a way to move forward from this point. Understanding concepts as existing in relationships provides a way for managing these concepts and using them in practice, all the while remembering that the meaning associated with these terms are infinite and open to change. Using Prokhovnik's relational thought model, connections amongst ideas are understood in much the same way as relationships amongst people, an ever-present, constant component of society yet always containing possibilities for change and a level of uncertainty.

Dualism endeavors to remove this uncertainty by establishing fixed understandings of particular ideas. As part of this process, dualism separates concepts that in fact exist in close relationship with one another. In contrast, Prokhovnik highlights that relational thought seeks to emphasize the connections that exist within these dichotomous pairings, arguing that there are numerous "intellectual and social benefits" in recognizing the relationships that are present both within and across existing dualisms (Prokhovnik 2003, 14). In contrast to dualism's restrictive 'either/or' pattern, relational thought proposes a 'both/and' approach, assisting transcendence of barriers established across existing dualisms.

Prokhovnik's model deals primarily with gender relationships, but translates easily to religion and politics. Politics has been situated within the public sphere of domestic state societies and the public international sphere. Largely since the Peace of Westphalia, religion has been considered a private state affair and within states, a private individual affair (Thomas 2000). Relational thought enables recognition of relationships amongst these traditionally separated dimensions of human activity. Thus, using a relational thought model, it is not a question of whether politics and the public realm should be 'secular' or 'religious.' Elements of both exist within the public political realm and should be recognized as such. The secular and the religious shape and define one another, so that what is considered secular is affected by what is considered religious and vice versa (Asad 2003). Further, regarding religion itself, it is not a question of whether religion is primarily institutional or ideational, primarily individual or communal, primarily 'irrational' or rational. Religion is made up of all six of these elements, and many others besides. At different times and in different contexts, some aspects will be more important to consider and analyze and will have more significant influence on aspects of politics than others, but all should be incorporated into the way in which religion and its relationship with politics are understood within political science and IR.

Combining Kristeva's dialogism and Prokhovnik's relational thought develops a framework that acknowledges connections amongst elements in religion that are not fixed, but are fluid, shifting, and changing as they interact with each other, with other ideas, other texts, and with people's practical experiences, past, present, and future. This opens up possibilities for rethinking and reassessing traditional secularist assumptions about the relationship between religion and politics and the nature of religion that have restricted much international relations analysis on this issue. Below, I highlight some specific words and phrases associated with the six elements of a relational dialogist discursive approach that can be applied to the study of religion in political science and IR.

4.1 Institutional

Four main types of religious institutions are included in this dimension: organized churches, religious lobby groups, religious charity groups and religiously affiliated political parties. The traditional focus on religion's institutional dimension suggests it exercises influence primarily through religious institutions and organizations. Institutional understandings of religion are perhaps the most easily identifiable of all the elements of religion within texts. When writers use words and phrases such as 'church' and 'faith-based organization,' or the name of a specific religious denomination, they tend to refer to the institutional element of religion. Reference to leaders of specific religious institutions or organizations also relates to religion's institutional element. Clearly, though, a primary focus on religion's institutional aspect leads to a neglect of religious traditions and communities where the institutional dimension is less significant or indeed is entirely absent. The dominant focus on institutional religion within political science and IR helps to explain why scholars have, until recently, neglected religion in general and religions beyond Christianity in particular within their analysis.

4.2 Ideational

The ideational element of religion is perhaps the most important of those factors that have been excluded from the dominant political science and IR understanding of religion. The neglect of this dimension has detrimentally affected understandings of the relationship between religion and politics.

'Ideational element' refers to key doctrines or core tenets of the beliefs of a particular religion. These effect how believers interpret, make sense of, and respond to the world around them. Taking Christianity as an example, ideational influences include assumptions relating to the fallen nature of the world (Romans 3:23), the existence of good and evil in an antagonistic relationship (Lewis 2002 [1952], 42), the idea of a Savior or Messiah (McDowell 1993, 248–249), concepts of unmerited grace and mercy (Yancey 1997, esp. chapter 4), the existence of Heaven and Hell (1 Peter 1:4; Matthew 10:28), an eschatological view of world history (Erickson 1998, 1155–1247), resulting in the eventual destruction of the present world and the creation of a new, perfect world (Revelation 20), the division of history into before Christ and after Christ, the idea of being chosen or of possessing a specific calling (stronger in some Christian denominations than in others) (Romans 8: 28–30), and the need for redemption from sin (Lewis 2002 [1952], 55).

Taking the USA as an example, the ideational dimension provides implicit influence on the construction and maintenance of US national identity, interpretations of events in global politics and justifications of US foreign policy. These include references to the USA as the 'city on a hill,' 'the last best hope of mankind [sic],' 'the bearer of the world's burdens,' all of which resonate with ideas about Christ found within the Christian scriptures (Cherry 1971, 21; Wilson 2012, 120). However, this influence often goes unnoticed, because it has become embedded in the "deep culture" of many Euro-American societies, part of the "collectively held subconscious ideas" that underpin what are thought to be "typical patterns of political behaviour" (Galtung 1996, 211; see also Osiander 2000, 762).

The language associated with the ideational element of religion also has close links with the discourse of nationalism. Smith observes "religious traditions, and especially beliefs about the sacred, underpin and suffuse to a greater or lesser degree the national identities of the populations of the constituent states" (Smith 2000, 795). Words such as 'sacrifice,' 'purpose,' 'destiny,' 'mission,' and even ideas of 'favor,' being 'blessed,' and possessing 'responsibility' often carry religious connotations, linking the nation to a deity or supernatural force in powerful ways. Although neither God nor a specific religious tradition may be explicitly referenced, there is an underlying assumption or linkage to a general religious theme. This tacit knowledge can have powerful implications for the social construction of the nation and for the justification of foreign policy.

Considering the long history of Protestant influence in the USA, the connections that words such as 'sacrifice,' 'destiny,' and 'mission' have with the Jewish and Christian traditions are especially important to take into account when exploring religion's influence on US national identity and foreign policy. David Campbell and Michael Barnett's work, discussed previously, highlights further the significant role religion can play in shaping national identity and foreign policy, particularly through such discursive knots. Other words that may also form part of this religion's ideational discursive entanglement are 'faith,' 'belief,' 'unique,' 'special,' 'chosen,' 'devotion,' 'hope,' 'spirit,' 'serve' or 'be of service,' 'devotion,' 'giving,' and especially 'sacrifice.'

While on their own, these words do not necessarily carry religious connotations or indicate a particular instance of religious influence each time they are used, collectively they constitute a powerful discursive knot where religious and nationalist discourses are entangled. Consequently, whether intentionally or not, these words play an important role in constructing a particular understanding of the nation, its role and purpose in world politics and, accordingly, in the justifications employed for certain policy choices and actions.

Building on this, it then becomes possible to determine the ways in which ideas about 'religion' influence the identification and development of options available for state action. Not only does the ideational element of religion influence meaning on its own but, combined with the other five elements, it works in conjunction with nationalism to promote a particular ideology or worldview, opening up certain interpretations of and responses to events in world politics, as well as closing off others. This occurs both consciously at the level of policy development and subconsciously at the level of embedded cultural assumptions.

4.3 Individual

The individual element of religion acknowledges a level of personal involvement or choice in relation to religion. The degree of this personal involvement and choice will vary across specific contexts and religious traditions. It suggests, however, that there is always some component of religious belief that exists within the individual. The individual chooses who and/or what they believe and why. Even if this choice is made on a highly limited basis or in the context of coercion to choose a particular belief system over another, some level of personal, individual agency and engagement exists within religion. Within secularist understandings of religion, the tendency has been to emphasize personal choice, to the extent of almost denying communal, public expressions of religious belief or devaluing the role of community in the development of personal religious beliefs. This preoccupation with individual religious freedom stems in part from the liberal emphasis on the individual and the importance of individual freedom.

The influence of the individual element of religion can be difficult to assess. If religion is mentioned, the text will use words such as 'personal,' 'private,' or 'individual' in conjunction with words mentioned above as possessing ideational connotations – for example 'faith' and 'belief.' Interestingly, though, spirituality, which arguably has less clear connections with institutionalized religions, is not often referenced. This implies that an acknowledgement of the influence of religion's ideational aspects at an individual level is acceptable and even relatively common. It is quite a different matter, however, when the individual concerned holds a public role and the beliefs become public also. The possibility then opens up for religion to influence politics through the personal beliefs of the public individual. This situation is problematic for secular liberal politics, where the separation of church and state is rigorously defended and (at least in theory) enforced. If the public individual has a close affiliation with an organized church or other religious institution, this circumstance becomes even more problematic, since it potentially offers a way for that religious institution to influence politics through its close relationship with the public individual (a concern that affected the presidential campaign of John F. Kennedy and that also arose as part of criticisms of George W. Bush's presidency).

4.4 Communal

The communal element of religion often operates in conjunction with the ideational, contributing to the construction and maintenance of a sense of national community or identity. Although traditionally the communal element of religion operates primarily amongst religious believers, the same effect is transferable to a community established on different grounds. The communal element of religion works to establish a community of believers and/or practitioners, joined together by their beliefs in the same doctrines and/or their participation in the same institutions or rituals. In this way, the communal element of religion is similar to nationalism and other political ideologies that establish a sense of community. It is important to observe, however, that such an understanding of religion's 'communal' aspects reflects the strong influence of Euro-American Protestant Christian religious experiences on the formation of contemporary scholarly approaches.

The communal element of religion is observable within texts in two main ways. Firstly, references to specific religious communities or communal activities focused on religion indicate the influence of the communal element of religion. Bellah (2005) provides several examples of such "public rituals," including national memorial services and prayers. Secondly, the communal element of religion may influence the construction or creation of a community based not on affiliation with a religion or religious group, but through the use of words and symbols implicitly associated with a particular religion. While membership of the group or community is not contingent upon religious beliefs, religious language is used to create a close-knit community. Anthony Smith (2000), Mark Juergensmeyer (2000), and Jeffrey Seul (1999) note religious communal language is often used in the construction of national identity. Religion contributes to the creation of communities through shared values, norms, customs and practices. Religion also provides a shared sense of heritage, history and of direction and purpose for the future. Juergensmeyer and Seul (ibid.) both note that religion can link individuals and communities to an identity and destiny that exists outside of the boundaries of time and space. As such, whether it is claimed by or assigned to individuals and groups, religion is a powerful marker of individual and collective identity. This second function of the communal element of religion is again demonstrated in the 'civil religion' of the USA (Bellah 2005). Affiliation with a theistic religion is not imperative for membership in the American civil religious community but the language of religion, and of a particular type of religion (predominantly Protestant Christianity, with some elements of Judaism) is still utilized to create that sense of community and belonging.

The same words that indicate religion's ideational influence are often used to construct a community, especially when used in conjunction with references to the collective (for example 'we,' 'our,' 'America' or 'the United States,' 'the West,' 'Western civilization'). Ideas of destiny and purpose as well as shared values and goals are powerful ways through which religion contributes to the development of a community.

This, too, has strong links to nationalism. Yet these ideas are also used to create a sense of community that extends beyond the borders of the nation-state. Through its relationship with otherworldliness and its capacity to transcend political borders, religious language has the capacity to create a sense of community that extends beyond the confines of time and space. As Smith (2000, 795–796) has highlighted, nationalism can operate in the same way, with members of nationalist groups and populations believing they are part of an historical legacy and building an eternal future. As such, there is arguably a continuation of discourse from different locations in society – religious to political and back again – stabilizing and supporting one another in a co-dependent relationship. Much of this imagery is borrowed from religion. The ideational and the communal elements of religion may also be utilized to construct an idea of community that goes across borders. Political leaders attempt to do this during times of conflict so as to clearly identify the states that are allies and those that are enemies. Examples of this include the Franklin Roosevelt's references to the United Nations in opposition to the axis powers in World War II during his 1942 State of the Union, and uses of terms such as 'Western' civilizational identity or the 'free world' in opposition to communism by US political elites during the Cold War (for more detailed discussion of these, see Wilson 2012, chapter 5).

4.5 Irrational

The irrational and rational elements of religion are the most problematic of all six elements of a relational dialogist approach to religion. Both 'irrational' and 'rational' are highly contested (and highly gendered) terms. There is much debate over what is deemed 'irrational' and 'rational' and what criteria are used to decide this. More importantly, however, irrational and rational form a central component of how religion and its relationship with politics in Euro-American contexts have been understood, regardless of how contested both terms are. Rational and irrational are categories that emerge out of a secularist worldview, whereas religion itself holds a completely different understanding of the world. Understanding it as a different world entirely from that viewed from a secular perspective may in fact be more accurate (Blaser 2013; Wilson 2017a). A 'religious' ontological perspective may hold that belief in God and/or life outside the natural, physical realm is not 'irrational' but is entirely logical, plausible, and 'rational.' Describing religion as 'non-rational' rather than irrational, as is the practice of some authors in an effort to acknowledge this difference in perspective, is also not entirely satisfactory. Such an approach still privileges the secularist worldview by describing religion as simply being something that is not rational. Perhaps the most helpful perspective is that of Immanuel Kant, who suggested that religious faith was in fact *beyond* the limitations of human reason (Bernstein 2009, 1037), making it neither rational nor irrational, but something else entirely. Alternatives exist, such as replacing 'irrational' and 'rational' with 'spiritual, emotional, physical, and cognitive rationalities,' also with their own obvious shortcomings. Thus, 'rational' and 'irrational,' like all the other components of the relational dialogist understanding of religion, should not be seen as fixed permanent categories, but rather as temporary terms within one approach that is endeavoring to move us away from a conceptual bias in favor of secularism towards different ways of thinking about the world that allow greater space for religion.

The 'irrational' element, or strand, of religion discourse operates both on its own and in conjunction with other strands to influence interpretations and representations of events in world politics. The irrational element of religion refers to the potential for justifying thoughts, policies, and actions, whether personal or in relation to the nation as a whole, through the use of 'transcendental' or 'otherworldly' ideas or doctrines. In liberal Enlightenment terms, such justifications are 'irrational' because they are not based in human reason alone but rely on belief in a higher being or in some other reality that is not demonstrable in this world. The liberal secular emphasis on the irrational element of religion is perhaps the least obvious yet most pervasive of the three traditionally emphasized elements of religion in IR. The irrationality of religion has not always been explicitly stated in studies that have considered religion. However, until the post-Cold War era, the majority of IR scholars did not engage with religion at all, largely as a result of religion's assumed irrationality (Fox 2001, 55–56). The lack of reference to religion in texts, then, is indicative of religion's presumed irrationality and the need to exclude religion from politics and public life.

Yet, the irrational elements of religion have also been and continue to be significant influences in politics and public life. This is in part because the elements of religion that are generally viewed as irrational by liberal scholars are highly effective tools in the construction of identity, especially national identity. The irrational element of religion is particularly useful in the construction of categories of 'self' and 'other.'

An author or speaker may utilize irrational linguistic characteristics of religion to construct a particular interpretation of actors and events in world politics that represents identity in terms of self and other, privileges certain courses of action over others, and leaves little room for negotiation or compromise. These linguistic characteristics of religion include highly emotive language, intolerance, advocating violence, and open discussion of spirituality (for example, referring to God, Satan, evil, demons, and angels; George W. Bush's infamous use of the term "axis of evil" in his 2002 State of the Union is a clear example; see Juergensmeyer 2000, 171–172).

4.6 Rational

The rational element of religion is highly complex for a variety of reasons. Liberal secular observers hold that religious belief is incompatible with rationalism because at some level, religion requires the implementation of faith (which itself betrays a narrow understanding of 'religion' amongst liberal secularists). Faith is considered unreliable (Eberle 2002, 313–314), viewed as directly contrasting with rationalism. Rationalism focuses on those things that can be observed and for which significant evidence exists to support their reality, without the need to exercise faith. Thus, because accepting the existence of God, for example, must, at some point, occur on the basis of faith, liberal secular rational enquiry cannot acknowledge God's existence.[4]

The position of religious thinkers on this issue is quite different, largely because they do not view belief in God as irrational (or even necessary). The late Pope John Paul II articulated this view in his letter to the bishops on the relationship between faith and reason (John Paul II 1998). According to this view, any rational search for truth and reason must begin and end with God. The argument is based on the belief that God is omnipotent and therefore it is only through knowing God that humans can begin to understand and know themselves and the world they live in. Pope Benedict XVI reiterated this view, arguing that faith and reason are not mutually exclusive, but rather compliment and complete one another (Zenit Catholic News Service 2007).

Eberle (2002, 313–314) has highlighted that the assumptions surrounding the acceptability of secular grounds over religious grounds, by secular political science and IR scholars particularly, are misleading. He argues: "'secular' connotes 'natural' and 'universal', whereas 'religious' connotes 'supernatural' and 'particular'" (313). He goes on to observe, however, that 'secular' justifications for particular beliefs, values, and principles are not universal and natural, but are in many cases culturally specific. Social scientists, including political scientists and IR scholars, argue that secular grounds are the only acceptable justifications because they are rational and universal. Yet, as Eberle points out, secular grounds are seen to be rational and universal precisely because they are made within a particular cultural setting that establishes secular thought as rational, universal, and acceptable. "Secular grounds, then, are cultural grounds, grounds we find plausible, in large part, because we have been socialized into one culture and not another" (314). Thus, Eberle suggests, there are problems with valuing the secular over the religious that may lead to errors in public political decisions, particularly decisions concerning public ethics and morality (316).

Eberle's broad critique of secular assumptions in liberal society supports Elizabeth Shakman Hurd's more specific arguments regarding IR. Hurd (2008, 14) suggests that secularism "is a normative formation that is widely perceived as legitimate" part of the broader set of assumptions within IR that drive how political authority and state action are understood and deemed legitimate or illegitimate. "Secularism produces

---

[4] This debate about the existence of God is a foundational debate in the traditional form of philosophy of religion, which itself is challenged by contemporary debates in the same field incorporating post-colonial and feminist critique.

authoritative settlements of religion and politics, while simultaneously claiming to be exempt from this process of production. This is a formidable exercise of power" (16). Following on from Hurd's observation, secularism produces an 'authoritative settlement' concerning what is 'rational' and common sense as well as determining what is 'irrational.' Secularism produces these authoritative settlements because of its assumed universality and rationality which, as Eberle noted, are in fact culturally embedded, particular assumptions about the nature of secularism (2002, 314). This again calls into question traditional categories of 'rational' and 'irrational.'

While these differences are potentially unresolvable, this does not necessarily hinder analysis, as both secular and theological interpretations of the rational element of religion are pertinent to the discursive study of religion in politics and IR. From a theological perspective, when a text acknowledges the existence of God and the importance of religious faith, it is a manifestation of the rational element of religion, although from a liberal secular perspective, this may be perceived as influence from the irrational element of religion. Consequently, references to God may be classified as both irrational and rational, consistent with the both-and approach of relational dialogism.

From a secular perspective, the rational element of religion manifests when authors of texts utilize calls for tolerance, peace, 'do unto others,' generosity to the poor, respect for authority and the law, equality, even discussions of sovereignty and the separation of church and state. All of these references reflect the more rational teachings of various religious traditions. Many secular thought traditions also promote these values. In some situations, it is possible to argue that these value commitments are also not 'rational,' since they may go against the self-interest of the state. As such, I suggest that these values should also be classified as both 'rational' and 'irrational.' Such classification is also important in order to avoid falling into the trap of characterizing religion as only 'good' or 'bad.'

5 Contributions of Discursive Analysis to the Study of the Power Politics of Religion in Political Science and IR

The discursive study of religion within political sciences and IR has opened up significant avenues for analysis and understanding previously unacknowledged within these fields. Discursive analysis of religion has contributed to more nuanced understandings of the ways in which different identity markers are entangled and molded by a variety of actors across different contexts and policy issues, including conflict, migration, climate change, humanitarianism, trade, and gender (Wilson 2017a; 2017b). One of the most significant areas where concern with the discourse of religion has contributed is in analysis of the right to freedom of religion or belief and the politics surrounding who is able to claim this right and who is not (Hurd 2015; Gruell and Wilson 2018), and how emphasis on this right by different actors can have entirely different and at times contradictory meanings (Castelli 2007; Gruell and Wilson 2018). In other words, the discursive study of religion has enabled the recognition of yet another dimension to power politics in political science and International Relations: the power politics of religion.

References

Agensky, Jonathan. 2017. "Recognizing Religion: Politics, History and the 'Long 19th Century.'" *European Journal of International Relations* 23 (4): 729–755.
Appleby, Scott. 2000. *The Ambivalence of the Sacred: Religion, Violence and Reconciliation*. Lanham, MD, USA: Rowman and Littlefield.
Asad, Talal. 2003. *Formations of the Secular: Christianity, Islam, Modernity*. Stanford: Stanford University Press.
Barnett, Michael. 1999. "Culture, Strategy and Foreign Policy Change: Israel's Road to Oslo." *European Journal of International Relations* 5 (1): 5–36.
Bellah, Robert. 2005. "Civil Religion in America." *Daedalus* 134 (4): 40–55.
Bernstein, Richard J. 2009. "The Secular-Religious Divide: Kant's Legacy." *Social Research* 76 (4): 1035–1048.
Blaser, Mario. 2013. "Ontological Conflicts and the Stories of Peoples in Spite of Europe: Towards a Conversation on Political Ontology." *Cultural Anthropology* 54 (5): 547–568.
Campbell, David. 1998. *Writing Security: United States Foreign Policy and the Politics of Identity*. Minneapolis: University of Minnesota Press.
Carr, Edward Hallett. 1946. *The Twenty Years' Crisis 1919–1939: An Introduction to the Study of International Relations*. London: Macmillan.
Castelli, Elizabeth. 2007. "Theologizing Human Rights: Christian Activism and the Limits of Religious Freedom." In *Non-Governmental Politics*, edited by Michel Feher with Gaëlle Krikorian and Yates McKee, 673–687. New York: Zone Books.
Cherry, Conrad. 1971. "Introduction," in *God's New Israel: Religious Interpretations of American Destiny*, edited by Conrad Cherry, 1–24. Englewood Cliffs: Prentice Hall.
Eberle, Christopher. J. 2002. *Religious Conviction in Liberal Politics*. Cambridge: Cambridge University Press.
Erickson, Millard J. 1998. *Christian Theology*. Second Edition. Grand Rapids: Baker Books.
Foucault, Michel. 1996. "The Order of Things." In *Foucault Live: Interviews 1961–84*, edited by Sylvere Lotringer, 13–18. New York: Semiotext(e).
Fox, Jonathan. 2001. "Religion as an Overlooked Element of International Relations." *International Studies Review* 3 (3): 53–73.
Galtung, Johan. 1996. *Peace by Peaceful Means: Peace and Conflict, Development and Civilization*. London: Sage Publications.
Godinho, Luisa. 2016–2017. "Discourse and International Relations: A Theoretical and Methodological Approach." *Janus: E-Journal of International Relations* 7 (6): 1–13.
Gruell, Christoph, and Erin K. Wilson. 2018. "Universal or Particular? Or Both? Understanding the Right to Freedom of Religion or Belief in Cross-Cultural Perspective." *Review of Faith and International Affairs* 16 (4): 88–101.

Hurd, Elizabeth Shakman. 2008. *The Politics of Secularism in International Relations*. Princeton: Princeton University Press.

Hurd, Elizabeth Shakman. 2015. *Beyond Religious Freedom: The New Global Politics of Religion*. Princeton: Princeton University Press.

John Paul II (Pope). 1998. "Fides et Ratio (Faith and Reason)." *Encyclical Letter of the Supreme Pontiff John Paul II to the Bishops of the Catholic Church on the Relationship Between Faith and Reason*, available online at http://w2.vatican.va/content/john-paul-ii/en/encyclicals/documents/hf_jp-ii_enc_14091998_fides-et-ratio.html (accessed 5 December 2018).

Juergensmeyer, Mark. 2000. *Terror in the Mind of God: The Global Rise of Religious Violence*. Los Angeles: University of California Press.

Kristeva, Julia. 1986. "Word, Dialogue and Novel." In *The Kristeva Reader*, edited by Toril Moi, 34–61. New York: Columbia University Press.

Lewis, Clive Staples. 2002 [1952]. *Mere Christianity*. London: Harper Collins.

Mamdani, Mahmood. 2004. *Good Muslim, Bad Muslim: America, the Cold War and the Roots of Terror*. New York: Doubleday.

Mattern, Janice Bially. 2001. "The Power Politics of Identity." *European Journal of International Relations* 7 (3): 349–397.

McDowell, Josh. 1993. *A Ready Defense*. Nashville: Thomas Nelson.

Milliken, Jennifer. 1999. "The Study of Discourse in International Relations: A Critique of Research Methods." *European Journal of International Relations* 5 (2): 225–254.

Morgenthau, Hans J. and Kenneth W. Thompson. 1985. "Politics Among Nations: The Struggle for Power and Peace" New York: Knopf.

Osiander, Andreas. 2000. "Religion and Politics in Western Civilisation: The Ancient World as Matrix and Mirror of the Modern." *Millennium* 29 (3): 251–287.

Philpott, Daniel. 2002. "The Challenge of September 11 to Secularism in International Relations." *World Politics* 55 (1): 66–95.

Prokhovnik, Raia. 2003. "Rational Woman: A Feminist Critique of Dichotomy" Manchester and New York: Manchester University Press.

Seul, Jeffrey R. 1999. "'Ours in the Way of God': Religion, Identity, and Intergroup Conflict." *Journal of Peace Research* 36 (5): 553–569.

Shapiro, Michael J. 1989. "Representing World Politics: The Sport/War Intertext." In *International/Intertextual Relations: Postmodern Readings of World Politics*, edited by James Der Derian and Michael J. Shapiro, 69–96. Lexington: Lexington Books.

Smith, Anthony D. 2000. "The 'Sacred' Dimension of Nationalism." *Millennium* 29 (3): 791–814.

Snyder, Craig A. 1999. "Contemporary Security and Strategy." In *Contemporary Security and Strategy*, edited by Craig A. Snyder, 1–12. London: Macmillan.

Strenski, Ivan. 2010. *Why Politics Can't Be Freed from Religion*. Chichester: Wiley-Blackwell.

Thomas, Scott M. 2000. "Taking Religion and Cultural Pluralism Seriously: The Global Resurgence of Religion and the Transformation of International Society." *Millennium* 29 (3): 815–841.

Waltz, Kenneth N. 1959. "Man, The State and War: A Theoretical Analysis" New York: Columbia University Press.

Weldes, Jutta and Diana Saco. 1996. "Making State Action Possible: The United States and the Discursive Construction of 'The Cuban Problem', 1960 –1994." *Millennium* 25 (2): 361–395.

Wilson, Erin K. 2012. *After Secularism: Rethinking Religion in Global Politics*. London: Palgrave Macmillan.

Wilson, Erin K. 2017a. "'Power Differences' and 'the Power of Difference': The Dominance of Secularism as Ontological Injustice." *Globalizations* 14 (7): 1076–1093.

Wilson, Erin K. 2017b. "The Socio-Political Dynamics of Secularism and Epistemological Injustice in Global Justice Theory and Practice." *European Societies* 19 (5): 529–550.

Wilson, Erin K. and Luca Mavelli. 2016. "The Refugee Crisis and Religion: Beyond Conceptual and Physical Boundaries." In *The Refugee Crisis and Religion: Secularism, Security and Hospitality in Question*, edited by L. Mavelli and Erin K. Wilson, 1–22. London: Rowman and Littlefield International.

Yancey, Philip. 1997. *What's So Amazing About Grace?* Grand Rapids: Zondervan.

Zenit Catholic News Service. 2007 (28 January). "Angelus: On the Faith-Reason Synthesis – A Precious Patrimony for Western Civilization." Zenit – the World Seen from Rome. Online available at http://www.zenit.org/english Code: ZE07012804 (accessed 29 January 2007).

Guy Redden
Religion, Discourse, and the Economy Question: Fraught Issues in Market Societies

As Dominique Maingueneau notes in this volume, discourse analysis of religion poses the problem of exactly how to achieve the main aim of discourse analysis, which is linking the linguistic and the social. Discerning the social significance of religious discourses involves particular challenges because – unlike those related to other institutional domains such as politics, media, education, or law, those concerning theological and supernatural matters can less readily be seen to convey representations of the social. And yet, religion, like science, is simultaneously an 'ultimate discourse' that rationalizes the foundations of society. It is deeply concerned with life and how it may be lived. Maingueneau avers that drawing upon utterances produced under particular circumstances it responds to the demands for sense from people who are always put in new situations.

Maingueneau's account captures my interest in religion as a cultural studies scholar. From a Foucauldian viewpoint there is no social institution or practice that does not involve sense making and the discourses through which it operates. Religion is living culture that responds to its surrounding world, even when it does so in a heuristic relationship with authoritative texts produced in other social settings (Bailey and Redden 2011). Interpreting its contemporary significance is an alluring prospect because as Bové (1992) points out, discourse analysis in the Foucauldian approach highlights the historical specificity of languages, their truth claims, and their institutional production. This means that ultimate discourses that offer universal principles or assert the ahistorical essence of states of affairs may be open to a certain kind of scrutiny through the interpretation of ways that they depend upon historical contingencies and institutional settings.

In this chapter, I narrow this frame to consider ways in which religious discourses (and discourses about religion) might be contingent upon economic relations and languages. However, this is not a straightforward enterprise. If religion has generally been neglected in discourse analytic circles as Maingueneau argues, its discursive imbrications with the economic are even more marginal to inquiry. Work in this area faces an additional fundamental problem, which is the influence of longstanding depictions of economy and religion as distinctively incompatible spheres. For Fitzgerald (2007), since its inception economics has been seen as a secular rationalist modern discourse held in contradistinction to religion, thus helping to reinforce the idea that the two are separate fields and only 'externally,' rather than constitutively, connected. Work advocating close attention to relationships between religion and economy risks upsetting such received ideas that each has its special logics that do not reduce to the terms of the other. And this situation is compounded by the success of economics in developing abstract models about the efficient allocation of resources that have considerable appeal to business and government elites, meaning that the contemporary discipline has little need for cross-disciplinary engagements (Fourcade, Ollion and Algan 2015).

The impasse seems a powerful one. A tradition of thinking about religion that disembeds it from the worldly economy is on one side, and a contemporary discipline that disembeds languages about the economy from those other disciplines is on the other. Indeed, the discursive study of the relationships between the religious and economic is inchoate, and has been approached in various and often incomplete or controversial ways.

However, before surveying some of these to indicate possible approaches, I would propose that scholars of religion should take the potential of questions about economy seriously, and that we can take inspiration from other disciplines in doing so. Not only do religious discourses respond to the economic dimensions of society and languages concerning them to help members of religious communities make sense of the world. Contemporary economic relations can also be expected to have some kind of bearing upon the ways religious discourses are produced and the forms that they take. The broad revival of interest in economy outside economics in fields such as economic sociology, economic geography, and cultural economy give some pointers as to how such issues can be broached.

From the 1980s the new economic sociology responded to the imagined disembedding of the economy from society that had been effected by economics, emphasizing instead that economic and social action and structures overlap at multiple scales (Granovetter 1985). The premise that actors act and are situated both socially and economically through the *same networks* created different ways to understand the interconnection of between the apparently separate realms. Meanwhile, the new field of cultural economy emerged in the late 1990s as the 'cultural turn' finally addressed economic issues. This was partly driven by the apparent culturalization of the economy in a consumer/information society where extensive symbolic components are discursively attached to goods via media and marketing, plus the increased commodification of cultural and leisure practices through which people seek personal meaning. But it was also sparked by the view that the economic itself is not a stable independent realm, but subject to modification by the performative power of discourses that are applied to, rationalize and shape economic action (Du Gay and Pryke 2002).

A mark of this recent work is refusal to accept the reification of markets or 'the economy' as though they operate through ahistorical principles or purely through their own logics sequestered from other influences. Instead it suggests that while heuristically there will always be some necessary separation of the constructs of economy, culture and society, in practice they interpenetrate each other. Theoretically this recognizes the possibility of multidirectional influences: economic relations can have an impact on discourses, and discourses can have an impact on economic relations, and a priori neither the discourses nor the relations are purely social, cultural, or economic. Take, for instance, how these dimensions converge in tourism, now the world's largest international trade, which accounts for 10.4% of global GDP. The industry centers upon symbolic production of representations that spur people to experience places and cultures as part of personal biographical narratives that involve numerous kinds of activities and social encounters.

If then religion is also living culture that shifts in form and language, and religious institutions are social ones, analysis that brings in the economy question has great potential to contribute to the new social and cultural disciplinary engagements with economy. But in order to do so it must it interrogate received meanings around religion and the economic in order to open up inquiry into the historically specific range of forms either could take in relation to each other. Currently, conversations among scholars of religion are too often hamstrung by undertheorized preconceptions that associate the sacred with higher orders of value seen as fundamentally incompatible with somewhat limited conceptions of the economic as a pecuniary realm of purely instrumental values such as accumulation of wealth and profit-seeking (Redden 2016).

Paradoxical as it may sound, a possible starting point for cultural economy of religion that refuses such simplistic distinctions might be to acknowledge that all religion is *inherently* economic. All action has an economic basis as it requires that resources necessary to act be available to actors, and this can only take place if those resources are distributed through socially organized production and distribution, and discourses that articulate them. While 'economics' today has become a language dominated by concerns about maximizing income and wealth, the broader idea of economy refers at root to any allocation of resources in society. *How* such allocation happens is always changing and how it should happen, open to interpretation. The systematic study of economy started when thinkers including Smith, Riccardo, and Marx considered how relationships between factors of production – including land, capital, and labor – may be arranged with various possible consequences. Today, however, resources in question are increasingly intangible, driven by the investment of capital in information technologies and the transformation of wages into expanded markets of symbolically differentiated goods through which consumers may make lifestyle choices.

Here then we may be able to start to identify some of the dimensions of economy imbricated with contemporary religion in a consumer society that involves much marketing of informational, symbolic and experiential goods.

1 Commodification and Marketization

It should come as little surprise that most research into religion and the economic is structured around the question of change, particularly concerning how the emergence of particular kinds of commerce might alter religion and its significance. The cover image of Steve Bruce's book *God is Dead* (2002) captures what happens when the accumulated wealth of religious organizations seems insufficient to offset the decline in their ability to garner resources necessary to maintain scale and influence: churches get converted into carpet superstores. For Bruce, such developments articulate the onward march of secularization: the shared meaning systems of religion that used to bind communities together and effect the related mobilization of resources for their institutional prominence are in apparently terminal decline. However, others stress that the economic basis of religion is itself changing, and new conceptions of religious activity have been generated with the rapid emergence of the disciplines of business and marketing (see Redden 2016). The key insight of such work is that in the modern world religion is increasingly imbricated with activity that would normally be categorized as commercial, calling into question settled notions about the separation of the sacred and profane (Durkheim 2012; Eliade 1959).

Before examining some of those perspectives, in order to take some first steps towards thinking about what difference 'commercialization' might make in the spiritual realm it is necessary to define commodification and marketization because an apparent the shift towards them is largely at stake. From norms for sharing food, tools and work in small-scale tribal structures to specialized, financialized, and high-tech markets of contemporary global capitalism, exchange of goods and services is universal to human life. But from Marcel Mauss onwards, economic anthropology has theorized the implications of different ways of conducting exchange. As Mauss (2002) showed, gift exchange – in which no immediate and direct return for resources distributed is expected – is common in communities distinguished by ongoing relationships among people that allow for reciprocation over time. However, commodity exchange with direct compensation allows reciprocation to be completed at the time of the transaction, and thus fosters the expansion of markets for exchange between strangers (Carrier 1991).

In most societies, things accorded a special aura such as sacred items are often considered the least exchangeable: saleability suggests commonness (Kopytoff 1986, 69). Indeed, the particular contemporary issue of cultural appropriation of spiritual traditions largely revolves around the threat to their sacred value for custodian communities when they become distributed more widely through commodity exchange (Redden 2012). Historically speaking religions have rarely been principally organized through markets – the social institutions through which commodity exchange is routinely conducted, but which may also vary, for instance, between different kinds of barter and money economies. Markets are themselves historically variable arrangements through which information flows, goods are circulated and people act in ways amenable to exchange transactions (Garcia-Parpet 2007).

A key contemporary challenge is to grapple with the apparent oxymoron that religion now appears routinely to be 'for sale' in *some kind* of marketplace, and what this might mean. Religious items may literally be for sale in the form of religious commodities exchanged between their producers and consumers via money economies. But it may also mean that institutional practices and discourses of commerce (such as marketing and finance) ingress into existing religious organizations in social environments where making choices between brands and commodities has become normalized as a mode of action for populations. Given that religion is a sphere of production in which symbolic goods play a vital role in institutional power to define the meaning and conduct of life, for discourse scholars this raises complex questions about potential economic influences upon the formation of religious languages, when religion 'comes to market.'

2 The Spiritual Marketplace

Although there is hardly yet a field of religious economy in which scholars debate related theories, there are multiple discourses on the market turn in religion. In one of the more influential accounts of recent religious change, Wade Clark Roof (1999) emphasized (on the basis of extensive interviewing in the U.S.) the contemporary pursuit of self-realization through the kind of religious questing that is "facilitated by the rise of an expanded spiritual marketplace" (10). According to Roof, in a religious market situation the "new spiritual suppliers" (inside and outside of religious establishments) "take religious pluralism for granted and play to themes of choice, individuality, and the desirability of a cultivated, spiritually sensitive self" (91). On the flipside people increasingly act as 'seekers' less interested in received obligatory traditional religious affiliations than exploration through choosing what is right for them from the range of symbolic options.

For Roof (1999), it is not the case that there is a single kind of response to such a pluralized scene – some may move from option to option frequently while others may commit to one in a fundamentalist fashion – but the inevitability of choice and its personal nature form the common element. Not only can, in this view the religious scene of the later twentieth century be characterized as a consumer marketplace, but crucially, in Roof's argument, markets have certain qualities that influence religion. Above all, when free from coercive forces, they give authority to individuals who become arbiters of their fortunes, while providers fashion spiritual messages through an expanded range of media to attract their attention. In other words, markets are consistent with individualization and expression of subjective preferences. In such a situation, diverse suppliers come to cater for niches symbolically representing seekers' different needs, consumer expectations and desires in ways that vary from the controlled discourses of traditional religions, further embedding the pluralization tendencies (Roof 1999, 109).

3 Economics of Religion

This is also a key insight of what has become termed 'the economics of religion,' which has been one of the most significant theoretical approaches to the study of religion in recent decades. However, unlike Roof, whose arguments are based on observations of the Baby Boomer generation in the United States, proponents suggest *all* religious phenomena can be understood by modeling them as following patterns of economic exchange. Pioneers in the field such as Stark, Bainbridge, Finke and Iannaccone (see Stark and Bainbridge 1996; Stark and Finke 2000; Iannaccone 1998) have applied fundamental concepts of economics to explain the social and behavioral dynamics of religion.

In this view, its forms are attributable to the balance between supply and demand. People are seen to desire religious goods, but, consistent with neoclassical economics, they are also considered to do so in line with subjective preferences. From this premise the most well-known prediction of the economic approach is that religion flourishes when a range of providers are permitted to compete in order to meet the diverse forms that demand may take. The high levels of religious participation in the United States – often taken as a country closest to the ideal of a free religious market – is used as empirical evidence for this claim, which, in turn is the basis for a critique of secularization theory. The apparent decline of religion in Europe is seen to result from the smothering of pluralism by state-backed religions that fail to cater to religious choice adequately. Thus, the decline of religion in some places is thought to be a local supply failure caused by the quintessentially economic problem of market monopoly – and not an expression of an irreversible decline in the religiosity of populations.

One assumption of such views is that *underlying* demand for religion is stable. In an influential essay that predates the formation of the economics approach from the 1980s onwards, Azzi and Ehrenberg (1975) propose that religion offers people three distinctive kinds of goods: spiritual goods (personal edification), social goods (secondary benefits of belonging to a religious community) and afterlife goods (metaphysical and ontological assurances). Religions are seen to offer specific combinations of them and, insofar as social environments allow freedom of choice, followers seek access to the benefits religious options offer in ways that maximize personal utility (Iannaccone 1998, 1479).

In other words, an individualistic economistic view of action, usually labeled 'rational choice,' underlies the theory. People (both providers and followers) are seen as motivated by rewards and expected to bear only certain reasonable costs (use of personal resources) in pursuing them. Where the balance of rewards and costs makes sense to actors a rational choice is possible and an exchange between producers and consumers is likely to take place. In this way, religious providers are seen to act like any other business that caters to people's needs in the marketplace. Discursive aspects include the ways that providers make their offers to people, catering to specifically religious needs while addressing other needs that consumers could satisfy from non-religious providers. In this sense then, religious education rivals secular, making certain kinds of claims about the moral cultivation of children, and church services can be expected to provide entertainment (such as drama and music) to rival that on offer in theatres, and recreation services that rival country clubs and tourism (Iannaccone and Bainbridge 2010, 462).

Much work in the field highlights how *different* personal, social, and afterlife goods are linked to expectations around costs and benefits among followers. These varying cost-benefit calculations can be said to explain the emergence of organizations that configure religion in different ways. However, these are not confined only to 'consumerist' or entertainment discourses of mainstream groups that permit lighter touch participation and seek to attract involvement and voluntary monetary contribution. The economic model extends to sects that provide goods in the form of high levels of belonging and doctrinal certainty in exchange for deep follower discipline and time/labor commitment. This means that the discursive implications are different from those of Roof's conception of spiritual marketplace, which emphasize individualism and quasi-religious spiritual registers of languages catering for a generation of consumer seekers. Indeed, unlike doctrinally flexible and experimental cults, strict sects seem inimical to modern consumerist sensibilities and instead make doctrinal offers of benefits very different from the seeker model – for instance that deprivation and restriction of personal freedom pay greater dividends in an afterlife (Stark and Bainbridge 1980).

4 A Secularized Marketplace?

Critics suggest that advocates of rational choice approaches read largely unsupported presuppositions of economics onto religion while cherry picking weak, often U.S.-centric, data sets for empirical back up (Bruce 2014). The economics of religion can also be considered an example of the hegemony of neoliberalism through supposing that market models replace other ways of thinking that consider the range of historical, cultural and social factors that shape society (McKinnon 2013). Indeed, it is effectively the universalistic application to religion of a historically specific neoliberal discourse about free-markets, utility maximization, and competition.

But advocates of secularization theory have *also* used market models to construct arguments contrary to the economics of religion approach. Instead they have suggested that increased resemblances between religion and consumer markets over recent decades indicate the dilution of belief and the collapse in the authority of religion itself. Peter Berger (in earlier work) argued that religion in general with the demise of religious monopolies, has increasingly come to follow market-style dynamics.

In a 1963 paper, Berger uses market metaphors to describe the promotional strategies of Christian denominations that sought members from a suburban U.S. population "that is highly mobile, highly literate, and highly selective in its patterns of consumption" (79). Such people could not be expected to have denominational loyalties as a matter of course. Hence, in attempting to recruit worshippers denominations faced challenges similar to "those faced by organizations marketing more secular commodities" (83). In the absence of state funding, the need to recruit (and therefore promote) was integral to the survival of these organizations. Berger describes how, under these circumstances, co-operation and rivalry between denominations followed market dynamics. On the one hand, there were advantages in interdenominational co-operation (to the extent that some 'mergers' took place) and in ecumenism, which defined an established group of denominations that would appeal to a mainstream suburban constituency. Yet, on the other, and partly as a consequence of the product standardization effects of co-operation, there was a need for each denomination to establish a unique profile that could be identified by consumers from this range of options, i.e. marginal symbolic differentiation of products took place as required by marketing. Each church sought to market a unique "denominational image" through their publicity (89). Though Berger adds the qualification that market forces do not override all other considerations – doctrinal commitments within denominations still provided discursive limits to the "packaging" of image (90).

According to Berger, the ability of people to choose affiliations cedes power to the religious consumer, and religious groups must accept this reduction in their symbolic authority and engage in marketing in order to remain current (1973, 142–149). Berger's sometime academic collaborator, Thomas Luckmann, also applies market metaphors in his concept of the 'invisible religion.' In 1967 he made the contention that:

> The social form of religion emerging in modern industrial societies is characterized by the direct accessibility of an assortment of religious representations to potential consumers. The sacred cosmos is mediated neither through a specialised domain of religious institutions nor through other primary public institutions. It is the direct accessibility of the sacred cosmos, more precisely, through an assortment of religious themes, which makes religion today essentially a phenomenon of the "private sphere." (1967, 103)

For Luckman, religion is marked by ever-shrinking transcendences as the sacred becomes less about large metaphysical claims than commensurate with secular lifestyle options for self-development (1996). For Berger, rather than expressing the kinds of obligation that are required for societies to be led by religion, "religious institutions have accommodated themselves to the moral and therapeutic 'needs' of the individual" (Berger 1973, 150). In this view, in polar opposition to the economics approach, religion catering to private preferences of the individual is a sign of its effective demise as its languages merge with secular expectations of market societies.

5 Postmodern Consumerism?

Yet, not all outside the economics of religion camp suggest that religious pluralism and consumerism denote the declining social importance of religion. Another interpretation is that they demonstrate its adaptability to changing social contexts. David Lyon (2000) argues that the consuming of religion should not be mistaken for social insignificance. Instead the increase in 'private' chosen belief that leads to religious pluralism should be understood as consistent with the social centrality of both consumerism and pluralized media to 'postmodernity.' In other words, tailoring of religion to consumer searches for personal meaning and experience is precisely significant because of the increasing organization of society around such norms. In developing this position Lyon agrees with much of what Berger argues about the religious marketplace, but denies it constitutes secularization. Instead the idea that religion is socially significant only when it binds groups of people to a single orthodoxy through its hold over public institutions is seen as erroneous as it takes one form it may have in particular socio-historical formation as the standard for all religion. And this concern with the historical specificity of market-like religiosity is also what differentiates his argument from economics of religion approaches.

The notion that consumption has superseded production as the central organizing principle of capitalist economy plays a key role in theories of postmodern and post-industrial society (Slater 1997, 174–176). Economic growth is increasingly driven by the *creation* of new and novel opportunities for consumption, rather than expanding capacity to produce existing products. Among the consequences of this shift have been changes in the symbolic dimension of capitalism, with the proliferation of promotional discourses that construct meanings throughout contemporary media for varied commodities on offer. Another has been the intrusion of commercial relations into an increasing number of aspects of social life that were previously organized through redistributive and gift economies (Keat et al. 1994, 5). In short, in a consumer society, more and more things are brought to the marketplace including experiential services, leisure and aesthetic practices, and commodities become inscribed with cultural meaning in becoming part of people's lifestyles and life narratives (McCracken 1986).

It is widely accepted among theorists of consumer culture that "the search for self-identity is a key determinant of postmodern consumption" (Elliot and Wattanasuwan) in an environment where goods and services are symbolically imbued not only with functional utility, but with the imagined power to transform consumers lives towards idealized states. Advertising often plays upon how a product supposedly fits with idealized identifications of persons and their lifestyles – products are presented as vehicles of self-realization. According to T. J. Jackson Lears (2000) the idea that they are means to therapeutic outcomes for the consumer first became pervasive in the marketing cultures of the late nineteenth and early twentieth centuries. It can therefore be said that consumer culture shares a broad affinity with religion: a focus on representations of the *good in life* and claims that practices (consumerist or religious) provide the key to unlocking it.

In this vein, several scholars have made arguments proposing that, due to their affinities, consumption and religion may converge in certain ways. After empirical work in the English town of Kendal, Heelas et al. (2005) suggest that a range of services and products available on the high street offer consumers sacred experiences or higher wellbeing values associated with spirituality. This is arguably one constituent of a 'spiritual revolution' in which religiosity is expressed in unexpected ways inimical to hierarchal religious authority, but consistent with the finding that many people today identify as spiritual and not religious (Fuller 2001).

For some commentators consumerism itself follows psycho-social patterns of religion in the sense that it addresses people's urge to find ultimate fulfillment by channeling it into consuming the promises expressed in the 'sign value' assigned to commodities (Rittenshouse 2013). The work of Russell Belk and collaborators has been particularly influential in establishing the idea that nominally 'secular' consumer behavior can become sacralized. Adapting Bellah's (1967) civil religion thesis – which identifies religious elements in secular domains that express higher values, such as nationalism – Belk, Wallendorf, and Sherry (1989) argue that the 'sacred' so defined (and distinct from substantive concerns with deities and the supernatural) is also consumed through popular culture, tourism, the secular cathedral of the department store, cars, collecting and any other consumption that offers the possibility of self-transcendence, deep meaning or heightened experience. This tendency to attribute personal life meaning to commodities extends also to the ways people may follow some brands they share 'values' with – in ways that resemble how they might commit to religions. The 'cult of mac' computers, for example, may be considered to show how consumers can adopt devotional and belief behaviors in relation to consumer brands that resonate with personal value orientations (Belk and Tumbat 2005).

6 Marketing Christianity

It would certainly be misleading to conflate consumerism and religion entirely, but such perspectives suggest ways in which 'higher values' considered sacred may in fact be compatible with economic relations, not separate from them. Of course, identifying how such imbrications plays out regarding religion is not straightforward. The latter takes many forms and has multiple dimensions, and neither is all consumer activity identical. Any affinities between religion and commercial realms should be read as a starting point for inquiry. Surely, at some level, relationships between them must affect the forms of religious practices and discourses on the ground, but also how we think about religion. Ultimately theoretical work only gets us so far without empirical and analytical research.

One of the main themes in recent work interested in economy and religion has been the adoption of marketing communications by Christian religious groups, which raises questions about how religious discourse might be shaped by the need to promote it. In *Selling God* (1994), Moore stresses that "Religion in Western societies has always had commercial aspects" (255). Indeed, Luther was responding in part to the selling of indulgences which offered recipients remission from sin without the need for severe penance. However, this was a use of commerce to shore up monopoly power, something different from the commercialized contemporary US religious scene in which the first amendment ensures competition. It is this and similar liberal milieux that attract much attention among scholars. While there are examples of collaborative promotion among mainstream groups such as the Alpha course (Hunt 2013), much attention is now given to 'branding' of different kinds of Christianity, that is defining what is unique about their symbolic 'offer' in a cluttered marketplace of religious styles and belief options (Twitchell 2007; Einstein 2008).

Consumption choices can clearly be influenced by other parties. Indeed, this is the discursive function of marketing. The very fact that consumers can make choices, however constrained, encourages those who promote commodities to acknowledge consumer agency, and attempt to 'mobilize' it by addressing criteria through which people may choose. In the world of marketing, this is done by forming symbolic connections between people's hopes, interests and anxieties, however quotidian, and the putative features of products (Miller and Rose 1997, 30–31). Promotional discourses are often conversational and advisory, constructing the consumer as an individual who responds positively to a product's convenience, applicability and usability in terms of their life, rather than someone who is commanded to accept something on terms other than those that are apparently their own (Fairclough 1994, 253–261).

This is particularly well borne out in the phenomenon on Christian megachurches that can be said to embed the gospel in a broader service that aims to persuade and satisfy on multiple levels. An ideal of contemporary marketing communications is that they are both omnipresent and seamless, i.e. they are active in any discourses where there is potential to mobilize consumers, but they are integrated with everyday life without marking themselves out. 'Below-the-line' techniques such as product placement, sponsorship, store design, and relationship marketing seek to take promotion beyond the more obvious genres of advertising that clutter much media space. It is along these lines that megachurches build an integrated all-encompassing consumer experience. Stewart M. Hoover describes the efforts of U.S. Protestant megachurches to attract seekers through 'pull' marketing strategies, not only in the attempt to address "hungers and needs" not catered for by other religious providers (150), but also in adding the infrastructure of consumer convenience: good onsite parking, childcare, shops, coffee bars, and other recreational facilities (152).

In his autoethnographic encounter with Southland Christian Church in Kentucky Battista (2010) identifies the subtle promotional hooks at every turn. Initially he is invited to an "after-tax dinner" that falls just after the deadline for IRS tax returns and is "designed to help you forget your IRS woes" (84). This is a much more savvy way to inform people than just describing religious content on offer. It turns out that it perfectly inserts the Southland brand into the lifeworlds of its target consumers. Hard-working, middle-class family members are offered a kind of therapy, laced with knowing humor, that makes them feel good about themselves as Christians and citizens who do their duty (paying to Caesar what is Caesar's) while at another level 'preferring' to take the opportunity serve God offered by the Church. From this entry point Battista finds a chain of interrelated texts and experiences that constitute not just a series of persuasive messages but a deeper symbolic world. The traditional imagery of crosses and bibles is deemed inappropriate on the basis of market research, and the out-of-town site contrasts with the hemmed-in urban setting of mainline churches. Inside the church is a theater for cultural amplification that generates numinous experiences, while the landscaped grounds create a bucolic sanctuary contrasted with urban degradation (a sanctuary that is literally out of reach to the working classes as no public transport serves the area). Ultimately, for Battista, the church is branded as a kind of religious country club that sacralizes the escapist cultural fantasy of the literary pastoral and links it to the lifestyle aspirations of the congregation.

For Einstein (2008), megachurches combine the evangelical impulse with the market imperative to grow the enterprise. Indeed, the largest US examples such as Lakewood and Willow Creek have congregations of twenty to thirty thousand. They are usually led by charismatic figures whose celebrity persona becomes part of brand representations, enabling the creation of a range of products, from the educational courses to media channels and Christian entertainment products that all bear the entrepreneur's imprimatur while further spreading the brand in a virtuous cycle of publicity.

But it is an Australian brand, Hillsong, that probably best exemplifies the market potential of megachurches. Starting out as a small church in the Australian suburb of Baulkham Hills it overcame the limits of its original location, initially by creating services across Sydney. However, it has now become a global organization with bases in 14 countries, driven by a scrupulous attention to user experience and networking combined with Christian rock, television and digital media created by leading professionals at the highest production standards to brand-conforming specifications. Economically, the buzz of participation is buttressed by a best of both worlds approach to funding. Churchgoers are expected to gift a portion of their income to the Church but are also encouraged to express their piety through purchase of Hillsong branded products.

If the mainstream churches observed by Berger (1963) were undertaking marketing communications consistent with their time, so is Hillsong. In Berger's study the impact of marketing was limited to the need to create a public facing 'brand image' to differentiate mainstream churches from each other. This, however, did not involve market engineering of doctrine or products of the kind that would deeply shape the religious discourses of each church. Hillsong, however, can be considered the most successful of all contemporary 'growth churches' that conjoin evangelism and the entrepreneurial ideology of neoliberal capitalism with the aim of maximizing growth – both the personal growth demands of its consumers, and growth of its own corporate enterprise (Maddox 2012). As Wagner (2017) shows, it does this by building the intangible asset of its brand at every moment of possible interrelation between itself and worshippers across the value chain it manages, including customer acquisition, messaging across numerous media platforms, the branded service experience, and the integration of elements to create a 'brand story.' Hillsong, then, takes the discursive practice of contemporary marketing to its highest level of sophistication. It sees the styling of symbolic and sensorial elements to form an inspirational worship brand experience that carefully steers Christian discourse away from emphasis on affects such as suffering and guilt towards fulfilling subjective desires to live an empowered, blessed, loving life – as reinforced scrupulously across its events and media (Wagner 2017). In short, Hillsong has found a perfect brand offer for its largely urban, cosmopolitan, middle-class target consumers, whose own evangelical testament then becomes the kind of brand advocacy that expands Hillsong's constituency.

7 The New Age

While megachurch participants consume allied Christian goods to express piety to a religion that still has membership-like dynamics, the New Age is often thought of as the quintessence of a contemporary spiritual marketplace. It presents a smorgasbord of spiritual belief and practice options derived from a wide range of cultural and religious traditions. According to Moore, New Age providers sell many practical techniques for self-improvement in "a market of intense product differentiation" (Moore 1994, 258). Distinctively, commodification is not an adjunct to traditional church or sect like gift giving norms as it with even Hillsong, whose celebrity pastors, (despite the wide range of branded products also sold) sprinkle services with constant reminders that donations and tithing are expected from congregants to help deliver the miraculous blessings of a particular creed (Reagan 2017).

However, brand loyalty is not expected in the New Age. The *main* mode of participation is purchase of goods and services (such as media, workshops, and therapies) on a fee-for-access basis that does not imply commitment beyond the transaction, as per the social relations of commodification. Bainbridge and Stark (1980) suggest it comprises a patchwork of 'audience cults' and 'client cults' through which consumers interact with teachers by privately consuming their media and therapists through buying services individually or in group settings such as workshops. The term 'New Age' then refers not to a given religion or variant, but the liberal milieu in which people move between them in a way inimical to any kind of fundamentalism. As Bloch (1998, 1) found in in-depth interviews, participants move between numerous contemporary and traditional knowledge traditions, and they cross paths unpredictably with similar individuals as they navigate the range of media and consumption options presented in New Age settings.

New Age goods and services often blur the boundaries between sacred and secular by offering direct therapeutic benefits to consumers. Metaphysical and supernatural claims concerning the holistic nature of the cosmos and the potential to reveal divine powers within the person are often linked to claims that tapping such powers allows one to improve outcomes in practical areas of one's life, from health and better careers to achieving sacred sex. Authors, entrepreneurs, publishing houses, seminar and workshop conveners, therapists, editors, and designers innovate products designed to appeal to consumer markets in a range of areas of everyday life. As Kimberly Lau notes, with regard to aromatherapy, "The proliferation of spin-off fragrance therapies exemplifies the capitalist necessity to divide the product line as well as the body and mind and spirit into as many parts as possible to ensure a continually growing market and consumer base" (2000, 35). Any interests in wellbeing a person may have can result in New Age products addressing them.

If, as Belk suggests, some consumer behavior is now marked by pursuit of higher values and experiences to enrich the self, the New Age would seem to cater directly to such impulses. The personalist modes of evidence employed in New Age discourse – especially the use of personal testimonies and vignettes about transformed lives – serve to illustrate the potential utility of the kind of knowledge on offer, in terms of enhanced personal experience. In other words, it reproduces the common optimistic 'before and after' trope of commodity promotion: "Buy this product and change your life" (Rosen 1988, 270). Often allied with the promise of better outcomes in specific aspects of one's life is the promise that such specific outcomes further enhance one's ability to be a freely self-fashioning being. Hence, New Age discourse respects not only the agency of the participant, but also offers to help increase it. As Johannson (1994) puts it: "Reading New Age books, magazines and adverts is like wandering through a hall of mirrors where all the images of the true self compete in telling you that you are absolutely wonderful and omnipotent" (222).

Such claims to be able to transform the self here and now also indicate transformed relations of religious authority. The 'epistemological individualism' of New Ageism has been widely noted as a core feature (Heelas 1996). It is held that in their spiritual quest a person should have freedom to choose the tools, practices and beliefs that they believe will facilitate their own spiritual development. This is highly compatible with the ethos of promotion that Keat et. al. (1994) named the 'authority of the consumer.' This is a cultural stress on the rights of consumers to determine value. It arises because the relations of free market economy require that goods and services "be responsive to their demands" (2). Roy Wallis has shown that religious groups that rely upon commodification tend to appeal to a wide array of interests because of a shift in power towards consumers (1974, 306). The New Age consumer of ideas is in a *literal* position of having to select 'what is right for them' from a range of marketed alternatives. As Bruce puts it, "In the market for ideas, the individual New Ager maximises his or her returns by exercising free choice and synthesising his or her best orientation of preferences" (2000, 231). Self-spirituality, the New Age discourse of subjective authority, corresponds with the actual authority of participants to choose which goods and services they will buy on the basis of their personal preferences. The subjectivist value-relativism expressed by New Agers is one dimension of the discourse that is congruous with its marketization (Hamilton 2000, 191). As Bruce puts it, "eclecticism requires an appropriate epistemology" (2000, 228).

Along these lines, New Age discourse could not be more distant from attempts to 'convert' people to accept a single creedal orthodoxy, observance the absolute sovereignty of a religious figure, or universal moral standards dictating their way of life. These are hallmarks of membership type groups that tend to accumulate their own capital and invest it in organizational hierarchies that control ideology. New Age has no such institutional basis and instead depends upon allowing diverse expressions of core philosophies, such as perennialism which finds spiritual value in numerous traditions, unlike fundamentalism (Aupers and Houtman 2006). Instead, the New Age more closely resembles the 'mobilization of the consumer' via appeals to higher personal benefits offered in a range of options. New Age producers incorporate the authority of the user-consumer into their promotional language.

The diffuse character of the New Age means it appears far from what is traditionally considered religion. There is no obligation to follow any creedal orthodoxy or external authority. Instead one may combine elements from a range of traditions as one sees fit. This novel form has led some to see it as paradigmatic of their favored theories. For Bruce (2000) it is an enormous 'cafeteria' of cultural products that illustrates how religiosity has been *reduced* to consumerism as a result of secularzsation. For Possamai (2003) and Urban (2000) it is quintessentially postmodern religion that denotes the breakdown of tradition and the pursuit of personal gratification above capital T truth.

8 Making Sense of Religious Markets

Such perspectives serve to remind us that once market or consumer dimensions are attributed to religions, questions of value are inevitably raised. Not only has the sacred previously been seen as a realm of higher transcendent value inimical to secular concerns including the economic, consumption in particular is often seen as something frivolous, as, in the words of Don Slater (1997), contrary to "all that is of lasting value in culture" (65). With regard to religion, the consumption-as-trivializing line of thought has influenced contemporary versions of the secularization thesis. According to Wilson, commodification reduces the significance of religion to that of "pushpin, poetry, [and] popcorn" (quoted in Heelas 1994, 103).

Mackian (2012) gives an overview of 'spiritual supermarket' critiques that tend to suggest that commerce overrides authentic religious values. These approaches stress supposed inflection of religious language with hedonism and quick fix solutions that are presented to participants, who are apparently manipulated by those seeking to make a buck. Such approaches are similar to early critiques of advertising which viewed it as the deliberate attempt to dupe audiences (Packard 1957). Certainly there are grounds upon which market-oriented religion can be critiqued. Carrette and King (2005) view spiritual commerce as a quiescence to the political status quo of mainstream neoliberal capitalism through sacralizing its consumer roles, and thus also as inimical to progressive religion that seeks social change. Heidi Marie Rimke (2000) argues that the particular style of guidance being offered presupposes "free" self-determining subjects putatively able to govern themselves. She argues that such models of personal responsibility ultimately "reproduce the social subject of liberal governance" (63) as they privilege liberal truths of choice, autonomy and freedom (62). Above all, they encourage the individual to take personal responsibility for creating a "productive self in private concerns" (72). Craig Martin (2014) has more recently extended such arguments to suggest the spiritual marketplace reproduces and sacralizes a largely fictitious neoliberal message about the benefits of choice, enterprise and self-empowerment that was promoted by the likes of Ronald Reagan (to the actual benefit not of ordinary people but of economic elites who make the profits in capitalism). For Martin, commodified spirituality is the new opiate of the masses, who would actually be better off with government welfare than unrealistic myths of self-realization.

However, is this always and inherently the case? Makian's interviews with contemporary spiritual seekers lead her to question whether commercial elements really override philosophical or sacred aspects that might underpin spiritual engagement. She finds that participants in the contemporary spirituality scene seek profound relationships with spirit that belie generalized assumptions that commerce dumbs religion down. Aupers and Houtman (2006) similarly argue that the New Age should not be reduced to its commercial dynamics, finding on the basis of interviews with teachers that seekers express profound holistic connection to others in search of universal wisdom inherent in the world's spiritual traditions. As Douglas Ezzy (2001) points out in his study of the commodification of witchcraft, not all aspects of commodified religious activity are subordinated to a marketing rationale (41). Yet, on the other hand, surely the market is "not a neutral influence on contemporary religious practices" (43).

Ezzy's conundrum captures nicely the one thing that is guaranteed when the economy question is asked in relation to religion: it generates conceptual problems. For instance, my own research field of New Age studies pretty much reached an impasse around the concept of the spiritual supermarket. As Sutcliffe and Gilhus (2014) note, the first wave of New Age studies tried to make sense of the movement's emergence and distinctive form in relation to its social environment and religious morphologies. The second wave turned away from macro questions towards detailed contextual ethnographies and histories. Among the concerns of those who advocated this shift was the idea that the generalization 'New Age' (a term rarely used by participants) evoked reductive ways of thinking formed in the first wave that belied the complexity of things labeled with the term. Ways of thinking that reduced the New Age to 'pick and mix' consumerism were particularly implicated (Sutcliffe and Bowman 2000).

The second wave led to many excellent studies, often conducted under the rubric of 'alternative spiritualities' rather than that of 'New Age.' However, from a cultural economy viewpoint, the impulses to go 'beyond' New Age, and 'spiritual supermarket' thinking lead to other problems. Aupers and Houtman (2006) recognize that depictions of the 'pick and mix' nature of New Age – and related discursive syncretism and individualism – are accurate at one level. However, they regard this as a *superficial* level such that dwelling on it distracts from the holism, perennialism and ethical commitments of those involved. While there is much to commend about this desire to take the New Age seriously rather than dismiss it on the grounds of its consumerism, it comes at the paradoxical cost of dismissing the conceptual significance or shaping power of the kinds of marketization the movement relies upon. It implicitly accepts the underlying view of people like Bruce that consumerism is socially insignificant or just essentially incompatible with religion, and suggests instead that meaningful social analysis of the New Age can only come by transcending concerns about its economic dimensions. Once again we find an implicit vision of society that does not include economy.

Reinstating the supposition that religion and economy have little to do with each other cuts off numerous lines of inquiry. For instance, what if the 'individualistic' desire to seek wisdom and achieve higher levels of subjective wellbeing are not some straightforward play for business, but expressive of the need to be responsible for one's own welfare that neoliberal political economy increasingly *foists upon* individuals, just as the power of collective solidarities and traditional sources of assured fate and identity are diminished (Redden 2011). In this sense New Age is not some arbitrary consumer distraction but a classed and gendered means through which some of those who experience fractured life courses and a degree of alienation from mainstream institutions of late modernity seek more meaningful lives. The marketplace is the institutional site that allows their generation of alternatives in terms that established religious discourses and institutions are not well placed address.

The problem is that simplifying metaphors such as spiritual supermarkets and (to use Bruce's term) 'cafeterias' are just that: metaphors used to simplify complex, multi-dimensional and distinctive developments of religion and economy in market societies. In fact, while some global branded New Age products from celebrity gurus might evoke mass markets and product standardization strategies of supermarkets or cafeterias, most New Age commerce does not. New Age business is driven largely by ethically committed sole traders active in socio-economic networks with their peers, not by business corporations. There is no evidence of elaborate marketing or that profit is the overriding motive of their careers. And there is every reason to consider that the spiritual consumer lifestyles constructed demonstrate how consumption can be a means by which ultimate life meanings are pursued in a consumer society.

In short, there is every reason to consider New Age consumption sacred consumption. It is not the practice itself but the terms in which many scholars have understood it that are banal. The level of nuance with which they have been routinely applied by some has been akin to considering a vegan diet adopted for ethical and environmental reasons as sharing 'just the same' social, cultural and economic implications as fast food – just because all foods can be purchased as 'commodities.' In light of the paralyzing effects of such limiting preconceptions about the 'non-sacred' status of the economic, it is unsurprising to find that some of the best work about New Age commerce has been conducted in business disciplines that suffer from no such complex. For instance, Nurit Zaidman sheds light on how New Age shop owners and consultants conduct commercial decision making and spiritual deliberation simultaneously in the ways they source, organize, and present their inventories of meaningful goods and services to their communities (Zaidman 2007a and 2007b; Zaidman, Goldstein-Gidoni and Nehemya 2009).

The aim of this essay has not, however, been to arrive at the conclusion that any one approach to discourse, economy, and religion is the correct one. Rather, it is in fact a plea that scholars be more reflexive about multiple possible approaches, forms, and questions in order that dialogues can develop. Indeed, the *main* problem is the continued prevalence of relatively fixed and uncritical conceptions of economy in the interpretation of religious phenomena, and the associated tendency that scholars who want to take religion seriously thus turn away from the economy question (Redden 2016). Instead, if we accept, in the words of John Frow (135), that in recent history there has "a continual, if uneven, extension of commodification" throughout society, numerous possibilities should be considered regarding the kinds of social and ideational change this may entail – including the possibility that religious goods may be brought to markets in different ways, with different implications, and with multiple impacts upon the discourses about the meaning of the world that religions so distinctively specialize in throughout history. For example, what does it mean to create new inflections of existing knowledges that are sold on the open market? Is it 'cultural appropriation' that infringes rights of custodians of sacred traditions who have kept them from broader circulation? Or does it give those traditions new contemporary relevance that creates connections across boundaries? Or both? How we frame such issues depends both on the particularities of cases – not all market religion is the same – and on how we consider traditional religious languages can be cultural or intellectual property in knowledge economies (Redden 2012).

For those not already committed to strong theories that explain all marketization in advance, such ambivalence is key. It suggests that patient empirical inquiry into the range of ways that religions may have commercial and economic aspects is needed to ground interpretations of their significance. Religions formations will always be complex and multidimensional, and new religious discourses (even if they prove to contain many elements from previous ones) will always combine elements that reject, accommodate and affirm aspects of the contemporary social milieux in which they arise (Dawson 2011, 312). Likewise, religions that embrace aspects of consumerism may do so in quite selective ways. Neo-Pentecostalism may share impulses of evangelism and a focus on experience with mainstream megachurches, but its 'prosperity theology' is much more directed at the global poor than the comfortable middle class audiences of churches like Hillsong, for whom it is a little gauche, despite the discourses about blessings and success that permeate their gospel. And the significant contemporary field of Muslim marketing articulates specific questions about the relationship between Islam, the secular, and modernity.

Relationships between religion, economy and commerce are studied in ever greater detail. This is to be welcomed, and discourse scholars can be guided by a range of questions in the face of diverse, palpable expressions of their interconnection. How might commerce influence the ethical codes of religion, or vice versa? Does the marketing impulse displace other religious rationalities or help to advance them? To what extent do religious languages in market societies come to stress 'this-worldly' benefits and diverse preferences of possible consumers? To what extent and in what ways might such languages be shaped by broader discourses about the economy, such as neoliberalism, or the material experiences and desires of different groups in market societies? Where does the imperative to convert become the imperative to persuade along lines of marketing communications? When and how might symbolic worlds conjured up by religions operate like brands, or be literally structured through the discursive practice of branding?

While most work so far in the field has taken place within the sociology of religion, increasingly scholars in commercial disciplines such as marketing are examining such questions (see Rinallo et al 2013; Usunier and Stolz 2014), and this can enrich work in this emerging research field. If nothing else this suggests religious markets have arrived – in the sense that they are recognized by specialists in both religion and market activity. Given that their disciplines have formed around the sacred and worldly spheres respectively, increased border traffic between them in coming years would no doubt lead to interesting and valuable new terrain.

References

Aupers, Stef, and Dick Houtman. 2006. "Beyond the Spiritual Supermarket: The Social and Public Significance of New Age Spirituality." *Journal of Contemporary Religion* 21(2): 201–222.
Azzi, Corry, and Ronald Ehrenberg. 1975. "Household Allocation of Time and Church Attendance." *Journal of Political Economy* 83 (1): 27–56.
Bailey, Michael, and Guy Redden. 2011. "Editors' Introduction: Religion as Living Culture." In *Mediating Faiths: Religion and Socio-Cultural Change in the Twenty-First Century*, edited by Michael Bailey and Guy Redden, 1–21. Surrey: Ashgate.
Bainbridge, William Sims, and Rodney Stark. 1980. "Client and Audience Cults in America." *Sociology of Religion* 41 (3): 199–214.
Battista, Andrew. 2010. "After the Garden is Gone: Megachurches, Pastoral, and Theologies of Consumption." *disClosure: A Journal of Social Theory* 19 (1): 83–96.
Belk, Russell W., Melanie Wallendorf, and John F. Sherry. 1989. "The Sacred and the Profane in Consumer Behavior: Theodicy on the Odyssey." *Journal of Consumer Research* 16 (1): 1–38.
Bellah, Robert N. 1967. "Civil Religion in America." *Daedalus* 96 (1): 1–21.
Belk, Russell, and Gülnur Tumbat. 2005. "The Cult of Macintosh." *Consumption Markets & Culture* 8 (3): 205–217.
Berger, Peter L. 1963. "A Market Model for the Analysis of Ecumenity." *Social Research* 30 (2): 75–90.
Berger, Peter L. 1973. *The Social Reality of Religion*. Harmondsworth: Penguin.
Bloch, Jon P. 1998. *New Spirituality, Self, and Belonging: How New Agers and Neo-Pagans Talk about Themselves*. Westport: Praeger.
Bové, Paul. 1992. *Mastering Discourse: The Politics of Intellectual Culture*. Durham: Duke University Press.
Bruce, Steve. 2002. *God Is Dead: Secularization in the West*. Oxford: Blackwell.
Bruce, Steve. 2000. "The New Age and Secularisation." In *Beyond New Age: Exploring Alternative Spirituality*, edited by Steven Sutcliffe and Marion Bowman, 220–236. Edinburgh: Edinburgh University Press.
Bruce, Steve. 2014. "Authority and Freedom: Economics and Secularization." In *Religions as Brands: New Perspectives on the Marketization of Religion and Spirituality*, edited by Jean-Claude Usunier and Jörg Stolz, 191–204. Aldershot: Ashgate.
Carrette, Jeremy R., and Richard King. 2005. *Selling Spirituality: The Silent Takeover of Religion*. New York: Psychology Press.
Carrier, James. 1991. "Gifts, Commodities, and Social Relations: A Maussian View of Exchange." *Sociological Forum*, 6 (1): 119–136.
Dawson, Andrew. 2011. "Consuming the Self: New Spirituality as Mystified Consumption." *Social Compass*, 58 (3): 309–315.

Du Gay, Paul, and Mike Pryke. 2002. "Cultural economy: an introduction." In *Cultural Economy: Cultural Analysis and Commercial Life*, edited by Paul Du Gay and Mike Pryke, 1–19. London: Sage.

Durkheim, Emile. 2012. *The Elementary Forms of the Religious Life*. Newburyport: Dover Publications.

Einstein, Mara. 2008. *Brands of Faith: Marketing Religion in a Commercial Age*. New York: Routledge.

Eliade, Mircea. 1959. *The Sacred and the Profane: The Nature of Religion*. New York: Harcourt Brace Jovanovich.

Ezzy, Douglas. 2001. "The Commodification of Witchcraft." *Australian Religion Studies Review* 14: 31–44.

Fairclough, Norman. 1994. "Conversationalisation of Public Discourse and the Authority of the Consumer." In *The Authority of the Consumer*, edited by Russell Keat, Nigel Whitelely, and Nicholas Abercrombie, 253–268. London: Routledge.

Fitzgerald, Timothy. 2007. *Discourse on Civility and Barbarity*. Oxford: Oxford University Press.

Fourcade, Marion, Etienne Ollion, and Yann Algan. 2015. "The Superiority of Economists." *Journal of Economic Perspectives*, 29 (1): 89–114.

Frow, John. 1997. "Gift and Commodity." In *Time and Commodity Culture: Essays in Cultural Theory and Postmodernity*, 102–217. Oxford: Clarendon Press.

Fuller, Robert C. 2001. *Spiritual, But Not Religious: Understanding Unchurched America*. Oxford: Oxford University Press.

Garcia-Parpet, Marie-France. 2007. "The Social Construction of a Perfect Market." In *Do Economists Make Markets?: On the Performativity of Economics*, edited by Donald A. MacKenzie., Fabian Muniesa, and Lucia Siu, 20–53. Princeton: Princeton University Press.

Granovetter, Mark. 1985. "Economic Action and Social Structure: The Problem of Embeddedness." *American Journal of Sociology* 91 (3): 481–510.

Hamilton, Malcolm. 2000. "An Analysis of the Festival for Mind-Body-Spirit." In *Beyond New Age: Exploring Alternative Spirituality*, edited by Steven Sutcliffe and Marion Bowman, 188–200. Edinburgh: Edinburgh University Press.

Heelas, Paul. 1994. "The Limits of Consumption and the Postmodern 'Religion' of the New Age." In *The Authority of the Consumer*, edited by Russell Keat, Nigel Whitelely, and Nicholas Abercrombie, 102–115. London: Routledge.

Heelas, Paul, 1996. *The New Age Movement: The Celebration of the Self and the Sacralization of Modernity*. Oxford: Blackwell.

Heelas, Paul, Linda Woodhead, Benjamin Seel, Bronislaw Szerszynski, and Karin Tusting. 2005. *The Spiritual Revolution: Why Religion Is Giving Way to Spirituality*. Oxford: Blackwell.

Hoover, Stewart M. 2000. "The Cross at Willow Creek: Seeker Religion and the Contemporary Marketplace." In *Popular Religion in America*, edited by Bruce David Forbes and Jeffrey H. Mahan, 145–159. Berkeley: University of California Press.

Hunt, Stephen. 2013. *Religion and Everyday Life*. London: Routledge.

Iannaccone, Laurence, 1998. "Introduction to the Economics of Religion." *Journal of Economic Literature*, 36 (3): 1465–1495.

Iannaccone, Laurence R., and William S. Bainbridge. 2010. "Economics of Religion." In *The Routledge Companion to the Study of Religion*, edited by John R. Hinnells, 461–475. London: Routledge.

Johansson, Lars. 1994. "New Age: A Synthesis of Premodern, Modern and Postmodern." In *Faith and Modernity*, edited by Philip Sampson, Samuel Vinary, and Chris Sugden, 208–251. Oxford: Regnum.

Keat, Russell, Nigel Whitelely, and Nicholas Abercrombie. 1994. "Introduction." In *The Authority of the Consumer*, edited by Russell Keat, Nigel Whitelely, and Nicholas Abercrombie, 1–19. London: Routledge.
Kopytoff, Igor. 1986. "The Cultural Biography of Things." In *The Social Life of Things*, edited by Arjun Appadurai, 64–91. Cambridge: Cambridge University Press.
Lau, Kimberley J. 2000. *New Age Capitalism: Making Money East of Eden*. Philadelphia: University of Pennsylvania Press.
Lears, TJ Jackson. 2000. "From Salvation to Self-Realization: Advertising and the Therapeutic Roots of the Consumer Culture, 1880–1930." *Advertising & Society Review* 1 (1). doi:10.1353/asr.2000.0009.
Luckmann, Thomas. 1967. *The Invisible Religion: The Problem of Religion in Modern Society*. New York: MacMillan.
Luckmann, Thomas. 1996. "The Privatization of Religion and Morality." In *Detraditionalization: Critical Reflections on Authority and Identity*, edited by Paul Heelas, Scott Lash, and Paul Morris, 72–86. Oxford: Blackwell.
Lyon, David. 2000. *Jesus in Disneyland: Religion in Postmodern Times*. Cambridge: Polity.
MacKian, Sara. 2012. *Everyday Spirituality: Social and Spatial Worlds of Enchantment*. Basingstoke: Palgrave Macmillan.
McCracken, Grant. 1986. "Culture and Consumption: A Theoretical Account of the Structure and Movement of the Cultural Meaning of Consumer Goods." *Journal of Consumer Research* 13 (1): 71–84.
McKinnon, Andrew M., 2013. "Ideology and the Market Metaphor in Rational Choice Theory of Religion – a Rhetorical Critique of 'Religious Economies.'" *Critical Sociology* 39 (4): 529–543.
Maddox, Marion. 2012. "'In the Goofy Parking Lot': Growth Churches as a Novel Religious Form for Late Capitalism." *Social Compass* 59 (2): 146–158.
Mauss, Marcel. 2002. *The Gift: The Form and Reason for Exchange in Archaic Societies*. London: Routledge.
Martin, Craig. 2014. *Capitalizing Religion: Ideology and the Opiate of the Bourgeoisie*. London: Bloomsbury.
Miller, Peter, and Nikolas Rose. 1997. "Mobilizing the Consumer: Assembling the Subject of Consumption." *Theory, Culture and Society* 14 (1): 1–36.
Moore, R. Laurence. 1994. *Selling God: American Religion in the Marketplace of Culture*. New York: Oxford University Press.
Packard, Vance, and Roy Payne. 1957. *The Hidden Persuaders*. New York: D. McKay Company.
Possamai, Adam. 2003. "Alternative Spiritualities and the Cultural Logic of Late Capitalism." *Culture and Religion* 4 (1): 31–45.
Reagan, Wen. 2017. "'The Music That Just About Everyone Sings': Hillsong in American Evangelical Media." In *The Hillsong Movement Examined: You Call Me Out Upon the Waters*, edited Tanya Riches and Tom Wagner, 145–161. Palgrave Macmillan.
Redden, Guy. 2016. "Revisiting the Spiritual Supermarket: Does the Commodification of Spirituality Necessarily Devalue It? *Culture and Religion*, 17 (2): 231–249.
Redden, Guy. 2011. "Religion, Cultural Studies and New Age Sacralization of Everyday Life." *European Journal of Cultural Studies*, 14 (6): 649–663.
Redden, Guy. 2012. "'The Secret', Cultural Property and the Construction of the Spiritual Commodity." *Cultural Studies Review*, 18 (2): 52–73.
Rimke, Heidi Marie. 2000. "Governing Citizens through Self-Help Literature." *Cultural Studies* 14 (1): 61–78.
Rinallo, Diego, Linda M. Scott, and Pauline Maclaran. 2013. *Consumption and Spirituality*. London: Routledge.

Rittenhouse, Bruce P. 2013. *Shopping for Meaningful Lives: The Religious Motive of Consumerism*. Eugene: Wipf and Stock Publishers.

Roof, Wade Clark. 1999. *Spiritual Marketplace: Baby Boomers and the Remaking of American Religion*. Princeton: Princeton University Press.

Rosen, Jay. 1988. "The Occult Establishment." In *Not Necessarily the New Age: Critical Essays*, edited by Robert Basil, 271–291. Buffalo: Prometheus.

Slater, Don. 1997. *Consumer Culture and Modernity*. Oxford: Polity Press.

Stark, Rodney, and William S. Bainbridge. 1980. "Networks of Faith: Interpersonal Bonds and Recruitment to Cults and Sects." *American Journal of Sociology*, 85 (6): 1376–1395.

Stark, Rodney, and William Sims Bainbridge. 1996. *A Theory of Religion*. Brunswick: Rutgers University Press.

Stark, Rodney, and Roger Finke. 2000. *Acts of Faith: Explaining the Human Side of Religion*. Berkeley: University of California Press.

Sutcliffe, Steven, and Marion Bowman, eds. 2000. *Beyond New Age: Exploring Alternative Spirituality*. Edinburgh: Edinburgh University Press.

Sutcliffe, Steven J, and Ingvild Sælid Gilhus. 2014. "Introduction: 'All mixed up'–Thinking about Religion in Relation to New Age Spiritualities." In *New Age Spirituality*, edited by Steven J. Sutcliffe and Ingvild Sælid Gilhus, 7–22. London: Routledge.

Twitchell, James B. 2007. *Shopping for God: How Christianity Went from in Your Heart to in Your Face*. New York: Simon and Schuster.

Urban, Hugh B. 2000. "The Cult of Ecstasy: Tantrism, the New Age, and the Spiritual Logic of Late Capitalism." *History of Religions* 39 (3): 269–304.

Usunier, Jean-Claude, and Jörg Stolz, eds. 2014. *Religions as Brands: New Perspectives on the Marketization of Religion and Spirituality*. Burlington: Ashgate.

Wagner, Tom. 2017. "The 'Powerful' Hillsong Brand." In *The Hillsong Movement Examined: You Call Me Out Upon the Waters*, edited by Tanya Riches and Tom Wagner, 253–269. Palgrave Macmillan.

Wallis, Roy. 1974. "Ideology, Authority and the Development of Cultic Movements." *Social Research*. 41: 299–327.

World Travel & Tourism Council. 2019. *Travel & Tourism Economic Impact 2019* (Report). Online available at https://www.wttc.org/-/media/files/reports/economic-impact-research/regions-2019/world2019.pdf (accessed 12 April 2020).

Zaidman, Nurit. 2007a. "New Age Products in Local and Global Contexts." *Culture and Religion*, 8(3): 255–270.

Zaidman, Nurit. 2007b. "The New Age Shop—Church or Marketplace?" *Journal of Contemporary Religion*, 22(3): 361–374.

Zaidman, Nurit, Ofra Goldstein-Gidoni, and Iris Nehemya. 2009. "From temples to organizations: The introduction and packaging of spirituality." *Organization*, 16(4): 597–621.

Hans G. Kippenberg
Dynamics of the Human Rights Discourse on Freedom of Religion – Observed from the Religious Studies Angle

This chapter is based on a study that was inspired by the article on religious freedom in the 1948 Declaration of Human Rights and its repercussions, to which scholars of religion have paid little attention to date (with the exception of an eminently valuable collection of sources and commentaries by Bielefeldt, Ghanea, and Wiener 2016). The juridification of religious freedom led to an expansion of the legal domain and to an intertwinement of law and religion (Årsheim 2016). I have investigated this topic from the perspective of the regulation of religious plurality in society (Kippenberg 2019). In this chapter, I want to address the legal discourse on freedom of religion within the UN, which developed in sustained interaction with an independent field of actions and institutions which people claimed were religious. Studying the legal framing of religion sheds light on attempts to regulate the religious field in times when intolerance and violence pervade it. Just as the freedom of the market functions only on the presupposition that the movement of goods is regulated (for example, by currency, money, wages, measurements, and rules to prevent monopolies), so too the freedom of religion, as delineated in the 1948 Universal Declaration of Human Rights (UDHR), requires a discourse on regulations. The fundamental Article 18 has already introduced regulatory rules:

> Article 18: Everyone has the right to freedom of thought, conscience and religion; this right includes freedom to change his religion or belief, and freedom, either alone or in community with others and in public or private, to manifest his religion or belief in teaching, practice, worship and observance.

Article 18 constructs religion as a social phenomenon requiring a legal right to be manifested in society's public sphere(s). Every citizen is entitled to manifest religion in public—not only church officeholders and theologians, but every citizen, either alone or in community with others. In addition, changing one's religion is right and proper.

The article specifies four such manifestations: teaching, practice, worship, and observance. These notions refer to activities in the realm of religion. Religion and law are independent of each other, but each is able to conceive of the other's actions in its own terms. Both are cultural systems. As Clifford Geertz formulated it: "Law [. . .] is part of a distinctive manner of imagining the real" (1983, 184). Legal representations confront religion with distinctions that are not its own, as Niklas Luhmann observes (1993, 263). Law either legalizes religious manifestations or rejects them as illegal. Article 18 regards religious plurality in a society or nation-state as normal and sees it as a building block of every genuine democracy. The secular nation-state is responsible for guaranteeing religious plurality and regulating freedom of religion.[1]

Legal notions of religious practices are derived from legal reasoning, and as such they are "invented." But "showing that a concept is a social construction says nothing about whether or not that concept identifies something real," as we learn from Kevin Schilbrack. He calls this a "critical realist" view of concepts (Schilbrack 2010, 1125). Gustavo Benavides likewise points out that the notion of "inventing a concept" wrongly suggests that there are no data to which the concept refers (Benavides 2000, 113–122; 2003, 895–903). The discourse on freedom of religion refers to empirical and historical data as well as to concepts of religion such as rituals, religious doctrines, tradition, and the formation of religious communities.

In 1993, more than 45 years after the UDHR, the UN Human Rights Committee added General Comment No. 22, exemplifying which kinds of activities – those which practitioners claim constitute worship or the teaching, practice, and observance of religion – are covered by Article 18, and which are not. Thus the committee tried to delineate the field of freedom of religion (Årsheim 2018, 106–112):

> 22 (4) The freedom to manifest religion or belief in worship, observance, practice and *teaching* encompasses a broad range of acts. The concept of *worship* extends to ritual and ceremonial acts giving direct expression to belief, as well as various practices integral to such acts, including the building of places of worship, the use of ritual formulae and objects, the display of symbols, and the observance of holidays and days of rest. The *observance* and *practice* of religion or belief may include not only ceremonial acts but also such customs as the observance of dietary regulations, the wearing of distinctive clothing or head-coverings, participation in rituals associated with certain stages of life, and the use of a particular language customarily spoken by a group. In addition, the practice and teaching of religion or belief includes acts integral to the conduct by religious groups of their basic affairs, such as the freedom to choose their religious leaders, priests and teachers, the freedom to establish seminaries or religious schools and the freedom to prepare and distribute religious texts or publications.
> (Kippenberg 2019, 141 Emphasis mine)

Here we note a preference for common religious activities and institutions that directly express religion, to the disadvantage of activities which flow from individual religious convictions.

Initially in 1948, freedom of religion was a moral right. Subsequently, however, the International Convention on Civil and Political Rights (ICCPR), adopted in 1966 and ratified in 1976, made the Declaration of Human Rights legally binding on all

---

[1] "Regulation" denotes an intervention by the state – for example, to maintain free markets. This is a process or policy that is intended to reduce the formation of monopolies and the undesired external effects of economic decisions through state intervention. In the sphere of religion, the action of the state consists in maintaining the free choice of religion and curbing undesired effects linked to this choice.

the signatory UN member states. It declared these nation-states to be the guarantors of human rights, responsible for encouraging a plurality of religions by regulating their cohabitation in one legal system. Thus freedom of religion becomes a subject of juridification. Secular law acquires competencies regarding religion; it regulates a number of different religious and secular activities; it is expected to resolve religious conflicts (Årsheim 2016, 291–292). In this context, the category of religion is a secular legal concept, construed by legal scholars and politicians, and practically enforced by statutes that compel the secular state to allow believers to observe different religious prescriptions. Kocku von Stuckrad has pointed out that the discourse on religion can integrate other discourses – in this case, a legal one – and vice versa. He argues that "[w]e have to take seriously the impact factors (such as 'materiality') that are outside of the discourse as well as systems of knowledge," and he defends "the appreciation of a plurality of knowledge systems" (von Stuckrad 2016, 218).

When the International Convention on Civil and Political Rights attributed to signatory UN member states the task of guaranteeing each citizen the fundamental right to invoke this freedom, it also empowered these states to place legal restrictions on the freedom to manifest religion publicly, provided certain national conditions are fulfilled:

> ICCPR article 18 (3): Freedom to manifest one's religion or beliefs may be subject only to such limitations as are prescribed by law and are necessary to protect public safety, order, health, or morals or the fundamental rights and freedoms of others.

Thus there are three criteria: national laws forbidding manifestations of religion (*legality*); prohibitions justified on the basis of protecting the common good in a particular society – its internal security, its morality, its health, and the basic rights and freedoms of other persons (*legitimacy*); and the question of whether such laws and prohibitions are necessary (*necessity*). Making judgments with regard to these three criteria is the responsibility of individual nation-states, allowing them to integrate religions in accordance with state interests.

This juridification altered the familiar categories of "religion" and the "public sphere." If religion is understood as a purely private matter, then the public sphere can be purely secular. But if this sphere becomes the place where manifestations of religions rightly take place, then religion also becomes public (*public religion*), thereby modifying the allegedly secular character of public space. Jürgen Habermas' notion of religion in a "post-secular society" (2009, 387–407; 2011, 15–33) and José Casanova's notion of a "public religion" (1994) both have their legal equivalents here. While the state's power is secularized, society becomes the sphere, where religions are revitalized. As Saba Mahmood has shown in her sophisticated study (2016), religious difference is conceived in secular terms.

In 1960, when the UN was discussing the ICCPR, the Sub-Commission on Prevention of Discrimination and Protection of Minorities, part of the Committee on Human Rights, published a related study (Lerner 2000, 9–39) written by Arcot

Krishnaswami. This study investigated cases of discrimination around the world in which concerned believers claimed that their freedom to manifest religion had been violated. Since Krishnaswami regarded religious communities as embodiments of the UN's spirit of fraternity and peace, he identified which communal religious practices, from this perspective, were justly or unjustly prohibited. He argued that practices such as human sacrifice, mutilation, slavery, prostitution, the formation of a caste of untouchables, or suttee/sati (the funeral custom in which a widow immolates herself on her husband's pyre) should be excluded from legal protection, since they are "so obviously contrary to morality, public order, or the general welfare that public authorities are always entitled to limit them, or even to prohibit them altogether" (Krishnaswami 1960, 24). On the other hand, he compiled a catalogue of activities that believers felt complied with what is prescribed or authorized by a religion or belief: namely, worship, processions, pilgrimages, equipment and symbols, arrangements for disposal of the dead, observance of holidays and days of rest, dietary practices, celebrations of marriage and its dissolution by divorce, the dissemination of religion or belief, and the training of personnel. When the nation-state subjected these practices to state control, religious adherents (and likewise Krishnaswami) regarded such state interventions as unjustified and discriminatory. Here a broad notion of religion emerged, based not on a functional or substantiv definition, but on a variety of believers' claims – supported by Krishnaswami – that their practices were religious and socially beneficial. The claims of these religious adherents were crucial in limiting the field of freedom of religion. Wilfred Cantwell Smith has already argued that 'religion' should be studied and defined not as a noun, but as the social practices which believers characterize as religious (1991, 20). Talal Asad has reiterated this claim, arguing that we should think of religion as an adjective (2001, 205–222). The concept of religion as an adjective is related to practices that are not religious in themselves. Thus 'religious' – in philosophical language – is not an analytic, but rather a synthetic notion.

Krishnaswami's catalogue and his 16 basic rules for legislation on religion later formed the basis of the UN Declaration on the Elimination of all Forms of Intolerance and of Discrimination Based on Religion or Belief (1981). The preamble to this declaration expresses its appreciation for religion as a "conception of life." It states: "Disregard and infringement of human rights and fundamental freedoms [. . .] have brought, directly or indirectly, wars and great suffering to mankind." It continues: "Religion or belief is one of the fundamental elements in the conception of life, and freedom of religion or belief should be fully respected and guaranteed," especially "considering that it is essential to promote understanding, tolerance and respect." By avoiding a definition of religion and focusing instead on religiosity as a subjective principle, the declaration expanded the number of cases in which activities are unjustly prohibited.

The declaration authorizes religious communities to carry out a variety of social activities and provides legal protection for the foundation of charitable or humanitarian organizations (Bielefeldt, Ghanea, and Wiener 2016, 242–257) and for the dissemination of publications; religious communities are entitled to receive donations, to train personnel, and to maintain both national and international relations. These rights generated a new social reality with regard to religion. In the Netherlands, the outcome of translating these religious rights into a social reality has been called "pillarization" (known as *Versäulung* in German); thus religions are shaping the cultural, civil, and communicative sectors of societies (Molendijk 2007, 307–327). M. Rainer Lepsius coined the term "social-moral milieu," indicating a fusion of region, economy, values, and religion that has affected German national elections (1973, 68). Gunnar Folke Schuppert (2012) speaks of "religious governance," pointing out that religion is establishing a public sphere of its own that could act independently of state institutions. In all of these cases, religious institutions could potentially act as rivals to or in competition with the state.

The article on freedom of religion in the ICCPR balanced freedom in one's choice of a faith (including the freedom to apostatize) with a freedom to manifest one's faith (including founding humanitarian organizations): "Rights of the source, rights of the target," as Tad Stahnke put it (1999, 254). But the balance between the two has tilted over the course of the years since 1960. Humanitarian organizations became an incentive for conversion and were accused of unfair proselytism. In 1993, the Committee on Human Rights discussed the question of what types of coercion were prohibited in Article 18 (2) of the ICCPR:

> ICCPR Art. 18 (2): No one shall be subject to coercion which would impair his freedom to have or to adopt a religion or belief of his choice.

Comment 22 (5) refers to "physical violence" and "penal sanctions," but also to "limiting access to education, medical care, work, or to participation in the political process" (see Bielefeldt, Ghanea, and Wiener 2016, 75–91). The power to provide social services has made religious communities powerful national and global actors, and thereby also potential partisans in political, societal, and religious conflicts. This kind of *unfair proselytism* is not content simply to propagate the faith; it also promises advantages to converts. A number of further declarations made by the UN General Assembly spoke out against any kind of intolerance or discrimination – above all, violence against citizens of different religions and beliefs, or violence that was justified on religious grounds. This debate has become increasingly intense and fundamental in the last decade of the twentieth century and the first two decades of the twenty-first, as the Report of the UN Special Rapporteur on Freedom of Religion or Belief shows (Bielefeldt 2017, 249–278).

Despite this cautious evaluation of their social activities, religious communities have been recognized and accredited by the UN as national and international religious non-governmental organizations (NGOs) and thus as partners in the realization of fraternity and peace, the main goals of the UN. Initially, it was Christian associations that were recognized as partners; from the 1980s onwards, Islamic and other religious associations followed suit. In 2003, for example, religious NGOs amounted to 10% of a total of circa 3,000 NGOs with consultative status at the UN (Berger 2003; Juul Petersen 2010, 2015; Lehmann 2016). This percentage remained constant in later years as well. Though these religious associations were granted autonomy in all of their activities, there was still a need to orchestrate their activities for the benefit of the UN's goals. In this process, the discourse on freedom of religion has fundamentally expanded, as Karsten Lehmann has shown. Freedom of religion, which was once intended to prevent close links between church and state, has become a requirement for religious communities; they must act independently of the state and be tolerant in secular social and political fields.

The USA also propagated the granting of religious freedom globally via its foreign policy, but it often enforced this abroad through violence and coercion. Thereby the USA helped American Christian missionary organizations (such as the Pentecostal movement, fundamentalism, and the sister church movement) to gain entrance into countries with other religions (Amsturz 2004; Herztke 2004). Islamic countries reacted by rejecting Christian missionary efforts as a threat to their societal cohesion and increasing the penalty for apostasy. Islamic NGOs which took the side of Muslims in political conflicts and gave their coreligionists aid and support in their *jihad* against the infidels (in Afghanistan, Palestine, Bosnia, and Chechnya) were banned by the US. In view of the worldwide phenomenon of religious violence in all exclusive religious communities from the end of the 1970s onward (Juergensmeyer, Kitts, and Jerryson 2013), the UN Human Rights Council resolved in the 2013 Rabat Plan to identify the conditions under which religions that are otherwise peaceful might become violent (UNHRC 2013). Thus international law concerning freedom of religion has become a source of political, social, and legal conflicts.

One particular issue in any analysis of the discourse on freedom of religion as a global fundamental right is the question of how this right, which claimed universal validity, came to be seen as the protector of particular, local religious practices. Which of these practices did it cover, and which not? Krishnaswami had already excluded certain practices as damaging to a society's common good. But what qualified other contingent religious practices for protection under the human right to freedom of religion?

The manner in which the standard of this "human right" was generated was itself already contingent. Its two specific places of origin, in France and in the USA, had different roots: namely, the philosophy of the French Enlightenment and American Nonconformist Protestantism. Neither Judaism, nor Christianity, nor Islam, nor other religions or cultures had acknowledged a concept of universal human rights antecedent to the state. And when the concept was finally developed, it was necessary to determine who was entitled to this right: Only male citizens, or also women? Only the free, or also slaves? Only citizens, or also foreigners and refugees? And to what were they entitled, when they benefitted from this human right? Up to the present day, studies of human rights are obliged to confront the problem of the contingency of any claim to universal validity.

Over the course of time, scholars have proposed several solutions. Jack Donnelly, one of the experts in this field, argues that the concept of human dignity, which arose in the West, should be accorded universal validity. It is possible to appeal to this concept anywhere, but this does not ensure the same substantial rights in every place. This means that human rights are both universal—the authorization of claims—and particular, since the contents of these claims differ from one epoch and culture to another (Donnelly 2003; 1999).

There is another empirical approach to the nexus between the universality of a claim and the particularity of its implementation: namely, to see human rights as enforceable basic rights. Christoph Menke has presented this approach, pointing to the distinctive public legal relationship between the individual and the state, which was established through the juridification of the right to freedom of religion and led to a new definition of the right to take legal action. The individual can appeal to a competent national court or, at the next level, to the human rights committee or to a transnational court, if the individual believes that his or her subjective rights are being infringed upon by the nation-state (Menke 2013). Menke develops a distinction first made by Michael Walzer: human rights do not lay claim to acceptance everywhere and by everyone as a "fully comprehensive law"; rather, they lay claim to a "continually changing and regenerating repetition," to an exemplary quality (Walzer 1990). In this process, human rights are differentiated. One and the same claim will be realized in different particular practices, if the complaint is successful.

When the European Human Rights Convention was approved by the European Council in 1950 and came into force in 1953, the signatory member states agreed that, according to Article 19, a European Court of Human Rights (ECtHR) should be set up, and according to Articles 34 and 35, that court could settle claims from persons or organizations claiming to be victims of violations of their right to religious freedom. The court's task would be to hear appeals against sentences handed down in national courts, ascertaining whether a person's rights had been violated. Here, people could appeal against what they perceived as unjustified verdicts that restricted their freedom to manifest their religion and convictions. Between 1962 and 2012, 213 verdicts were issued (Evans 2009; Weber 2009).

The court was faced with the problem that different member states have different understandings of morality and religion, as well as the fact that their constitutions were different. It was necessary to offer some leeway in acknowledging these differences between nation-states when evaluating complaints about alleged violations of human rights. The court found a solution by granting national authorities a "margin of appreciation" in restricting public manifestations of moral and religious practices and convictions (Mahoney 1990, 1998). For example, a British publisher complained that his school textbook – which was intended to teach pupils the facts of life, particularly sexual ones – was banned, but his complaint was rejected on the grounds that the book was inappropriate for English pupils for moral reasons. Similarly, the court rejected a complaint concerning the refusal to grant a license to screen a film in Austria, on the grounds that it offended the religious feelings of Austrian Catholics. The European Court judges held that the national authorities were better able to assess the moral or religious grounds for a ban. This prompted vigorous discussions about the consideration given to the views of national minorities in these verdicts (Brems 1996).

On the other hand, with a view to realizing human rights in signatory member states, the court made some exemplary decisions in cases which became precedents for future decisions. It handed down decisions about which public manifestations of religion offended freedom of religion and were therefore inadmissible, and also about when this was the case (for example, the obligation to take a special religious oath when assuming a state office). When a pacifist protested against the use of English troops in Northern Ireland by calling on them to refuse to serve and was convicted by an English court under the Incitement of Disaffection Act 1934, her appeal to the European Court did not help her. The majority of the judges held that the right only applied to private convictions, not the act of handing out leaflets openly appealing to soldiers to desert (Evans 2001, 105–106).

Various appeals to the European Court of Human Rights ensured the independence of religious communities, protected them from state interventions, and made their autonomy inviolable. The validity of religious freedom in states with official state churches was also the subject of a court case that has repeatedly been cited as a precedent (Kokkinakis vs. Greece 1993; see Evans 1997, 281–314). The court ruled that mutual tolerance between citizens of different faiths, as demanded by the human right to freedom of religion, was more important than obeying the specific tenets of a state constitution (as regards, for example, a state religion, laicism, or cooperation between church and state) (Evans 2009, 45–46). In view of the religious plurality of European nation-states, the court saw its task as protecting religious pluralism, and thereby democracy, on behalf of European citizens. In this way, the tension between universal human rights and local practices was resolved in Europe. The state's task is to enable and even foster religious pluralism. Malcolm D. Evans speaks of "the state's responsibility as the neutral and impartial *organizer* of the exercise of religions, faiths and beliefs" and of "the state as 'facilitator of organizational and individual religious freedom'" (Evans 2009, 45). Thus the discourse on freedom of religion has consequences for a common European understanding of the tasks of the state.

However, the intricacy of this discussion intensified as a result of the increase in migration and the fact that many migrants practiced their own religions. Those who did not wish their children to have a Christian education complained about Christian practices, such as crosses displayed in state schools in Italy. When Italy rejected this complaint, the claimants appealed to the European Court of Human Rights. Despite initially wavering, the court ultimately approved the state's praxis. Muslim migration to Europe led to new claims regarding public manifestations of their religion. Islamic migrants claimed that their religious practices were local concretizations of the universal standard of the freedom to manifest religion and belief. The European Court did not find a common perspective in its evaluation of these claims. Doesn't Islam contradict the human rights norms necessitating a plurality of religions in the public sphere, as its ban on apostasy demonstrates?

Particularly instructive for the kind of protection offered by human rights law is a new interpretation of the prohibition of blasphemy in European caselaw and in the UN. In 1976, the English publisher of a gay periodical was condemned for disseminating blasphemous libel. When Muslims in England referred to this case in their demand to prohibit the dissemination of Salman Rushdie's novel *The Satanic Verses*, the case was dismissed with the affirmation that the prohibition of blasphemy only protected Christianity. The ECtHR also dismissed an appeal against this verdict. Nevertheless, a new interpretation of the prohibition of blasphemy could already be discerned in its treatment of Christian cases. The protection offered by the blasphemy law does not extend to the religion itself, but to its believers (including non-Christian believers), and it is meant to protect them against the public fomentation of hatred. It is not the criticism of religion that is forbidden, but rather the call to hate members of other religions. Indeed, criticism of religion must be permitted.

Nilüfer Göle has given a new shape to the European dilemma which we see here (Göle 2017). Controversies over Islamic practices have broken out again and again in the European public sphere, sometimes intensified by legal verdicts. Göle and her collaborators have examined these controversies in places where they once raged and have brought those involved to sit together around a table, with the intention of forming an "experimental public sphere" in which they could discuss the disputed facts of the case once more. In this way, they transformed the controversial phenomena into a new public sphere shared by non-European migrants and other Europeans.

These unresolved controversies can be linked to studies concerning the special characteristics of European culture and nation-states. Rémi Brague (2002) sees Europe's identity as "ex-centric" since it is rooted not in Europe itself, but outside of Europe – in Greece and the Middle East. The fact that Greek culture and the religions of Judaism and Christianity (and later Islam) entered the Western sphere from the eastern Mediterranean region and remained perennial markers of orientation for the culture of the inhabitants of the West has contributed to the formation of this cultural consciousness. Similarly, Edgar Morin (1991) sees Europe's unity as consisting in a complexity that brings great differences together without blending them. He lists the numerous contradictions between religion and reason, faith and doubt, mythical and critical thinking, and other antagonisms, describing their interactions as situations of perennial dialogue. One could apply the same model to the European discourse on human rights with regard to freedom of religion. It has promoted an antagonistic pluralism.

To sum up, the human rights discourse on freedom of religion has developed since 1948 along the lines of public manifestations of religion. The legal framework transformed a private faith into a public performance, and public performance shaped private belief. Teaching, practice, worship, and observance are religious activities that happen to take place among citizens in a secular society, and the issues of the secular society shape private commitments. The interaction between religious activists and their social environment became the point of departure for new religious institutions and discourses: believers teach worldviews that reject the state; they run social institutions independent of the state; they produce networks and media of their own, inside nation-states and beyond national borders; they observe customs of their own, independent of the habits of the majority of a nation-state's inhabitants. In this process of an emerging public religion, the concept of religion cannot be subject to a definition, since it includes activities that not everyone acknowledges as religious; the ensuing conflicts contributed to increasing splits within and among nation-states. Thus religions and their positions in society became a disputed issue.

When we address the general discourse on the article of freedom of religion in the UDHR and within the UN, we see that the positive evaluation of religious communities as bearers of the values of fraternity and peace enabled these communities to expand their activities into new societal areas. They could be accredited as powerful NGOs and UN partners. As soon as this happened, however, some of these communities were drawn into national and international political conflicts. In one declaration after another, the UN General Assembly summoned the nation-states and religious communities to take action against discrimination and intolerance, but without lasting success. The necessity of regulating freedom of religion altered the position of religions in the context of these nation-states.

In Europe, the Convention for the Protection of Human Rights and Fundamental Freedoms developed legal instruments that made it possible to acknowledge diverse religious activities in worship, teaching, practice, and observance as protected by human rights. It established the plurality of religions in one and the same nation-state or society and enabled the integration of migrants with Islamic beliefs. Yet attempts to generate standards for the public role of religions have stimulated conflicts among citizens.

References

Amsturz, Mark R. 2004. *Evangelicals and American Foreign Policy*. Oxford: Oxford University Press.
Årsheim, Helge. 2016. "Whose Religion? Whose Freedom? Discursive Constructions in the Work of UN Special Rapporteurs on Freedom of Religion or Belief." In *Making Religion: Theory and Practice in the Discursive Study of Religion*, ed. by Kocku von Stuckrad and Frans Wijsen, 287–316. Leiden and Boston: Brill.
Årsheim, Helge. 2018. *Making Religion and Human Rights at the United Nations*. Berlin and Boston: De Gruyter.

Asad, Talal. 2001. "Reading a Modern Classic: W. C. Smith's 'The Meaning and End of Religion'." *History of Religions* 40: 205–222.
Benavides, Gustavo. 2000. "What Raw Materials Are Used in the Manufacture of Religion?" *Culture and Religion* 1: 113–122.
Benavides, Gustavo. 2003. "There Is Data for Religion." *Journal of the American Academy of Religion* 71: 895–903.
Berger, Julia. 2003. "Religious Non-Governmental Organizations: An Exploratory Analysis." *Voluntas: International Journal of Voluntary and Nonprofit Organizations* 14: 15–39.
Bielefeldt, Heiner, Nazila Ghanea, and Michael Wiener, eds. 2016. *Freedom of Religion and Belief: An International Law Commentary*. Oxford: Oxford University Press.
Bielefeldt, Heiner. 2017. *Freedom of Religion or Belief: Thematic Reports of the UN Special Rapporteur 2010–2016*. Bonn: Verlag für Kultur und Wissenschaft.
Brague, Remi. 2002. *Eccentric Culture: A Theory of Western Civilization*. South Bend, IN: St. Augustine's Press.
Brems, Eva. 1996. "The Margin of Appreciation Doctrine." *Max-Planck-Institut für ausländisches öffentliches Recht und Völkerrecht* 56: 230–314.
Casanova, José. 1994. *Public Religions in the Modern World*. Chicago: University of Chicago Press.
Donnelly, Jack. 1999. "Human Rights and Asian Values: A Defense of 'Western' Universalism." In *The East Asian Challenge for Human Rights*, ed. by Joanne R. Bauer and Daniel A. Bell, 60–87. Cambridge: Cambridge University Press.
Donnelly, Jack. 2003. *Universal Human Rights in Theory and Practice*. Ithaca and London: Cornell University Press.
Evans, Carolyn. 2001. *Freedom of Religion under the European Convention on Human Rights*. Oxford: Oxford University Press.
Evans, Malcolm D. 1997. *Religious Liberty and International Law in Europe*. Cambridge: Cambridge University Press.
Evans, Malcolm D. 2009. *Manual on the Wearing of Religious Symbols in Public Areas*. Strasbourg: Council of Europe Publishing.
Geertz, Clifford. 1983. "Local Knowledge. Fact and Law in Comparative Perspective." In *Local Knowledge: Further Essays in Interpretive Anthropology*, ed. by Clifford Geertz, 167–234. New York: Basic Books.
Göle, Nilüfer. 2017. *The Daily Lives of Muslims: Controversy and Islam in Contemporary Europe*. London: Zed.
Habermas, Jürgen. 2009. "Die Revitalisierung der Weltreligionen: Herausforderung für ein säkulares Selbstverständnis der Moderne?" In *Kritik der Vernunft*, vol. 5 of *Philosophische Texte*, ed. by Jürgen Habermas, 387–407. Frankfurt am Main: Suhrkamp.
Habermas, Jürgen. "'The Political': The Rational Meaning of a Questionable Inheritance of Political Theology", in: Eduardo Mendieta/ Jonathan VanAntwerpen (eds.), *The Power of Religion in the Public Sphere*. New York: Columbia UP 2011, 15–33; „‚Das Politische' – Der vernünftige Sinn eines zweifelhaften Erbstücks der Politischen Theologie", in: Eduardo Mendieta/ Jonathan VanAntwerpen (Hg.) *Religion und Öffentlichkeit*. Suhrkamp: Berlin 2012, 28–52.
Hertzke, Allen D. 2004. *Freeing God's Children: The Unlikely Alliance for Global Human Rights*. Lanham, MD: Rowman.
Juergensmeyer, Mark, Margo Kitts, and Michael Jerryson, eds. 2013. *The Oxford Handbook of Religion and Violence*. Oxford: Oxford University Press.
Juul Petersen, Marie, "International Religious NGOs at the United Nations: A Study of a Group of Religious Organizations", in: *The Journal of Humanitarian Assistance* 2010 https://sites.tufts.edu/jha/archives/847

Juul Petersen, Marie, *For Humanity or for the Umma? Aid and Islam in Transnational Muslim NGOs*. London: Hurst & Company 2015.

Kippenberg, Hans G. 2019. *Regulierungen der Religionsfreiheit. Von der Allgemeinen Erklärung der Menschenrechte zu den Urteilen des Europäischen Gerichtshofs für Menschenrechte*. Baden-Baden: Nomos.

Krishnaswami, Arcot. 1960. *Study of Discrimination in the Matter of Religious Rights and Practices*. New York: United Nations. http://www.ohchr.org/Documents/Issues/Religion/Krishnaswami_1960.pdf.

Lehmann, Karsten. 2016. *Religious NGOs in International Relations: The Construction of 'the Religious' and 'the Secular'*. Abingdon: Routledge.

Lepsius, M. Rainer. 1973. "Parteiensystem und Sozialstruktur: zum Problem der Demokratisierung der deutschen Gesellschaft." In *Deutsche Parteien vor 1918*, ed. by Gerhard Albert Ritter, 56–80. Cologne: Kiepenheuer.

Lerner, Nathan. 2000. *Religion, Beliefs, and International Human Rights*. New York: Orbis.

Luhmann, Niklas. 1993. *Gesellschaftsstruktur und Semantik. Studien zur Wissenssoziologie der modernen Gesellschaft*, vol. 3. Frankfurt am Main: Suhrkamp.

Mahmood, Saba. 2016. *Religious Difference in a Secular Age: A Minority Report*. Princeton: Princeton University Press.

Mahoney, Paul. 1990. "Judicial Activism and Judicial Self-Restraint in the European Court of Human Rights: Two Sides of the Same Coin." *Human Rights Law Journal* 11: 57–88.

Mahoney, Paul. 1998. "Marvellous Richness of Diversity or Invidious Cultural Relativism?" "The Doctrine of the Margin of Appreciation under the European Convention on Human Rights: Its Legitimacy in Theory and Application in Practice." Special issue, *Human Rights Law Journal* 19: 1–6.

Menke, Christoph. 2013. "Privatrecht, Klagerecht, Grundrecht. Zur Einheit der modernen Rechtsidee." In *Der Staat im Recht. Festschrift für Eckart Klein zum 70. Geburtstag*, ed. by Martin Breuer, et al., 439–452. Berlin: Duncker & Humblot.

Molendijk, Arie L. 2007. "Versäulung in den Niederlanden: Begriff, Theorie, *Lieu de Mémoire*." In *Religion und Gesellschaft: Europa im 20. Jahrhundert*, ed. by Friedrich Wilhelm Graf and Klaus Große Kracht, 307–327. Köln: Böhlau.

Morin, Edgar. 1991. *Europa denken*. Frankfurt am Main: Campus.

Schilbrack, Kevin. 2010. "Religions: Are There Any?" *Journal of the American Academy of Religion* 78: 1112–1138.

Schuppert, Gunnar Folke. 2012. *When Governance Meets Religion: Governancestrukturen und Governanceakteure im Bereich des Religiösen*. Baden-Baden: Nomos.

Smith, Cantwell Wilfred. 1991. The Meaning and Ende of Religion. Minneapolis: Fortress.

Stahnke, Tad. 1999. "Proselytism and the Freedom to Change Religion in Human Rights Law." *Brigham Young University Law Review* 251: 251–344.

Stuckrad, Kocku von. 2016. "Religions and Science in Transformation: On Discourse Communities, the Double-Bind of Discourse Research, and Theoretical Controversies." In *Making Religion: Theory and Practice in the Discursive Study of Religion*, ed. by Kocku von Stuckrad and Frans Wijsen, 203–224. Leiden and Boston: Brill.

Sullivan, Donna J. 1988. "Advancing the Freedom of Religion or Belief through the UN Declaration on the Elimination of Religious Tolerance and Discrimination." *American Society of International Law* 82: 487–520.

United Nations. 1981. "Declaration on the Elimination of All Forms of Intolerance and of Discrimination Based on Religious Belief." New York: United Nations. https://undocs.org/A/RES/36/55.

United Nations Human Rights Council. 2013. "Report of the United Nations High Commissioner for Human Rights on the Expert Workshops of the Prohibition of Incitement to National, Racial or Religious Hatred." New York: United Nations. https://www.ohchr.org/Documents/Issues/Opinion/SeminarRabat/Rabat_draft_outcome.pdf.

Walzer, Michael. 1990. *Thick and Thin: Moral Argument at Home and Abroad*. Notre Dame, IN: University of Notre Dame Press.

Weber, Anne. 2009. *Manual on Hate Speech*. Strasbourg: Council of Europe Publishing.

Morny Joy
Gender and Its Vicissitudes

1 Introduction

During the last fifty years, a revolution has occurred that modified the accepted meaning and application of the word 'gender.' Formerly, it had functioned simply as a term of grammatical attribution, indicating whether terms, usually nouns in non-English languages, were of a feminine, masculine, or neuter gender. Yet, more recently, the term 'gender' has been involved in intense debates concerning its problematic relations with the notions of 'sex' and 'sexuality.' Most traditional religions have either attempted to avoid what they regard as the resultant highly politicized exchanges on this topic or have vigorously condemned such unwelcome developments.

Certain secular feminist scholars, such as Judith Butler, Linda Nicholson, and Joan Wallach Scott, began in the 1980s to employ the term 'gender' in ways that helped to dismantle the former basic meaning of the term. Their explorations would play a crucial role in their own discursive analyses of gender, sex, and sexuality. As a result, 'gender' was employed as a powerful tool that helped them to expose the inequities that resulted from male dominance and had remained unchallenged until the present era. Yet it does need to be acknowledged that masculinity itself began to be questioned by scholars such as the sociologist R. W. Connell[1] (2005 [1995]) and David M. Halperin (1998; 2002) who have examined various forms of male conduct and discourse that were in dire need of clarification.

A number of feminists in religious studies, such as Darlene Juschka, were also influenced by secular women scholars and undertook to explore the terms, 'sex' and 'gender,' as they were understood in the discipline of the study of religion. Juschka appraised the forms of male domination and debasement of women, in addition to suggesting alternative perspectives that moved ultimately from the analysis of gender to semiotics. The theologian Mary McClintock Fulkerson critically examined the role of compulsory heterosexuality as mandated in scripture. In response, she reinterpreted a biblical text, where she proposes a more inclusive reading of human sexual relations.

These monumental shifts have occurred at the same time as the categories 'secular' and 'religious' have undergone intensive scrutiny of their own binary divisions. Certain advocates, e.g., Charles Taylor (2007) and Jürgen Habermas (2006, 1–25; 224–223), have endeavored to find ways of introducing religion into the public

---

[1] R. W. Connell, formerly known as Robert W. Connell, is now known as Raewyn W. Connell. Connell's early focus was on hegemonic masculinity and gender inequality. Later in life, Connell identified as a transexual woman.

https://doi.org/10.1515/9783110473438-011

sphere, while many secularists are strongly opposed to any move in this direction. Fundamentalists of various affiliations also support an agenda of a complete domination by religion in both public and private realms.

At the heart of these disparate, though not completely mutually exclusive interactions, a power struggle has arisen that seeks not only to challenge heteronormative sexuality and gendered stereotypes but also to introduce more flexible modes of gender identification. Such a change would lead to the replacement of former monolithic and hierarchical institutions, be they religious or secular, that have closely monitored gender identity and sexual behavior. In regards to religions, perhaps the greatest struggle is that of questioning the 'truism' that proclaims God's divine decree of heteronormativity with its inherent model of what is termed 'a gender binary,' as in 'Male and female he created them.'

In this chapter, I will not be able to explore all the multiple variations and complexities of both the historical and contemporary developments that have informed the changing dynamics and demise of gender as indicating a binary separation. If I were to take into consideration all the variant positions of masculine and feminine roles, with their resultant responses and interrogations, they would require a book. Each critical assessment, especially with regard to sex and gender, besides being both intriguing and challenging, needs a careful and detailed examination. As a result, I have initially chosen to focus my article, using a framework of discursive analysis, primarily on the field of women's sex and gender studies. In addition, I will also evaluate certain of the changes that have occurred in the aspects of 'sex' and 'gender' as they have been challenged by 'queer' and 'trans' observations.[2]

My presentation, though basically chronological, presents what I term, 'vignettes,' as a way of visiting the distinct topics as they feature in discourse analysis. In addition to secular theorists and philosophers, such as Judith Butler, Joan Scott, and Linda Nicholson, who laid the foundations for the revolutionary intervention of gender in feminist circles, interchanges with religious attitudes and practices will be appraised. There has obviously been a revolutionary impact on religion, although it has also received harsh criticism from conservatively inclined persons.

This chapter is a survey of the complex interactions involving gender, sex, and sexuality, which Judith Butler initially named the "heterosexual matrix" (Butler 1990, 184).[3] The phrase marks a time and place where extremely profound changes would occur both in society and religion. To begin, I will focus on the period of protests by women during the late 1980s and 1990s where the term 'gender' was associated with those women who rebelled against essentialist claims that had delegated

---

[2] While this paper scrutinizes the impact of sex and gender, it further entails interdisciplinary investigations in order to help clarify and assess the effects of these disciplines on the study of religion.

[3] Butler's depiction of the 'heterosexual matrix' combines attributes and categories including heterosexuality and male privilege that dominate and control social and cultural practices, most of which are strictly enforced.

women to a system of social and religious subservience. Later in the chapter, however, I will also pay attention to another dynamic and passionate movement that has emerged and altered the status and identities of many people. In more recent times, this movement has disputed 'gender,' and introduced its own spectrum of subjective identities. This has resulted in people claiming a right to affirm their own identities, with titles such as 'queer,' 'trans,' 'gender fluid,' and 'gender neutral.' Consequently, the status of the term 'gender,' designated as a type of provocation against the long-held, culturally gendered constraints, lost some of its strength, and could be described today as no longer occupying the predominant position it had achieved in the 1990s (Scott 2010, 7–14).

Nonetheless, the word 'gender' with its contemporary permutations and negotiations, can still make a claim to have provided the impetus for women to contest their status of inferiority. In this guise, gender was deployed to contest the superiority of the male of the species, which was acknowledged as virtually all-pervasive. To account for the existence of this disparity, specifically in what has been named as the 'western world,'[4] a short selection of the philosophical, metaphysical, and religiously oriented antecedents that have informed its development is necessary.

2 Aristotle and the Diminution of Women

From a contemporary perspective, it may seem to be somewhat arbitrary, even disparaging, to cast blame on Aristotle for introducing a precedent of a human hierarchy where the female is regarded as defective. It is mainly Aristotle's theoretical and metaphysical works, especially the *Politics* and the *Metaphysics* (1971 [1941]), with their problematic claims, that have informed much of western philosophy and theology until the twentieth century. Aristotle laid a foundation of misapprehensions about women that has resulted in misogynistic consequences. It is not only the disparity in the attribution of male and female characteristics that is at fault. It is Aristotle's underlying metaphysical system that cemented his assumptions. The term 'patriarchal privilege,' which is of relatively recent origin, designates its presumption.[5]

---

[4] The term 'western' has long outlived its original qualification as designating a specific region and tradition. However, when referring to the history of philosophy and also theology, it remains a relevant marker.

[5] Aristotle need not totally bear the brunt of the tradition that affirms the inferiority of women. Thomas Aquinas (ca. 1225–1274) was strongly influenced by Aristotle's legacy. His major work, the *Summa Theologicae*, raises the issue of whether women should have participated in the original creation, given their deficiency. He responded somewhat grudgingly, allowing that while women did not have equal status with the male, their presence was required for the generation of human beings (*Summa Theologicae* 1964, Part 1a, q. 92, a.1, Obj.1). This concession was seemingly censured by his further observation: "For the active power in the seed of the male tends to produce something like

One telling example of Aristotle's statements is found in the *Politics*: "The male is by nature superior, and the female inferior; the one rules, and the other is ruled; this principle, of necessity, extends to all mankind" (Aristotle 1971, p. 1132, 1254b: 10–15). In contemporary discourse analyses of views on gender, it is Aristotle's metaphysical system, with both its implicit and explicit assumptions, that have since been found wanting. His infamous dictum that "the female is as it were a deformed male" (Aristotle, *Generation of Animals*, Vol. II, 1943, pp. 174–175, 737a: 25–30), also contributed to establishing the origin of women's inferiority in the western philosophical and theological domains. It is this metaphysical regime that is finally being challenged, although much of the contemporary terminology involved differs from the actual categories that Aristotle himself employed.

Perhaps the most detrimental of Aristotle's indictments, however, was his remark that women were lacking in what was understood as the rational or deliberative faculty. Aristotle did allow that a woman may have an intuitive grasp of truth, but this insight was not reached by either deliberation or logic. It was a woman's purported 'lack of authority' over the irrational elements of her constitution that prevented her from exercising practical reason. It is in the *Politics* that Aristotle declares: "For the slave has no deliberative faculty at all; the woman has, but it is without authority, and the child has, but it is immature" (Aristotle 1971, p. 1144, 1260a: 10–15). It is pronouncements such as this that are deemed responsible for the stereotype of women's deficiency in both mind and body.

3 Gendered Observations by Women Scholars

In the discipline of the study of religion, the terms 'gender,' 'sex,' and 'sexuality' are words that, until quite recently, had not featured prominently. In previous centuries, religious decrees regarding sexual promiscuity were promulgated by clerical authorities, naming what sins to avoid so as not to incur any punishment that entailed divine retribution. There were specific formulas directed at men and women, respectively, defining appropriate chaste, gender-specific, and god-fearing conduct. It is a particularly recent development that scholars in religion have taken to investigating these rules and have submitted them to what could be termed a discursive mode of 'gender analysis' – examining in detail the complex interactions of 'gender,' 'sex,' and 'sexuality,' especially in connection with the dynamics of power.

---

itself, perfect in masculinity; but the procreation of a female is the result either of the debility of the active power, or some unsuitability of the material," *Summa Theologicae*, Ibid. Such a judgment simply reinforced women's already dismal reputation.

Maryanne Cline Horowitz published a comprehensive article entitled simply "Aristotle and Woman" (Horowitz 1976).[6] It was one of the first to interrogate rigorously Aristotle's attitude toward women as is reflected in his writings. It also marked the beginning of a resurgence of critical interest in Aristotle by feminists. Horowitz does not mince her words: "Aristotle's belief in the mental and biological superiority of free men to both women and natural slaves, which was his ultimate justification for male rule in the household and state, gave sanction to a hierarchy of servitudes, including wifedom and slavery" (Horowitz 1976, 188). Horowitz also found fault with what she describes as Aristotle's "biological–philosophical concepts of male and female," where maleness is active and spiritual while femaleness is passive and of a material nature (Horowitz 1976, 186–187). This categorization needs to be placed in the context of Greek philosophical thought, where that which was associated with the spiritual was held in far greater esteem than what pertained to matter.

A more recent book by Sister Prudence Allen, *The Concept of Woman: The Aristotelian Revolution, 750 BC – AD 1250* (1997 [1985]), provides further insights. In addition to a close exploration of Aristotle's own philosophy with its theological implications, Allen exhaustively examines the historical effects of certain of Aristotle's principal views on other influential philosophers.[7] At the core of her work is a concept that she names "gender polarity," which she views as still permeating much of Christian teachings. Allen relates her understanding of this usage in response to Aristotle's statement that "male and female are opposite as contraries." She observes:

> Aristotle claimed that in a pair of contraries, one must always be the privation of the other. Subsequently the female was interpreted as the privation of the male.
>
> Since the concept of privation involves a negative variation, it follows that this description of the female [. . .] provided the metaphysical framework for sex polarity. [. . .] For Aristotle, contraries also involved a mutual hostility. [. . .] Aristotle grounded this relation of hostile opposition between women and men within the most fundamental of his metaphysical categories. Within this framework, he gave sex polarity the power eventually to dominate all of western philosophy. (Allen 1997 [1985], 89)

Allen's final evaluation, states that she is inclined to abandon Aristotle's version of the concept of woman, given its many misrepresentations. She then remarks that the errors evident in his version of sex-polarity need to be removed from his work on the subjects of biology, ethics, metaphysics, and politics. Nonetheless, Allen is willing to approve other topics in Aristotle's work, especially his move to reconcile

---

6 Maryanne Cline Horowitz observes: "The limiting of the feminist movement to the nineteenth and twentieth centuries reveals the myth of 'historical progress' at work, for the woman question has been a perennial question, rising in importance in particular historical epochs" (Horowitz 1976, 84, note 4).

7 A second volume was later published by Allen that surveyed other repercussions of Aristotle's work. In this volume, Allen included numerous medieval women's reactions. See Allen (2002).

soul with body, form with matter, and rationality with materiality. She appreciates these efforts as she believes they help to avert any tendency toward dissension between human beings (Allen, 1997 [1985], 124–125).

Unfortunately, however, Aristotle did not attempt to apply this insight of a compatible human alliance to the division he had wreaked between men and women. It is only in the present era that projects of possible restoration are being undertaken. Allen herself is a strong supporter of such developments. One message that can be gleaned from Allen's analyses is that although the early Jewish, and later Christian patriarchs, had their misgivings about Eve's conduct, which had already rendered women suspect, it was Aristotle, together with his later admirer, Thomas Aquinas, who consolidated the negative views of the female with their own respective philosophical and theological systematics.

Sophia M. Connell, a British philosopher, in her recently published book, *Aristotle on Female Animals: A Study of the Generation of Animals*, has provided other possible interpretations of particular books by Aristotle (Connell 2016; see especially chapter 1, "Feminism, Sexism and Aristotle," 17–52). Connell is troubled by the mainly negative reception of Aristotle's texts by a considerable number of contemporary feminists, who deem Aristotle as responsible for his founding of a philosophical approach based on the opposition of male and female (Connell 2016, 20). Connell cautions that this blanket judgment of Aristotle needs to be carefully appraised and revised within their specific socio-political contexts (Connell 2016, 28). In Connell's view, this procedure can help to delineate more accurately the source of Aristotle's sexism which, when analyzed, can be more explicitly defined.[8]

The main concern of Cornell is with certain contemporary women scholars' inaccurate interpretations of Aristotle's statements in *The Generation of Animals*. She worries that they are being transposed too hastily to Aristotle's other works, especially the *Metaphysics*, where they have been inaccurately conflated. In Connell's estimation, such scholars have not read the other texts of Aristotle with sufficient precision, particularly those dealing with his physiological descriptions. She is also wary, however, of a number of contemporary male classical scholars, and disagrees strongly with those who defend Aristotle's views, arguing that he was not sexist.[9]

Connell's close reading of biological matters in Aristotle's *The Generation of Animals*, in connection with what she names as "gender issues" (Connell 2016, 42), confirms that Aristotle's "female principle" (2016, 28), refers solely to animals. She does not agree that this phrase has any reference to actual women. Connell states that, according to Aristotle, although the "female principle" is connected to matter,

---

[8] Connell also states that: "Feminism benefits through the fact that a serious discussion of gender in Aristotle's works opens up, and highlights the importance of, areas of his philosophy that have been consistently marginalized in the past" (Connell 2016, 51).
[9] Connell does not accept this position where these scholars "consciously attempt to provide a non-sexist rationale for his [Aristotle's] assigning an inferior role to women" (Connell 2016, 40–41).

the female herself is never regarded by Aristotle as solely representing an inferior material element.[10] This latter remark becomes particularly relevant in Aristotle's discussions of the female's activity in her contribution to the conceiving of an embryo.

On this charged topic of conception, Aristotle has been accused of confining women to a passive receptivity, where the male is presented as both the initiator and the agent of the form/soul in any embryo conceived. (For Aristotle, the soul, when aligned with substance, forms the essence of a living being [Aristotle *On the Soul*, 1971, pp. 555–556, 412b: 5–10]. Such an interaction has been widely criticized by feminists as typical of Aristotle's disregard of women. In response, Connell counters that, in Aristotle's biological descriptions, matter and form are interactive, and that, without this connection, no conception occurs (Connell 2016, 28). Such a conclusion also supports Connell's own position, where she claims there is "no explicit justification for the oppression of actual women in Aristotle's biology" (Connell 2016, 33).

In contrast to her defense of Aristotle's position on matter in *The Generation of Animals*, it is in another section of the same volume that Connell does not hesitate to denounce Aristotle of "undeniable sexism" (Connell 2016, 42). She accuses him of "a stark and undeniable sexism which enters his explanation of the division of the sexes" (2016, 42). This sexism is also obvious in Aristotle's *Metaphysics* and *Politics*, where he denies women positions of equality, both in the home and in politics. Connell states that "a male-based attitude pervades many parts of Aristotle's thought" (2016, 47). For Connell, this negative disposition, especially in relation to probity, needs to be challenged. Her final judgment is that Aristotle should not be simply excused by the cliché that he was 'a man of his time' and did not deliberately intend to be sexist.

Connell's work thus situates Aristotle as a perplexing figure; one whose work in many areas still needs meticulous attention to determine his actual position on the fraught issues of sex and gender. It would be an intriguing exercise to consider what Horowitz's, Allen's, and Connell's responses to each other's studies might be, given their distinctive disciplinary affiliations and approaches to the topic. In addition, 'gender,' as a recent critical term, has changed the ground rules of debate by its disturbance of the strict binary division between male and female. As such, gender has become a debatable issue in contemporary discursive exchanges both within and outside of philosophy and religion. It is not immediately clear in such uncharted territory, however, whether these initiatives can assist in revising Aristotle's legacy. There is the prospect, however, that they could contribute to innovative advances in both theory and practice with regard to the status of women.

---

10 Given the contentious viewpoint where Aristotle aligns women with inert matter, Connell, with her careful reading of *The Generation of Animals*, responds that: "Aristotle does not identify women, or even the female contribution to generation, with matter in any straightforward manner" (Connell 2016, 28).

4 Innovative and Problematic Directions: The Separation of Gender and Sexuality

It is a major leap from Aristotle to the present-day's volatile debates on the topics of gender, sex, and sexuality. Undoubtedly, one could employ a thorough genealogical inquiry in the mode of Michel Foucault. This discursive practice could supply a number of appropriate references indicating important precursors. In fact, in *The History of Sexuality* (1980), Foucault does indeed supply references dating back to the Fourth Lateran Council (1215 CE) and the names of various moralists in later centuries. This, however, is not the main focus of his work. Foucault's inquiry begins with the seventeenth century, where, in its early stages, "shameless discourse" about sex still existed (1980, 3). By the end of the century, such language had begun to disappear. A period of repression, which Foucault defines as "the monotonous nights of the bourgeoisie," followed (1980, 3). Yet Foucault was not particularly interested in a basic historical documentary about this change and its possible deviations. Instead, he introduced a new method, which he named "discursive analysis." Foucault describes his approach:

> The central issue, then (at least in the first instance), is not to determine whether one says yes or no to sex, whether one formulates prohibitions or permissions, whether one asserts its importance or denies its effects, or whether one refines the words one uses to designate it; but instead to account for the fact that it is spoken about, to discover who does the speaking, the positions and viewpoints from which they speak, the institutions which prompt people to speak about it and which store and distribute the things that are said. What is at issue, briefly, is the over-all discursive fact. (1980, 11)

The problematic issue with Foucault's explorations in these matters, however, is that, as Carolyn J. Dean has eloquently expressed, "Foucault's work presumes a construction of men's but not women's subjectivity" (Dean 1994, 271–296). Nonetheless, many women scholars adopted Foucault's mode of discourse analysis to clarify their own versions of how repressive regimes have manipulated the lives of women. They were mainly interested in Foucault's own locating of the machinations of power that could interfere with their own existence. Such a detailed analysis can reveal deep insights and an awareness that, in turn, promotes resistance. As a result, Foucault's findings on sexuality did mark a milestone for women in that he introduced an "analysis of power" (Foucault 1980, 81). This encouraged women scholars to examine their own insights and concepts that would, in time, assist them in theorizing and implementing their critique of male domination – something which Foucault himself had never considered.

Another approach is undertaken by Kim Phillips and Barry Reay, the authors of the book, *Sex before Sexuality: A Premodern History*. They make a trenchant observation: "In the period dealt with in this book, ca. 1100–1800, there was sex but no sexuality" (Phillips and Reay 2011, 7). With this statement, the authors imply that, while there were certainly sexual couplings of diverse persuasions during this period, the intense interest in contemporary sexual preferences, identities, performance, and perversions, was not necessarily evident. The authors also warn that employing current terms, i.e., those dating from the late-nineteenth century, could distort definitions and interfere with an accurate understanding of premodern practices. (This could possibly be understood as an implicit warning against Foucault's own innovative vocabulary.)

It was in the 1950s, however, that certain thinkers from different disciplines would begin to propose ideas and concepts that would, in time, rearrange and 'complexify' contemporary awareness on the subject of sex and gender. John Money, a psychologist and sexologist working at the Johns Hopkins Hospital, Baltimore, describes how in the 1950s he had realized that the word "sex" bore the brunt of what he called a "terminological overload" (Money 1985, 72). He came to this conclusion from his early studies of children born with birth defects affecting their sexual organs. (Today the term 'intersex' is mostly employed in these situations.) In a later article, Money reminisced that, at that time, "there was no concept of 'gender identity disorder,' nor was there any recognition of the term 'gender' as a human attribute" (Money 1994, 163). He had first introduced the term "gender role," as a substitute for the former all-embracing concept of "sex role" in the *Bulletin of the Johns Hopkins Hospital* (Money 1955, 253). In a later article he stated: "So far as I have been able to ascertain, I was the first person to use the term, gender role, in print, and certainly the first person to define it in print" (1973, 397). In his further work at the Gender Identity Clinic, established at Johns Hopkins in 1966, Money continued to refine his understanding of this term with the additions of "gender identity" and "gender-identity role" (Money 1985, 71). In addition, he declared that the term "gender" and its qualifications, when separated from the concept of sex, marked an attempt to evade "gender determinism" (1985, 77). Consequently, the word 'gender' became an indicator of cultural affiliations and distinct from being identified with biological 'sex.' 'Gender' was also gradually integrated into scientific documents and usage. In addition, 'gender' also began to be adopted in literary works. Finally, it made its disruptive entrance into philosophy, theology, and the aptly named 'gender studies.'

Another pioneer was Robert Stoller, a professor of psychiatry at University of California, Los Angeles, who, in his book, *Sex and Gender: The Development of Masculinity and Femininity* (Stoller 1968), expanded on Money's statement. He was perhaps the first to state that 'gender' was definitely associated with culture, as distinct from 'sex,' which was solely biological. Stoller observed: "Gender is a term that has psychological and cultural rather than biological connotations; if the proper terms for sex are 'male' and 'female,' the corresponding terms for gender are 'masculine' and 'feminine'; these latter might be quite independent of (biological) sex" (Stoller 1968, 9–10). This declaration would resonate with mixed reactions in many disciplines in the years that followed.

Ann Oakley, a British sociologist, mentions Money's insightful work, *Sex, Gender, and Society*, (Oakley 1972, 7). Yet Oakley's own work headed in quite a different direction. She first noted that, in the growing controversy about sex roles, the majority of people used the term 'sex differences' when, in fact, they were actually referring to what she understood as 'gender differences' (Oakley 1972, 189). Oakley was one of the first women to make such a distinction. Her research findings led her to introduce the term "gender differentiation" (Oakley 1972, 203). She declared that it was women's alleged difference, including her purported inferiority when compared to men, that was central to the heated debates concerning the nomenclature of sex and gender. Oakley claimed that such disagreements were evidence that designations of cultural characteristics still retained a patriarchal privilege (Oakley 1972, 208). This situation continued because, rather than acknowledging gender as a "social ascription" (Oakley 1972, 204), most researchers still held strongly to views that gender differences were definitely innate.

In her own subsequent substantial body of work, Oakley's aim was to uncover the prejudices at work in this ingrained mode of gendered differentiation. Her future publications investigated the intricate cultural processes that influenced institutionalized power and thus inhibited women from attaining the parity and respect that she regarded as their due (Oakley 2005, 7–20). Oakley's work was extremely insightful about women's roles and conditioning. She devoted her research to depicting the unjust conditions of women's lives, e.g., especially economic dependence (2005, 22–23), as well as the travails of domesticity that restricted their lives (2005, 109–116). Although she recognized how the maneuvers of powerful males had severely affected women (2005, 196–205), Oakley did not address how women could strategically challenge this systemic deprivation of independence. Such an initiative was manifestly needed. This aspect would be undertaken in the work of Gayle Rubin, Judith Butler, and Joan Wallach Scott, but Oakley was unimpressed by their appeal to poststructuralism, and what she described as their "overdependence on theory" (2005, 208).

5 Feminist Developments in Sex and Gender

The anthropologist, Gayle Rubin, in her article, "The Traffic in Women," initiated a radical shift in the way that the "sex/gender system," as she described it, had functioned in North America (1975, 157–210). Initially, Rubin was suspicious of the intertwined dependency of sex and gender. She described her understanding as: "A 'sex/gender system' is the set of arrangements by which a society transforms biological sexuality into products of human activity, and in which these sexual needs are satisfied" (1975, 159). At the same time, however, Rubin was also suspicious of "the socially imposed division of the sexes," i.e., sexual dimorphism (1975, 179).

She also took to task the theories of Freud, Lacan, and Lévi-Strauss for their restrictive definitions and their denigrating observations about women. Finally, she advocated a revolution that would "liberate human personality from the straight-jacket of gender" (1975, 200). Rubin's work marked the beginnings of the gay and queer movement that would, in time, ignite an activist reaction.

In a later work, "Thinking Sex: Notes for a Radical Theory of the Politics of Sexuality" (1984, 267–319), Rubin altered her earlier thoughts as she continued to expand her awareness. This work in particular, would establish Rubin's reputation. She proposed that prescriptive rules, governing both sexuality and mandated gender roles, would become irrelevant. Rubin declared, "The new scholarship on sexual behaviour has given sex a history and created a constructivist alternative to sexual essentialism" (1984, 276). This change was inspired by her encounter with Foucault, both with the man himself and his work. It was her admiration for his avoidance of biological determinism and his emphasis on the "generative aspects" of sexuality that inspired Rubin to envisage a different future.

Rubin determined that in order to better understand the existing dynamics of the sex/gender system, which she judged to be regulated by "sexual essentialism" (1984, 275), she needed to explore alternative positions. She declared that, "In contrast to my perspective in *The Traffic in Woman*, I am now arguing that it is essential to separate gender and sexuality analytically to reflect more accurately their separate social existence" (1984, 308). This change was viewed as imperative by Rubin because, at that time, many people still continued to conflate the terms, "sex" and "gender."

However, Rubin's radical proposals were not universally acclaimed, and she was criticized by a number of feminists on different counts. The principal rebuke was that by severing biology/matter from socially constructed gender, biology would maintain a determinant role. A number of women scholars also accused Rubin of launching an attack on feminism.

There is a fascinating exchange in an article, "Sexual Traffic: An Interview with Gayle Rubin" (Butler 1994, 62–99), where Judith Butler and Rubin discuss their respective thoughts on the issues of sex, sexuality, and gender. Their exchange helps to clarify Rubin's reasons for separating sex from gender. In her responses to Butler's questions, it becomes obvious that Rubin did not regard herself as reprimanding feminism nor rejecting her own ideas as presented in "Traffic in Women." Rubin stated: "There was a different set of concerns that generated *Thinking Sex* (1984). I wasn't looking to get away from 'Traffic in Women'" (Rubin, in Butler 1994, 97). Instead, Rubin was proposing to replace the limitations she had diagnosed in the theory that had previously connected gender and sexuality. One of Rubin's most pressing issues was that she did not think feminism had yet dealt satisfactorily in addressing issues of "sexual difference and sexual variety" (Rubin, in Butler 1994, 97) Her intention was to clear "space for work on sexuality that did not presume feminism as the sole obligatory and sufficient approach" (Rubin, in Butler 1994, 88).

Subsequently, Rubin had to defend her version of sexuality and its queer dynamics from accusations of being lacking in morality, because her view of sexuality was regarded by some as unabashed self-indulgence or worse.[11] Ultimately, however, it was Foucault's influence that prompted Rubin's move to poststructuralism as an antidote to structuralism which had simply reinforced binary divisions. Given her strong criticisms of conventional theories, especially feminist theory's heterosexual bias and structuralism's intransigence, it was not surprising that Rubin would be attracted by constructivism.

Judith Butler was enthusiastic in her appreciation of Rubin's accomplishments, declaring:

> [W]hat interested me in "The Traffic in Women" was that you, by using a term that comes from American sociological discourse – "gender" – by using that term, you actually made gender less fixed, and you imagined a kind of mobility to it which I think would be quite impossible in the Lacanian framework. (1994, 68)

Butler then continued with a surprising admission that Rubin's work had so impressed her that it was one of the formative influences in her own change of direction: "I went with gender myself in *Gender Trouble*" (1994, 68).

In the closing section of the interview, when Butler somewhat playfully suggests that they return to the term "gender," Rubin appears to be somewhat apologetic about her own responses. It was as if she interpreted Butler's remark as intimating there had been no extensive discussion on the topic of gender during their exchange. Rubin simply replied to Butler: "I will only say that I never claimed that sexuality and gender were always unconnected, only that their relationships are situational, not universal, and must be determined in particular situations. I think I will leave any further comments on gender to you, in your capacity as the reigning 'Queen of Gender'!" (Rubin, in Butler 1994, 97).

It is intriguing that, in this context, Rubin, who herself was no stranger to queer theory and its deviations, refers to Butler as the "Queen of Gender." Although Butler had not made any explicit reference to 'queer' in her initial venture of subverting gender in *Gender Trouble* (1990), she was taken by surprise when the book was declared as "one of the founding texts of queer theory" (Butler 1999, vii). Yet the term "gender" had not featured prominently in Rubin's and Butler's conversation. This was because both Butler and Rubin had, by this time in 1997, already moved beyond 'gender' as a means of providing incentives to dislodge existing gendered affirmations. Rubin's negative attitude certainly served to present evidence that she did not hold current definitions of gender in high regard. Nevertheless,

---

11 See Jacobson and Pellegrini (2003, 134–35), who provide a reflective depiction of Rubin's position.

Rubin's work was a vital impetus that helped both women and men to experiment with alternative models of queer theory, such as 'trans,' 'gay,' 'gender neutral,' and 'gender fluid,' in addition to queer (Rubin 2011).

The two ground-breaking books of Butler's, *Gender Trouble* (1990) and *Bodies that Matter* (1993), had also introduced variations, such as parody and performativity, that created interruptions which 'disturbed heteronormativity.' Both Rubin and Butler, with their distinct contributions, had helped to realign the meanings and attributes of 'gender' so that the term was no longer identified with the static categories of a binary model that had dictated the restrictive terms of sexual difference.

There were, however, two objections made by a number of feminist critics about these developments. One, as observed above in Rubin's work, was the separation of nature/biology from culture/gender, thus virtually rendering these two categories mutually exclusive. The other charge, aimed at Butler's work, was that of her deregulated constructivism which encouraged infinite possibilities. (These topics will be addressed later in this essay.)

6 Gay and Lesbian Interventions in Religion

Inevitably, the question arises as to whether the work of poststructuralist feminists, such as that of Rubin and Butler, had a marked influence on scholars in the field of the study of religion. Another question that needs to be posed, given Butler's explicit commitment to queer diversions, concerns what kind of reception such a movement had generated, especially in the study of religion. One of the first feminist scholars in religion to engage with Butler's work was Mary McClintock Fulkerson, a theologian at Duke Divinity School. Among her academic specializations was the contemporary study of Protestant theology. Fulkerson's essays, "Changing the Subject: Women's Discourses and Feminist Theology" (1996, 131–146) and "Gender – Being It or Doing It? The Church. Homosexuality, and The Politics of Identity" (1997, 188–201), appeared in a series of publications that marked a distinct challenge to certain Protestant religious congregations with their ambivalent attitudes especially toward gay and lesbian members in their respective communities. Fulkerson's studies were set against the background of two Protestant denominations, the Presbyterian Church USA, and the United Methodist Church, both of whom, in the early 1990s, undertook extensive and divisive surveys that examined the divergent views of their followers, mainly concerning the religious status of gay and homosexual members.

In the opening pages of her essay, "Gender – Being It or Doing It?," Fulkerson asks a thought-provoking question that raised the possibility of a revised reading of Paul's statement in *Galatians* 3:28. She inquires: "What would it mean to claim that there really is 'neither male or female [. . .] in Christ' in the light of poststructuralist critiques?" She also questions whether a person who claims to be non-heterosexual will be welcomed by God or not (1997, 189). Fulkerson's questions indicate that she is deeply concerned with issues of sexual identity – specifically with those people who identify as lesbian and gay.

Fulkerson acknowledged the work of both Butler and Foucault as influential poststructuralists, and she approves of the challenges they declared against the regulations pronounced by rigid heterosexists. These moves disconcerted those with inflexible gendered definitions and attitudes. Fulkerson declares: "Any assumption that our notions of real sexual identity are somehow identical with the categories and world-views of ancient or biblical communities – if that is our theological authorization – is simply naive" (1997, 198).

Elaborating on this assessment, Fulkerson details other aspects of Butler's and Foucault's work that she had found instructive. She surveys Butler's analysis of the sex/gender problematic and her theory of social construction, which dismisses notions of predetermined sexual identity (Fulkerson 1997, 192). At the same time, by examining other gendered designations, such as heteronormativity, Fulkerson affirms the need for a Foucauldian genealogical analysis. Such a discursive approach helps to disclose the way that certain configurations, together with power, can dictate both social structures and definitive rules. Fulkerson viewed this discursive approach as assisting the detection of specific manipulations of power that are pervasive in the discourse of sexuality. Fulkerson's views are very much in agreement with Foucault's statement: "Sexuality must not be thought of as a kind of natural given [. . .] It is the name that can be given to a historical construct" (Foucault 1980, 105).

It is in another article, "Changing the Subject: Feminist Theology and Discourse," that Fulkerson justifies her adoption of this poststructuralist approach (1996, 131–147). First, Fulkerson describes her own understanding of poststructuralism.

> Poststructuralism, as used here, refers to a set of discussions within the broader currents of postmodernism initiated around language. The constituting character of discourse in this account is a move away from the view that language reflects reality. Poststructuralism enables recognition of the *made* – the socially coded – character of realities – of nature as well as culture, sexed bodies as well as gendered roles. (1996, 135)

In addition, Fulkerson declares that she does not agree that discourse operates solely on a verbal and theoretical level. Nor does she believe that feminist discourse analysis is merely immaterial. She carefully distinguishes her appreciation of what counts as a discursive practice. It can be appreciated as communicating a number of processes and activities, which Fulkerson lists as "bodily, oral, and not simple ideational or linguistic. Meaning may be spoken, written, gestured and/or performed" (1996, 138). In effect, discourse can have both material and practical results.

Perhaps Fulkerson's most important contribution, however, is her support of Butler's poststructuralist critique of substance metaphysics, especially as it has been applied to theology and, by extension, to feminist theology. Fulkerson affirms Butler's taking issue with a "substantialist notion of the subject," where the identity of "one's sex/gender" is aligned with an "essential self" (1997, 191–192).

Fulkerson also rejects what she terms the "metaphysical threesome of sex, gender and desire," and, in quoting Butler, she indicts the "metaphysical unity of the three, [that] is assumed to be truly known and expressed in a *differentiating desire for an oppositional gender – that is, in a form of oppositional heterosexuality*" (Butler 1990, 22, quoted by Fulkerson, 1997, 192; italics original). Yet, in adapting Butler, Fulkerson's aim is not only to eliminate this harmful combination of sex, gender, and desire which she judges as decisive for maintaining the male–female binary. She also appeals to Butler's position when she states that "[W]omen/men are not 'natural' and fixed entities. They exist not by ontological truth, but by virtue of 'repetition' and difference" (1997: 195). In this way, Fulkerson corroborates that gender cannot claim any idealized ontological status. Instead, she proposes, in agreement with Butler, that "genders are only produced as the truth effects of a discourse of primary and stable identity" (Butler 1990, 136).

In order to disempower this firmly established heterosexist regime, Fulkerson also assents to Butler's use of parody as an effective strategy in a process that Butler names the "denaturalization" of gender (Butler 1990, xxx). This intervention proposes that parody, as a mode of resistance, in connection with performance and performativity, can interrupt prescribed norms of bodily conduct (Butler 1990, xxxi).

When *Gender Trouble* was first published by Butler in 1990, however, she was strongly criticized for introducing such a strategy. Consequently, Fulkerson is extremely careful in her defense of Butler's approach, declaring that she appreciates Butler's work because it does not intend to eliminate the subject of 'women.' Nor did Fulkerson view it as anti-feminist. Instead, Fulkerson appreciates Butler's goal that such a move would permit alternative possibilities of self-formation to be introduced (Fulkerson 1997, 195). In this way, Fulkerson intends to unsettle Christianity's complacent and self-defensive attitudes toward gender.

Fulkerson was motivated to write this essay by the reluctance of the mainline Presbyterian and Methodist Protestant traditions to implement fully the recommendations resulting from their respective committees' study reports. These were both tabled in 1991 (See Fulkerson 1997, 500n1–501n4). Agreeing with Butler's arguments, Fulkerson sought to protest Christianity's own biased attitudes. She accuses both society and religious traditions – despite stalwart efforts by gays and lesbians for their inclusion – of still presuming that the normative ideals of traditional binary sexual identity should predominate.

It was for this reason that Fulkerson had recourse to Butler's and Foucault's work as a stimulus to awaken in her readers an alternative vision of how things could be otherwise. In the concluding section of "Changing the Subject," Fulkerson justifies her turn to poststructuralism:

> Poststructuralism, understood as a way to look at discourse is useful because it opens up the instability of meaning, its exclusions, and its connections with desire, power and location. By appropriating its refusal of fixed meaning, whether the "real woman" or the real meaning of male language, feminists can shift from the notion that everything is fluid to look at the arrangements of actual situations. (Fulkerson 1996, 146)

At the same time, Fulkerson proposes a "theological grammar" or discourse that refuses to endorse any "natural identity" (1997, 194), be it of metaphysical or scriptural derivation. She also invokes an "iconoclastic criticism" (1997, 198), which she describes as a form of scripture directed toward a radical love. Fulkerson's description of this transformative interpretation is based on a discourse of fallibility that encompasses human finitude and error. Such an evocation, in turn, summons relations that admit to weaknesses, yet expand with accountability, kindness, respect, and *agape* toward others who are similarly susceptible (1997, 198). It is then that Fulkerson affirms that this orientation can further enlarge its range so as to encompass new modes of gender identity. This development, enhanced by her deft textual analysis, allows Fulkerson to return to her opening remarks. She now ventures to repeat her initial enquiry with an increased emphasis that has become an exhortation: "[I]t is time to read Galatians 3:28 with a new literalness, admitting that we are all performing our sex/gender" (1995, 199).

Fulkerson's engagement with sex, gender, and desire launched an important movement in subjecting religion and gender to a close analysis from a poststructuralist perspective. Since Fulkerson's iconoclastic essay, and her own strategic emendation of *Galatians*, the topic of gender and religion, has been enhanced by the publication of numerous volumes in the last twenty-five years. They have been authored and edited by multi-identified scholars who have further advanced respect for gay, lesbian, queer, and trans orientations. These volumes include titles such as: *Que(e)ring Religion: A Critical Anthology Religion* (Gary David Comstock and Susan E. Henking, 1997). This volume was where Mary McClintock Fulkerson published her article, "Being It or Doing It"; *The Gender/Sexuality Reader* (Roger N. Lancaster and Micaela di Leonardo, 1997); *The Transgender Studies Reader* (Susan Stryker and Stephen Whittle, 2006) and *The Routledge Queer Studies Reader* (Donald E. Hall and Annamarie Jagose, 2013).

7 Variations on a Theme of Gender in Religion

As late as 2005, there was still some confusion among women scholars in religion as to the manner in which the word 'gender' was to be incorporated into the study of religion.[12] This became obvious to me when I was invited to address the issue of "Gender and Religion" at a conference (Joy 2006, 7–30). To my surprise, when I did an online search, I found at least thirty titles of books published in the past five years in connection with women, religion, and gender. This inspired me to familiarize myself with such diverse usages. Firstly, I discovered that the English term "gender," even from its grammatical perspective, is not available in many languages, e.g., it does not exist in Chinese or Finnish. Consequently, the word "gender" is usually transliterated, with occasional odd results (Li Xiao-Jian 2004, 87–103). It was not my intention at that time, however, to become entangled in such linguistic technicalities concerning "gender." My task was rather to investigate the types of meaning of gender that were then in circulation. It became both a wide-ranging and challenging task as I explored these variations.

Example 1: Gender as Equivalent to the Word "Woman"

Many of the books I read did not explicitly theorize, let alone problematize, the concept of 'gender.' The word was being used in a general sense, and was virtually equivalent to women. It was also employed as a descriptive term, referring to women's roles in society. To give one example, and to show that I was not immune from such a tendency, I will cite an article of my own called "God and Gender: Some Reflections on Women's Invocations of the Divine" (Joy 1995, 17–30). From my present stance, I can admit that, at that time, I was employing the term in a general way, without any precise definition of 'gender.' The chapter explored the recent modes of 'God-talk' by feminists who were resisting the attribution of male qualities to the divine. In other articles, 'gender' had varying connotations that were associated with the qualifier 'female.' Basically, at that time, 'gender' was being employed in a nebulous, though vaguely feminist, fashion.

Example 2: Gender as Indicative of Culturally Accepted Behavior

A number of books understood 'gender' as referring to both 'male/masculine' and 'female/feminine' roles and characteristics as representative of society's view of requisite behavior for men and women. Such books indicated an awareness that

---

12 This section of my essay was previously published in *Temenos*, the *Journal of the Finnish Society of Religion*, Vol.21/1 (2006): 7–30, with the title "Gender and Religion: A Volatile Mixture." It appears here under the title "Variations on a Theme of Gender in Religion." Another short section of this essay was separated and appears in the section named, "The Vatican's Objection to Gender." Both essays have been revised and adapted. They are printed with the permission of the editors of *Temenos*.

these roles could change in time, but there was no enquiry into the origins or the genealogy of such roles – it was enough to describe their present situation. In certain historical studies, this descriptive task was sufficiently demanding to preoccupy the author's attention. As a consequence, however, there was little in-depth analysis of such changing conventions and their consequences. Occasionally, such descriptions, whether intentionally or not, intimated directions for further intensive enquiries but these suggestions never seemed to be examined in detail.

An example of such an approach can be found in *Patterns of Piety: Women, Gender and Religion in Late Medieval Reformation England* by Christine Peters (2003). This historical study traces certain effects of the Reformation on women, which Peters refers to as having a "gender impact." In describing the changing practices of Christian piety, Peters depicts a gradual movement after the Reformation towards a Christocentric mode of parish piety. This differed markedly from the former monastic and mystical variety. It also seemed that the paradoxical viewpoint of medieval times, where women were simultaneously characterized as more prone to piety, yet also more liable to sin – especially the sins of the flesh – were fading. Other traditional gender stereotypes that characterized men as rational and self-controlled, and women as weak and emotional, became less emphatic. Nevertheless, sin was still judged in proportion to the degree of responsibility one held within the prevailing patriarchal system. Peters observed:

> The weak, emotional temptress could be viewed as less culpable than the man who succumbed to her sexual charms, and her husband who had failed his duty to guide and control her. Moreover, that both interpretations were present in varying degrees in late medieval culture added to the ambiguities of gendered experience, as so did the apparently contradictory stereotype of the godly woman. (2003, 346)

This was a succinct and largely accurate assessment of what Peters viewed as ambiguities. Yet, because the book's purpose was principally to give an historical account of this change, there was little on-going genealogical inquiry of the relevant implications for the status of women. With few exceptions, women appeared to remain subjects of a male-dominated religious hierarchy that continued to control their existence.

Example 3: Gender as Essentialism

In contrast, however, there were various works that criticized the previously limited descriptive approach toward gender roles in historical settings that adopted a discursive mode. This move can be appreciated as marking the beginning of an explicit mode of 'gender criticism.' It questioned the normativity of specific cultural attributions or designated roles. It was also especially concerned with understanding the way that 'gender' had been identified with what, in time, had become enforced behavioral ideals. In this way, such ideals had come to represent timeless or essential qualities that were identified with women.

By questioning such idealist models of women, Kathleen Biddick, in her essay "Genders, Bodies, Borders: Technologies of the Visible" (1993), undertook a critique of Carolyn Bynum's book *Holy, Feast, Holy Fast* (1987). It examined the lives of medieval Christian women mystics. Biddick questioned both Bynum's notion of the body and her seeming acceptance of the myth of a triumphant *Christianitas*, with its elisions and omissions. In her scrutiny, Biddick documents how Bynum's treatment of a medieval woman saint's body unproblematically accepts the characterizations of women as reflecting, not just an historical, but a predetermined maternal reality. As Biddick notes: "The model of gender in *Holy Feast, Holy Fast* assumes that gender is an essence that appears prior to other categories and informs them; that the feminine mirrors, indeed reduces to, the female reproductive function; that the female body is the originary, foundational site of gender" (1993, 397).

Biddick's claim is that neither gender nor sex is inherently inflexible – indeed, for her, each term is first imagined and then culturally constructed. Rather than taking Bynum's study at face value, Biddick reads her work as a case-study of the construction of a definitive gendered regime. As such, her analysis contains invaluable insights for a contemporary application (1993, 390). Instead of simply equating a women's body with the maternal, Biddick asks: "How can we write these histories such that in making women 'visible' we do not blind ourselves to the historical processes that defined, redefined and engendered the states of the visible and the invisible?" (1993, 390). In other words, Biddick was concerned with the exclusions in Bynum's ostensibly gendered portrayal. Biddick wondered specifically what had been elided by Bynum's unquestioning acceptance of women's maternity, in both its spiritual and physical senses. Biddick's work helps to introduce a mode of historical exploration of a discursive nature, with gendered inflections, that does not accept an historical depiction as necessarily a definitive account. In concluding, she indicates that further exacting enquiries are definitely needed.

Example 4: Gender as a Critical Analytic Category

Another approach was evident in a volume edited by Kari Elisabeth Børresen, *The Image of God: Gender Models in the Judaeo-Christian Traditions* (1995). This work was a response to the way particular facets of the feminine gender had been designated not simply as essentialist, but also as mandatory for women. The different contributors to this edited volume all evaluated the manner in which the concept of *imago dei* had been interpreted over the centuries. The predominant view was that it is man alone who is regarded as *theomorphic*, i.e., made in the image of God. As her main analytical category, Børresen, employed the phrase "human genderedness." She described this as "the sense of a combined biologically given and a socio-culturally shaped female and male existence" (1995, 1). She stated that such assigned gender attributes are neither innate nor normative, but culturally established.

Børresen's principal intention, which was theologically motivated, was to decipher, through a close reading of Christian scripture and tradition, that revelation could be understood as a continuous process rather than an obligatory fiat. In her own interpretation of the creation of the sexes, Børresen appealed to the biblical passage where both male and female are created in the image of God (Genesis 1: 26–28). For Børresen, this passage supports the full inclusion of women in humanity's god-likeness. Consequently, she argues that it is not only men who are presumed to be *theomorphic*. By employing gender as an analytic tool of interpretation – where gender was not prescriptive – Børresen dismantled centuries of exegesis. Her conclusions had important theological resonances. She affirms that women also are created, both body and soul, in the image of God. They are not necessarily inferior. Børresen's work supports contemporary claims by women that they be fully accepted as equals within the Christian religious tradition.

Example 5: Gender as a Tool of Comparative Analysis

The next study is of an anthropological nature. Nevertheless, it fits neatly within the scope of the study of religion. It also adds to the growing repertoire of meanings of the term 'gender,' where gender roles and qualities are not regarded as either intrinsic or universal. In her book, *Spirited Women: Gender, Religion, and Cultural Identity in the Nepal Himalaya* (1996), Joanne Watkins used the word 'gender' in what would initially appear to be primarily a neutral sense. She described what she terms the "egalitarian gender configurations," i.e., the roles and relations of the Nyeshangte people of Nepal. Watkins describes the gender relations and roles adopted by men and women in this Buddhist society as complementary and non-hierarchical. In addition, however, there is a practice that Watkins named "gender variance," where the identity of 'male' or 'female' do not always follow expected gender roles. This indicates that certain social roles were interchangeable. Watkins describes how, in such a setting, "neither men nor women are [. . .] prevented from participating in their society's two central institutions: international trade and Buddhist ritual practice" (Watkins 1996, 16). Thus, women could perform religious rituals because they are not "denigrated nor are they regarded as polluting" (Watkins 1996, 17). Though Watkins made no explicit binary commentary, she was employing gender as a tool of subtle cultural analysis and contrast. Her position was thus not entirely neutral, as it suggested a comparison with western religious practices where 'gender variance' roles have not been commonly accepted. By comparison, in most prominent western religions, it has proven extremely difficult for women to be allowed to act as ritual specialists, ostensibly because of the allegation that menstruation is polluting.

Example 6: Gender as a Mode of Subversive Disturbance

The next example marks a definite change in approach, particularly because the author has employed 'gender' in both a theoretically sophisticated and a critical mode. Biblical scholar Deborah Sawyer had been influenced by Judith Butler's work on gender. As mentioned earlier, Butler had rejected the accustomed frames of reference that aligned sex with specific gender characteristics and roles that were viewed as natural, if not metaphysically ordered, from a religious perspective.

Sawyer introduced certain ideas of Butler, as well as those of the early Luce Irigaray (1985), in her book, *God, Gender and the Bible*. Her intention was to disturb traditional gender categories in the Bible. By using Butler's concept of gender as 'performative' from *Gender Trouble*, Sawyer deemed that, because prescribed gendered behavior had often depended on political and/or religious mandates, rather than on any intrinsic characteristics, it could be challenged. Such a strategy however, as in Butler's work, also depended on acknowledging the category of gender as performative – i.e., that it is acquired by repetitive enactment of roles (Butler 1990, 25). Yet Butler's intent was also one of parodying such established normative roles. This is similar, in some respects, to Irigaray's device of critical mimesis. As a mode of deconstructive, philosophic, and psychoanalytic reading of texts, this tactic was deployed to reveal the mechanisms controlling gendered assignments. It especially targeted those that privileged the male position – be it associated with intellectual, social, or religious contexts (1985, 76). What both these approaches advocated was the disturbance of accustomed gendered priorities. Their intention was to encourage a more fluid construction of gender. This would then replace the traditional gender dimorphism of specific male and female roles. Such a tactic would also allow gender to become a multivalent category, thus liberating sex from its primary identification with the procreative functions. In both of these models, one could ideally – though to my mind, not unproblematically – choose one's gender identity from a spectrum of possibilities.

By arguing that the Bible provided grounds for such gender modifications, Sawyer applied this theory to the story of the pious widow, Judith, in the Hebrew Bible. Judith deliberately adopted the wiles of a seductress to at first beguile, and then to decapitate the Assyrian general Holofernes, an arch-enemy of Israel. Sawyer stated: "The chorus of women recognize the achievement of [this] unconventional warrior, and we are able to observe how gender games have been employed to subvert the expected, entrenched norms of this ancient socio-political context" (Sawyer 2002, 97).

The ultimate irony of this story, however – and this does not escape Sawyer's notice – was a further latent message embedded in this text. It warns men to beware of siren women, for it may ultimately cost them their heads. Unfortunately, however, in the context of the Bible, this particular incident falls into insignificance over the years. It is overwhelmed by a predominantly male ethos that, until recently, has understood itself as alone being divinely ordained as superior in the order of creation.

Example 7: Gender as an Historically Disruptive Strategy

If such deconstructive mimesis and parodic disturbances can only help women to advance a limited distance in their explorations, the question becomes: are there other potentially effective strategies that can assist women in a period when the prefix 'post-' has become prolific? One book that could provide further assistance is *Playing for Real: Hindu Role Models, Religion and Gender*, edited by Jacqueline Suthren Hirst and Lynn Thomas (2004). In surveying certain prescribed role models for Hindu women, whether they appeared in sacred texts, myths, or popular stories, Hirst and Thomas investigated the interventions of authority and power latent in these stories. They were particularly concerned with the directives prescribed for the proper conduct of women. What was of marked interest to them was the social and political regimes that determined these assigned gendered roles. In their introduction to the volume, Hirst and Thomas recognized the complexity of both the reception of, and resistance to, such role models, inflected as they are in India by caste, age, economic status, and political allegiances, in addition to religion.

Suthren and Hirst acknowledged their theoretical debt for this intricate social analysis to the postcolonial feminist writings of, among others, Kumkum Sangari (1990), where phrases such as "cultural imperialism" and "gender essentialism" were often evident. Initially, these phrases had been deployed to challenge colonialism and its imposition of gendered regulations that resonated with discipline and power. Originally, gender rules, similarly to colonial regulations, were principally designed to control women or the conquered/marginalized peoples who needed to be trained to be obedient and subservient.

In reviewing all of the above articles, however, it becomes quite evident that, during the 1980s and 1990s, studies by women in religion were slowly maturing and moving in the direction of a critical awareness that introduced discursive analyses. This gave rise to a forceful rebuttal of many religions' extremely controlling attitude to women and their closely monitored gendered behaviors.

8 History, Discourse, and Gender Analysis

Ever since her first essay on the topic, "Gender: A Useful Category of Historical Analysis" (1986), Joan Wallach Scott, the American historian and critical theorist, continued to propose both demanding questions and innovative prospects for the term "gender." In the revised introduction to her book, *Gender and the Politics of History* (1999 [1988]), Scott introduces the principal concerns that have thus far guided the orientation of her work. She states:

> As a historian I am particularly interested in historicizing gender by pointing to the variable and contradictory meanings attributed to sexual difference, to the political processes by which those meanings are developed and contested, to the instability and malleability of the categories, "women" and "men," and to the ways those categories are articulated in terms of one another, although not consistently or in the same way every time. (1999, 10)

Although she acknowledged that 'gender' had been adopted by feminists in the 1970s with the goal of exposing the way that history had treated women (1999, xi), Scott was committed to clarifying the distinctive role that 'gender' could contribute to an analysis of historical texts and their biases. She forged a path that was to revolutionize how one could both engage with and promote a heterodox use of the term. Scott was not content to accept a stark separation of biological sex from the cultural construction of gender. Her intention was to contest even this crucial move by encouraging women to scrutinize attentively the trajectory by which sexual difference had dictated the terms of women's lowly status.

Scott proposed her own understanding of gender: "The core of the definition rests on an integral connection between two propositions: gender is a constitutive element of social relationships based on perceived differences between the sexes, and gender is a primary way of signifying relationships of power" (1986, 1067). She added a qualification that, although these two aspects are related, they must remain analytically separate (1067). Although gender is understood as intertwined with power, it is not identified with power *per se*. Scott described gender as "a field within which or by means of which power is articulated" (1986, 1069). She understood that this field of gender involved a manipulation of power that deployed sexual difference in a manner that excluded and belittled women. Yet Scott was also aware that gender could be activated as an instrument of change. To initiate such a disconcerting process, Scott introduced a mode of gender analysis that shattered views of standardized sexual difference and their associated essentialist claims. Scott's confrontation with these obstacles resulted in an awakening of women's resistance to such well-established norms.

Initially, Scott was influenced by Jacques Derrida, but it was Foucault's poststructuralist approach, as well as his insights of the exercise of power, that had the strongest influence on her work. Refusing to accept causal arguments and normative ideals as irrefutable, she examined the mechanics of power in a discursive manner. This enabled her to detect a prescribed code of behavior which controlled the status of women. As a result, Scott advocated a strategy where 'gender' featured as an analytical aid that supported women in their quest for recognition. In time, this move would acknowledge women as participants in history, rather than being automatically dispatched to the periphery. Scott first explains her reasons for adopting 'gender' as a specific and useful category: "'Gender' seemed the best way to realize the goal of historians of women in the 1970s; to bring women from the margins to the center of historical focus, and, in the process, transform the way all history was written" (1999, xi–xii). This strategy was based on her adaptation of Foucault, especially his work on genealogy.[13]

It is extremely enlightening to follow Scott's trail as she first demonstrates how gender constructs can first be contextualized by employing a Foucauldian discursive analysis. She then illustrates the way these tenets can then be subjected to a further dissection that exposes their own inadequacies, as well as their severely restricted views of women's abilities. Finally, in her move from text to action, Scott introduces tactics that help to form a radical activist response to counter such distortions. This would allow women to defy conventions with critical moves such as acts of resistance, reinterpretation, and other emancipatory endeavors.[14]

Scott would nonetheless differ in one aspect from Foucault's model of discourse and his notion of a "discursive field."[15] As her work delved more deeply into the situation of women, Scott became aware of the limits of theory and realized that she needed to encourage a mode of support for women's own agency. As noted earlier in this chapter, this was not advocated by Foucault.

When she implemented gender as a disruptive category, Scott first asked two basic theoretical questions: "How does gender work in relationships? And How does gender give meaning to the organization and perception of historical knowledge?" (1986, 1055). It was only later, in her "Revised Preface" to the second edition of her 1988 volume, *Gender and the Politics of History* (1999), that she detailed the

---

13 Scott (1991, 796) cites Michel Foucault's description of genealogy, which has implications for her own work: "[I]f interpretation is the violent or surreptitious appropriation of a system of rules, which in itself has no essential meaning, in order to impose a direction, to bend it to a new will, to force its position to a different game, and to subject it to secondary rules, then the development of humanity is a series of interpretations. The role of genealogy is to record its history: the history of morals, ideas, and metaphysical concepts, the history of the concept, of liberty or of the ascetic life; as they stand for the emergence of different interpretations, they must be made to appear as events on the stage of historical progress" (Foucault 1977, 151–152).
14 Scott did not position 'gender' as the only analytic category. Scott acknowledged race and class were also just as capable a lens through which to view the inequities of social designations, but her preferred emphasis was that of gender.
15 For Foucault, 'discourse' or 'discursive analysis' was not confined to words and texts. Instead, the field was widened to cancel the division between words and things. As a result, any system or structure that was influenced by cultural formation such as habits, constructions of various types, attitudes and behaviours, were all modes of meaning that could be discursively investigated. A 'discursive field' indicated overlapping discourses that could interact, influencing gradual changes. Scott's work enabled women to participate in 'discursive analyses' aided by her insightful inclusion of 'gender,' which Foucault did not acknowledge.

exacting questions that she viewed as necessary to move from theory to praxis. These are:

> How and under what conditions [have] different roles and functions been defined for each sex; how [have] the very meanings of the categories "man" and "woman" varied according to time and place; how [were] regulatory norms of sexual deportment created and enforced; how [have] issues of power and rights played into questions of masculinity and femininity; how [do] symbolic structures affect the lives and practices of ordinary people; how [were] sexual identities forged within and against social prescriptions. (1999, xi)

In Scott's view, all of these behaviors and movements, when filtered through the lens of gender, aided the detecting of how the misapprehensions that have diminished women were configured. She observed: "When historians look for the ways in which the concept of gender legitimizes and constructs social relationships, they develop insight into the reciprocal nature of gender and society and into the particular and contextually specific ways in which politics constructs gender and gender constructs politics" (1986, 1070). These in-depth investigations aided Scott to confirm that any official status of definitions and proclamations of gender were not sacrosanct. Such a realization implied that they could be realigned to support innovative gendered relations that would not only foster equity but also allow divergent modalities of gender.

An engaging comparison can be made between the work of Scott and her comrade in dissension, Judith Butler, about their respective views on the category of gender and gender difference. A further and even more compelling account is the manner in which Butler described their differences in an essay, "Speaking Up, Talking Back: Joan Scott's Critical Feminism," which appeared in a book that Butler co-edited with Elizabeth Scott (2011).

Butler relates that it was she who was most opposed to the term "sexual difference" (1993, 21), as basically sustaining heteronormativity and thereby reinforcing the static categories in a binary gendered system. In taking issue with this construct, Butler began to use the term "queer" in her attempt both to disempower its former abusive connotations and also to disconnect binary gender dogmatism. In introducing "queer," Butler intended to employ the term as galvanizing a site of contestation. She declares that the word "queer" was distorted or "twisted" in its former use, where it indicated an insult or a degrading epithet. Instead, Butler proposed to mobilize "queering" by supporting its deconstruction of fixed meanings and directing them toward more constructive political engagements and alliances. However, Butler was wary of any meaning that might assume control and dictate new rules or norms. Instead, she suggests: "The term will be revised, dispelled, rendered obsolete to the extent that it yields to the demands which resist the term precisely because of the exclusions by which it is mobilized" (1993b, 17).

In comparison, Scott did not regard 'gender' as having any ambitions to attain an absolute status as 'truth.' Nor did she align it with any metaphysical status. Consequently, Scott considers 'sexual difference' as a particular structure located within an historical context, which is not immutable. Her approach was to discover the collusion at work in cultural and political maneuvers so as to repudiate the claims of such constructs.

Although there are a number of similarities in the work of Butler and Scott, it would appear that their views on the issue of 'sexual difference' were dissimilar. This difference, however, did not lead to any major friction between them. In fact, Butler admits that Scott was one of her close interlocutors and she describes her own position in relation to Scott's:

> And though I certainly set out to upset normative accounts of gender, and to question the restriction of binary thinking on our conceptualization of gender, I worried that sexual difference was itself normative within feminism [. . .] Although these were, and remain, different approaches, the commitment to coming up with a critical feminism clearly bound us together in a common project, one that we understood at the time to require and to specify poststructuralism. (2011, 21)

Butler and Scott were clearly mutually supportive of each other's work. Their theories encouraged many feminists to follow their lead in a ground-breaking project that advocated introducing new perspectives about issues involving sex, gender, and their entanglement with notions of truth and power. By investigating the origin of such major items, they both looked to Foucault's analysis of what he termed, 'régimes of truth.'[16] In short order, however, they were both severely taken to task by religious authorities for their work, which was judged as being offensive, if not profane.

9 The Vatican's Objections to 'Gender'

It was the unsettling of gender norms and roles by an intervention of the term 'gender,' as undertaken by both Butler and Scott that upset fundamentalist Christians in the United States. It also troubled the late Pope John Paul II, as well as conservative elements in other religions. Butler describes her astonishment when she learned of the maneuverings of the Vatican in the lead-up to the Beijing world conference on the status of women in 1995, sponsored by the United Nations: "The Vatican not only denounced the term 'gender' as a code for homosexuality, but insisted that the platform language [of the conference] return to the notion of sex, in an apparent effort to secure

---

16 Both Butler and Scott were also influenced by Foucault's insight on what he describes as 'régimes of truth.' In such regimes, truth and power were interwoven and functioned as forms of 'regulatory control.' (Foucault 2000, vol. 3, 111–133). However, both Butler and Scott introduced other elements into their disruptions of such régimes, such as Butler's use of 'queer' and Scott's use of 'gender', especially in relation to their respective views on the regulative norms that did not recognize women's integrity and decision-making as part of their identities.

a link between femininity and maternity as a naturally and divinely ordained necessity" (Butler 2001, 423). Scott, reported on another occurrence in the United States around the same time, when a sub-committee of the U.S. House of Representatives entertained submissions that warned morality and family values were under attack by "gender feminists" (1999, ix). It would appear that both the Vatican and the neoconservative groups in the United States had been informed of Butler's work, if not Scott's approach as well, with their respective questioning of traditional gender roles.

Scott reports that the American speakers in the House of Representatives, in their own depiction of this threatening situation at the Beijing conference, also described it as having been hijacked by so-called "gender feminists" (1999, ix). They further portrayed such women as believing "everything that we think of as natural, including manhood and womanhood, motherhood and fatherhood, heterosexuality, marriage and family [as] only culturally created 'fixes,' originated by men to oppress women" (Scott 1999, ix). Nonetheless, in one sense, the critics of this disruptive use of gender were perceptive because they did sense that 'gender,' as it was being used by Butler and Scott, had become, for a time, a key term for women who no longer wished to assume that biology dictated destiny.

The United Nations, however, did not capitulate to the Vatican's pressure. Statements were issued at the Beijing conference, reflecting on the findings of a special group designated to investigate the usage of the term 'gender.' A motion at the UN meeting was passed, allowing that the term 'gender' would be retained, in accordance with its accepted usage in numerous other UN forums and documents. The UN declared that there was no indication of any new meaning or connotation of the term 'gender' that differed from prior usage. Nevertheless, one could well ask, what is this ordinary, commonly accepted prior usage of 'gender' that the United Nations accepts? A careful reading of the UN conference resolutions indicates that 'gender' refers to the basic differences between men and women that are simply taken for granted. It could thus appear that the UN was not necessarily on the side of the alleged "gender feminists" but still regarded gender as a neutral descriptive marker, designating the male and female of the species as belonging to different biologically determined sexes.

There were, nonetheless, numerous scholars and activists who wondered if it was worth continuing the struggle for gender and women's rights at the UN, so effectively organized had the opposition become (Posadskaya-Vanderbeck 2004). The Vatican continued to promote a conservative block and formed alliances with other countries to oppose what they deemed as anti-marriage, anti-family, and antiprocreation measures. In recent years, however, such movements have not been quite so effective, though they have certainly not disappeared. Their tactics, however, were politically targeted to keep women in their proper place, as the unsullied guardians of a nation's morality. It is extremely telling that, in many of these religions, a nation's fall from grace is often blamed on women's waywardness, especially sexual deviance. They judged that women were in need of being rescued from their fallen state and returned to supervision and subservience. Gender, as it is interpreted by Joan Scott, continued to oppose such a divinely ordained decree. Many activist women in the study of religion have since both followed and refined the work of Scott and Butler on the analysis of gender.

10 Further Adventures of Sex and Gender in the Study of Religion

One of the more prolific scholars in the study of religion who had closely followed the development of the term "gender" as presented by Butler and Scott is Darlene Juschka. In her publications (1999; 2005 [2009] 2014; and 2016), Juschka has written from a mainly critical perspective when it comes to religion. In her initial essay, "The Category of Gender in the Study of Religion" (1999), she presented an outline of the period from approximately the 1980s to the 1990s, sampling diverse theories of gender and their implications. She also included book reviews of two recent volumes by scholars in religion: John S. Hawley's *Fundamentalism and Gender* (1994), and Ursula King's *Gender and Religion* (1995). It appeared, however, that Juschka felt that she needed to introduce "a map of the terrain of feminist analyses" (1999, 77) to clarify the situation. This was provided by an overview of mainly secular feminists' analyses of gender, especially by those who had attempted to introduce innovative theories concerning the dynamics of sex and gender. Certain scholars cited by Juschka in her essay were from diverse disciplines, e.g., an anthropologist, Sherry Ortner (1974; 1996); a psychoanalyst, Nancy Chodorow (1978); a psychologist and ethnologist, Nancy Jay (1991) and a philosopher, Moira Gatens (1991). It is also apparent that, in her later work, Juschka was also influenced by the work of feminist scholars such as Butler, Christine Delphy, Linda Nicholson, and Scott, to name the most prominent. Yet such was the diversity of the above views, the gender theories proposed were not necessarily in agreement, given the complexities of the variable definitions involved.

In her reviews of the works of Hawley (1994) and King (1995), it soon became evident that Juschka was disappointed with what she found. Her assessment of the two books, whose titles both included the word 'gender,' indicated that vital factors were lacking. As a result, while Juschka did commend some significant changes, she also specified deficiencies in the theorizing of 'gender' as it was presented in the study of religion.

Her verdict declared that great care needed to be exercised in the subtle process of disentangling the multiple influences in any study where sex and gender are involved. Instead of generalizations that result in a singular, sweeping diagnosis, what is required is a precise analysis of each specific context. Such a critical analysis would pay close attention to the personal, social, temporal, and geographical contexts. This move would also help to define particular regional differences and to prevent facile generalizations.

In her review of Hawley's book on fundamentalism, Juschka detects two major problems. Her first concern is that the basic term 'gender,' as understood by Hawley, is not contested. As a result, a heterosexual formula is firmly entrenched. There is no attempt to question the history or structure of gender with its specific properties and values, let alone examine any intermingling of gender with sex. The consequence of such a failure to appraise gender, is that a western patriarchal model, with its stark gendered division, is automatically assumed.

Juschka surmises that such a lack of insight occurs because it is not gender itself, but fundamentalism, that is of prime interest to Hawley. Yet even on this topic, Hawley does not impress Juschka. In her view, his second failing is that he regards fundamentalism as a static category. Hawley situates degrees of fundamentalism, each spaced in a static position, along a continuum spread between liberal and conservative extremes. As a result, this continuum is mapped in terms of western definitions. The problem then arises that any study of non-western religions will suffer from the imposition of such western categories. This occurs at the expense of non-western religions' own distinct orientations and definitions. For Juschka, the word 'gender,' as treated in Hawley's book, does not appear to introduce any new understanding of the terms 'sex' and 'gender,' but simply reinforces the standardized prevailing system.

The second book, edited by Ursula King (1995), does seem initially to receive Juschka's approval. This is because, in her Introduction, King does acknowledge that gender is a cultural construction. King also agrees that there has been a distinction drawn between sex and gender. It appears, however, that King, instead of examining both of these categories and their theoretical significance, intends to maintain a sharp separation of sex and gender. Juschka does concede that the essays in King's book do raise intriguing issues about women, gender, and religion, especially as they pertain to sexist ideology and religious hierarchies. She is troubled, however, that King fails to address the troublesome issue of sex and its relation, gender. Juschka states that, by not examining the "bedrock naturalism of sex," King appears to assign gender as being complicit with sex. This, in turn, supports the reification, rather than a deconstruction of sex, as a distinctive agent (1999, 103–104).

Juschka responds to such obstacles, remarking that such a composite of sex and gender could become extremely problematic. The main result would be a type of biological foundationalism, where gender continues to yield to the primacy of sex. Another possibility is that gender, separated from sex, is left alone to languish and is regarded as being of lesser significance. In Juschka's view, this latter separation could sustain a form of gender polarity. This view was also proposed earlier by Prudence Allen in the section on Aristotle (1995, 81). It is also not difficult to detect in these formulations a latent influence of Aristotle's devaluations of women, also described earlier by Allen, as possibly lurking in the shadows. Linda Nicholson aptly summarizes the basic influences affecting this situation:

> When the Bible or Aristotle is the source of authority about how the relationship between women and men is to be understood, any asserted differences between women and men are to be justified primarily through reference to these texts. When, however, the texts of Aristotle and the Bible lose their authority, nature and the body become the means for grounding any perceived distinction between women and men. This means that to the extent that there is a perceived need for the male/female distinction to be constituted as a deep and significant one, the body must "speak" this distinction loudly, that is, in every aspect of its being. The consequence is a two-sex view of the body. (1994, 88)

Juschka, in a seemingly exasperated rejoinder, inquires why this continued usage of a two-sex dichotomy needs to be assigned constantly to human sexual difference. She had explored such aspects of sex, sexuality and gender in a chapter entitled "What is Gender? What is Sex? What is Gender/Sex?" (2005 [2009]). However, it is as if Nicholson's above diagnosis responds to Juschka's question. She agrees with Nicholson's further analysis, where she clarifies the two inconsistent viewpoints of sex and gender as they had been inherited from the 'second wave of feminism' during the 1960s and 1970s. The first of these aspects is that of biological foundationalism and its connection with sex, and the second aspect regards gender as a cultural construct, implying that gender can be chosen at will. Nicholson criticizes both of these, especially the construct of gender which she names as a "coatrack" model where cultural characteristics can be hung, i.e., assumed at will in a non-deterministic way (1994, 81–2). Nicholson strongly disapproves of such moves, declaring: "Biological foundationalism and the coatrack view of identity in general stand in the way of our truly understanding differences among women, differences among men, and differences regarding who gets counted as either" (1999, 82).

In concluding her own remarks, Juschka reviews the results of her earlier survey of current developments in the study of sex and gender in her 2005 [2009] chapter. Her severest commentary occurs toward the conclusion: "Feminism cannot counter the hegemonic understanding of sexed behavior if it continues to use a category [gender] which was created by that hegemony [male] in order to oppress/repress and control the female, and in that women" (103). For Juschka, it is imperative that the dialectical interactions of the categories of sex and gender, or 'gender/sex,' as she preferred to call them, become the central elements that are in need of vigilant analyses. As such, there is a demand to not only investigate the dynamics of power at work in any such interactions, but also to clarify the role of institutions which, by wielding such power, uphold or even dictate their terms of reference.

Juschka both recapitulates and amplifies her findings with certain qualifications (2005 [2009], 231–233). She also outlines what she considers to be viable results from a critical modification of the study of religion. This is the outcome of her version of discourse analysis as introduced by Foucault which she has adapted. She states: "The interrelated categories of gender and sex [or gender/sex as she had regarded them] provide a means and a way to understand not only the how and why of religions, but equally the how and why of social organization and the manufacturing of culture in and of itself" (2005 [2009], 235). Juschka regards this innovative advance as enabling not only a careful investigation of cultural systems with their accompanying structures, including religion, but also as perhaps encouraging of transformation. Her final injunction warns that it is imperative for feminist scholars in religion to be alert and to intervene in any offensives of power-plays attempted by male hierarchies. She views such collusion as still being endemic in most religious institutions with their hierarchical regimes that either debase or exclude women. It is this insight that will influence her rejection of religion as being a detrimental hindrance.

From the beginning of her writings, it seemed that Juschka was seeking to comprehend the function of gender/ sex in relation to religion. This resulted in her construct of a theoretical model that had helped to explain the problems and distortions in the work thus far undertaken in the study of religion. Her chapter, entitled *What is Gender? What is Sex? What is Gender/Sex?* (2005 [2009]), was mainly animated by Juschka's realization of religious dogmatism, especially in matters concerning women. It also led to a somewhat blunt statement that summarized the harsh restraints that religion had imposed on women: "[R]eligion has been one method to ensure the subordination of women . . . and the absence of women as living persons within the development and disseminations of religions" (2009, 235).

In a later volume, *Political Bodies/Body Politic: The Semiotics of Gender* (2014 [2009]), Juschka describes how she had been perplexed by the potent influence of what she described as "gender/sex ideology." She realized that this development required further investigation in order to discern its specific machinations (2014, 1). To assist in this task, Juschka then proposed to adopt a 'semiotics of gender.' Such a theoretical approach would assist in providing insight into the entanglements of human behavior, when they are combined with particular rules and traditions, especially those dominant in religion.

Juschka's stance, however, did not simply consist of an analysis of the subjugation of women. She had also become fascinated by the obscure weavings of myth, ritual, and sign-symbol. Inevitably, her search extended beyond religion to include a much wider investigation, which incorporated both social and cultural conventions together with their regulative demands. Juschka describes this development:

> My interest is to better understand how gender/sex is coded in the modern world, and how particular discourses such as history, evolutionary biology, primatology, medicine, and popular culture in the novel, film, and art are central to the discursive formation of gender/sex. This discursive formation, I have argued and continue to argue, is then deployed through myth, ritual, and symbol providing gender/sex with a concreteness and reality that is, as any good Marxist would contend, mystified. (2014, 133)

With this declaration, Juschka affirmed her neo-Marxist orientation. One result of this preference was that Juschka redirected her use of language, thus rejecting the dubious nature of religious expressions. She declared, "I resist using the term 'religion' throughout this text and instead opt to use the phrase 'system(s) of belief and practice', as I feel this latter allows me more latitude" (2014, 19). (In this case, "system" indicates "a collection of independent but interrelated constituents that comprise a unified whole" [2014, 39].)

Juschka added a number of further qualifications to this position. In her view, myth, symbol, and sign-symbol may not be evident in certain forms of religious expression. In order to identify these terms, Juschka expanded her framework so as to integrate them with sex/gender analyses in order to help evaluate the "system(s) of belief and practice" (2014, 19). Her other concern involved a situation that could occur when systems of belief and practice, with their myths, rituals, and sign-symbols, are still accepted as implementing a divine ordinance, rather than assessing social and cultural categories (2014, 191). Juschka adopted a strategy to intercept any automatic inclusion of a religious nature. Such a procedure is also in keeping with her removal of what she describes as "the ideological mystification of gender/sex" (2014, 12).

Given these modifications, it can be argued that Juschka has rejected the confining elements of religion. Henceforth, her work could be identified as that of a secular scholar employing multi-disciplinary approaches, e.g., sociological and anthropological methods, in addition to semiotics. What has become obvious, however, is Juschka's resistance to the intransigence with which religion has implemented its doctrines. Her intense study of these practices, primarily intended for women, were directed toward to providing alternative possibilities for those interested in redefining their identities. This procedure was not only obvious in a secular society, but also in women's growing dissent from rigid religious edicts.

It was in this ambience, somewhat surprisingly, that Juschka acknowledges the work of three major feminist Catholic scholars, Mary Daly (1987), Elisabeth Schüssler Fiorenza (1985), and Rosemary Ruether (1983), who were intent on reclaiming their status as independent women. In so doing, Juschka expanded on her depiction of these three feminists about whom she had written in her PhD thesis, entitled *Feminist Encounters with Symbol, Myth and Ritual* (1998). Juschka expressed how each women, in their distinctive ways, had challenged the patriarchal autocracy of religion by reintroducing the history of women in the early church. This paved the way for women's efforts to introduce a form of Catholic Christianity that promoted "a system of belief and practice" where peoples of all dispensations could support each other in a just and egalitarian relationships. However, as theologians, they were not especially interested in discourse analysis, nor in the theoretical debates that analyzed sex and gender (2009 [2005], 251–253). At the same time, African American women were also making their presence felt with their adoption of what they termed a womanist rebellion. (See especially Katie Cannon [1998] and Dolores S. Williams [1993]).

Juschka was also resolute in her demand that any reanimated categories of gender and sex "must be submitted to an ongoing social and historical analysis" (2009,

249). At the same time, she advises women that it is imperative to remain wary of the interventions of power that persist in many religions. In a more recent publication, "Feminism and Gender Theory" (2016), Juschka provides, after many years of exacting effort, her latest refinement of the term 'gender,' where she again refrains from acknowledging 'religion.' Instead she endorses her phrase, "systems of belief and practice":

> Gender is a central and primary concept – fluid, constructed, and ever-changing – deployed in and through human signifying systems toward establishing epistemological and metaphysical narratives of existence. Some might argue such a claim is immoderate, but many would not. Gender plays a key role in all aspects of human existence be it in language, education and knowledge production, social organization, or systems of belief and practice (aka religions). It is no surprise that gender is a hotly contested subject. (2016, 137)

This definition appears to be a open-ended explication that resembles the fluidity of contemporary gendered fluctuations where gay, queer, trans, and gender-neutral identities, among others, have destabilized traditional norms of gender. In the present era, however, it would appear that 'gender' no longer represents "a hotly contested subject", as it did in the 1990s. It has also been forsaken by its former advocates, Butler and Scott. It remains to be seen how the status and understanding of gender, as it has been presented by Juschka, will emerge from the multiple variations that have since continued to appear and to demand their own rightful space and recognition.

11 The End of Sexual Difference?

Judith Butler also supplies her own concise overview for the future of both sexual difference and gender in an article entitled "The End of Sexual Difference?," published in *Feminist Consequences: Theory for the New Century* (2001, 414–434). Her contribution also encompasses an open-minded viewpoint that would encourage diverse arrangements about sexual differences, though it differs from that of Juschka. Thus far, Butler's position on these issues had not been fully developed. As a result, it was Butler herself who began to question the relevance of gender and sexual difference and explore other modalities of identity. She declared:

> This human will not be "one," indeed, will have no ultimate form, but it is one that is constantly negotiating sexual difference in a way that has no natural or necessary consequences for the social organization of sexuality. By insisting that this will be a persistent and open question, I mean to suggest that we make no decision on what sexual difference is, but leave that question open, troubling, unresolved, propitious. (2001, 432)

In the years that followed, Butler examined other emerging issues of gender as they appeared, including developments in queer theory. Surveying the territory, she remarked that "the term 'gender' has become a site of contest for various interests" (2001, 425). She situated this observation especially in relation to queer theory, stating that: "[S]exual difference is clearly out of favour within some reigning paradigms of queer theory" (2004, 426). Butler did not intend, however, to assess the respective merits of these competing factions, nor to accept any precise definitions. She believed that it was more important to consider the diverse meanings that the word 'gender' had acquired:

> My purpose is not to win a debate, but to try to understand why the terms are considered so important to those who use them, and how we might reconcile this set of felt necessities as they come into contact with one another. I am here as interested in the theoretical reasons proffered for using one framework at the expense of another as in the institutional possibilities that the terms alternatively open and foreclose in varying contexts. (2001, 416)

Butler sought to identify the ways that a specific word could alter gender's meaning and to appraise the results that ensued. Yet she cautioned that, while the meanings of terms can be disputed, they need not necessarily be discarded. Butler's main concern was that, if only words that were deemed acceptable were employed, the energy and curiosity sparked by challenging outdated definitions would be lost. At the same time, however, she made an astute evaluation of the present situation that raised the conversation to a higher level. She states:

> I want to suggest that the debates concerning the theoretical priority of sexual difference to gender, of gender to sexuality, of sexuality to gender, are all cross-cut by another type of problem, a problem that difference poses, namely, the permanent difficulty of determining where the biological, the psychic, the discursive, the social begin and end. (2001, 426)

These decisions certainly marked a shift away from the previous preoccupations that solely analyzed the meanings of gender, sexuality and sexual difference. However, these terms did not definitively disappear from Butler's vocabulary. In pursuing this issue, Butler inquired: "What does this way of thinking sexual difference do to our understanding of gender?" (2001, 427). One response could be that it indicates gender would no longer remain at the center of Butler's attention. She would move the topic of 'gender' into a completely different terrain. This would place Butler at a distance from those countries or regions where gender was still considered as a contentious site. In these domains, gender norms would continue to function, not simply as regulative ideals, but often as fixed and non-negotiable items (2001, 429–431). Butler, however, would continue to expand her range of interests to include innovative aspects of social, political, and ethical matters.

The new topics that emerged from Butler's reflections addressed issues such as those of vulnerability, precariousness, precarity, grievability, and the conditions that support what is considered as a 'livable/bearable life.' Such topics introduce serious ethical and political dilemmas. In *Frames of War* (2009), Butler confirms this definite change of direction, acknowledging that she has moved away from her former main concern with sexuality and gender to the politics of war (2009, 1–32).

In this context, precariousness and precarity specify the vulnerability of human existence, no matter what sexual identity is involved. Butler states: "Precariousness and precarity are intersecting concepts. Lives are by definition precarious: they can be expunged at will or by accident; their persistence is in no sense guaranteed. [. . .] Precarity designates that politically induced condition in which certain populations become differentially exposed to injury, violence and death" (2009, 27).

Such matters can also determine whose lives count and who are excluded, as, for instance, those who identify with LGBTQI+, and who are ostracized. Yet, similarly to her thoughts on gender matters, Butler does not seek watertight definitions, nor exact solutions. Instead, she supports a watchful awareness that would detect and carefully appraise any restrictive pronouncements with their harmful effects.

This move is in keeping with Butler's thinking that began when she first replied to criticisms of *Gender Trouble* (1990). One major concession was that she later acknowledged that she may have played too fast and loose with her ideas of gender, materiality, and the body. This was clarified in her new "Preface" to the tenth anniversary edition of *Gender Trouble* (1999 [1990], vii–xxvi). She observed that "*Gender Trouble* had sought to uncover the ways in which the very thinking of what is possible in gendered life is foreclosed by certain habitual and violent presumptions" (1999, viii). She also emphasized the main purpose of this exercise:

> The point was not to prescribe a new gendered way of life that might then serve as a model for readers of a text. Rather the aim of the text was to open up the field of possibility for gender without dictating which kinds of possibilities ought to be realized. One might wonder what end "opening the possibilities" finally is, but no one who has understood what it is to live in the social world as what is "impossible, illegible, unrealizable, unreal, and illegitimate is likely to pose that question." (1999, viii)

In a 1998 interview with Irene Costera Meijer and Baukje Prins that Butler stated in simple words the incentive that lies at the heart of her commitment to this humanitarian cause: "My work has always been undertaken with the aim to expand and enhance a field of possibilities for bodily life" (1998, 277). One could agree that this remark would remain at the center of Butler's work, where, in addition to 'mattering,' the body would now feature as an element of central importance, no matter what form of human identity is involved.

There was no surprise, then, in the 1999 the republication of *Gender Trouble*, where, in the "Preface," Butler named the topics that she would now include if she were to rewrite the earlier volume. These represent extremely relevant topics: transgender and intersexuality, racialized sexuality, gender dimorphism, and taboos against miscegenation (1999, xxvi). Butler also addressed the topic of queer studies in more detail. Her conclusion to the "Preface" makes it emphatically clear how her activist sympathies are now being mobilized in both ethical and political directions. Her focus emphasizes the vulnerability of those persons whose bodies are excluded from a heteronormative regime. She concludes: "This book is written then as part of the cultural life of a collective that had, and will continue to have, some success in increasing the possibilities of a livable life for those who live, or try to live, on the sexual [and racial] margins" (1999, xxvi). Such a statement indicates a significant change in Butler's approach to the modes of suffering and conflict that she has continued to witness as the struggles of peoples' lives in what can be an intimidating and dangerous world.

12 The Demise of Gender's 'Cutting Edge'

Joan Scott, Butler's comrade in their early passionate exchanges about 'gender,' had also begun to lose interest in the topic of gender in the late1990s. Scott noted that "gender seems to have lost its ability to shock and provoke us" (1999 [1998]: xii). There was also a lack of the enthusiasm that had previously animated rebellious ways of thinking and living. In the "Preface" to her own revised edition of *Gender and the Politics of History*, Scott admitted that, as the 1990s came to a close, 'gender' also seems to have lost its critical expertise (1999 [1988], xii). Scott then conceded that her original 1988 edition was a product of the 1980s, an era when 'gender' had become a trouble-maker. Gender analysis had disorganized the customary gender arrangements by indicating the discrepancies between distinctive male and female codes of behavior. The marked shift away from gender feminism during the 1990s, however, was extremely disheartening to many. Scott turned her attention elsewhere, continuing her disruptive tactics in other contested areas, such as academic freedom.

In her article, entitled "Gender: Still a Useful Category of Analysis?" (2010), Scott revisited her original article on this topic (Scott, *Gender and the Politics of History*, 1988). She states frankly: "[D]espite much innovative research on sexuality, gender – at least in historical discourse – most often refers to an enduring male/female opposition, a normatively (if not distinctly biological) heterosexual coupling, even when homosexuality is the topic being addressed" (2010, 10). Scott expresses her disquiet that the sex/gender binary remains extant, despite a combative generation of scholarship aimed at dislodging the fixture of sexual difference. Her conclusion is frank. "Gender is, I would argue, the study of the vexed relationship (around sexuality) between the normal and the psychic, the attempt at once to collectivize fantasy and to use it for some political or social end, whether that end is nation-building or family structure" (2010, 13). Scott implies, however, that gender could possibly reclaim its former status, if it were still sufficiently energetic to summon the strength to undertake a strict self-critical diagnosis. But even this remark seemed jaded.

Scott also invited a number of respected feminist scholars from diverse backgrounds to provide their own views in a volume as to how women's studies and its flagship, 'gender,' had gone astray. In *Women's Studies on the Edge* (2008), Scott fully supported the strategy of turning "feminism's critical edge against itself" (8), requesting the participants that they offer their criticisms and recommendations for the future. She observed that feminists had previously employed such a critique on numerous issues. Perhaps the most crucial contemporary questions that she posed were: "What does it mean to make 'woman' the object of our studies? What are the exclusions performed by insisting on a homogeneous category of 'women?'" (2008, 7). It is somewhat intriguing that Scott even provided the requirements needed for engaging in such a task but, surprisingly, she did not specify gender as playing a major role in the proceedings.

The responses of the contributors of the invited volume were certainly not hesitant. Criticisms came from all directions, including such problems as: institutionalization; fragmentation into subcultures; standardization. One scholar, Gayle Salamon, Professor of English at Princeton University, raised a vital question at the beginning of her article on: "Transfeminism and the Future of Gender" (2008, 115–136). She asks: "What is the relationship between women's studies, feminism, and the study of transgenderism and other normative genders?" (2008, 115). She follows this by remarking that trans-teaching and scholarship have not necessarily been received with open arms in women's studies. Salamon observes that "transgenderism" is perhaps the latest addition to a list of disparate identities, e.g., women of color, lesbians, queer, and sex radicals, who have not been admitted into the closed ranks of gender studies with their exclusive feminist categories (2008, 116). Salamon also suggests that trans studies could rejuvenate gender studies. This would result from the fact that trans categories do not fit easily into established 'gender' definitions. Just as 'gender' disrupted the staid rules and regulations that had governed gender binarism, transgender studies could deliver an invigorating debate that "requires a new articulation of the relation between sex and gender, male and female" (2008, 117).

Scott herself, at the end of her "Introduction" (2012, 13), endorsed a revolutionary change where intellectual connections could be reassembled. She proposed a cross-disciplinary approach, which she promotes as being of an indeterminate orientation, an approach that would be "on the edge of discovering new possibilities" (2012, 13). The salient issue, however, is whether there would be a consensus among scholars who are willing to collaborate in such a perilous venture, or whether 'gender' would submissively be absorbed by what looms in a *terra incognita*.

13 Further Reflections on Queer, Transgender, and Other Identities

There is one vital observation that needs to be taken into account when considering the above interactions. This is that many of the women involved, Judith Butler, Mary McClintock Fulkerson, Darlene Juschka, Gayle Rubin, and Joan Scott, all attest to the influence of Michel Foucault. This is in accord with their own understanding of his work, especially discourse analysis. Yet perhaps it is time for a divergence from the previous intensive commitment to the causes of sex and gender. It does appear, however, that Butler is the only one who is determined to build a bridge to the other forms of identity that have emerged as viable alternatives to the fading support for sex and gender, i.e., identities such as 'queer,' 'trans,' and more recent terms such as asexual, non-binary, and bisexual.

In an interview with Judith Butler by Sara Ahmed (2016), Butler states that, because the terms of gender normativity can function in an autocratic fashion, they need no longer be accepted as irrevocable – "one can now decline, deride, and 'queer' them" (2016, 485). In answer to another question posed by Ahmed about her attitude to the words, 'feminist' and 'queer,' Butler affirms: "I would not deny or refuse such terms. I would only dedicate myself to not letting them become ossifying in their effects" (2016, 488). It is in this context that Butler adds names for the conditions that would help to render life livable for all people. They include equality, freedom, and justice, and are directed toward attaining these outcomes for the vulnerable, i.e., especially those who have been excluded by gender norms and other sexual irregularities. What is also evident in Butler's work is that she does not discriminate in her empathy for all types of human identity.

During recent years, however, an interesting anomaly has developed with regard to Butler's work. Regardless of her ongoing support of attempts to "depathologize queer and trans lives" (2016, 483), she has been the subject of a number of criticisms. Butler's own position on 'queer,' however, has stayed basically in keeping with her definition in *Bodies that Matter*: "[It] will have to remain that which is, in the present, never fully owned, but always and only redeployed, twisted, queered from a prior usage and in the direction of urgent and expanding political purposes, and perhaps also yielded in favor of terms that do that political work more effectively" (1993a, 228). At that earlier time, 'queer' had been deployed initially to counter the stabilized, if not severe, imposition of gendered roles and prescribed identities. Yet, in her interview with Sara Ahmed (*Sexualities*, 2016), Butler's comments reveal thoughts that may have led to a misinterpretation, if not disagreement with her words.

It was in her interview with Ahmed, that Butler also describes in a retrospective reflection how she was somewhat troubled with the advent in 'queer studies' of a need to introduce a "queer identity" (2016, 489). This demand to identify oneself within the parameters of queer and trans configurations was disconcerting. Butler admits that she had been more inclined toward a type of queer work that helped to promote alliances but not to emphasize identity. However, she did acknowledge this dilemma, and reflected: "But then again, I have to ask myself: why should we not be startled by the directions that a term like 'queer' takes? It has travelled far and wide, and who knows what next permutation it will have?" (2016, 489).

Yet even further complications were to intervene in connection with 'transgender' protests. Butler states that many 'trans' and 'intersex' people, and their supporters, had charged that 'queer' has become restrictive, even an exclusive term, by not acknowledging a 'trans' way of living (2016, 490). In her response Butler admits that versions of 'queer' had been justly accused with being "presumptively white and classist." As if to promote a balance in this situation, Butler also states her respect for the growing Queer People of Color (QPoC) movement that incorporates colonialism, class, gender, race, and sexuality in its studies (2016, 491–492). Finally, there was the issue of identity itself. As 4part of her reflections, Butler poses a question:

> If "queer" means that we are generally people whose gender and sexuality is "unfixed" then what room is there in a queer movement for those who understand themselves as requiring – and wanting a clear gender category within a binary frame? [. . .] Many people with intersexed [and "trans"] conditions want to be categorized within a binary system and do not want to be romanticized as existing as "beyond the categories." (2016, 490)

In answering this hypothetical question, Butler does not dismiss the claim that, for some trans people, the issue of autonomy is important. Neither does she regard this request as individualist, but as an issue of recognition. In Butler's view, all of the above controversies are in need of very attentive deliberation by all concerned.

Recent years have witnessed the proliferation of disparate queer and trans identity claims that contribute to 'gender variance,' i.e., the diverse titles such as 'gender queering,' 'gender non-binary,' 'gender-fluid,' and 'gender-neutral,' that has prompted disagreements. It is helpful in this context to quote the wise words of Susan Stryker, an openly lesbian trans person, who observes in her book, *Transgender Studies*: "Neither feminism nor queer studies, at whose intersection transgender studies first emerged in the academy, were quite up to that task of making sense of the lived complexity of contemporary gender at the close of the last century" (2006, 7). It seems that today, as gender becomes qualified by unfamiliar words, that a generation gap has emerged. Butler herself understands that these issues, as they relate to ways of addressing others, no matter what their identity, will assist in making life livable. She concludes her reflections with a further astute question that addresses the heart of the issue:

> How do we think about bringing feminism into a closer relation with queer and trans and with anti-racist struggles without letting those who conduct trans phobic diatribes monopolize the meaning of feminism, or those who continue to believe that feminists must continue to defend themselves against the claims of cultural difference? Can we still own queer – or any of these terms – without letting them monopolize difference, allowing for a certain movement of thought that is grateful to its critics for letting us think something new, that is glad to be in the mix of emerging alliance and not the ultimate sign of its unity? (Butler 2016, 492)

As a result, during recent years gender has morphed into many divergent identity claims, as well as some rejections. There have been ugly clashes between anti-trans feminists and transsexuals. At the same time, there are also other queer groups who remain content sheltering under a capacious and diverse LGBTQI+ umbrella.

Many of the younger generation prefer to identify simply as nonbinary, thus allowing for more fluid forms of sexuality and gender. In the background there are the theorists such as Butler who have attempted to provide insights into the extremely problematic issues that abound without imposing any absolutist declarations. Yet very little of these developments has been made welcome in religious circles until quite recently. In the following sections of this chapter, I will address certain of the inroads that have come to be either acknowledged or disparaged as part of the complexities that inform contemporary issues.

14 Gender, Trans, and the Predicament of Religion

Collaborative agreements, however, are not ubiquitous in this day and age. In October 2018, the prime minister of Hungary, Viktor Orbán, announced that he was cancelling accreditation of courses in gender studies at two universities: Central European University and Eötvös Lorand University. He is quoted as stating: "the government's standpoint is that people are born either male or female, and we do not consider it acceptable for us to talk of culturally constructed genders rather than biological sexes." Shortly afterwards, the *New York Times* reported that Donald Trump was considering a similar intervention where he would announce a definition of gender that would be "grounded in science, objective, and administrable." In one sense, these statements do not bode well for other-than-binary genders, even if they are reminiscent of the earlier debates about strict gender norms. There was, however, an immediate refutation of Trump's proposal in the *New York Times* by Anne Fausto-Sterling, emerita professor of Biology and Gender Studies at Brown University, to the effect that: "It has long been known that there is no single biological measure that unassailably places each and every human into one of two categories – male or female" (*New York Times*, 25 October 2018). While the term 'religion' did not feature in either of these right-wing politicians' remarks, there is no doubt that the influence of religion played some part in the appeal to their base.

There are a number of responses that could be directed at such a viewpoint with its biased emphasis on heteronormativity. One would be that of distress in queer and trans people for whom the impact of such a rigid ruling could have dire repercussions. Another would be to inquire as to whether it is worth experiencing another round of interminable debate about a conundrum that has been resolved in many quarters. Finally, it could be asked if such an attitude foreshadows the end of gender's contribution to knowledge. Is it time to dismiss 'gender' as a commonplace term and to devise other models that meet the needs of gay, queer, and transgender and otherwise identified people? While the prospect of the latter is not inevitable, it is obvious that there remain many formidable issues to be addressed in connection with 'quasi-religious' mandates that could precipitate another round of 'gender discord.'

15 Transgender Advances

It is undeniable that transgender people have often been ignored, abused, and refused access to religious groups, including the scholarly study of religion. Yet, over the years, activist outreach and support programs have increased. Nevertheless, given the evidence of the negative experiences that contributors of the following narratives have described, religious studies still suffers from major omissions. The principal problem is a reluctance to welcome transgender scholars into hallowed territory. Nevertheless, there was a remarkable move made two years ago when the *Journal of Feminist Studies in Religion* (31, no. 1, 2018) invited transgender scholars to contribute to a special issue. Many of their narratives are heart-rending in their depictions of rebuttal and exclusion; yet others provide hope with a glimmer of collaboration. It is not possible to include the work of all the contributors to this special issue, nor even to name the many topics presented. Instead, I have included selections from a number of papers that provide evidence of the long-overdue welcome of trans persons to the study of religion.

The first presentation was that of Judith Plaskow, professor emerita of Manhattan College. She introduces her paper as being prompted by similarities she has discerned in Max Strassfeld's paper, "Transing Religious Studies" (2018, 37–53). Strassfeld specializes in Rabbinic Literature, Transgender Studies, and Jewish Studies at the University of Arizona. His book project, *Transing the Talmud: Androgynes and Eunuchs in Rabbinic Literature*, explores eunuchs and androgynes in Jewish law, and pairs classical Jewish texts with intersex autobiography, transgender studies, and theories of queer temporality, in order to argue that the rabbis use these figures to map the boundaries of normative masculinity. In his paper, Strassfeld charges that religion and, in particular, the study of religion, especially in North America, is not only gendered but cisgendered. Strassfeld is even more striking in his declaration that: "A feminist religious studies without transfeminism is not feminist at all" (2018, 49). He then stresses the need for a thorough process of a "transing of religious studies" (2018, 37). Plaskow is supportive of this move, insofar as it assists the study of religion in unfettering its restrictive boundaries to include transgender issues, which can enrich its ways of knowing and being.

Plaskow's own paper, "Transing and Gendering Religious Studies" (2018, 75–79), is insightful in proposing a comparative review between the battles that can be found of lesbian, gay and queer feminists in religion with those of Strassfeld's own trans struggles. Plaskow's review issues a strong challenge to essentialist elements that still unfortunately infiltrate the study of religion.

Melissa M. Wilcox, who is Professor and Holstein Family and Community Chair in Religious Studies at University of California, Riverside, tells the disheartening, yet so familiar, narrative of rejection by senior women scholars during her journey toward acceptance as a transgender scholar in the study of religion. She vividly describes the experience, together with other transgender people, of "shouting into the silencing vacuum of active ignorance" (2018, 87). For Wilcox, the task is not only one of persisting to shout into the vacuum but of interrupting firmly those transphobic voices that continue to maintain their malicious campaign. She remains resolute in her support of the voices of trans* scholars in the study of religion and their enhancement of the discipline.

At the beginning of her paper, "Multiplicity and Contradiction: A Literature Review of Trans* Studies in Religion" (2018, 7–23),[17] Siobhan M. Kelly remarks: "The field of trans* studies began making inroads in gender/queer theory and studies in the early 1990s, but within the field of religion, progress toward this (sub)discipline's place, acceptance, and legitimacy has been a much slower journey" (2008, 7). One way to illustrate this somewhat slow but increasingly steady process of 'trans studies' in the study of religion is Kelly's extensive compilation of a literary review of relevant books that have been published in the last thirty-five years. She divides the publications into different categories that comprise a significant survey. Anthologies, autobiographies, biographies abound, revealing intimate accounts of trans* peoples' lives that illustrate their divergent "personal, religious, spiritual, and sex and gender experiences" (2018, 8). Such intimate disclosures flout prescribed or expected formats, particularly those firmly established in the study of religion. One powerful book Kelly names, which addresses colonial/imperial issues, is Afsaneh Najmabadi's *Professing Selves: Transsexuality and Same-Sex Desire in Contemporary Iran* (2013). It is recommended as a must-read "for students of gender and of sex, of post-, de-, and anti-colonial thought, and of cultural studies" (2018, 16). Kelly's compendium of titles of trans* gender literature provides a powerful and capacious survey of trans* studies that enriches the awareness of contemporary insights in the domain of the study of religion.

16 Deviations from a Theme

The multiple theories that have been advanced in this chapter, be they linguistic, conceptual, philosophic, and political, have helped to understand the grounds on which definitions of 'gender' were made and evaluations determined. The

---

17 Kelly notes: "Sometimes, this field is called trans studies or transgender studies. I follow the lead of University of Arizona's 2016 Trans*Studies Conference, using the asterisk to denote an openness to a wide variety of embodiments, practices, and methodological approaches" (2018, 18).

addition of 'religion' into this mixture, and the judging of its efficacy, did, at times, create heated disputes. There are many scholars of gender, however, who still remain staunchly at a distance from religion. Nevertheless, this chapter has attempted to convey how secular definitions of gender influenced the manner with which deficiencies in religion's attitudes and expressions could be corrected. What has not been addressed in this chapter are the views of those scholars who deliberately refrain from any such interaction. However, their work can still provoke questions that can lead to further awareness of secular ideas in relation to religious topics. One example of this position is the work of Elizabeth M. Wilson.

17 Elizabeth Wilson and Bodily Interferences

During the recent years of experimentations in sex, gender, and transgender, mostly within the territory of social constructivism, there have always been a number of scholars who have remained unwilling to abandon the physical body and its diverse interfaces with other processes. In her book *Gut Feminism* (2015), Elizabeth A. Wilson represents those who do not regard the body as dictating "obligatory sexualities and sex roles" (2015, 35). Wilson assesses this move as forsaking biology in favor of an androgynous and genderless society, which she implies Gayle Rubin promoted. She has carefully examined the effects of Rubin's work in order to diagnose how it came to be that "biology became the underbelly of feminist theory" (Wilson 2015, 23–35). The result of Wilson's findings in *Gut Feminism* provides a comprehensive overview of more recent analyses of sex and gender in particular ways that signal a possible reintroduction of the physical body with its unanticipated interruptions.

Wilson has detected a reticence in feminist studies to confront biology with its physiological dimensions, an omission that she plans to amend. Yet Wilson does not intend to return to the days of sexual essentialism. Indeed, she claims that her work "does not endorse biology" (2015, 27). Nor does she aim to supply a solution, especially one that would be of a reparable nature. What is at stake for Wilson is the virtual elision of the volatile body itself. Wilson wants to restore an awareness of ways that moods, bodily modalities, and other interventions, such as depression, aggression, guts, pain, pills, and placebos, react and interact with the body in unpredictable ways. Wilson encourages involvement in the learning of new ways that disclose how such elements "annex each other, how they bind, braid, branch and cleave" (2015, 150). At the heart of her work is a challenge to feminist theorists who have baulked at transgressing their own boundaries of social and discursive analysis.

This endeavor is definitely not a basic empirical or physiological investigation. It probes the *psyche/soma* problem with an innovative perspective that has significant political implications. Wilson explains her understanding of this sense of the political: "We need these kinds of alliances with biology not just in relation to depression; more generally they help to unsettle political certainties of what we think we stand for, and what we stand against, and where we stand when we make political gestures" (2015, 35). Wilson's explorations, as described above, could be viewed as quite contentious in their disputing of the status quo. They continue to problematize the dyadic configuration of mind and body in ways that suggest the body still conserves resources that could be plumbed in multiple interactive ways. Wilson's analyses also help to destabilize the hard-core aspects of feminist theory, which Wilson describes as "so instinctively antibiological" (2015, 1).

Religion, however, does not make an appearance in Wilson's analyses, which is not surprising. One could, however, question its exclusion from her evaluation. Before proceeding with such an interrogation, it would be appropriate to position Wilson's insights within a specific context.

During the 1990s and early 21st century, the theoretical battles between "essentialists" and "constructivists" consumed much energy in feminist circles. Subsequent ventures in sex and gender appeared to avoid the physicality of the body from fear of being labeled deterministic. Wilson's work is a reminder that such exclusions have come at a price. It also illustrates the segregation that can so easily arise between alienated factions. Wilson's approach introduces "pathways by which biological data can become critically mobile" (2015, 175). This statement appears as an incentive to recuperate possibilities that have remained peripheral, yet which could help to revitalize ignored aspects of bodily conditions. This is definitely not an approach that the study of religion has attempted to undertake, especially in the context of contemporary biological knowledge which Wilson supports.

Nevertheless, would it be possible for the study of religion to begin to explore a topic that addresses negative biological aspects? One possible contemporary issue is that of the physical and mental harm religious regulations have inflicted on certain of its followers. These have mainly resulted from the repercussions of the rigid control of sexuality. There have been many critical books and articles published within the framework of sociological, psychological, and psychoanalytical approaches that document religion's failure to address this issue. What has been missing, however, is a collaborative and interdisciplinary project. This would pay attention to the damage done to the physical body and the emotional havoc that has resulted. Such an initiative, however, would need to respect the disparate conceptual methods involved, as well as to query discipline-specific applications. This may appear to be too taxing a task, given the level of Wilson's critical arguments. Nonetheless, such an undertaking would be in keeping with what Wilson has termed "a more vibrant biologically attuned account of the body" (2004, 14). This would imply a demanding though salutary endeavor if a similar approach to the body were to be attempted within the confines of religion.

18 Concluding Observations

It is extremely difficult to bring this chapter to a satisfactory conclusion. In retrospect, the journey of accompanying the development of sex and gender over the past fifty years has exemplified a remarkable voyage of discovery and also of transformation. This is because many women have deserted the dictates of religion, especially in matters of sex and gender. In addition, male scholars have also charted their course of discovery, specifically their own encounters with dogmatic religion. Such demanding exercises have introduced many changes of direction. This is because initially, both sex and gender appeared to contain basic definitions of their meaning and advice for subsequent applications. However, explorations of scholars who were attracted by Foucault's discourse analysis came to understand that there can be no precise or definitive meaning for the term 'gender.' The discourse analysis introduced by Foucault sharpened the awareness of the dynamics of power as a controlling mechanism. As a result, new possibilities of knowledge emerged that were not connected with staid statements as being both true and binding. Instead, Foucault encouraged a sharp awareness that applied discourse analysis of the social circumstances in which specific concepts were conceived and introduced. This approach, with its open-ended disposition and its non-certainty, was adopted by many scholars who were influenced by Judith Butler and Joan Scott. As mentioned earlier, both women and scholars of that era appreciated the dynamic challenges that could be applied to formerly static rules and rigid regulations.

During the years that marked the unprecedented changes in behavior and attitudes, many women and men came to appreciate their mutual respect and support of one another. The role of religion, in its encounter with gender, culminated in a deepened awareness of the potentialities that can be realized when both men and women refuse to accept impositions that do not respect their integrity. What still lies in the future for religion and gender is difficult to predict. This is because diversity has arrived with all its permutations, including the expansive attitude that persons of queer, trans-gender, or gender-neutral variant identities invoke. Perhaps the most impressive achievement that has occurred is the weakening of the binary system that had so long dictated the terms of both gender and religious mores. Heteronormativity's hold has weakened, so that gender, formerly constricted in a binding contract with religious edicts, no longer dictates the terms of compulsory male and female roles. It is too soon, however, to rest assured that these changes will continue to operate as a mode of genuine liberation. Today, many people in the world are subjected to regimes of power that exclude them from exercising their autonomy and integrity.

References

Aquinas, Thomas. 1964. *Summa Theologicae*. Vols. 1–60. English Translation. New York: McGraw Hill.
Aristotle. 1971 [1941]. *The Basic Works of Aristotle*. English Translation. Edited by Richard McKeon. New York: Random House.
Aristotle. 1943. *Generation of Animals*, Vol. 2. English Translation: A. L. Peck. Cambridge, MA. Harvard University Press.
Allen, Sister Prudence. 1997 [First ed.: 1985]. *The Concept of Woman: The Aristotelian Revolution, 750 B.C. – A.D. 1250*. Grand Rapids, MI: William B. Eerdmans.
Allen, Sister Prudence. 2002. *The Concept of Woman*, vol. II, *The Earliest Humanist Reformation, 1250–1500*. Grand Rapids, MI: William B. Eerdmans.
Biddick, Kathleen. 1993. "Genders, Bodies, Borders: Technologies of the Visible." *Speculum* 68: 389–418.
Børresen, Elisabeth, ed. 1995. *The Image of God: Gender Models in Judaeo-Christian Tradition*. Minneapolis: Fortress Press.
Butler, Judith. 1990. *Gender Trouble*. New York: Routledge.
Butler, Judith. 1991. "Imitation and Gender Insubordination." In *Inside/Out: Lesbian Theories, Gay Theories*, edited by Diana Fuss, 13–31. New York: Routledge.
Butler, Judith. 1993a. *Bodies that Matter: On the Discursive Limits of "Sex."* New York: Routledge.
Butler, Judith. 1993b. "Critically Queer." *A Journal of Lesbian and Gay Studies* 1, no.1: 17–32.
Butler, Judith. 1994. "Sexual Traffic: An Interview with Gayle Rubin." *Differences: A Journal of Feminist Cultural Studies* 6, no. 2: 62–99.
Butler, Judith. 1998. "How Bodies Came to Matter: An Interview with Judith Butler." Irene Costera Meijer and Baukje Prins. *Signs* 23, no. 2: 275–286.
Butler, Judith. 2001. "*The End of Sexual Difference?*" In *Feminist Consequences: Theory for the New Century*, edited by Misha Kavka and Elizabeth Bronfen, 414–454. New York: Columbia University Press.
Butler, Judith. 2004. "The End of Sexual Difference?" In *Undoing Gender*. Revised version, 174–203. New York: Routledge.
Butler, Judith. 2009. "Introduction: Precarious Life, Grievable Life." In *Frames of War, When is Life Grievable?* 1–32. London: Verso.
Butler, Judith. 2011a. "Speaking Up, Talking Back: Joan Scott's Critical Feminism." In *The Question of Gender: Joan W. Scott's Critical Feminism*, co-edited with Elizabeth Reed, 11–28. Bloomington: Indiana University Press.
Butler, Judith. 2011b. "Lives Less Livable." An interview with Marcus McCann. *Briarpatch Magazine: Engendering Emancipation*. https://briarpatchmagazine.com/issues/view/may-june-2011.
Bynum, Carolyn Walker. 1987. *Holy, Feast, Holy Fast: The Religious Significance of Food to Western Women*. Berkeley: University of California Press.
Cannon, Katie. 1988. *Black Womanist Ethics*. Atlanta, GA: Scholars Press.
Comstock, Gary David, and Susan E. Henking, eds. 1997. *Que(e)ring Religion: A Critical Anthology*. New York: Continuum.
Connell, R.W. 2005 [1995]. *Masculinities*. Cambridge, UK: Polity.
Connell, R.W., and Rebecca Pearse. 2015 [2002]. *Gender in the World Perspective*. Cambridge, UK: Polity.
Connell, Sophia. 2016. *Aristotle on Female Animals: A Study of the Generation of Animals*. Cambridge, UK: Cambridge University Press.
Delphy, Christine. 1993. "Rethinking Sex and Gender." *Women's Studies International Forum* 16, no. 1: 1–9.

Foucault, Michel. 1976. *The History of Sexuality*, vol. 1, *An Introduction*. Translated by R. Hurley. New York: Vintage.
Foucault, Michel. 1977. "Nietzsche, Genealogy, History," *Language, Counter-Memory, Practice: Selected Essays and Interviews*, trans. Donald F. Bouchard and Sherry Simon, ed. Bouchard. Ithaca, N. Y.: 151–52.
Foucault, Michel. 2000. "Truth and Power." In *Essential Works of Foucault 1954–1984*. Series editor: Paul Rabinow, vol. 3, 111–133. New York: The New Press.
Fulkerson, Mary McClintock. 1996. "Changing the Subject: Feminist Theology and Discourse." *Literature & Theology* 10, no. 2: 131–146.
Fulkerson, Mary McClintock. 1997. "Gender – Being It or Doing It? The Church, Homosexuality, and the Politics of Identity." In *Que(e)ring Religion: A Critical Anthology*, edited by Gary David Comstock and Susan E. Henking, 188–201. New York: Continuum.
Habermas, Jürgen. 2006. "Religion in the Public Sphere." *European Journal of Philosophy* 14, no. 1: 1–25.
Halperin, David M. 1998. "Forgetting Foucault: Acts, Anxieties, and the History of Sexuality." *Representations*, No. 63: 93–120.
Halperin, David M. 2002. *How to do the History of Male Homosexuality*. Chicago: University of Chicago Press.
Hawley, John Stratton, ed. 1994. *Fundamentalism and Gender*. New York: Oxford University Press.
Horowitz, Maryanne Cline. 1976. "Aristotle and Woman." *Journal of the History of Biology* 9, no. 2: 184.
Hirst, Jacqueline Suthren, and Lynn Thomas, eds. 2004. *Playing for Real: Hindu Role Models, Religion, and Gender*. Oxford: Oxford University Press.
Irigaray, Luce. 1985. *This Sex Which Is Not One*. Translated by C. Porter with C. Burke. Ithaca, NY: Cornell University Press.
Jacobson, Janet R., and Ann Pellegrini. 2003. *Love the Sin: Sexual Regulation and the Limits of Religious Tolerance*. New York: New York University Press.
Joy, Morny. 1995. "God and Gender: Some Reflections on Women's Invocations of the Divine." In *Religion and Gender*, edited by Ursula King, 121–143. Oxford: Blackwell.
Joy, Morny. 2006. "Gender and Religion: A Volatile Mixture." *Temenos* 42: 17–30. Reprinted here with permission of the journal editors. (Revised and Adapted).
Juschka, Darlene. 1999. "The Category of Gender in the Study of Religion." *Method & Theory in the Study of Religion* 11, no. 1: 77–105. [Reprinted as a chapter in *Method & Theory in the Study of Religion*: *Twenty-Five Years On*, edited by Aaron Hughes, 239–265. Leiden: Brill, 2013].
Juschka, Darlene. 2005. "What is Gender? What is Sex? What is Gender/Sex?" In *The Routledge Companion to the Study of Religion*, edited by John S. Hinnells, 229–242. New York: Routledge. [2nd ed. 2009].
Juschka, Darlene. 2014. *Political Bodies / Body Politic: The Semiotics of Gender*. New York: Routledge. [1st edition, Sheffield, UK: Equinox, 2009].
Juschka, Darlene. 2016. "Feminism and Gender Theory." In *The Oxford Handbook of the Study of Religion*, edited by Michael Stausberg and Stephen Engler, 137–149. Oxford: Oxford University Press.
Kelly, Siobhan M. "Multiplicity and Contradiction: A Literature of Trans* Studies in Religion." *Journal of Feminist Studies in Religion* 34, no. 1: 7–23.
King, Ursula, ed. 1995. *Religion and Gender*. Oxford: Blackwell.
Korte, Anne-Marie. 2011. "Openings: A Genealogical Introduction to Religion and Gender." *Religion and Gender* 1, no. 1: 1–17.
Li, Xiao-Jian. 2004. "Xingbie or Gender." In *Gender, For a Different Kind of Globalization*, edited by Nadia Tazi, 87–103. New York: Other Press.

Money, John. 1955. "Hermaphroditism, Gender and Precocity in Hyperadrenocorticism: Psychologic Findings." *Bulletin of Johns Hopkins Hospital* 96, no. 6: 253–264.

Money, John. 1973. "Gender Role, Gender Identity, Core Gender Identity: Usage and Definition of Terms." *Journal of the American Academy of Psychoanalysis* 1, no. 4: 397–402.

Money, John. 1985. "Gender: History, Theory and Usage of the term in Sexology and its Relation to Nature/Nurture." *Journal of Sex & Marital Therapy* 11, no. 2: 71–79.

Money, John. 1994. "The Concept of Gender Identity Disorder in Childhood and Adolescence after 39 Years." *Journal of Sex & Marital Therapy* 20, no. 3: 163–177.

Nicholson, Linda. 1994. "Interpreting Gender." *Signs: Journal of Women in Culture and Society* 20, no. 1: 79–105.

Nicholson, Linda. 1999. "Interpreting 'Gender'," revised. In *The Play of Reason*, chapter 4, 53–76. Ithaca, NY: Cornell University Press.

Oakley, Anne. 1972. *Sex, Gender, and Society*. London: Maurice Temple Smith.

Oakley, Anne. 2005. *The Ann Oakley Reader: Gender, Women and Social Science*. Bristol: Polity Press.

Peters, Christine. 2003. *Patterns of Piety: Women, Gender and Religion in Late Medieval Reformation England*. Cambridge: Cambridge University Press.

Phillips, Kim, and Barry Reay. 2011. *Sex before Sexuality: A Premodern History*. London: Polity.

Plaskow, Judith. 2018. "Transing and Gendering Religious Studies." *Journal of Feminist Studies in Religion* 34, no. 1: 75–80.

Posadskaya-Vanderbeck, Anastasia. 2004. "International and Post-socialist Women's Rights Advocacy: Points of Convergence and Tension." In *The Future of Women's Rights: Global Visions and Strategies*, edited by Joanna Kerr, Ellen Sprenger, and Alison Symington, 186–96. London: Zed Books.

Rubin, Gayle. 1975. "The Traffic in Women: Notes on the Political Economy of Sex." In *Toward an Anthropology of Women*, edited by Rayna Reiter, 157–210. New York: Monthly Review Press.

Rubin, Gayle. 1984. "Thinking Sex: Notes for a Radical Theory of the Politics of Sexuality." In *Pleasure and Danger*, edited by Carole Vance, 267–319. London: Pandora.

Rubin, Gayle. 2011. *Deviations: A Gayle Rubin Reader*. Durham, NC: Duke University Press.

Sangari, Kumkum, and Sudesh Vaid, eds. 1990. *Recasting Women: Essays in Colonial History*. New Brunswick, NJ: Rutgers University Press.

Sawyer, Deborah. 2002. *God, Gender and the Bible*. London: Routledge.

Scott, Joan Wallach. 1986. "Gender: A Useful Category of Historical Analysis." *American Historical Review* 91, no. 5: 1053–1075.

Scott, Joan Wallach. 1988. *Gender and the Politics of History*. New York: Columbia University Press. [Revised edition with a new Preface, September 15, 1999].

Scott, Joan Wallach. 1991. "The Evidence of Experience." *Critical Inquiry* 17, no. 4: 773–797.

Scott, Joan Wallach. 2008. *Women's Studies on the Edge*. Durham, NC: Duke University Press.

Scott, Joan Wallach. 2010. "Gender: Still a Useful Category of Analysis?" *Diogenes* 57, no. 1: 7–14.

Stoller, Robert. 1968. *Sex and Gender: The Development of Masculinity and Femininity*. London: H. Karnac.

Strassfeld, Max. 2018. "Transing Religious Studies." *Journal of Feminist Studies in Religion* 34, no. 1: 37–53.

Stryker, Susan and Stephen Whittle. 2008. *Transgender History*. New York: Seal Press.

Stryker, Susan and Stephen Whittle. 2013 [2006]. *The Transgender Studies Reader*. New York: Routledge.

Taylor, Charles. 2007. *A Secular Age*. Cambridge, MA: Harvard University Press.

Wilcox, Melissa M. 2018. "Religion is Already Transed; Religious Studies is Not (Yet) Listening." *Journal of Feminist Studies in Religion* 34, no. 1: 84–88.

Wilson, Elizabeth A. 2015. *Gut Feminism*. Durham, NC: Duke University Press.

Williams, Dolores. S. 1993. *Sisters in the Wilderness: The Challenge of Womanist God-Talk*. New York: Orbis Press.

Jay Johnston
'Beyond' Language? Ecology, Ontology, and Aesthetics

1 Introduction

> [. . .] the laughter that shattered, as I read the passage, all the familiar landmarks of my thought – *our* thought, the thought that bears the stamp of our age and our geography – breaking up all the planes with which we are accustomed to tame the wild profusion of existing things, and continuing long afterwards to disturb and threaten with collapse our age-old distinction between the Same and the Other. (Foucault 2001, xvi)

This chapter seeks to stay in the moment (the 'event') of this shattering laughter; the point identified by Michel Foucault in his now infamous Preface to *The Order of Things* in which familiar systems of knowledge and the order and relations *between things* in their attendant worldview collapse. This is not an exercise in swapping one order for another: no matter how strange, illogical, disturbing or *different*. Rather, it is an exploration of the 'other' of discourse(s), their often unrecognized, unperceived yet nonetheless affective and impelling conditions. These are emotional, ontological, aesthetic aspects implicit to any discourse, yet also exceeding it. A laughter that ruptures, an experience of awe that delights, a vision that transmogrifies.

The understanding of any such experience is necessarily socio-culturally specific. While it is instructive to consider the dominant discourse of wonder, or of the sublime etc., this chapter seeks something less tangible, more difficult. It seeks the moment before absorption into the order of *a* discourse and the residue of that which accompanies its rendering – within – discourse. Discourse in this context is taken as "an ensemble of verbal and non–verbal practices of large social communities" (Angermuller et. al. 2014, 2). Albeit in this context "social communities" is not exclusive to humans, rather it is inclusive of nonhumans as well.

Many recent dominant 'turns' in the humanities are already exploring the non-linguistic aspects of discourse, including affect theory, new materialism, new animism, aesthetics of religion, material religion. This article will commence with a short overview of these approaches and their ramifications for 'thinking' religion/religious discourses (non-linguistic) in an interdisciplinary context. It will then turn to consider examples where that which remains 'beyond' yet implicit can be glimpsed and even utilized within research via methods of critical practice (in the visual arts) and creative engagement. Examples will be analyzed from within the domain of 'nature writing.' This is a highly fertile field (!) – although one that can only be touched on herein – due to the shared discursive tropes of human–nature engagement found in this discourse and that of religious experience. It is also of especial reference because of the contested term 'nature' itself. Historically, discourses of modernity, founded upon a logic of unequal binary oppositions (Lloyd 1993) defined and positioned nature as culture's 'other.' Whether romantically celebrated or denigrated (including being feminized) nature was crafted as distinct from culture and an object of disinterested analysis. That is, it was 'mute' and spoken about or for. However, many well-known critiques have thoroughly eroded and destabilized any such delineation, especially the work of Donna Haraway which has simultaneously challenged the belief in the pure ontological categories of 'human,' 'animal,' and 'machine' (1991). In parallel with these theoretical critiques artists and writers have produced work that illuminates, and seeks to critically respond to, the complex interrelationships between the human and nonhuman. The foundation of any such practice is the attribution of agency to the nonhuman (whether the act is one of attribution or perception of 'what's there' is dependent upon the perceiving subject's capacity to register and recognize alterity). Necessarily, this requires critical examination of the attendant non-linguistic discourses utilized to represent this other-than-human agency and its intersubjective affects.

2 Affects, Ontologies, Ecologies

> If religion is a massing of affects, a core response of bodies in the world prior to ideas, words, thoughts, then it is open to non-linguistic bodies. Animal religion overturns the sentence of solitary confinement imposed on human bodies by our own anthropocentric presuppositions, returning us to other bodies on and in the earth. (Schaefer 2015, 211)

In *Religious Affects: Animality, Evolution and Power*, Donovan O. Schaefer casts religion as a "massing of affects," and in doing so he has opened out the category to subjectivities other than the human (and well beyond linguistic definitions: a move also central to material and aesthetic approaches to religion). I have explored the ethics of this proposition with regard to the cultivation of perception elsewhere (Johnston 2017). However, in the context of this chapter, it is salient to re-emphasize the non-linguistic operations of affect. As in Foucauldian approaches to discourse, affect is embedded and emerges from "non-linguistic forms of power" (2015, 179).

Affect theory is suitably diverse in its interpretation and application. In a reductive overview there are two dominant 'paths' The first is associated with Gilles Deleuze (1925–1995) and his revivification of Henri Bergson's (1859–1941) work and the second is founded upon analysis and reconsideration of the psychologist Silvan Tomkins' (1911–1991) work. Both approaches understand affects as non-linguistic 'forces': for Deleuze affects are flows of forces (ontological forces) for Tomkins they are akin to emotions (and indeed, there is a continuing debate regarding the distinction between affects and emotions). For followers of both 'paths' affects are robust potencies that are not necessarily consciously perceived and are non-linguistic. They are both creative and potentially malleable. These forces are not specific to the human subject: they are considered constitutive of all animals and the multiple worlds in which they reside (Johnston 2017).

The physical body and its network of relations (forces and flows) is a locus of affect. Indeed, Schaefer argues that affect is the "material" out of which religion is formed and that "Religions build on a body's available repertoire of affective bodily technologies, bending them, deterritorializing them and reconstituting them in new configurations" (2015, 210). Affects are subject to, and generative of, forms of power and particular affective capacities are physiologically and socio-culturally inculcated in the body. That is, certain affects (and responses to affects) while non-linguistic can nonetheless be cultivated and privileged (consciously or unconsciously) while others can be minimized or ignored. Affect can be generated collectively and amassed through time. They are intimately related with subjective capacity – the limits of what a subject can and cannot do – and recognition.

Affect theory has been extensively explored in the discipline of cultural studies, however its application in religious studies has to date been more muted (see also Anne Koch's chapter in the present volume). However, the Religion, Affect and Emotion Group of the American Academy of Religion has been a prime facilitator of interdisciplinary dialogue.

In the wake of affect theories emphasis on the networks and productivity (creative and restrictive) of non-linguistic power, theories of other-than-human agency emerged and began to dominate discussion. Indeed, one (diverse) form, New Materialism, has been a strong interdisciplinary discourse for nearly a decade. In Religious Studies, its most marked effect has been the revivification and rethinking of animism, see for example Harvey (2013). In brief, New Materialists ascribe agency to matter that is not derivative from the human as causal agent. Jane Bennett's proposition of *vital matter* (2010) has been core to the development of many New Materialist frameworks. As I have argued elsewhere (2016), such concepts of matter (ontological and agential) are not new – in fact they are very 'old' concepts of matter – and may be found in bodies of knowledge historically excluded by the Academy: indigenous and esoteric traditions. However, Bennett and other New Materialists have successfully opened up a space within the humanities were such ideas can be analyzed and debated with due rigor and seriousness. This has allowed an increased presence of differing worldviews and epistemologies in academic 'space.'

Core to these arguments is the vexing issue of the apprehension of the other-than-human agency. I have detailed my concerns with Bennett's call to be "temporarily infected by discredited philosophies of nature risking the 'taint of superstition, animism, vitalism, anthropomorphism and other premodern attitudes'" (Bennett quoting Mitchell 2005, 149) previously, noting the implied denigration of indigenous and esoteric epistemologies that this statement appears to propose (Johnston 2016, 81–82). This issue of just how one does perceive other-than-human agency remains difficult and challenging and it is just the place where the utilization (and combination) of a wide range of methods – including creative practice – is most needed.

In a recent article, Arianne Françoise Conty (2018) has noted the dominance of affective and New Materialist approaches; indeed, these now form a dominant discourse in a number of Humanities disciplines. She writes:

> Subjects and objects, the infatuation of modernity, have gone out of fashion. Scholars today see agency, events, lines of flight and entanglements where they used to see subjects and objects, often leading to an indiscretion between the two that is celebrated as having finally overcome the anthropocentrism responsible for justifying a human subject over and against a world of things. (2018, 73)

In particular, the use of "indiscretion" in this quotation caught my eye: as indiscretions are wont to do! At first I mused that it was a slip, and that 'indistinction' should take its place. In the realms of intersubjectivity – and especially where concepts of ontological matter are concerned, as I have discussed in relation to subtle matter (Johnston 2008) – just where one 'subject' ends and another begins is a troubling matter (but good trouble – in a Haraway sense). The use of the term indiscretion, consciously or unconsciously, evokes issues of morality, it does after all commonly refer to: "a want of discernment or discrimination [. . .] a want of judgement in speech or action; injudicious, unguarded or unwary conduct; imprudence" (*OED*). That is, inappropriate boundaries have been crossed: so perhaps, despite the prevalence and fashionability of concepts of vital or ontological matter within the academy, such ideas continue to cause unease, even alarm.

Conty views New Materialism as the study of the "modern unconscious," that was distanced and repressed by modernity's commitment to subject–object distinction and the subject's superiority as the locus of agency (2018, 74–75). Interestingly, she characterizes the movement as seeking to "extend characteristics and values deemed uniquely human to the rest of the world" noting "they disagree on whether certain new distinctions should replace old ones, or whether all forms of agency should be treated equally" (2018, 75). However, in the context new materialism the term "extend" is not the best choice of term, because the recognition (perception) of other-than-human agency should not be an act of *allowing* or *bestowing* upon non-human materialities human forms of agency. Rather it should be the base acknowledgment that such agencies *all ready exist*, followed by the ethical imperative to explore how to 'hear' these agencies: to render them respect and where appropriate representation.

In esoteric traditions, there are always degrees of perceptive development that are understood to accord with and result in the increased perception of other-than-human agency (see Johnston on 'Esoteric Aesthetics' 2017; 2018). So again, the issue tussled over by new materialists and company with regard to the distinction between different agencies – and indeed their boundaries – is itself an inherently fluid one. It appears that while the subject–object boundary has been thoroughly problematized, the desire to fix borders between subjects (or agencies) remains. Conty notes the reinscription by Tim Ingold and Eduardo Kohn of an animate/inanimate binary within the vital environment posited by Bennett. The issues of these 'new' boundaries, (new dualisms even!), is a crucial one. However, this chapter has a different focus than an in-depth consideration of the new divides. Nonetheless, it is crucial to acknowledge that the moves of the affect theorists and new materialists enabled a space within the academy in which other-than-human agencies could be considered seriously (and without the invocation of the 'spiritual' word, of which many in the secular academy remain afraid). As such, it has pushed scholarly consideration – once again – to the edge of language. It is to this edge, particularly in relation to Kohn's work, that this chapter now turns.

3 Non-linguistic Languages and Ecologies

Non-linguistic aspects of discourse have been a focus of study in many disciplinary areas (see Reiner Keller's chapter in this volume) – including discourse studies itself. Christopher Hart's examination of the visual basis of linguistic meaning also stresses – with reference to David Machin's analysis (2013) – the "multimodal turn in discourse studies and critical discourse studies (CDS) with researchers addressing the way knowledge and values are constructed through images as well as language usages" (2016, 335). Hart's work particularly considers the substantial role that visual media plays in "shaping linguistically communicated meaning" (2016, 336). The analysis of visual media – and their relations of support or subversion to dominant discourses – has been a staple of art historical and theoretical analysis for decades, much analysis developing in the wake of Roland Barthes' works. Indeed, even within the traditional linguistic/literature field of storytelling analysis itself, attention has turned to consider the non-linguistic aspects of its discourse. Marta Sibierska argues, from a cross-disciplinary perspective but with particular eye to the ramification for evolutionary and narratological theory, that the "human ability to tell stories is not restricted to the verbal medium" (2017, 47).

Despite the rich and varied research in these areas, this short section is concerned with a move away from 'text' *per se* – even in a multimodal framework – to consider an account developed by Eduardo Kohn of intersubjective relations in an Amazonian forest. His account of ethnographic fieldwork – *How Forests Think: Toward and Anthropology Beyond the Human* (2013) developed in dialogue with concepts of vital matter which includes other-than-human ontologies but also utilized Charles Pierce's semiotic theory as a framework for understanding a complex ecosystem.

The term 'ecosystem,' as Conty has observed, is increasingly employed to designate contemporary analysis of intersubjective relations that undermine 'human/

nature' and subject/object divides and which also crosses (or troubles) the borders between 'human and natural sciences.' She writes:

> Since moral issues can no longer be separated from biological concerns, and politics can no longer be separated from nature, addressing the Anthropocene entails the dissolution of the nature/culture divide, but also of the disciplinary divide between natural and human sciences. Bridging the human and natural sciences, this new discipline must address the earthly (rather than global) complexities of our causally inter-dependent planet with an embodied semiotics of life capable of meeting the needs of the 21st century. (2018, 91)

Here we see the meeting of two discourses that are usually 'held' apart: that of embodiment and that of semiotics. "Embodied semiotics" is not a misnomer, but is integral to Kohn's work and can also be found in Charles Foster's experimental activities aimed at experiencing the perceptive worlds of particular animal species (2016). I have previously written about the way in which this cultivation of perception resulted in the development of new embodied narratives of possibility and agency (Johnston 2017, 15). Suffice to note here that discourse and embodiment are not alternatives but radically interrelated aspects of any ecology.

Eduardo Kohn develops concepts of selfhood, embodiment and soul in the context of anthropological study with the Runa, communities of the Ecuadorian Amazon. Central to his arguments is a concept of living beings being defined by thoughts and an attendant claim "that all thoughts are alive." This then is foundational to his core claim that "all living beings, and not just humans think" (2013, 72). Kohn understands the forest as animate; its agency is not tied to the human (ibid.). As a living being, it thinks. However, such thought is non-linguistic, yet for Kohn no less involved in a semiotic system. He particularly stresses Peirce's proposition that "signs stand for something in relation to a 'somebody'" (2013, 73). According to Kohn this relational semiotic structures the ecosystem: "The semiotic quality of life – the fact that the forms that life takes are the products of how living selves represent the world around them – structures the tropical ecosystem" (2013, 78).

Evolution – the developmental adaptation of living things to specific contexts and in specific lived relations over a sustained period of time – is viewed by Kohn as a semiotic relationship (2013, 76). Indeed, from such a perspective it could be understood as producing multiple ecological discourses. Significantly for Kohn it is not just humans who can create representations, but all other living beings as well.

> Language and the related discursive regimes that condition so much of our thought and action are not closed. Although we must of course be cautious about the ways in which language (and by extension, certain socially stabilized modes of thought and action) naturalizes categories of thought, we can venture to talk about something like life "itself" without being fully constrained by the language that carries this forth. (2013, 90–91)

It is here that the semiotic but non-linguistic emerges in Kohn's thought. He attributes unique "ontological properties" to nonhuman life and argues that their particular perspectives and properties can be known – to a degree – by humans (2013, 91).

However emergent meaning making agents are restricted in Kohn's view to "living beings" and contra new materialism – of which he is critical – that attribute is not extended to phenomena like snowflakes or rocks. Kohn's study is an exercise in striving to know these non-linguistic perspectives, which at the same time requires a radical rethinking of the dominant western categories of the human. His practice as an anthropologist is a lived intervention in these discourses.

Similarly, and to close this section, critical practice, sometimes referred to as 'practice-led research' is an approach taken particularly in the visual arts that aims to generate interventions in dominant discourses and create new, emergent (including non-linguistic) knowledges. It "constitutes the active exploration of critical concepts in practice: a process that draws on phenomenological experience as well as conceptual understanding, a process continually open to question, re-negotiation, re-interpretation and ultimately re-presentation" (Adams 2014, 218).

This is a process of simultaneous embodied awareness and theoretical reflection. The process of the art production (including performance) is considered integral to the emergence of new knowledge it generates, facilitates and represents it (bit it is no mere illustration). Adams notes that this practice is utilized to "explore multi–sensory understanding" (2014, 218); therefore it can also be considered to 'play' in the realms of the non-linguistic. To close this chapter, this next section takes up this spirit of practice-led research in the exploration of the non-linguistic and examines a work of creative writing; indeed, the turnings are more complex than that. The selected work is the critical examination by a creative writer of the limits of linguistic representation and the potential sites of emergence of the non-linguistic.

4 Words and Woodpigeons

In the article, "How Many Words Do You Need to Describe a WoodPigeon?," author Chris Arthur reflects on his writing practice and argues that there is an inherent simplicity in any linguistic presentation of the 'natural world.' This may seem obvious, for example 'platypus' designates a particular type of monotreme in its entirety and not in any particular specificity. However, it is the relation between language, perception and ethical responsibility that Arthur highlights which is particularly pertinent in this context. He notes:

> My worry is that the way in which we routinely apply language to that [natural] world may be a contributing factor leading to the mindset that allows us to wreak such damage on our environment. Verbal simplifications, and the superficial perceptions – or rather misperceptions – they foster, undermine the sense of wonder on which respect for nature is built. (2014, 32)

Taking the mundane example of "There's a woodpigeon on the lawn" Arthur contends that the way in which he would usually communicate this occurrence "seemed designed to hide" rather than to elucidate "what was really there" (2014, 33). In response to this realization Arthur strives to develop a "less blinkered account than that offered by our usual modes of discourse." To achieve this he proposes four "waves," each wave, he contends undermined the utility and accuracy of the common-sense statement "There's a woodpigeon on the lawn."

The first wave is a greater attentiveness to color. Arthur approaches this task with an artists' eye ("to sketch a picture") and reference to ornithological guidebook descriptions. Yet, still he finds these descriptors, for example "green" or "grey-brown lacking; no least because they impose an incorrect stasis (2014, 33):

> How differently it appears when standing breast-high amidst grass and daises, and when perched and preening in a nearby tree; when it's sitting with its feathers fluffed out and when it's flying, when it's caught in a burst of sunshine or seen under grey clouds heavy with the imminence of rain. (2014, 33)

Indeed, each of the nouns and adjectives in this sentence could reasonably be subjected to the same type of scrutiny afforded the woodpigeon: grass, daises, tree, sunshine, grey clouds (what kind of grey?). Arthur's call is for an increased attentiveness and an attendant creative–struggle to find discourse adequate to it. But even here, in this example, he has chosen to focus on the woodpigeon, leaving all else to "usual modes of discourse" (2014, 33).

Non-linguistic discourses of attention also need to be interrogated. We are culturally trained to perceive; directed to what is important to focus on and what can be ignored; to choose centers and therefore to create peripheries; to hear a melody more than a bassline. But what occurs if we redirect our attention from its usual patterns? Indeed, the popular surge of so-called 'mindfulness' practices can involve a type of somatic retraining (even if it is in the guise of 'stress management'). Therefore discourses of perception are physiological: they are embodied. Embodiment is not neutral as Pierre Bourdieu and Michel Foucault have demonstrated. The limitations, capacities and resistance of 'any' body is socio-culturally conditioned. Whilst Bourdieu (1990 [1980], 53) exemplified this via his proposition of *habitus* – a "system of durable, transposable dispositions [. . .] principles which generate and organize practices and representations" – and an examination of cross-cultural and generational difference; more recently Charles Foster (2016) sought to train his senses and body in order to get as close as possible to the experience of a non-human other (see also Johnston 2017). Here of course, the physiology is markedly different, hence the highly different sensorial capacities of badger contra human. Yet, Foster's project – which included to experience life as a badger as close as possible – demonstrated the large capacity humans have for altering and extending their perceptive range and capacity. However, of especial note in this context are his remarks regarding (un)conscious limiting of perceptive capacities:

> And I remembered Jack Swartz, who said that he could see auras around each of us and whose ability to detect light frequencies extended from 335 to 1,700 nanometres, which is

1,000 nanometres beyond the spectrum normally regarded as visible by humans. But I remembered in particular John Adams, the physiologist who tested Schwartz. Astonished at the results, he re-examined his own vision without the conventional presumptions about what humans could do, and found much of the theoretically invisible infra-red spectrum was in fact visible to him. (2016, 43)

In Foster's description normative belief about what was physiologically 'usual' or possible limited individual capacity. Therefore both the discourses and experience pertaining to the range and capacity of normative sense perception can also be considered as socio-culturally determined, and as such, should be a topic for sustained critical inquiry.

As I hope the previous discussion has demonstrated, Arthur's "first wave" opened a broad frame of questioning with regard to attention – its cultivation and focus – and the limits (or not) of particular perceptive capacities. His additional three "waves" build on this foundation. The second "wave" erodes the simplicity of the sentence "There is a woodpigeon on the lawn" which he calls a "dam wall." Behind this wall, he claims, is a rich multiplicity, a "tonnage of unspoken water that only trickles hints of its existence through the close-fitting blocks of our vocabulary" (2014, 34). To exemplify Arthur's invokes among other things the weight of a pigeon's skull, the organs of its anatomy, their scent and texture. In short, he enters within (or behind) the feathered surface to take account of a microscopic and interior view. As such, the previous point raised with regard to the focus of attention is even more acute. How can one maintain the equal depth and focus on each aspect of all this stimulus? Choices must be made. Such choices, about upon what to alight – and in what order – are made (albeit mostly unconsciously). Arthur's does not raise this issue; but he does argue that such consideration pushes perception 'beyond' language. Indeed, as the quotation below demonstrates, terms that have historically been employed to denote (certain types) of religious experience are invoked to articulate the inadequacy of language. "I picture words streaming towards the bird in jumbled, desperate profusion, scores of sentences formed to try to catch it. Each one is instead deflected, pulled into orbit around something about which a great deal can be said, but in the end it remains mysterious, ineffable, enchanted" (2014, 34).

Here is an acknowledgment of a 'remainder' that escapes linguistic denotation. The humble wood pigeon deemed "ineffable" and "enchanted." But here too, is the well-worn trope of nature mysticism. Developed through nineteenth century Romantic discourses, this 'nature' is one of immanent – albeit overwhelming experience of the divine. Its traditions are carried forward in contemporary so-called New Nature Writing (an example of which is discussed below). Suffice to note here the seeping residue of that familiar discursive construction of human–nature relations.

To these conjectures Arthur adds two more corrosive "waves," both pertaining to time. The first is built upon a lament for the incapacity of words to capture the "quantum of time" at an individual level; the sentences inability to capture the span of the woodpigeon's being through time (2014, 34) and the second (overall, the fourth "wave") refers to the erosion brought about by geological time. The latter is an impersonal duration, a "wave of deep time," evolutionary time that transmogrifies the woodpigeon into a "temporal chasm" (ibid.). "One of the tendrils from that ancient genesis stretches all the way from it to the moment when a woodpigeon landed on the lawn just outside my window" (ibid.).

I've been playing with Arthur and his woodpigeon to exemplify the simultaneous critical–creative methods that have developed to tune in to non-linguistic discourse. As is evident, this is not a project for the faint hearted, yet it is one – which numerous examples herein have attest – that is implicitly interrelated with the ethical imperative to perceive agencies (ontologies) other than the human.

5 Conclusion

> We simultaneously use different means of representation, the most prominent of which are language, gestures, feelings and scenic images. It is especially fruitful to investigate the scenic mode of daydreaming as a central form on non-linguistic thinking. (Lohmer 2013, 1)

'Beyond' is a bad word choice for this context. There is no beyond language, because there is no beyond if language is uncoupled from human spoken and written systems. Further, 'beyond' evokes a linear framework or progression while the relations discussed herein have focused on an immersive 'present' in which we – as active agents – have the choice to cultivate our awareness in order to perceive more clearly (but never entirely) and respect other-than-human agencies.

The crucial irony that haunts engagement with other-than-human agency in academic discourse is that it remains a predominantly linguistic form that renders these arguments legible: both in concept and case-study. Yet, incursions into this dominant mode of argumentation continue apace, for example, multi-modal expression (the use of textual, visual, aural mixed–media), and, challenges to the accepted styles of dominant linguistic argumentation developed from the integration of creative writing or the disruption of predictable structural elements of logical analysis (none of which are employed herein!). Ultimately however, the imperative is on scholars themselves to soften their grip on reason (which concomitantly undermines their vocational foundation). Only with a conscious opening to alternate epistemologies and modes of expression can agencies of the other-than-human more fully self-represent and be 'heard.' Yes: that amounts to an undermining of the very pillars upon which the Academy is constructed: most certainly its particular valuation of what constitutes legitimate knowledge. Nonetheless such an orientation does not mean an uncritical abandonment of reason, or its valuable insights and contributions. Rather, it calls for institutional regimes – including publication and assessment technologies – more accommodating of plural epistemologies and artistic incursions. None of this is simple or straightforward; indeed it cannot be anything other than challenging and disruptive. Taking non-human agency seriously should fracture the system. In response we should not be too eager to fill, or map over, the fissure it creates.

The creative–critical incursions discussed herein render the subject–object only every partially, problematizing attempts to generate cohesive discursive regimes; to pinpoint and encapsulate in language; to situate phenomena concretely in the 'order of things.' The chortle of derision for the illogical with which this chapter opened has come to signify our own conceptual limitations. Laughter, not at the bizarreness of an 'other' but at one's own folly. This is a foolishness to be celebrated if at its heart is the acknowledgement of that which elides order and necessarily troubles dominant systems of knowledge and representation.

The quotation that opens this section gestures to a different beyond, to that which was not considered herein – to a certain extent this consideration has remained squarely in the realm of reason(s) – that is, a vast range of epistemologies that are foundationally non-linguistic. To raise a last shattering laugh: the discourse of the day–dreaming woodpigeon remains beyond us all.

References

Adams, Suze. 2014. "Practice as Research: A Fine Art Contextual Study." *Arts & Humanities in Higher Education* 13 (3): 218–226.
Angermuller, Johannes, Dominique Maingueneau, and Ruth Wodak. 2014. "The Discourse Studies Reader: An Introduction." In *The Discourse Studies Reader: Main Currents in Theory and Analysis*, ed. by J. Angermuller, D. Maingueneau, and R. Wodak, 1–14. Amsterdam and Philadelphia: John Benjamins Publishing Company.
Arthur, Chris. 2014. "How Many Words Do You Need to Describe a Woodpigeon?" *Eathlines* 9: 32–36.
Bennett, Jane. 2010. *Vibrant Matter: A Political Ecology of Things*. Durham and London: Duke University Press.
Bourdieu, Pierre. 1990 [1980]. *The Logic of Practice*. Translated by Richard Nice. Stanford: Stanford University Press.
Conty, Arianne Françoise. 2018. "The Politics of Nature: New Materialist Responses to the Anthropocene." *Theory, Culture & Society* 35: 73–96.
Foster, Charles. 2016. *Being a Beast*. London: Profile Books.
Foucault, Michel. 2001 [1966]. *The Order of Things*. London: Routledge.
Haraway, Donna. 1991 *Simians, Cyborgs and Women: The Reinvention of Nature*. London: Free Association Books.
Harvey, Graham, ed. 2013. *The Handbook of Contemporary Animism*. London and New York: Routledge.
Hart, Christopher. 2016. "The Visual Basis of Linguistic Meaning and its Implications for Critical Discourse Studies: Integrating Cognitive Linguistic and Multimodal Methods." *Discourse & Society* 27 (3): 335–350.
Johnston, Jay. 2008 *Angels of Desire: Esoteric Bodies, Aesthetics and Ethics*. London: Equinox Publishing.
Johnston, Jay. 2016. "Slippery and Saucy Discourse: Grappling with the Intersection of 'Alternate Epistemologies' and Discourse Analysis." *In Making Religion: Theory and Practice in the Discursive Study of Religion*, edited by Frans Wijsen and Kocku von Stuckrad. Berlin: de Gruyter.

Johnston, Jay. 2017 "Rewilding Religion: Affect and Animal Dance." *Bulletin for the Study of Religion* 46 (3/4): 11–16.
Lloyd, Genevieve. 1993 [1984]. *The Man of Reason: "Male" and "Female" in Western Philosophy.* London: Routledge.
Lohmar, Dieter. 2013 [2012]. "Language and Non-Linguistic Thinking." In *The Oxford Handbook of Contemporary Phenomenology*, edited by Dan Zahavi. Online edition. Oxford: Oxford University Press.
Machin, David. 2013. "What is Multimodal Critical Discourse Studies?" *Critical Discourse Studies* 10 (4): 347–355.
Mitchell, W. J. Thomas. 2005. *What Do Pictures Want? The Lives and Loves of Images.* Chicago: University of Chicago Press.
Schaefer, Donovan O. 2015. *Religious Affects: Animality, Evolution, and Power.* Durham and London: Duke University Press.
Sibierska, Marta. 2017. "Storytelling Without Telling: The Non-Linguistic Nature of Narratives From Evolutionary and Narratological Perspectives." *Language and Communication* 54: 47–55.

Index of Key Terms

Affect theory 19, 118, 119, 231–235
African American 37, 61, 214
Agency/Agencies 11, 14, 117, 119, 136, 155, 232–236, 240, 241
American Academy of Religion 233
Apparatus 10, 62, 63
Archetexts 64, 65
Archive 62, 63
Arian 112
Articulation 28, 29, 49, 219

Baby Boomer generation 150
Benedictine 114
Bible 60, 61, 64–67, 156, 203, 204, 212
Biopolitics 115
Birmingham School 24, 26, 108, 109
Bodily modalities 225
Brown University 222
Buddhism 66, 118, 202

Capitalism 148, 153, 157, 158, 160
Central European University 222
Chaldean Church 66
Chicago tradition 25, 34
Christianity 64, 66, 67, 70–72, 110, 112–114, 129, 131, 134, 135, 137, 152, 155–157, 173, 174, 176, 177, 187, 188, 197, 200–202, 208, 214
Circuits of culture 24, 28
Cistercian orders 114
Classification 15, 29, 44, 45, 49, 82, 89
Cold War 126, 128, 129, 138, 139
Colonialism 15, 91, 100, 101, 112, 204, 221, 224
Communism 126, 138
Conflict transformation 127
Conversation(al) analysis 27, 40, 61, 93, 109
Critical Discourse Analysis (CDA) 4, 89, 90, 95–100, 102–104, 107, 110
Critical feminism 110, 207
Critical realist 170
Cultural turn 83, 108, 146

Definition of the situation 24, 26
Dialogical Self Theory 4, 89, 90, 94–104
Discipline 4, 40, 51, 71, 114, 115, 119

Discourse analysis 3, 7, 9, 14, 28, 82, 104, 107, 125, 126, 128, 129, 131, 141, 184, 190, 206, 225
Discursive field 7, 8, 16, 38, 49, 62–64, 206
Discursive formation 30, 36, 38, 101, 114, 125, 129, 213
Discursive practice 31, 40, 92, 93, 98, 101, 108, 111, 157, 163, 190, 196
Discursive study of religion 1, 4, 108, 126, 127, 132, 141, 142
Dispositif 1, 37, 41, 42, 50, 65, 109, 113, 116, 120
Dualism 113, 132, 133, 235
Duke Divinity School 195
Durkheimian 29, 33

Eastern Orthodox Church 66
Economic relations 145, 146, 154
Economics of religion 150, 151, 153
Embody 7, 19, 62, 72, 90, 95, 119, 120, 172, 236–238
Enlightenment 78, 139, 174
Entanglement 2, 4, 84–86, 234
Eötvös Lorand University 222
Esoteric 233, 234
Essentialism 79, 108, 120, 184, 193, 201, 204, 205, 223, 225, 226
Ethics of discourse 27
Ethnographic 34, 42, 50, 114, 156, 161, 235
Ethos 71, 72, 102, 204
European Court of Human Rights 175

Foucauldian 4, 24, 82, 107, 109, 113, 114, 119, 120, 145, 205, 232
Fourth Lateran Council 190
Frame 2, 43, 44, 49, 58, 63, 72, 111, 130
Freudian 11
Fundamentalism 149, 158, 159, 174, 184, 208, 210

Gaia 85
Gender Identity Clinic 191
Gender studies 5, 184, 191, 219, 221
Genealogy 3, 10, 16, 43, 81, 82, 108, 114, 120, 190, 196, 199, 200, 206

Genre theory 40
Globalization 103
Governance 4, 114–117, 120, 160, 173
Governmentality 41, 115, 116, 119
Grounded theory 26, 49, 50

Heaven 13, 134
Hegemonic 16, 28, 29, 38, 69, 90, 96, 101, 109, 118, 119, 129, 151, 212
Hell 13, 134
Hermeneutical 2, 33, 49, 81, 84
Heteronormative 184, 195, 196, 207, 217, 222, 227
Hillsong 156, 157
Hinduism 20, 66, 204
Historical 153, 200, 201, 205–207, 213, 214, 218
Historical analysis 4, 7, 10, 30, 77, 78, 79, 80, 81, 82, 85, 115, 214
Historicize 8, 11, 13, 16–18, 80, 108, 112, 205
Humanists 14, 68, 71

Identity/Identities 14, 62, 100, 103, 128–132, 135, 137, 139, 141, 153, 161, 184, 185, 191, 196–198, 203, 207, 212, 215, 217, 219–221, 227
Incitement of Disaffection Act 1934 176
Indigenous 16, 19, 94, 233
International Convention on Civil and Political Rights 170, 171, 173
Interpretation 1, 2, 8, 34–36, 39, 40, 45, 49, 50, 57, 58, 64, 66, 67, 69, 79, 93, 107, 111, 114, 118–120, 128, 129, 135, 139, 141, 145, 147, 153, 162, 163, 177, 188, 198, 202, 232
Interpretive analytics 29
Interpretive paradigm 23, 26, 27, 44
Interpretive repertoire 43
Interpretive scheme 43, 44, 45, 49
Interpretive sociology 26, 27, 29, 31, 36, 43, 50
Intersubjective 232, 234, 235
Intertextuality 90, 99, 104, 132
Islam 20, 64, 66, 69, 94–100, 102, 104, 114, 116, 129, 131, 163, 173, 174, 176–178

Jansenism 68, 71
Judaism 19, 66, 67, 69, 112, 131, 135, 137, 174, 188, 203, 223

Knowledge societies 24

Linguistics 3, 4, 5, 27, 28, 57, 59, 60, 73, 81, 89, 92, 93, 96, 103, 107, 108, 128, 130, 131, 139, 145, 196, 199, 239
Literary critical theory 7, 9

Manhattan College 223
Mappings 3–5, 47
Marxist 11, 16, 60, 109, 213
Material agency 4
Materialism 80, 82–84, 86
McMaster University 7
Meadian 33
Misogynistic 185
Modularity 65–67, 72
More-than-human 84, 86
Mystical 71, 200
Mysticism 69, 201, 239

Narrative structure 47, 77
Native Americans 112
Neoliberal 96, 101, 115–117, 119, 151, 157, 160, 161, 163
New Age 19, 119, 157–162
New Humanism 7
New materialism 18, 42, 231, 233, 234–236
New Nature Writing 239
Non-discursive practices 39, 118, 120
Nones 19
Non-governmental organizations (NGOs) 173, 174, 178
Nonhuman(s) 231, 232, 236, 238, 241
Non-human agency 118
Non-linguistic 231, 232, 235–238, 240, 241

Objective 2, 3, 33, 34, 37, 80, 222
Ontology/ontologies 10, 11, 83, 84, 110, 111, 138, 150, 197, 231–236, 240
Oslo Peace Accords 130
Other-than human 233–235, 240

Patriarchy 116, 185, 192, 200, 211, 214
Performative 42, 146, 196, 197, 203
Phenomenal structure 45, 46, 49
Phenomenology 25, 33, 35, 108, 237
Pluralism 112, 149, 150, 153, 169–171, 176–178, 240
Polemics 60, 110, 112
Political economy 161
Politics of knowledge 3, 27, 37, 50

Popular discourse 13
Postcolonial 110, 112, 113, 119, 121, 140, 204
Posthumanist 85
Poststructural 24, 111, 192, 194, 195, 198, 205
Power 2–4, 16–18, 28, 29, 38, 50, 84, 101, 111–114, 125, 126, 129–131, 141, 142, 149, 186, 190, 192, 205, 207, 212, 215, 227, 233
– power relations 205
– power/knowledge 120
– exercise of power 131
Practice 5, 8, 10, 11, 29, 30, 32–37, 39–42, 45, 57, 82, 90, 92, 107, 109, 113, 115, 118, 121, 125, 137, 146, 154, 158, 169, 170, 172, 176–178, 184, 214, 238
Pragmatism 23, 31, 34, 59, 80, 94
Presbyterian Church 195
Problematisations 30
Protestant 66, 67, 71, 112, 131, 135, 137, 155, 174, 195, 197

Queer theory 194, 215, 217, 220, 224
Qur'an 64, 69, 70, 114

Rabat Plan 174
Rational 133, 138–141, 145, 146, 150, 163, 186
Realism 14, 15
Reflexive 24, 70, 110, 111, 128, 162
Reflexive modernity 24
Relational 84, 133, 236
Relational dialogism 141
Relational dialogist 4, 126, 132, 134, 138, 139
Relationships of authority 17
Relativist 2, 110
Religious freedom 5, 169–178
Roman Catholic 10, 11, 61, 66–70, 72, 112, 176, 214
Romanticism 114, 239
Runa 236

Sacralising 160
Sacred 7, 8, 58, 67, 69, 71, 135, 147, 148, 152, 154, 158, 160, 162–164
Satanism 23, 131
Second Vatican Council 66, 70, 72
Secularization theory 111, 125–127, 150, 151, 171
Self-constituting discourses 58, 61–63, 65, 71

Self-representation 12
Semantic 108, 118
Semiotic(s) 60, 183, 213, 214, 235, 236
September 11 125, 126
Seventh-day Adventist 67
Situational 91
SKAD 27, 32, 34, 36–44, 47–50
Social actors 27, 33, 36, 37, 39–41, 92, 146
Social construction 15, 23, 25, 34, 37, 43, 80, 83, 84, 86, 90, 103, 109, 112, 120, 128, 135, 170, 193, 194, 196, 211, 222, 225, 226, 238
Social theory 8, 19, 58
Socialization processes 33, 35
Sociology of knowledge approach to discourse studies (SKAD) 3, 23
Socratic style 8
Soul 13, 85, 189, 202, 236
Southland Christian Church 156
Spiritual 19, 118, 119, 136, 148, 149, 151, 154, 157, 160, 161, 187, 201
Statement 30, 42, 43, 45, 50, 209
Structural 11, 31, 194
Subjective 30, 35, 40, 59, 72, 114, 117, 118, 120, 132, 149, 150, 157, 159, 172, 175, 185, 190, 232, 233
Symbolic horizons 33
Symbolic interactionism 24–26, 30–33, 35, 50, 156
Symbolic order(ing) 28, 33–38, 42, 43
Symbols 7, 18, 33–36, 128, 137, 172

Textual analysis 42, 198
Theology 9, 14, 60, 62, 64, 65, 67, 78, 108, 141, 145, 163, 169, 183, 185–188, 191, 195, 198, 202, 214
Theoretical sampling 49
Torah 69, 70
Transgender studies 219, 221, 223–224

United Methodist Church 195
United Nations (UN) 5, 138, 169–174, 177, 178, 208, 209
Universal 13, 18, 108, 112, 113, 140, 174, 175
Universal Declaration of Human Rights (UDHR) 169, 170, 178
Universe of discourse 25
University of Alabama 19, 20

University of California 191, 224
University of Toronto 7

Weberian 24, 33
Western 40, 108, 110, 112, 116, 137, 138, 155,
    177, 185–187, 202, 210, 237

Womanist 214
World War II 108, 138

Zen studies 114

Index of Places

Afghanistan 100, 174
Africa 16, 112
America 19, 29, 30, 66, 94
Asia 19, 114
Australia 156
Austria 28, 176

Baltimore 191
Baulkham Hills 156
Beijing 208
Bosnia 174
Britain 10, 23, 28, 108, 175, 188, 192

Cairo 116
Canada 7, 10, 14
Chechnya 174
China 23, 51, 199
Cuba 129

Ecuadorian Amazon 58, 236
England 177
Euro-American 110, 126, 131, 135, 137, 138
Europe 15, 62, 109, 110, 112, 113, 126, 150, 175–178

Finland 199
France 10, 11, 16, 26, 31, 39, 41, 46, 47, 49, 58–60, 68, 70, 71, 174

Germany 23, 25, 27, 28, 29, 33, 39, 41, 43, 46–49, 79, 173
Greece 58, 62, 66, 177, 187

Hungary 222

Indonesia 89, 94, 96–98, 100, 102, 104
Iran 126
Ireland 116, 176

Israel 130, 203
Italy 176

Japan 44, 51

Kentucky 156

Lakewood 156
Los Angeles 191

Mediterranean 177
Mexico 10
Middle East 177
Morocco 96–99, 100, 102

Nepal 202
Netherlands 15, 16, 89, 90, 95–98, 100, 102, 104, 173
North America 9, 59, 112, 192, 223

Palestine 174

Riverside 224
Romania 23
Russia 94

Sydney 156

Tanzania 89
Turkey 97, 99, 102

United States of America (USA) 11, 16, 17, 113, 126, 129, 131, 135, 137, 138, 156, 174, 195, 209

Vatican 208, 209

Willow Creek 156

Index of People

Adams, John 237, 239
Adams, Suze 237
Ahmed, Sara 220
Alexander the Great 112
Allen, Sister Prudence 187–189, 211
Althusser, Louis 10
Ambrose, Saint Aurelius 69
Appleby, Scott 127
Aquinas, Thomas 185, 188
Aristotle 185–190, 211–212
Arthur, Chris 237–240
Asad, Talal 114, 117, 119, 172
Augustine, Saint Aurelius 69
Aupers, Stef 160, 161
Austin, John L. 93, 107, 108
Azzi, Corry 150

Bainbridge, William Sims 150, 158
Bakhtin, Mikhail 59, 94, 97, 99, 103, 132
Barker, Eileen 119
Barnett, Michael 129, 130, 135
Barthes, Roland 18, 235
Battista, Andrew 156
Beck, Ulrich 24
Belk, Russell 154, 158
Bell, Catherine 110
Bellah, Robert N. 137, 154
Benavides, Gustavo 170
Benedict XVI, Pope 140
Bennett, Jane 233, 235
Benveniste, Émile 59
Berger, Peter 25, 32–34, 37, 83, 151–153, 157
Bergson, Henri 232
Berkeley, Bishop 14
Biddick, Kathleen 201
Bloch, Jon P. 158
Blumer, Herbert 31
Børresen, Kari Elisabeth 201, 202
Bosk, Charles L. 25
Bourdieu, Pierre 93, 118, 238
Bové, Paul 145
Bowker, Geoffrey S. 44
Brague, Rémi 177
Braun, Willi 9

Brinton, Laurel J. 81
Bruce, Steve 148, 159, 161, 162
Bush, George W. 136, 139
Butler, Judith 183, 184, 192–197, 203, 207–210, 215–222, 227
Bynum, Carolyn 201

Caesar, Gaius Julius 156
Campbell, David 129, 135
Casanova, José 171
Cassirer, Ernst 34
Castellani, Brian 31
Certeau, Michel de 15
Chidester, David 15, 16
Chodorow, Nancy 210
Clarke, Adele 26, 27, 31, 47, 111
Connell, Robert W. 183
Connell, Sophia M. 188, 189
Conty, Arianne Françoise 234
Coole, Diana 83
Corbin, Juliette 45

Daly, Mary 214
Daston, Lorraine 80
Dean, Carolyn J. 190
Deleuze, Gilles 232
Delphy, Christine 210
Denzin, Norman 26
Derrida, Jacques 205
Descartes, René 64
Dewey, John 31
van Dijk, Teun 27, 89
Donnelly, Jack 175
Dostoevsky, Fyodor Mikhailovich 94
Douglas, Mary 15
Dreyfus, Hubert 29
Durkheim, Émile 8

Eberle, Christopher. J. 140, 141
Eder, Franz X. 3, 82
Ehrenberg, Ronald 150
Einstein, Mara 156
Eliade, Mircea 7, 8, 114
Evans, Malcolm D. 176
Ezzy, Douglas 161

Fairclough, Norman 26, 28, 89–94, 96, 99–101, 103, 104
Faure, Bernard 114
Fausto-Sterling, Anne 222
Finke, Roger 150
Fiorenza, Elisabeth Schüssler 214
Fitzgerald, Timothy 9, 109, 110, 145
Foster, Charles 236, 238, 239
Foucault, Michel 7, 10, 24, 26, 28–31, 34, 36, 40, 41, 43, 44, 50, 57, 58, 65, 72, 81–83, 89, 90, 92, 95, 101, 107, 109, 110, 115–118, 190, 193, 196, 206, 208, 212, 220, 227, 231, 238
Fraser, Nancy 31
Freud, Sigmund 193
Frost, Samantha 83
Frow, John 162
Fulkerson, Mary McClintock 183, 195–198, 219

Galison, Peter 80
Gamson, William 43, 44
Garfinkel, Harold 38, 93
Gatens, Moira 210
Geertz, Clifford 169
Gell, Alfred 84
Giddens, Anthony 24, 93
Gill, Sam D. 80
God 68, 70, 71, 111, 131, 135, 138–141, 156, 184, 186, 196, 199, 201, 202
Goffman, Erving 93
van Gogh, Vincent 63
Goldenberg, Naomi 16
Göle, Nilüfer 177
Goodall, Jane 119
Gramsci, Antonio 101
Gray, Breda 116
Gregory the Great 69
Gusfield, Joseph 25

Habermas, Jürgen 27, 38, 91, 93, 171, 183
Hall, Stuart 24, 32
Halperin, David M. 183
Haraway, Donna 85, 232, 234
Hart, Christopher 235
Hawley, John S. 210, 211
Heather, Noel 89
Heathorn, Stephen 7
Heelas, Paul 119, 154

Hermans, Hubert 89, 97, 103
Hermans-Konopka, Agnieszka 97, 103
Herodotus 112
Hilgartner, Stephen 25
Hirst, Jacqueline Suthren 204
Hjelm, Titus 89, 111
Hodder, Ian 84
Holofernes, General 203
Homer 64
Hoover, Stewart M. 155
Horowitz, Maryanne Cline 187, 189
Houtman, Dick 160, 161
Hume, David 64
Huntington, Samuel 113
Hurd, Elizabeth Shakman 127, 140, 141
Husserl, Edmund 64

Iannaccone, Laurence 150
Ingold, Tim 234
Irigaray, Luce 203

Jackson, Stevi 31
Jäger, Siegfried 28
Jay, Nancy 210
Jerome, Saint 69
Jesus of Nazareth 63, 70, 134, 135, 196
Jóhannesson, Ingólfur Ásgeir 82
Johannson, Lars 158
John Paul II, Pope 140, 208
Johnston, Jay 5, 83, 107, 110
Jørgensen, Marianne 89
Joy, Morny 5, 110
Juergensmeyer, Mark 137
Juschka, Darlene 183, 210–215, 219

Kant, Immanuel 64, 82, 138
Keller, Rainer 3, 4, 107, 109, 111, 119, 235
Kelly, Siobhan M. 224
Kennedy, John F. 136
King, Ursula 210, 211
Kippenberg, Hans G. 1, 5, 108
Koch, Anne 4, 233
Kohn, Eduardo 234–237
Kohnen, Thomas 68
Koselleck, Reinhart 78
Koyré, Alexandre 78
Kress, Gunther 89
Krishnaswami, Arcot 172, 174

Kristeva, Julia 126, 132, 133
Kuhn, Thomas 38

Lacan, Jacques 82, 193, 194
Laclau, Ernesto 28, 29
Landwehr, Achim 82
Latour, Bruno 84, 85
Lau, Kimberly 158
Lears, T. J. Jackson 153
van Leeuwen, Theo 89
Lehmann, Karsten 174
Lévi-Strauss, Claude 193
Lincoln, Bruce 8, 12
Lock, Terry 89
Lovelock, James 85
Luckmann, Thomas 25, 32–34, 36, 37, 83, 152
Luhmann, Niklas 169
Luther, Martin H. 155
Lyon, David 153

Machin, David 235
Mackian, Sara 160
Mahmood, Saba 116, 171
Maingueneau, Dominique 4, 114, 145
Mannheim, Karl 45
Manning, Philipp 29
Martikainen, Tuomas 115
Martin, Craig 15, 160
Marx, Karl 147
Mattern, Janice Bially 130, 131
Mauss, Marcel 148
McCutcheon, Russell T. 3, 113
McMullin, Neil 7
Mead, George Herbert 25, 33–35
Meijer, Irene Costera 217
Menke, Christoph 175
Milliken, Jennifer 128, 129
Mills, Charles W. 24
Moberg, Marcus 89
Money, John 191, 192
Moore, R. Laurence 155, 157
Morin, Edgar 177
Mouffe, Chantal 28, 29

Najmabadi, Afsaneh 224
Newton, Isaac 78
Nicholson, Linda 183, 184, 210, 212

Oakley, Ann 192
Orbán, Viktor 222
Orsi, Robert 12
Ortner, Sherry 210

Paden, Bill 8
Park, Yoosun 81
Pascal, Blaise 10
Paul 69, 195
Peters, Christine 200
Phillips, Kim 89, 190
Pierce, Charles 235
Plaskow, Judith 223
Plato 64
Possamai, Adam 159
Prins, Baukje 217
Prior, Lindsay 31
Prokhovnik, Raia 126, 132, 133

Rabin, Yitzhak 130
Rabinow, Paul 29
Ramey, Steven 20
Reay, Barry 190
Redden, Guy 4
Riccardo, David 147
Ricoeur, Paul 45, 77
Rimke, Heidi Marie 160
Rivière, Pierre 30, 31, 45
Roof, Wade Clark 149–151
Roosevelt, Franklin 138
Rorty, Richard 31, 80
Rose, Nicolas 37
Rousseau, Jean-Jacques 63
Rubin, Gayle 192–195, 219, 225
Ruether, Rosemary 214
Rüsen, Jörn 79
Rushdie, Salman 177

Saco, Diana 128–131
Said, Edward 7, 112
Salamon, Gayle 219
de Sales, François 71
Sangari, Kumkum 204
Sarasin, Philipp 81, 82
Sawyer, Deborah 203
Schaefer, Donovan O. 119, 120, 232, 233
Schilbrack, Kevin 170
Schuppert, Gunnar Folke 173

Schütz, Alfred 25, 34, 36, 83, 107
Scott, Joan Wallach 183, 184, 192, 204–210, 215, 218, 219, 227
Scott, Sue 31
Searle, John 107
Sennett, Richard 37
Seul, Jeffrey 137
Shapin, Steven 78
Sherry, John F. 154
Sibierska, Marta 235
Simmons, Merinda 15
Slater, Don 160
Smith, Adam 147
Smith, Anthony 135, 137, 138
Smith, Cantwell 9, 172
Smith, Jonathan Z. 9, 12, 13, 17, 79, 80, 108, 111
Smith, Leslie Dorrough 15
Srubar, Ilja 34
Stahnke, Tad 173
Star, Susan L. 44
Stark, Rodney 150, 158
Stoller, Robert 191
Strassfeld, Max 223
Strauss, Anselm 25, 26, 31, 45
Strenski, Ivan 131
Stryker, Susan 221
Stuckrad, Kocku von 1, 4, 50, 107, 108, 110, 171
Sun, Jessie 81
Swartz, Jack 238

Taves, Anne 18
Taylor, Charles 183
Taylor, Mark 9
Thomas, Dorothy 24, 25
Thomas, Lynn 204
Thomas, William I. 24, 25
Tomkins, Silvan 232
Touna, Vaia 15
Trump, Donald 11, 222

Urban, Hugh B. 159

Wagner, Tom 157
Wallendorf, Melanie 154
Wallis, Roy 159
Wallop, Gerard 78
Walzer, Michael 175
Watkins, Joanne 202
Weber, Max 24, 25, 43, 50
Weldes, Jutta 128–131
White, Hayden 77
Wijsen, Frans 1, 4, 27, 58
Wilcox, Melissa M. 224
Wilson, Elizabeth M. 160, 225, 226
Wilson, Erin 4
Wodak, Ruth 28, 89

Žižek, Slavoj 8, 10

www.ingramcontent.com/pod-product-compliance
Lightning Source LLC
Chambersburg PA
CBHW030537230426
43665CB00010B/934